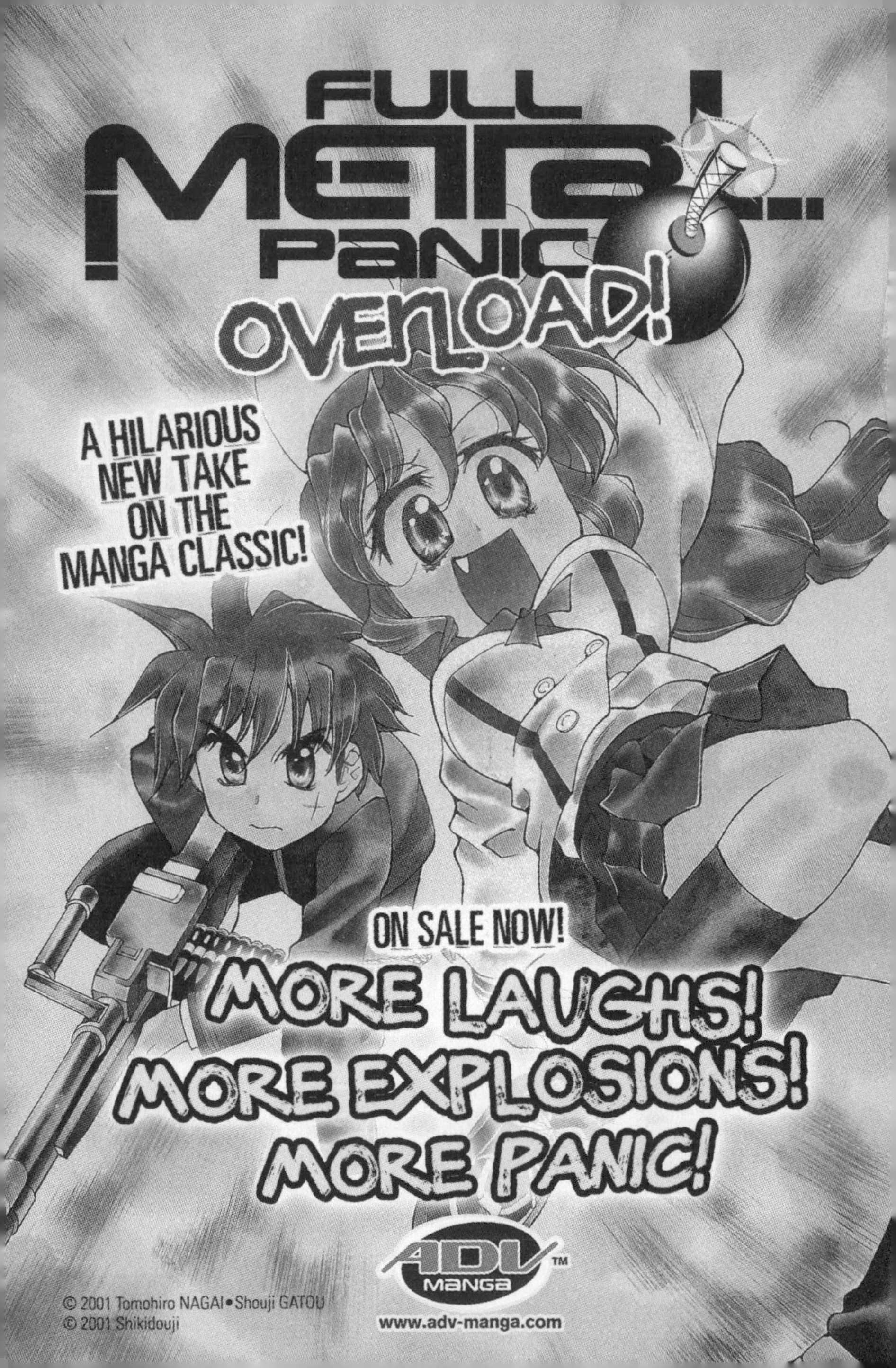
FULL METAL PANIC
OVERLOAD!
A HILARIOUS NEW TAKE ON THE MANGA CLASSIC!
ON SALE NOW!
MORE LAUGHS!
MORE EXPLOSIONS!
MORE PANIC!
ADV MANGA ™
© 2001 Tomohiro NAGAI • Shouji GATOU
© 2001 Shikidouji
www.adv-manga.com

FROM THE CREATOR OF *AZUMANGA DAIOH!*

YOTSUBA&!

1

KIYOHIKO AZUMA

A NEW SERIES FROM KIYOHIKO AZUMA!

INTERNATIONAL BEST-SELLING AUTHOR OF

AZUMANGA DAIOH

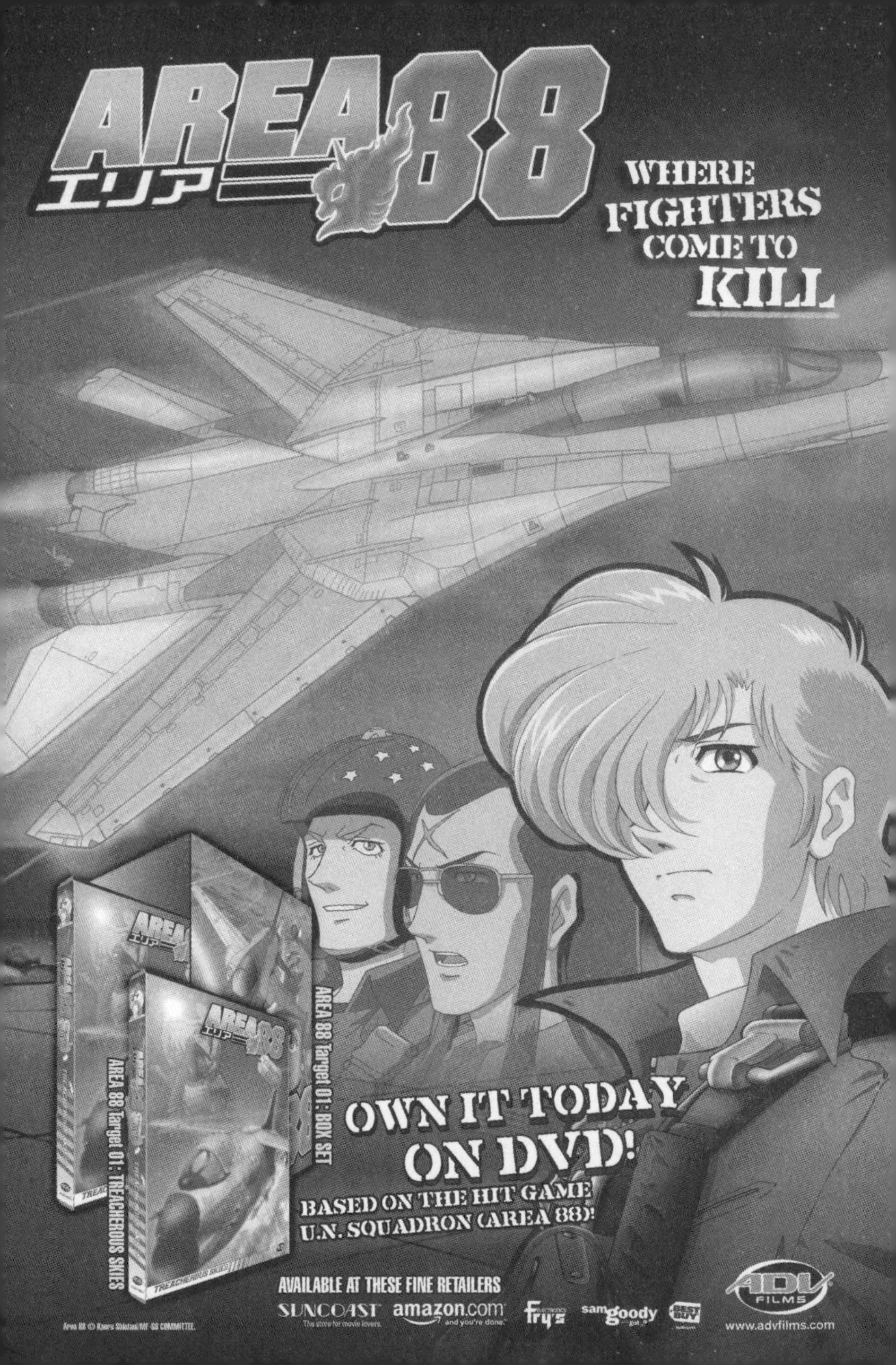
AREA 88
エリア88
WHERE FIGHTERS COME TO KILL
AREA 88 Target 01: BOX SET
AREA 88 Target 01: TREACHEROUS SKIES
OWN IT TODAY ON DVD!
BASED ON THE HIT GAME U.N. SQUADRON (AREA 88)!
AVAILABLE AT THESE FINE RETAILERS
SUNCOAST The store for movie lovers.
amazon.com and you're done.
Fry's
sam goody
BEST BUY
ADV FILMS
www.advfilms.com
Area 88 © Kaoru Shintani/MF-88 COMMITTEE.

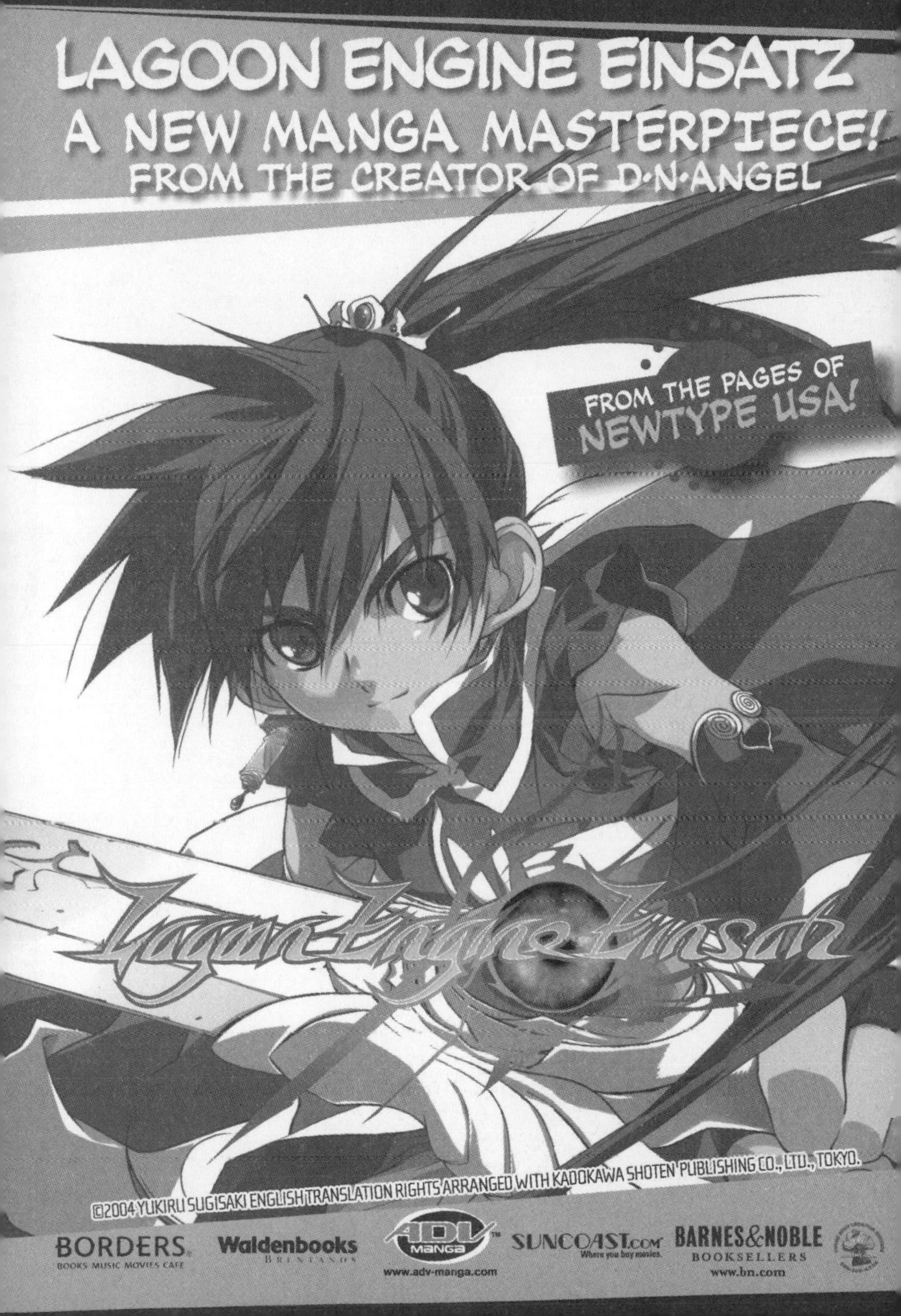

LAGOON ENGINE EINSATZ
A NEW MANGA MASTERPIECE!
FROM THE CREATOR OF D·N·ANGEL
FROM THE PAGES OF NEWTYPE USA!
©2004 YUKIRU SUGISAKI ENGLISH TRANSLATION RIGHTS ARRANGED WITH KADOKAWA SHOTEN PUBLISHING CO., LTD., TOKYO.
BORDERS
BOOKS MUSIC MOVIES CAFE
Waldenbooks
ADV Manga
www.adv-manga.com
SUNCOAST.com
Where you buy movies.
BARNES&NOBLE
BOOKSELLERS
www.bn.com

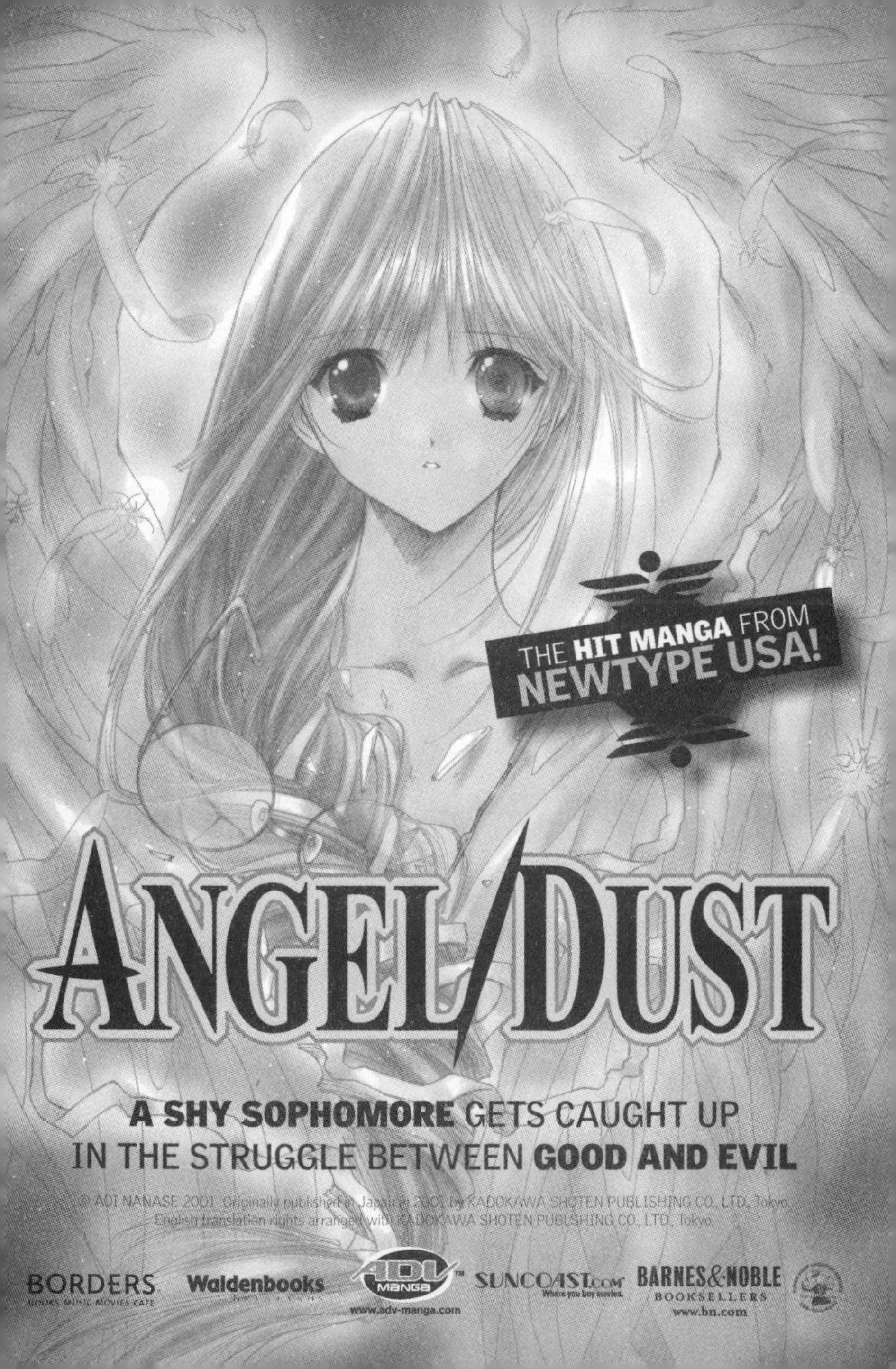
THE HIT MANGA FROM NEWTYPE USA!
ANGEL/DUST
A SHY SOPHOMORE GETS CAUGHT UP IN THE STRUGGLE BETWEEN GOOD AND EVIL
© AOI NANASE 2001. Originally published in Japan in 2001 by KADOKAWA SHOTEN PUBLISHING CO., LTD., Tokyo.
English translation rights arranged with KADOKAWA SHOTEN PUBLSHING CO., LTD., Tokyo.
BORDERS
BOOKS MUSIC MOVIES CAFE
Waldenbooks
ADV MANGA
www.adv-manga.com
SUNCOAST.com
Where you buy movies.
BARNES&NOBLE
BOOKSELLERS
www.bn.com

Times are tough, and with Orphen's pockets as empty as his stomach,

he's going to have to face his most daunting adversary yet---the workplace!

This sorcerer-turned-busboy takes to the taverns,

but there'll be little time for abusing the customers when Cleao is kidnapped by a fearsome gang that's out to put all magic-users under the blade. Orphen springs into action, but this time he may need a little help from a powerful new ally...

⊕RPHEN

Vol.4

Orphen Volume Three

© 1999 Yoshinobu Akita/Hajime Sawada
© 1999 Yuuya Kusaka
Originally published in Japan in 1999 by
KADOKAWA SHOTEN PUBLISHING CO., LTD., Tokyo.
English translation rights arranged with
KADOKAWA SHOTEN PUBLISHING CO., LTD., Tokyo.

Editor JAVIER LOPEZ
Translator BRENDAN FRAYNE
Graphic Artist MARK MEZA

Editorial Director GARY STEINMAN
Creative Director JASON BABLER
Sales and Marketing CHRIS OARR
Print Production Manager BRIDGETT JANOTA

International Coordinators TORU IWAKAMI & MIYUKI KAMIYA

President, CEO & Publisher JOHN LEDFORD

Email: editor@adv-manga.com
www.adv-manga.com
www.advfilms.com

For sales and distribution inquiries please call 1.800.282.7202

 is a division of A.D. Vision, Inc.
5750 Bintliff Drive, Suite 210, Houston, Texas 77036

English text © 2005 published by A.D. Vision, Inc. under exclusive license.
ADV MANGA is a trademark of A.D. Vision, Inc.

ISBN: 1-4139-0268-5
First printing, September 2005
10 9 8 7 6 5 4 3 2 1
Printed in Canada

STAFF

佐々木清彦 kiyohiko sasaki

牧野功 isao makino

星畑拓生 takuo hoshihata

浅川圭司 keiji asakawa

ORPHEN

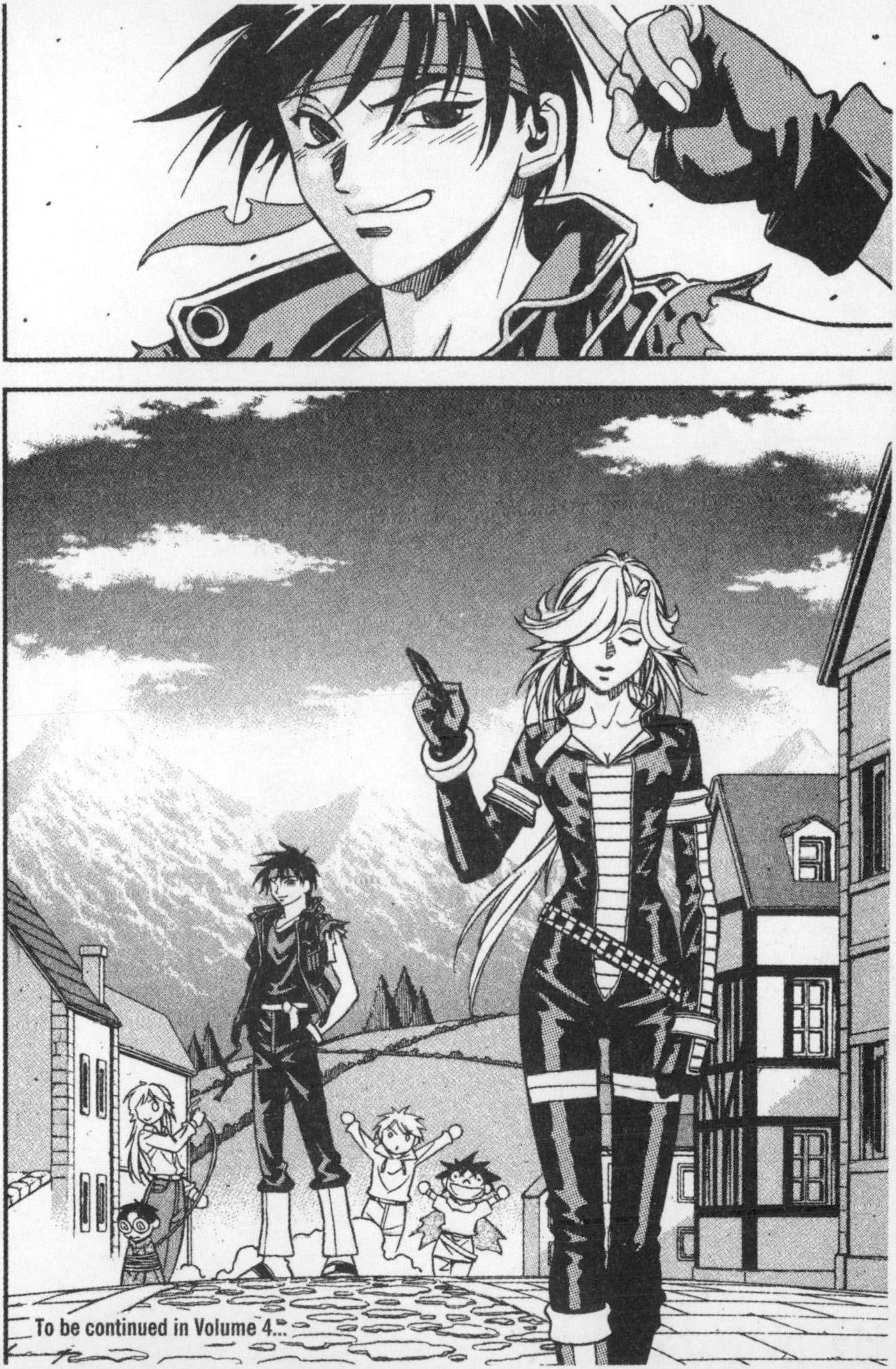
To be continued in Volume 4...

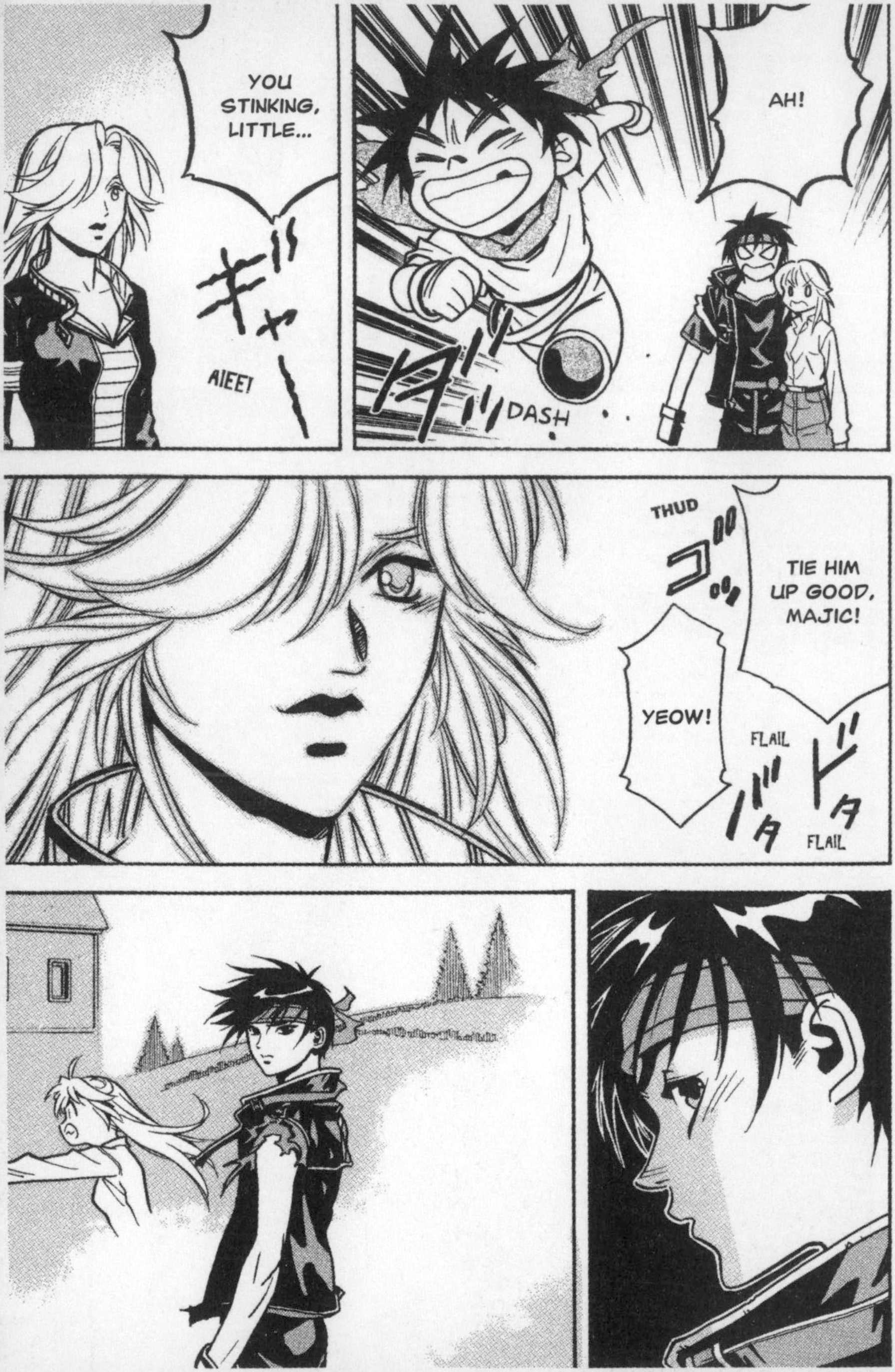
AH!
DASH
YOU STINKING, LITTLE...
AIEE!
TIE HIM UP GOOD, MAJIC!
THUD
YEOW!
FLAIL
FLAIL

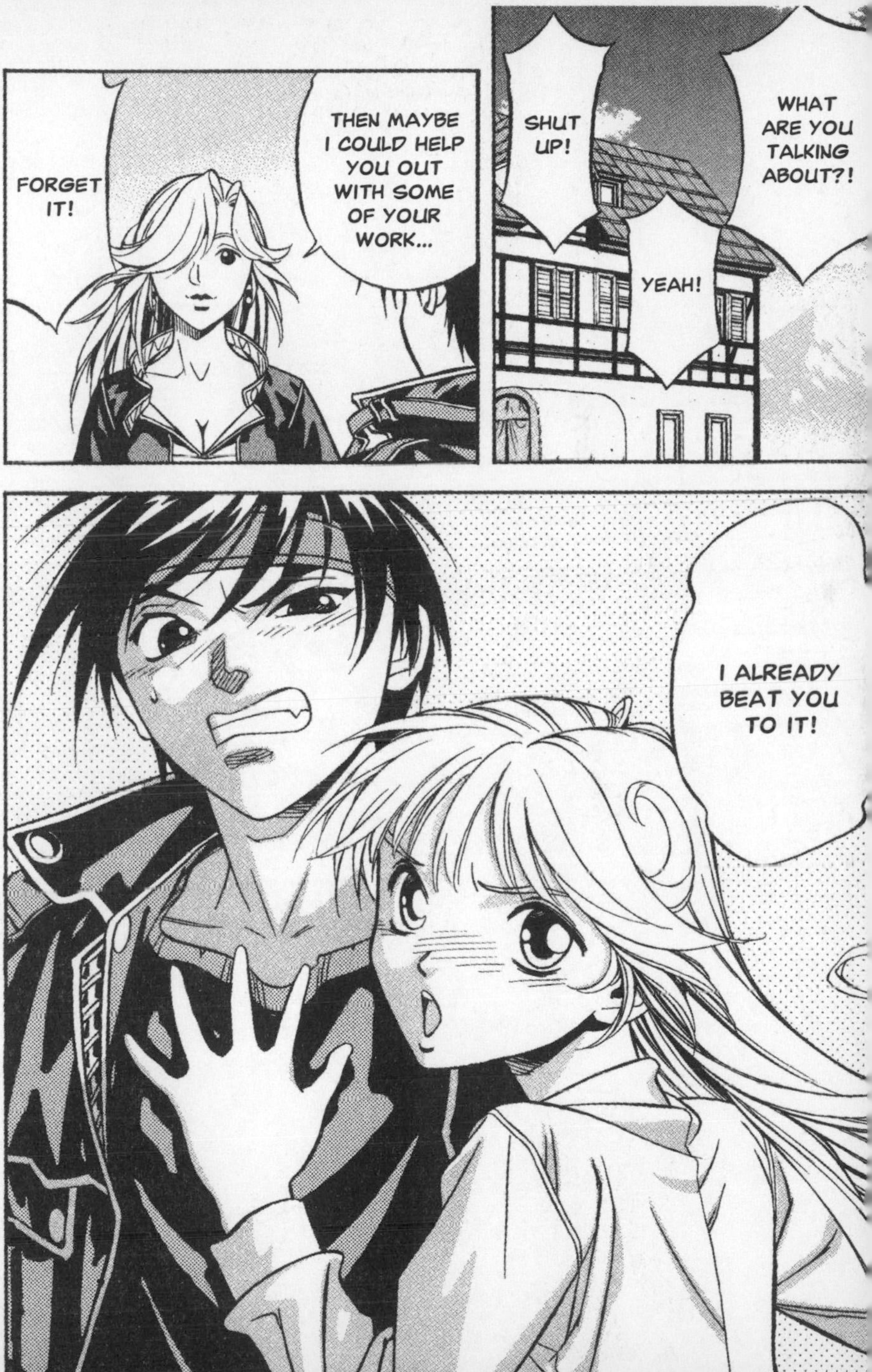
WHAT ARE YOU TALKING ABOUT?!
SHUT UP!
YEAH!
THEN MAYBE I COULD HELP YOU OUT WITH SOME OF YOUR WORK...
FORGET IT!
I ALREADY BEAT YOU TO IT!

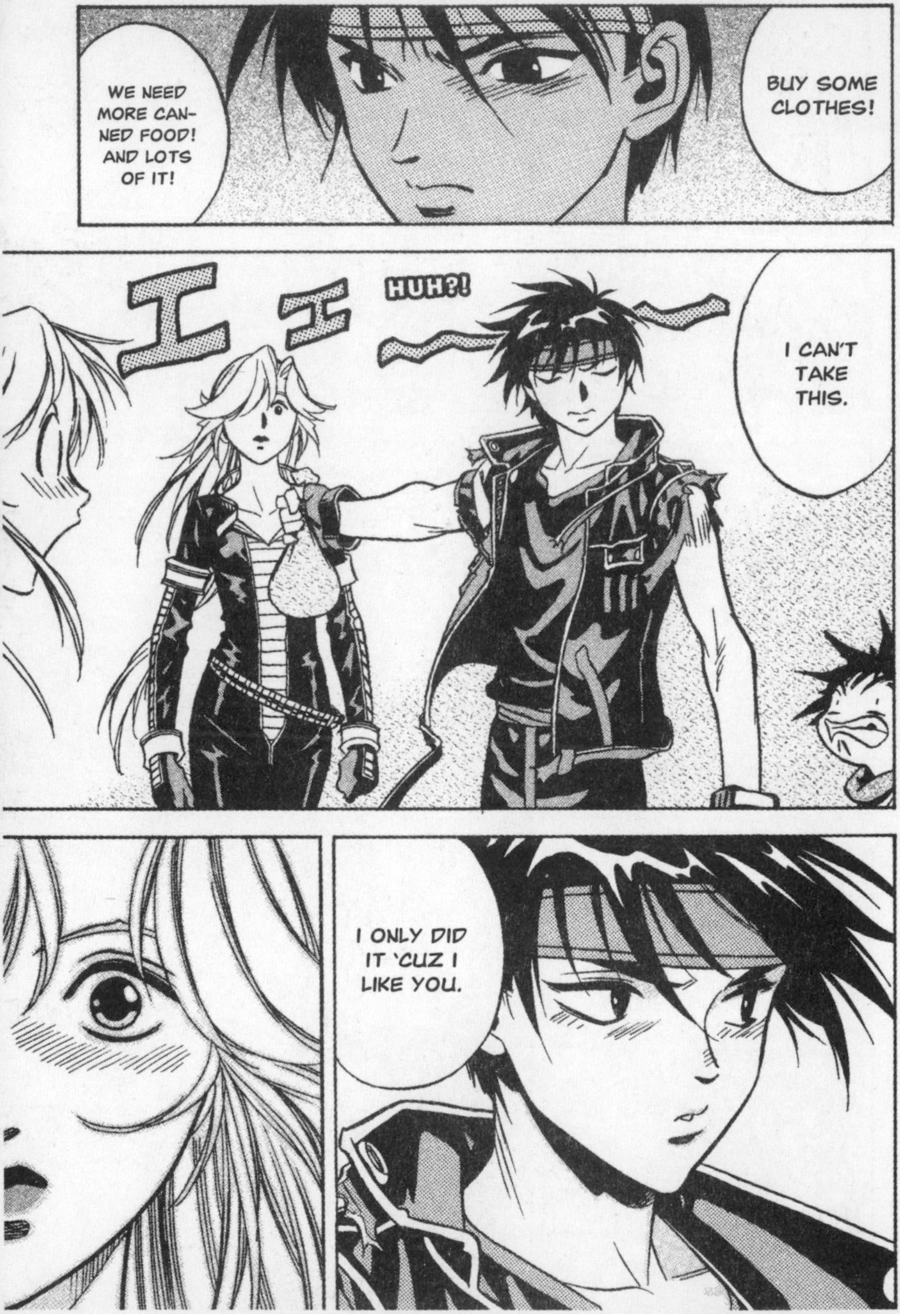
BUY SOME CLOTHES!
WE NEED MORE CAN-NED FOOD! AND LOTS OF IT!
I CAN'T TAKE THIS.
HUH?!
I ONLY DID IT 'CUZ I LIKE YOU.

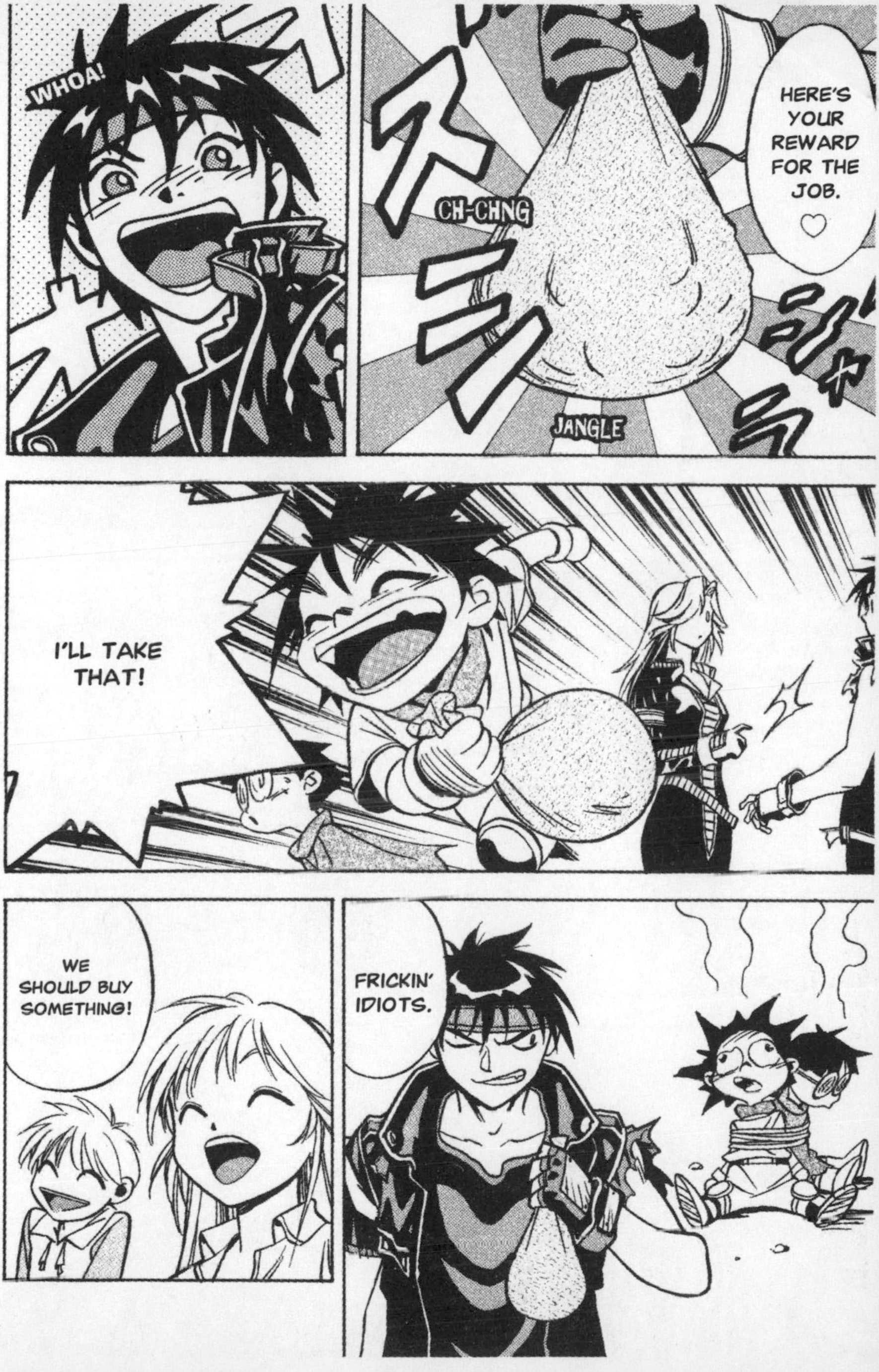
HERE'S YOUR REWARD FOR THE JOB. ♡
CH-CHNG
JANGLE
WHOA!
I'LL TAKE THAT!
FRICKIN' IDIOTS.
WE SHOULD BUY SOMETHING!

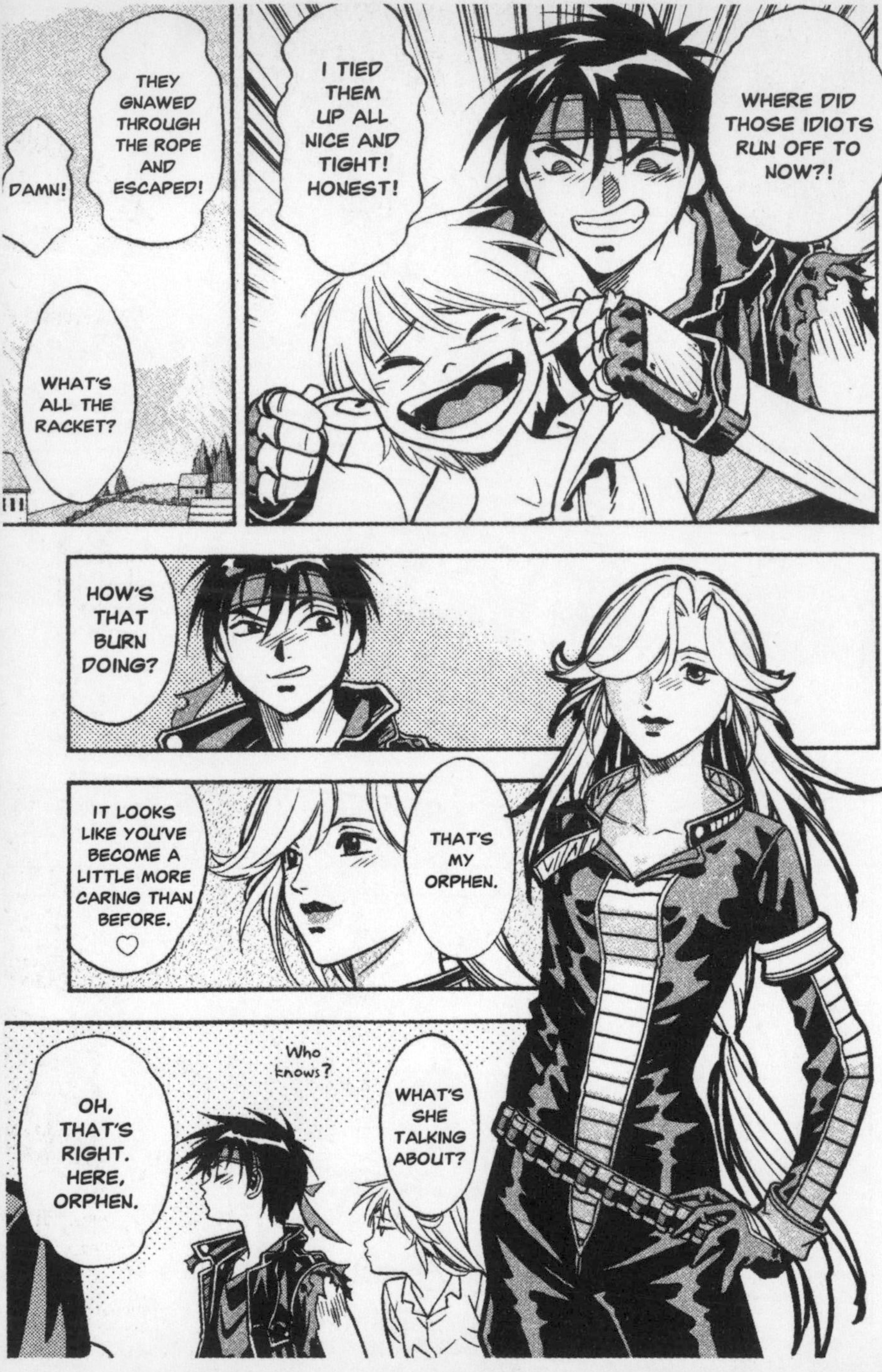
WHERE DID THOSE IDIOTS RUN OFF TO NOW?!
I TIED THEM UP ALL NICE AND TIGHT! HONEST!
THEY GNAWED THROUGH THE ROPE AND ESCAPED!
DAMN!
WHAT'S ALL THE RACKET?
HOW'S THAT BURN DOING?
IT LOOKS LIKE YOU'VE BECOME A LITTLE MORE CARING THAN BEFORE. ♡
THAT'S MY ORPHEN.
WHAT'S SHE TALKING ABOUT?
Who knows?
OH, THAT'S RIGHT. HERE, ORPHEN.

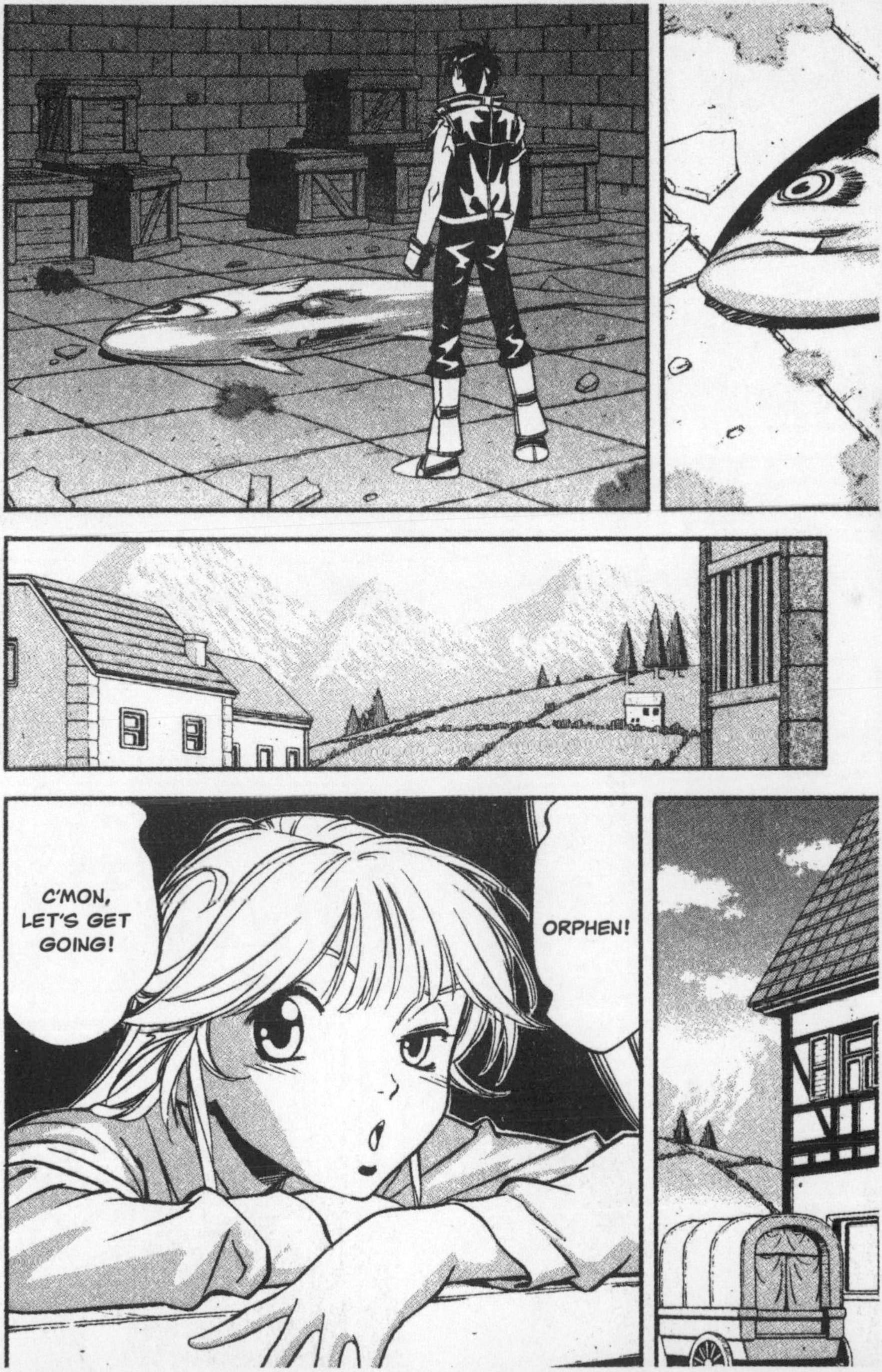
ORPHEN!
C'MON, LET'S GET GOING!

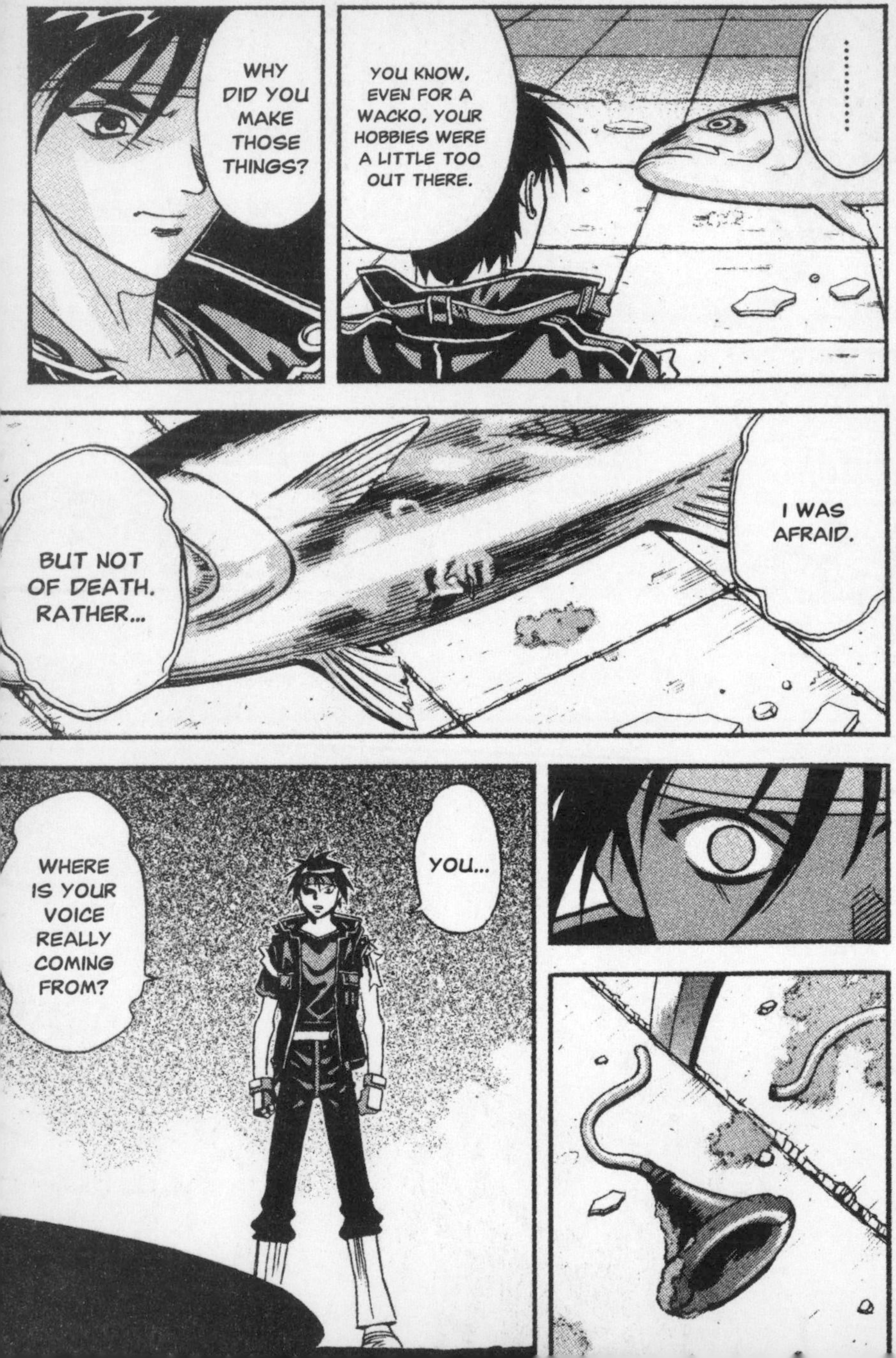
......
YOU KNOW, EVEN FOR A WACKO, YOUR HOBBIES WERE A LITTLE TOO OUT THERE.
WHY DID YOU MAKE THOSE THINGS?
I WAS AFRAID.
BUT NOT OF DEATH. RATHER...
YOU...
WHERE IS YOUR VOICE REALLY COMING FROM?

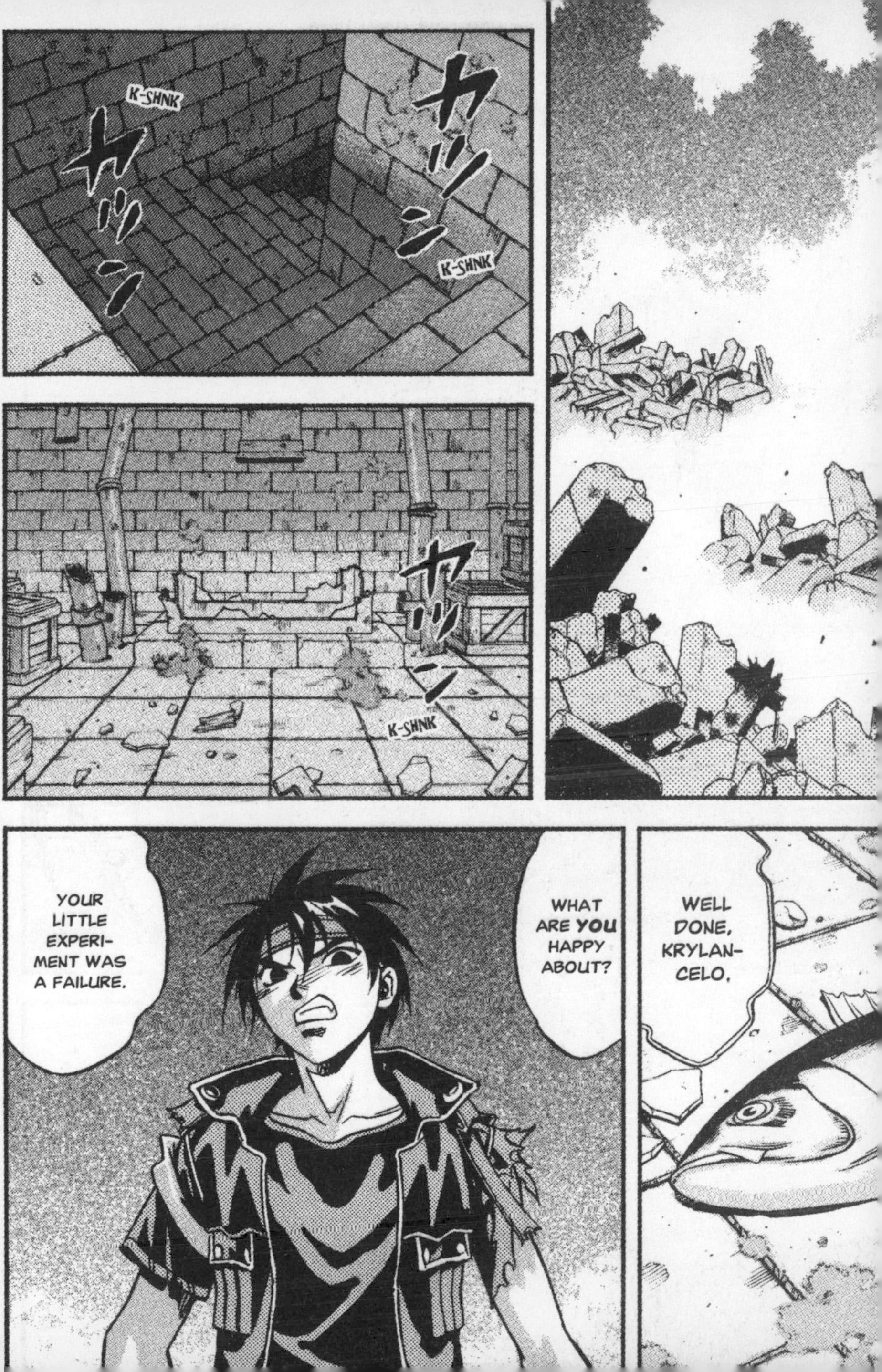
K-SHNK
K-SHNK
K-SHNK
WELL DONE, KRYLANCELO.
WHAT ARE YOU HAPPY ABOUT?
YOUR LITTLE EXPERIMENT WAS A FAILURE.

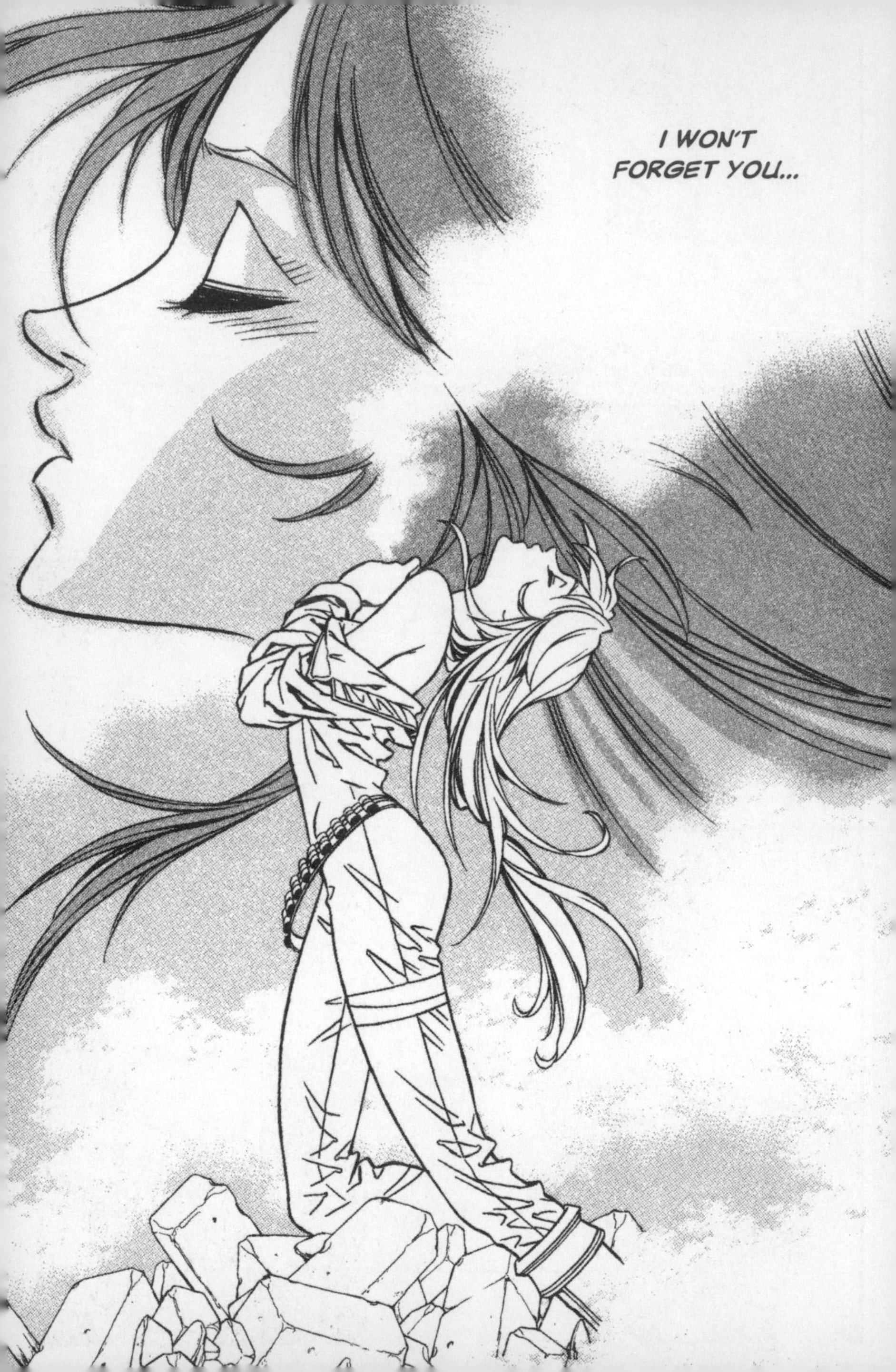
I WON'T
FORGET YOU...

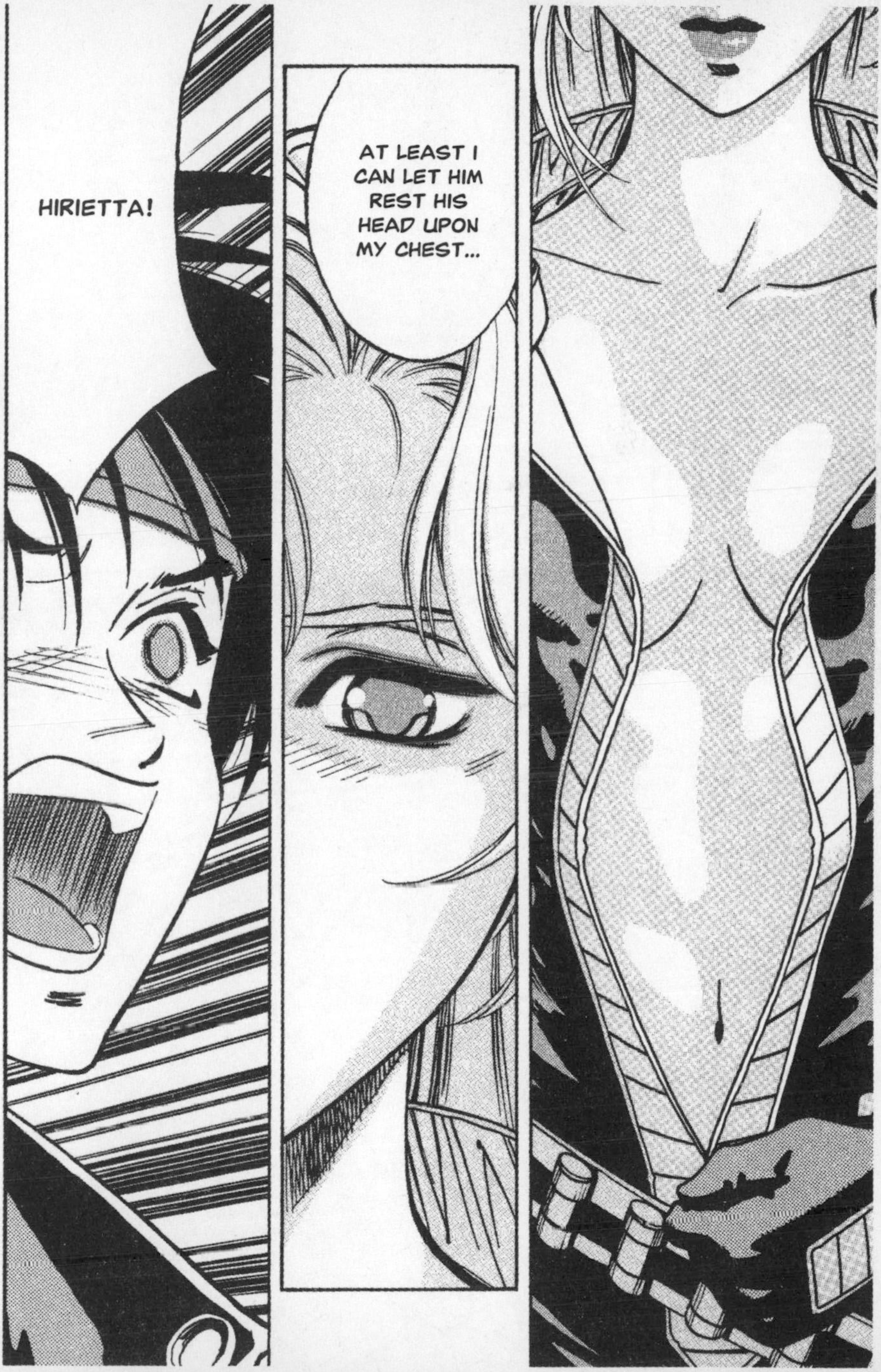
AT LEAST I CAN LET HIM REST HIS HEAD UPON MY CHEST...
HIRIETTA!

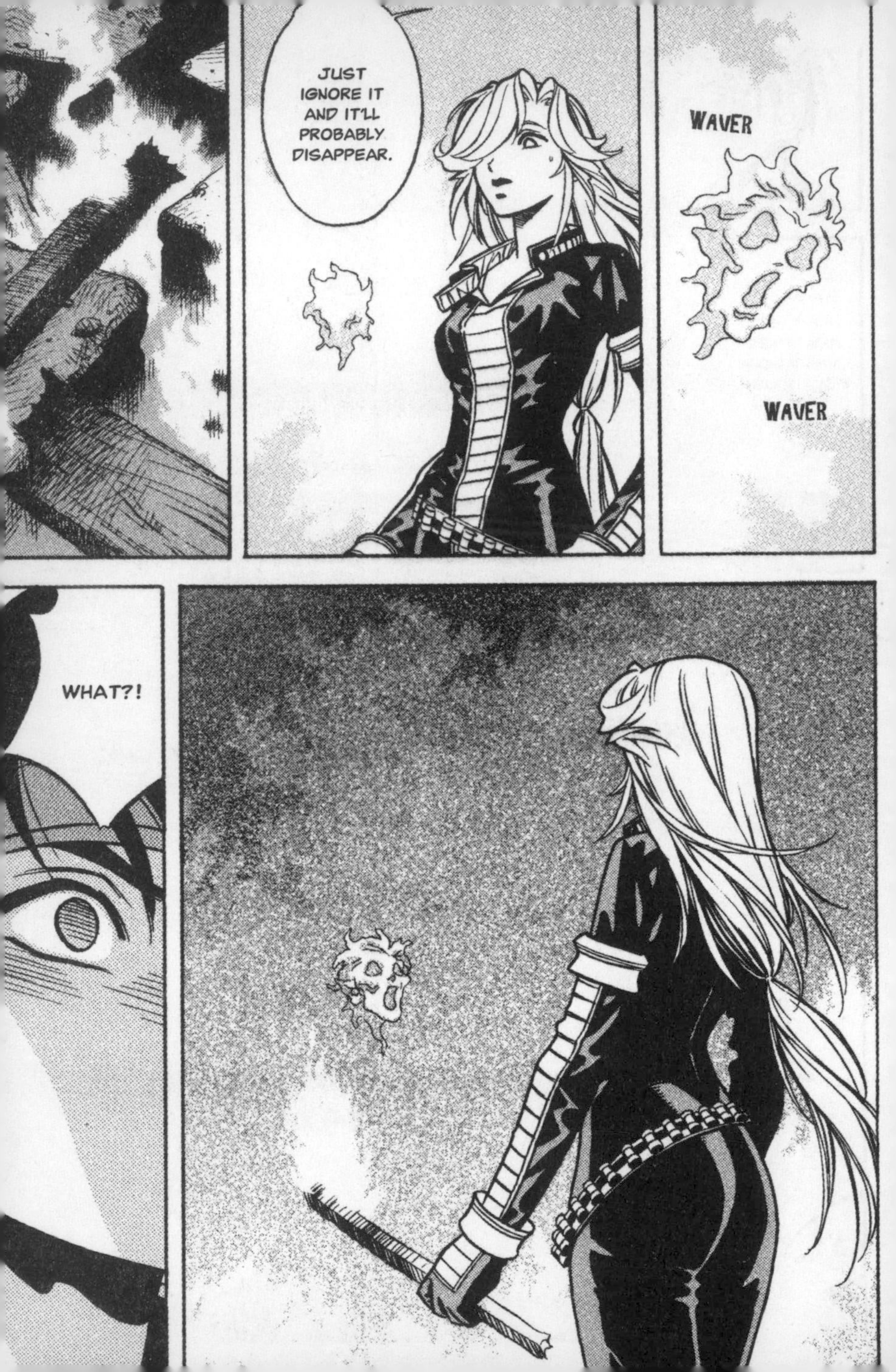
WAVER
WAVER
JUST IGNORE IT AND IT'LL PROBABLY DISAPPEAR.
WHAT?!

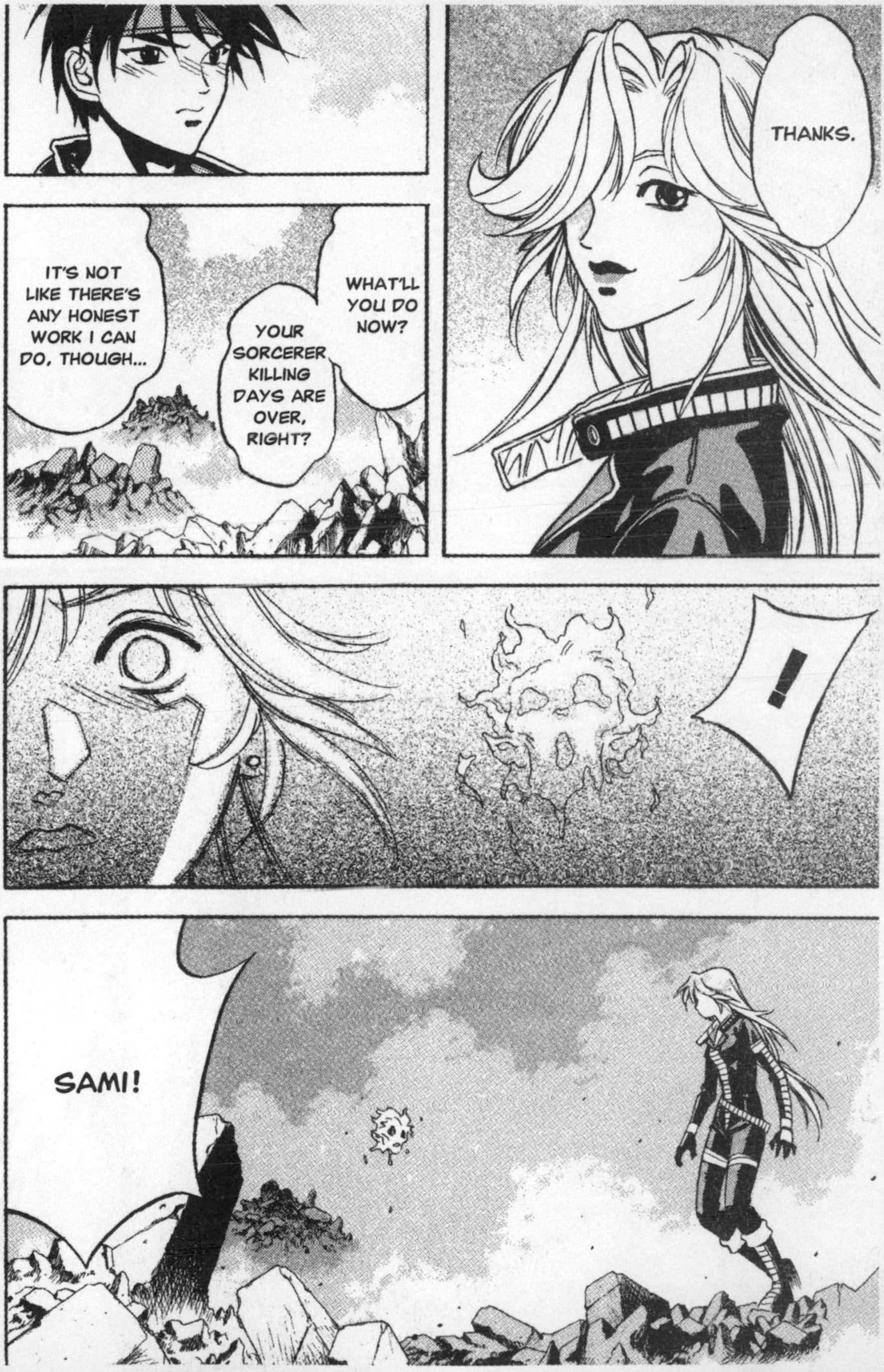
THANKS.
WHAT'LL YOU DO NOW?
YOUR SORCERER KILLING DAYS ARE OVER, RIGHT?
IT'S NOT LIKE THERE'S ANY HONEST WORK I CAN DO, THOUGH...
!
SAMI!

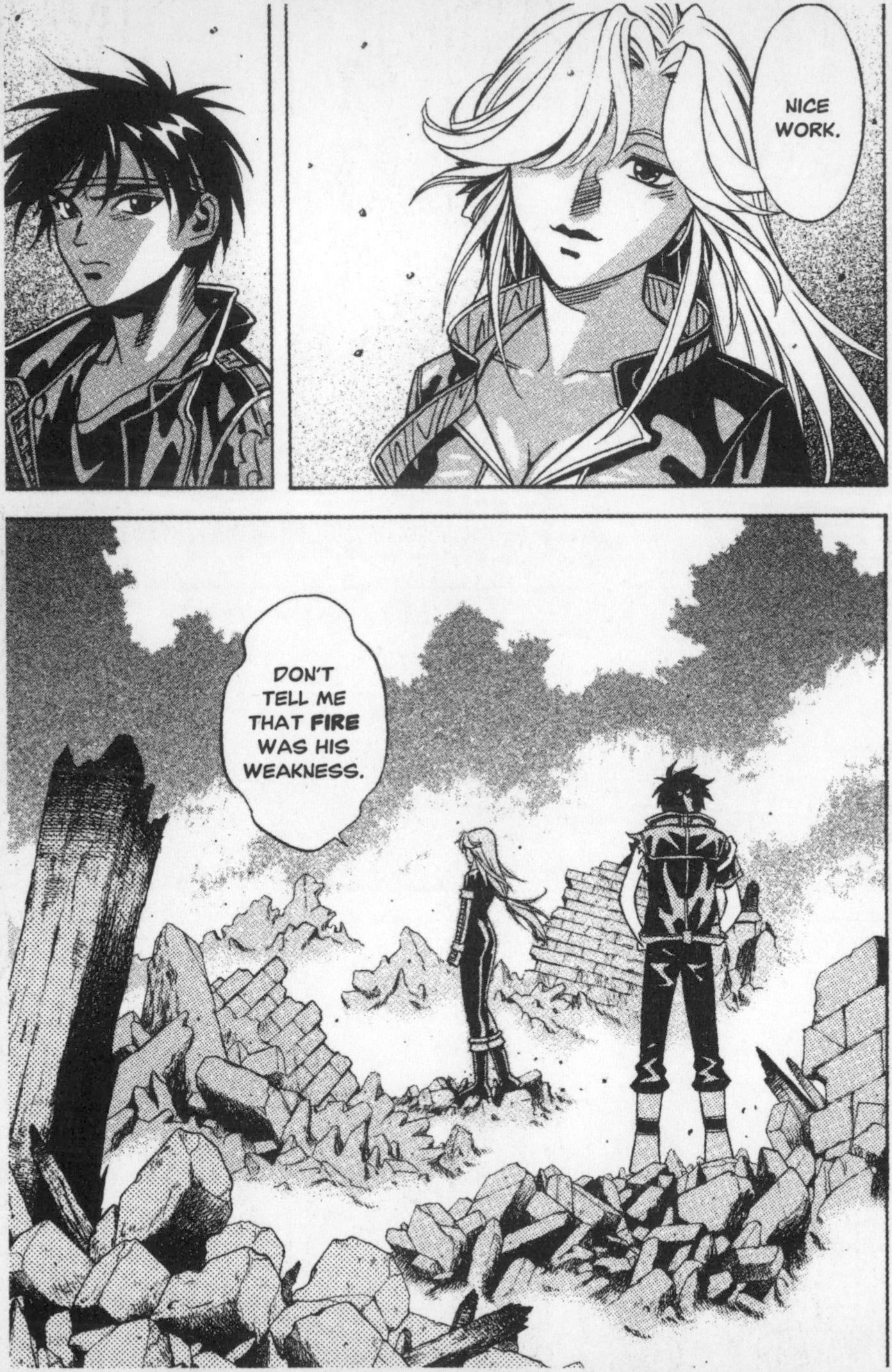
NICE WORK.
DON'T TELL ME THAT FIRE WAS HIS WEAKNESS.

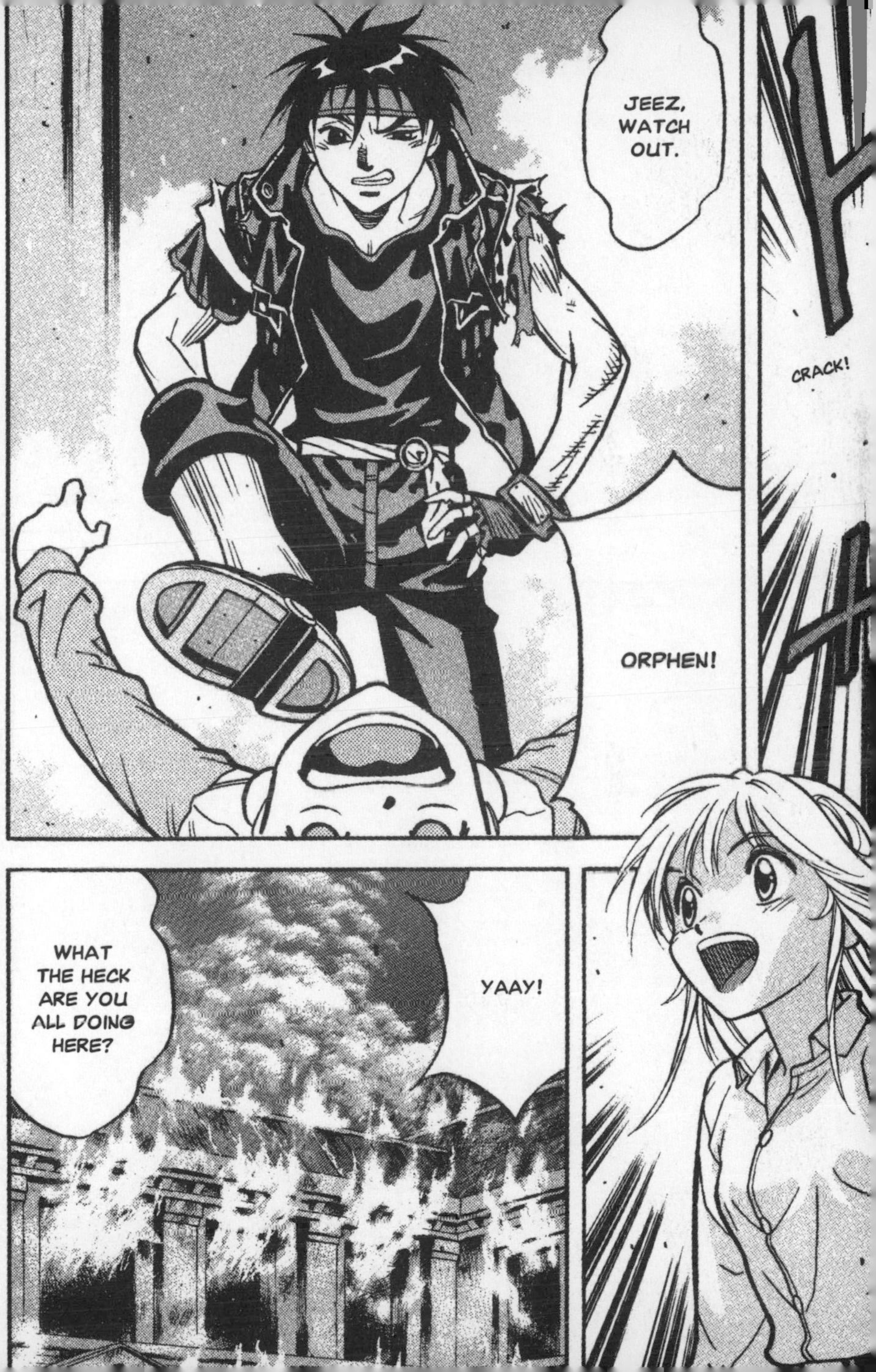
CRACK!
JEEZ, WATCH OUT.
ORPHEN!
YAAY!
WHAT THE HECK ARE YOU ALL DOING HERE?

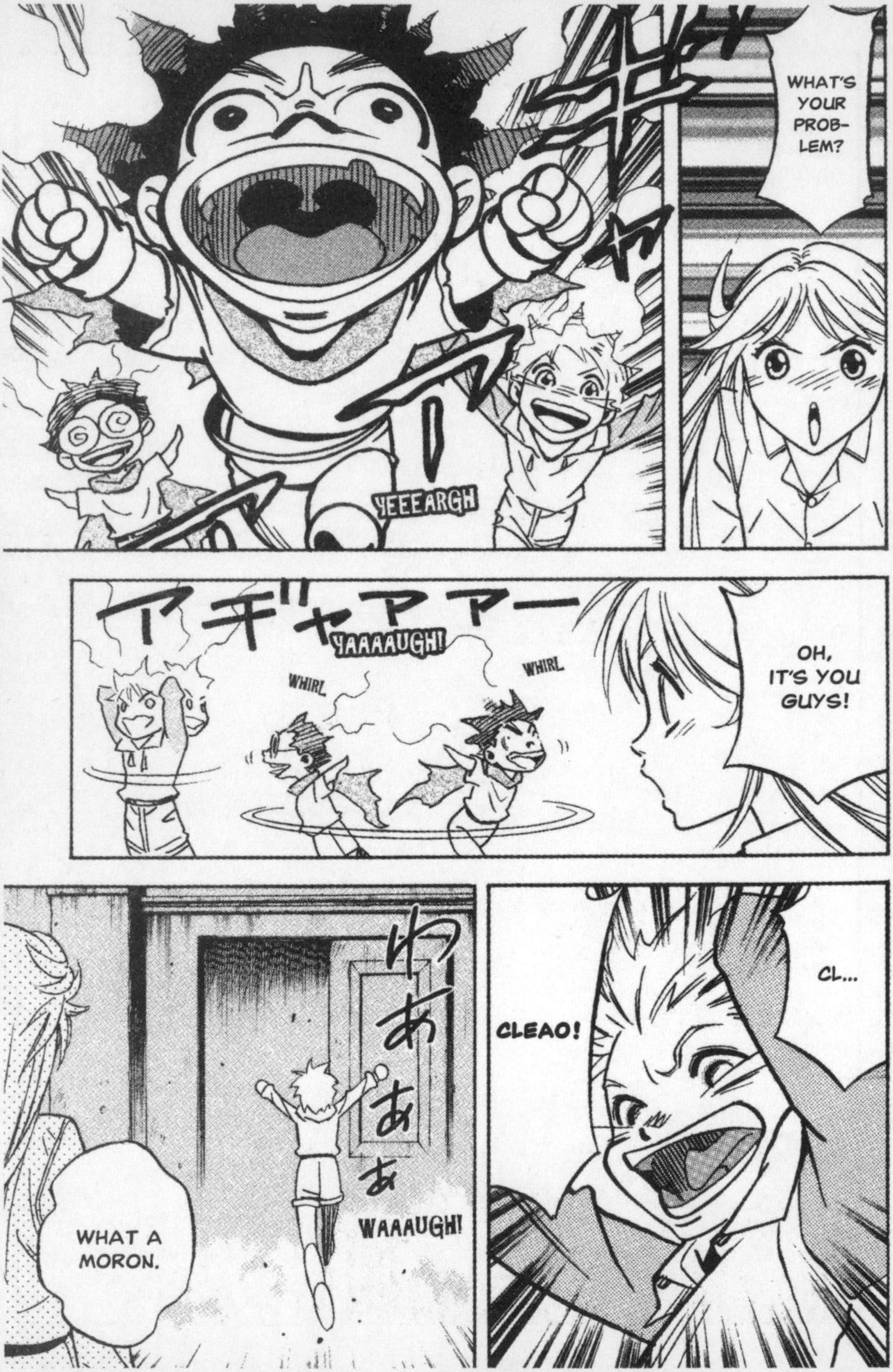

WHAT'S YOUR PROB-LEM?
YEEEARGH
アギャアアー
YAAAAUGH!
WHIRL
WHIRL
OH, IT'S YOU GUYS!
CL...
CLEAO!
わあああ
WAAAUGH!
WHAT A MORON.

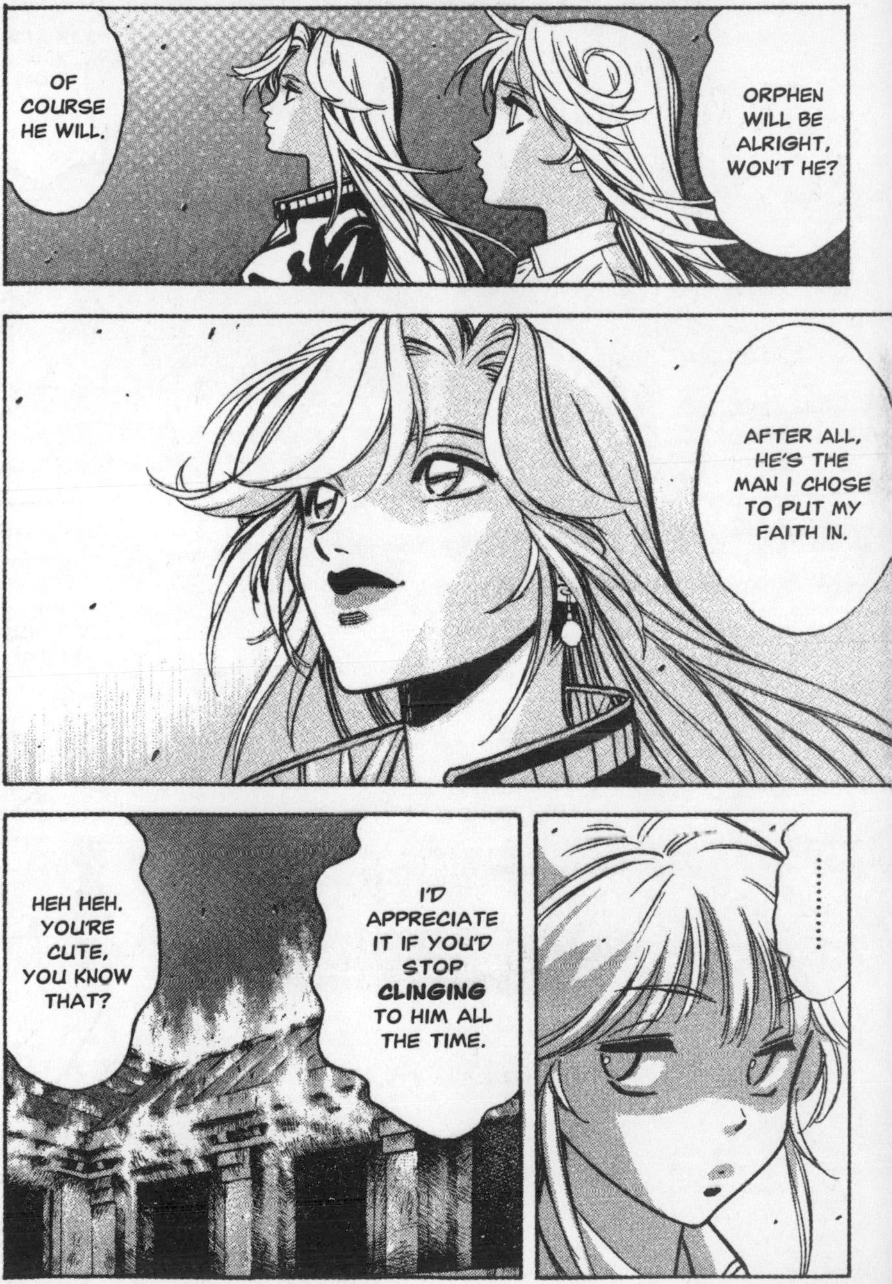
ORPHEN WILL BE ALRIGHT, WON'T HE?
OF COURSE HE WILL.
AFTER ALL, HE'S THE MAN I CHOSE TO PUT MY FAITH IN.
......
I'D APPRECIATE IT IF YOU'D STOP CLINGING TO HIM ALL THE TIME.
HEH HEH. YOU'RE CUTE, YOU KNOW THAT?

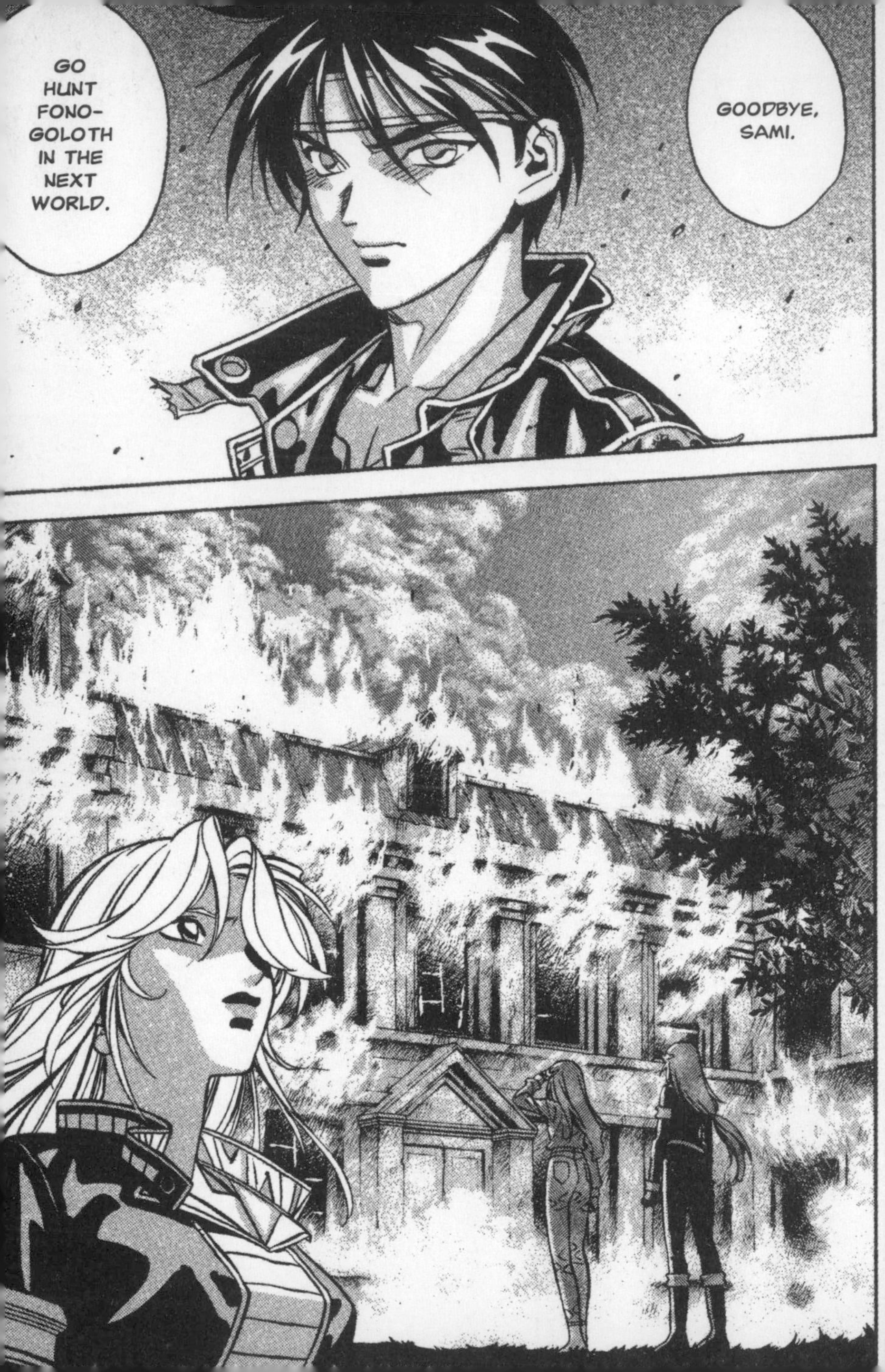
GOODBYE, SAMI.
GO HUNT FONO-GOLOTH IN THE NEXT WORLD.

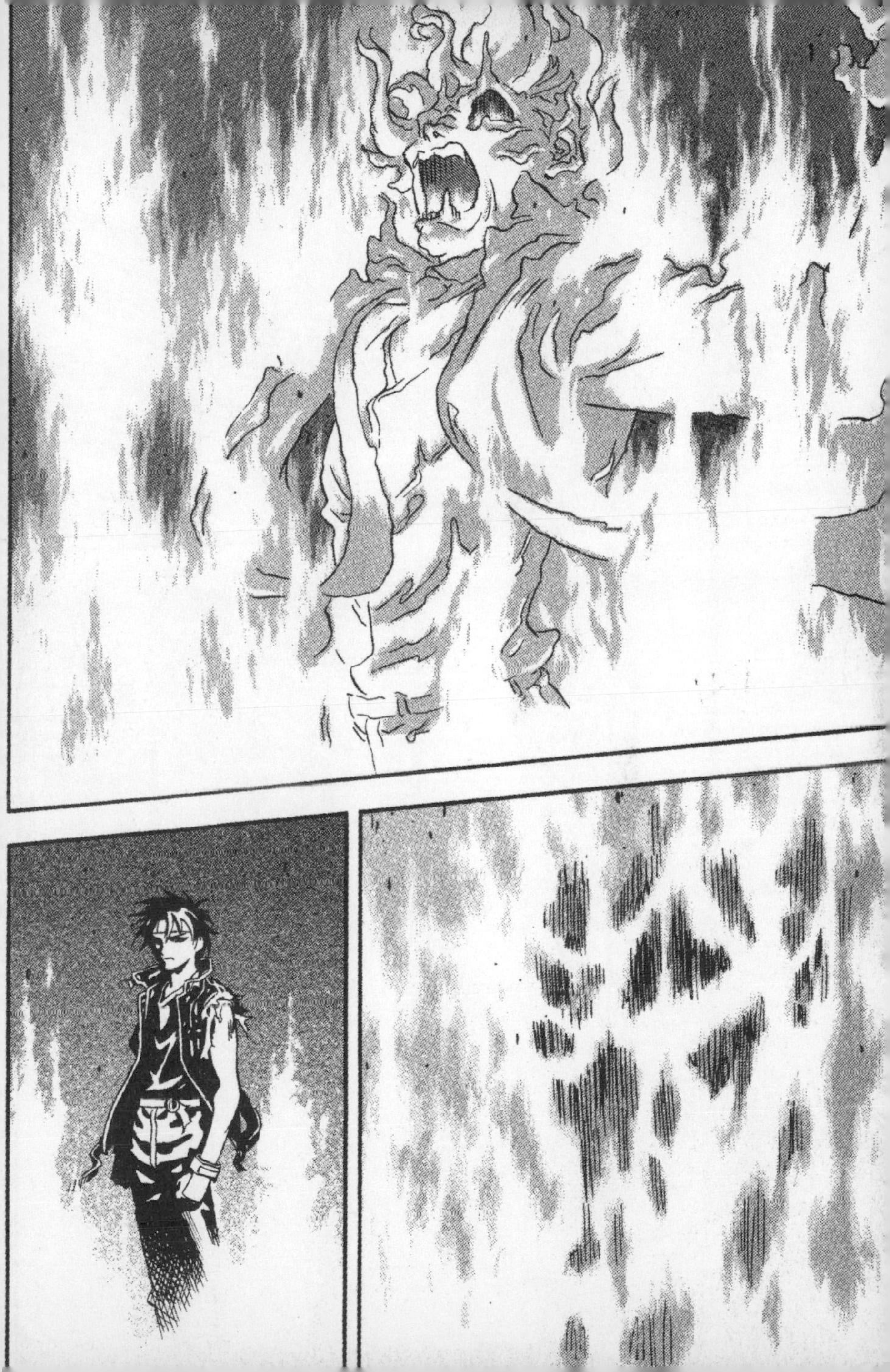

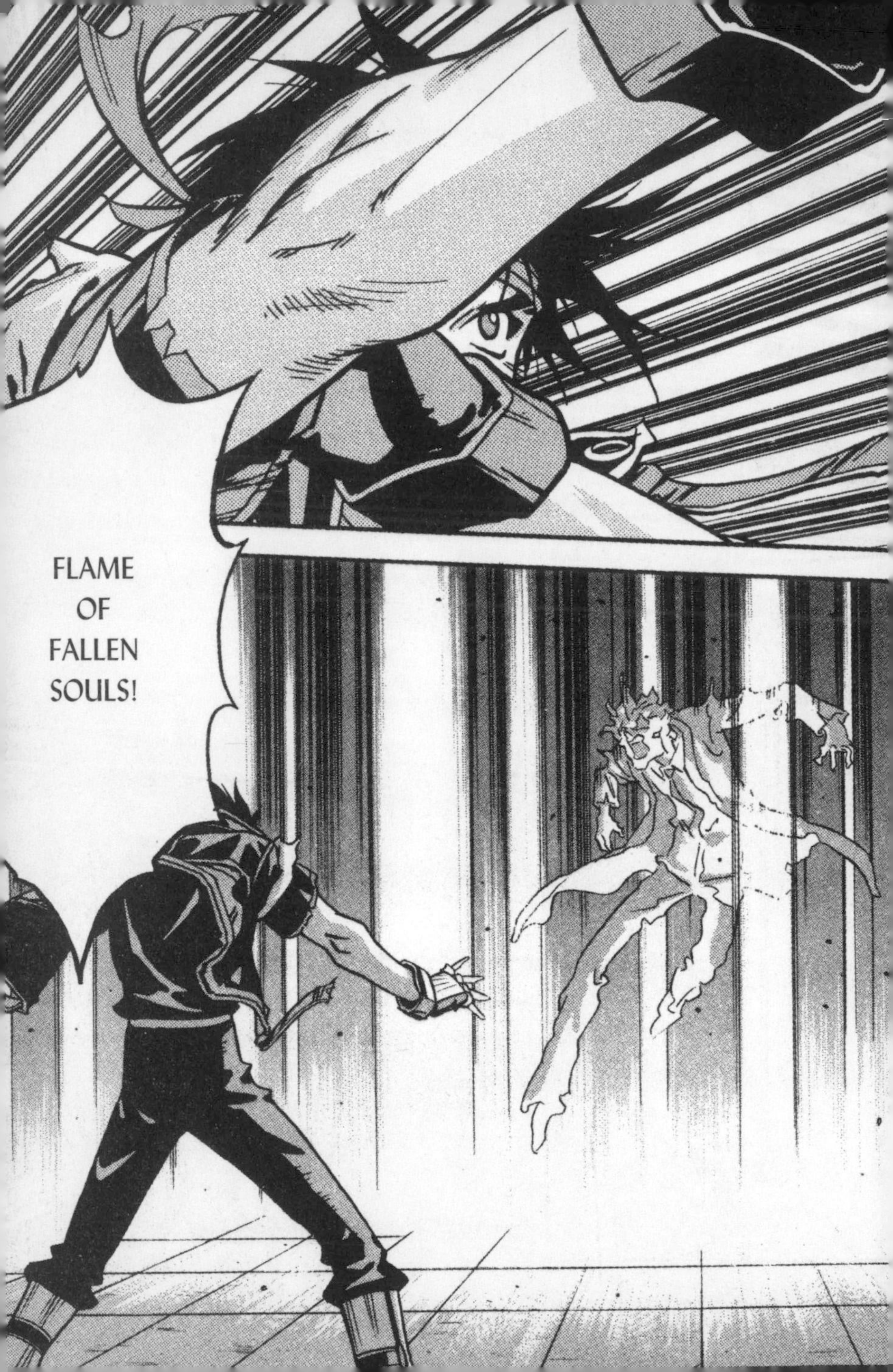
FLAME OF FALLEN SOULS!

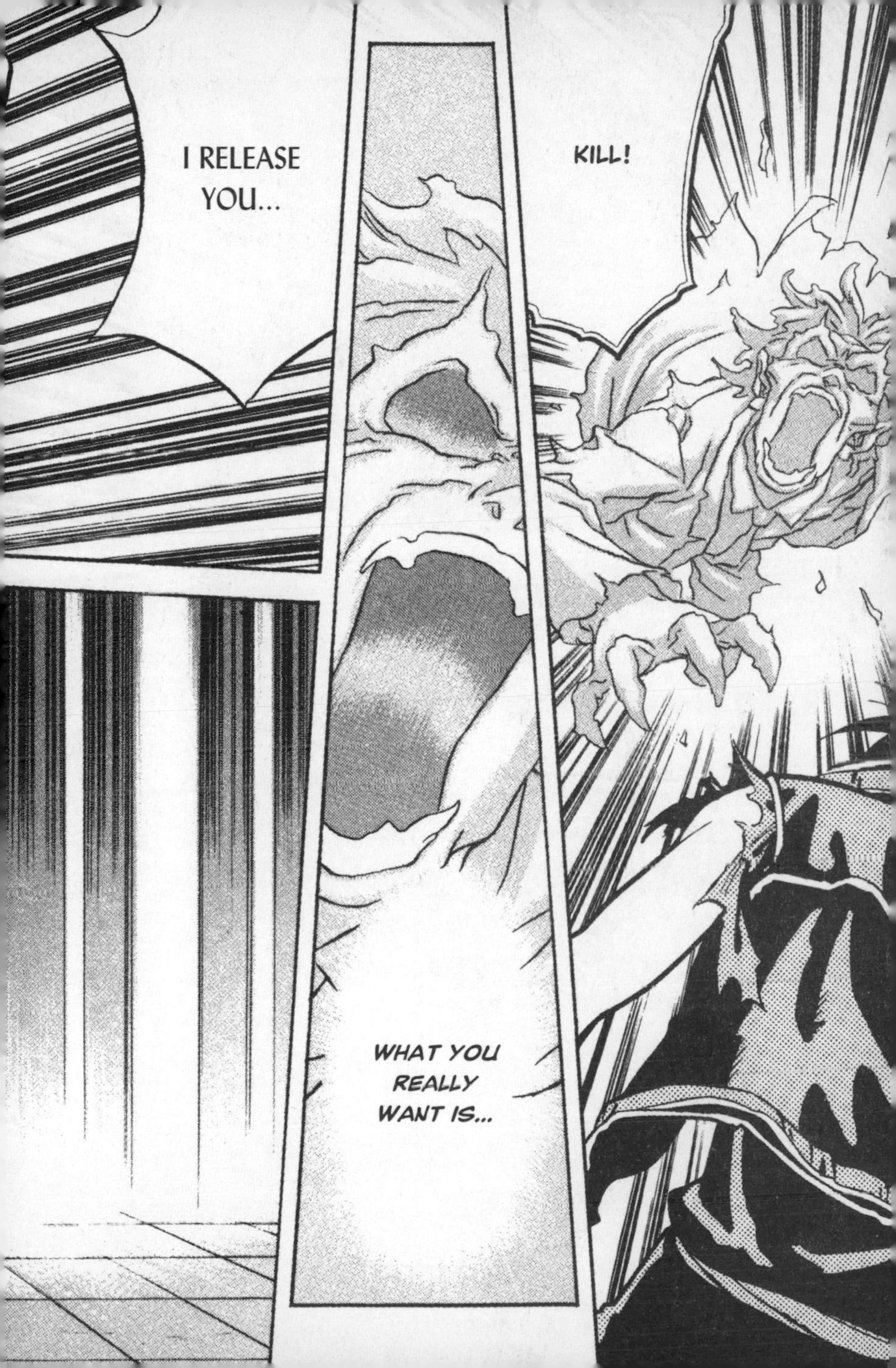
KILL!
I RELEASE YOU...
WHAT YOU REALLY WANT IS...

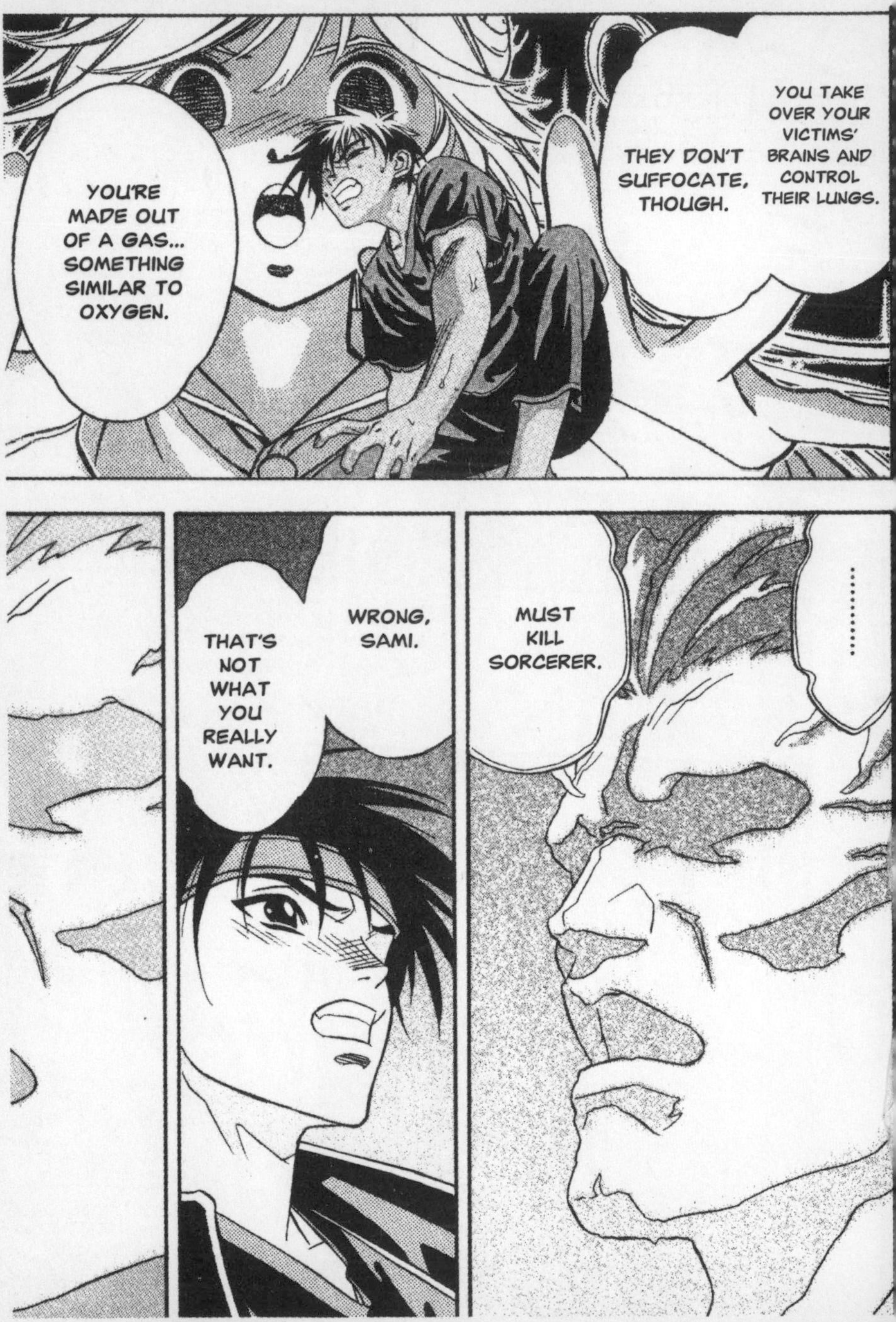
YOU TAKE OVER YOUR VICTIMS' BRAINS AND CONTROL THEIR LUNGS.
THEY DON'T SUFFOCATE, THOUGH.
YOU'RE MADE OUT OF A GAS... SOMETHING SIMILAR TO OXYGEN.
......
MUST KILL SORCERER.
WRONG, SAMI.
THAT'S NOT WHAT YOU REALLY WANT.

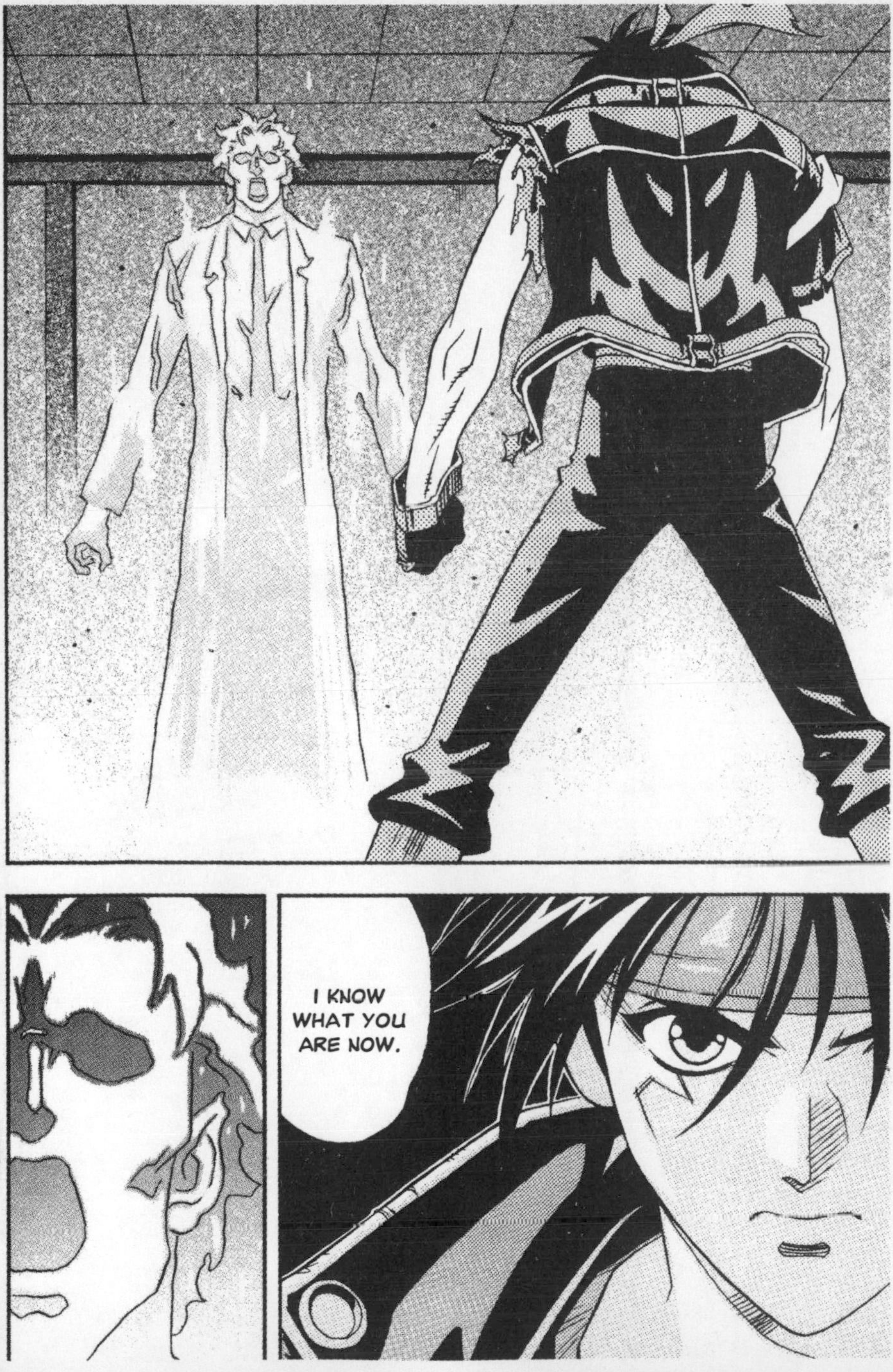
I KNOW WHAT YOU ARE NOW.

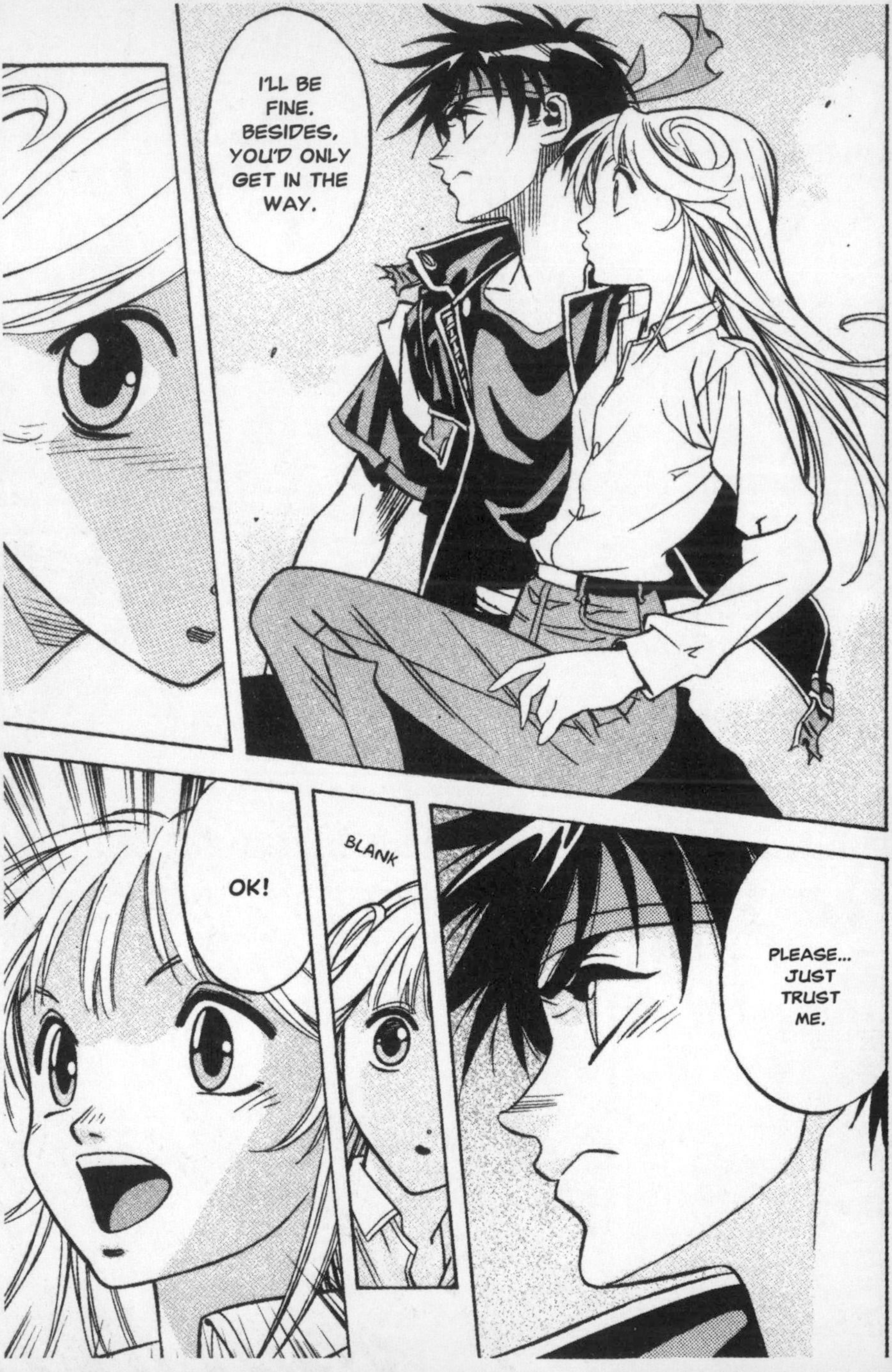
I'LL BE FINE. BESIDES, YOU'D ONLY GET IN THE WAY.
PLEASE... JUST TRUST ME.
BLANK
OK!

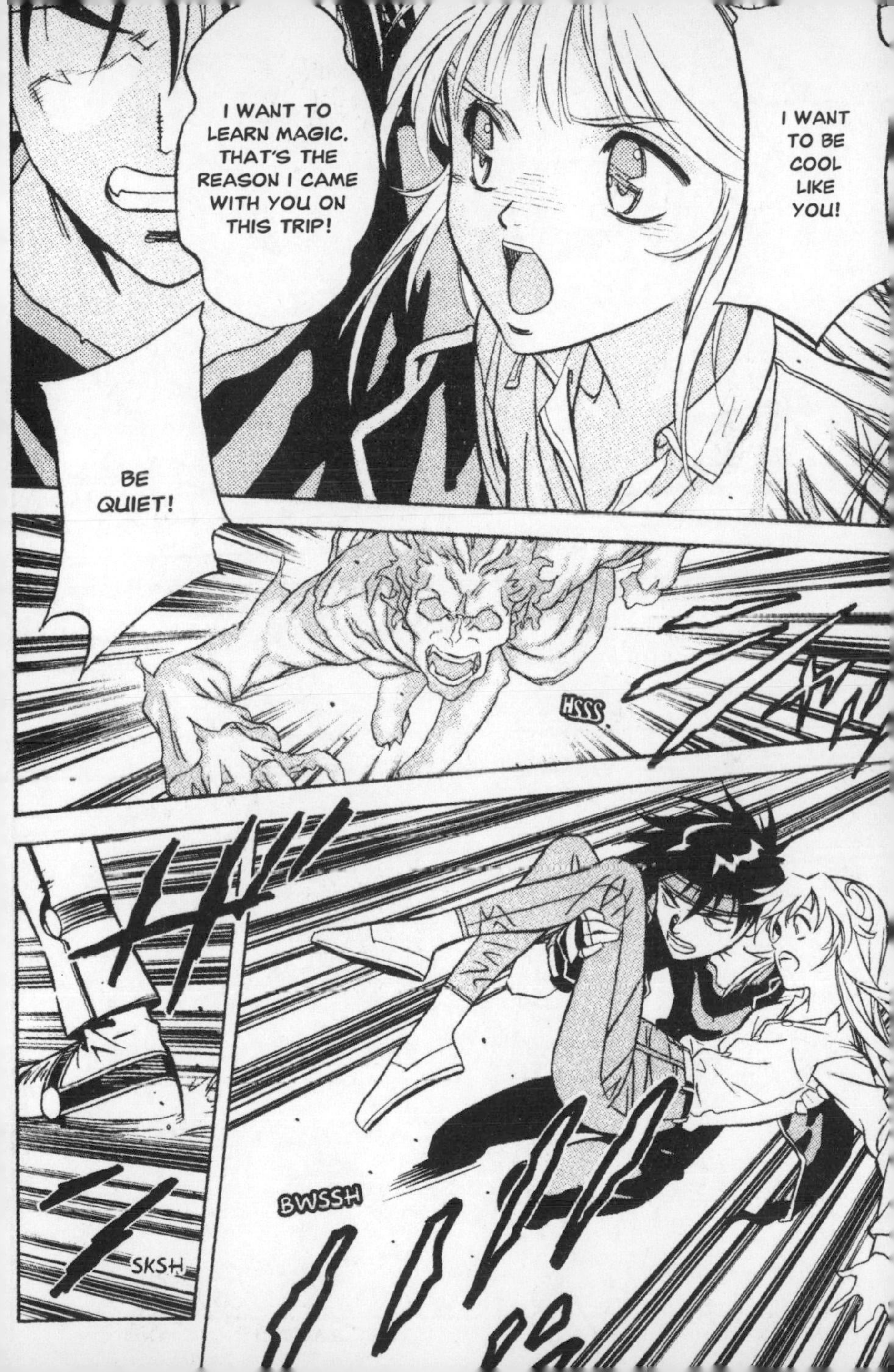
I WANT TO BE COOL LIKE YOU!
I WANT TO LEARN MAGIC. THAT'S THE REASON I CAME WITH YOU ON THIS TRIP!
BE QUIET!
HSSS
BWSSH
SKSH

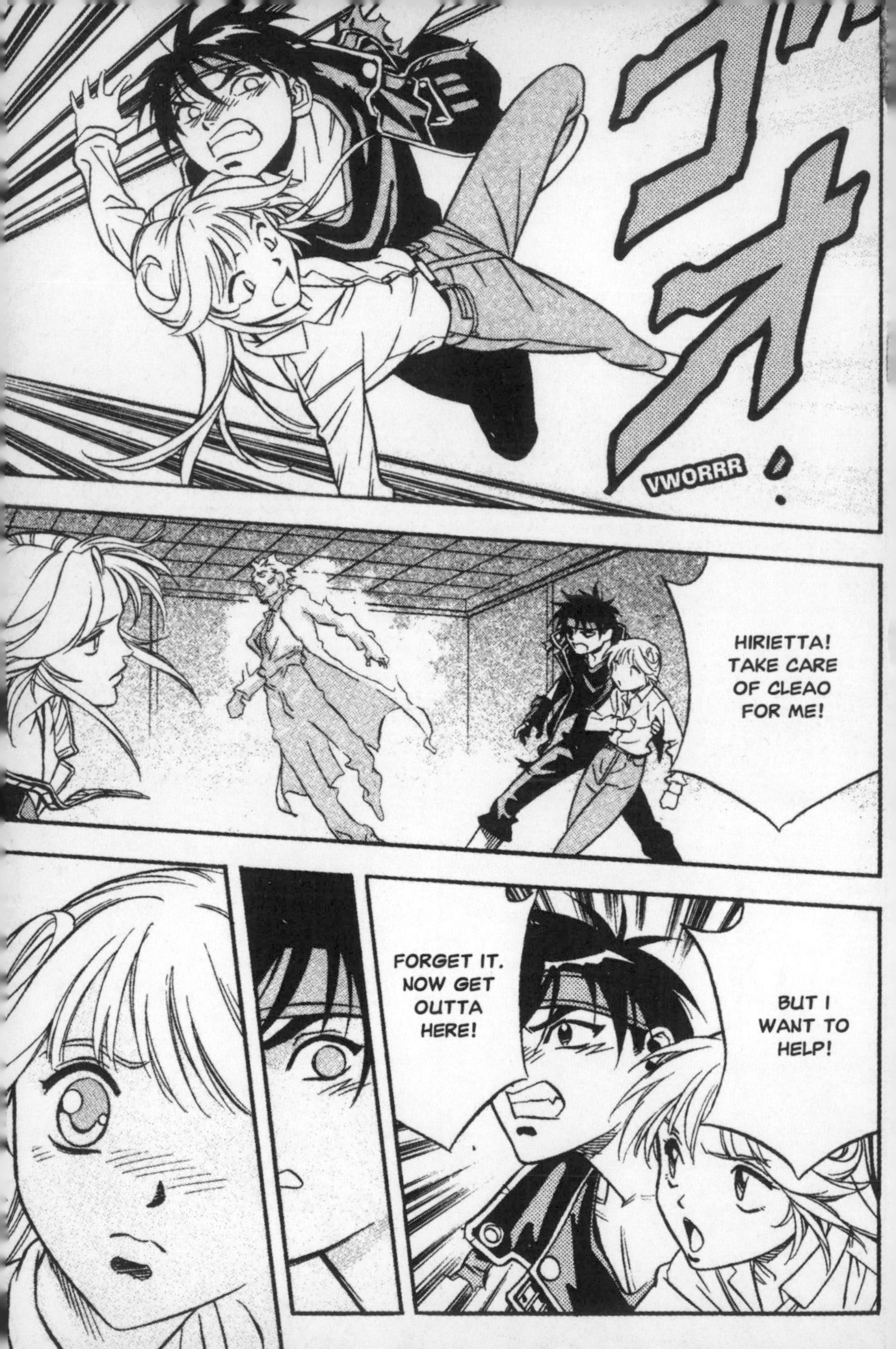
VWORRR
HIRIETTA! TAKE CARE OF CLEAO FOR ME!
BUT I WANT TO HELP!
FORGET IT. NOW GET OUTTA HERE!

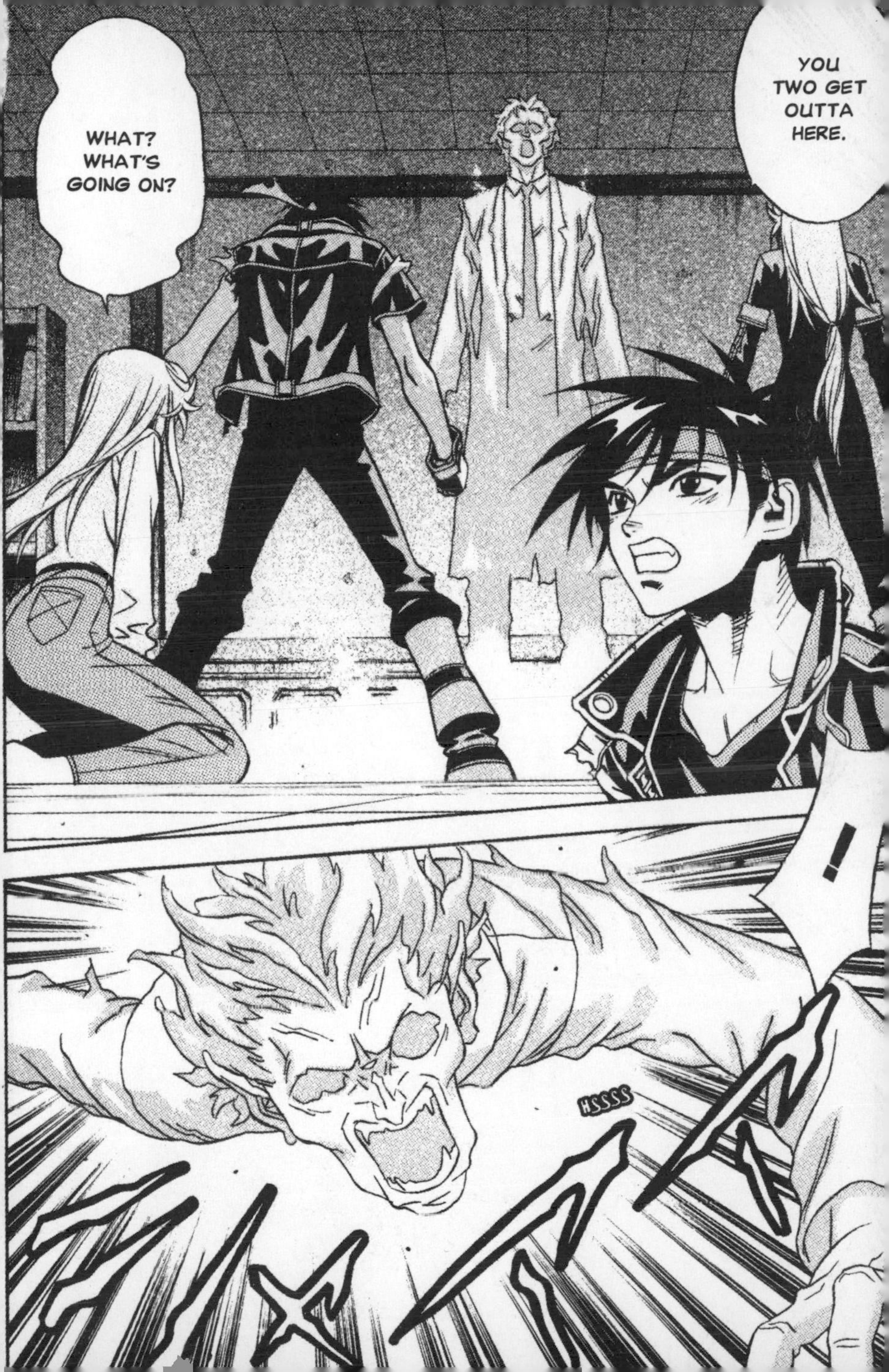
YOU TWO GET OUTTA HERE.
WHAT? WHAT'S GOING ON?
!
HSSSS

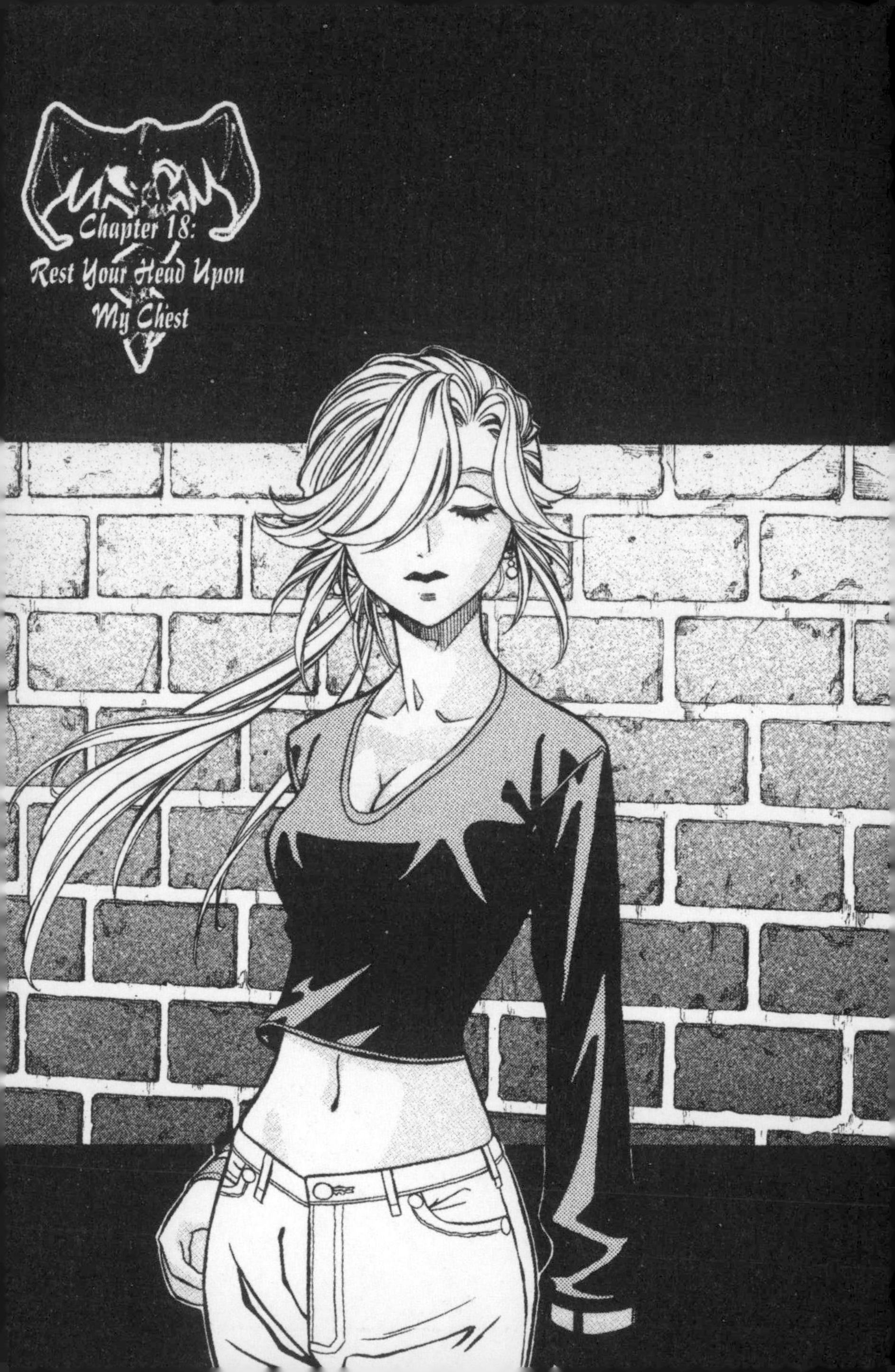
Chapter 18:
Rest Your Head Upon
My Chest

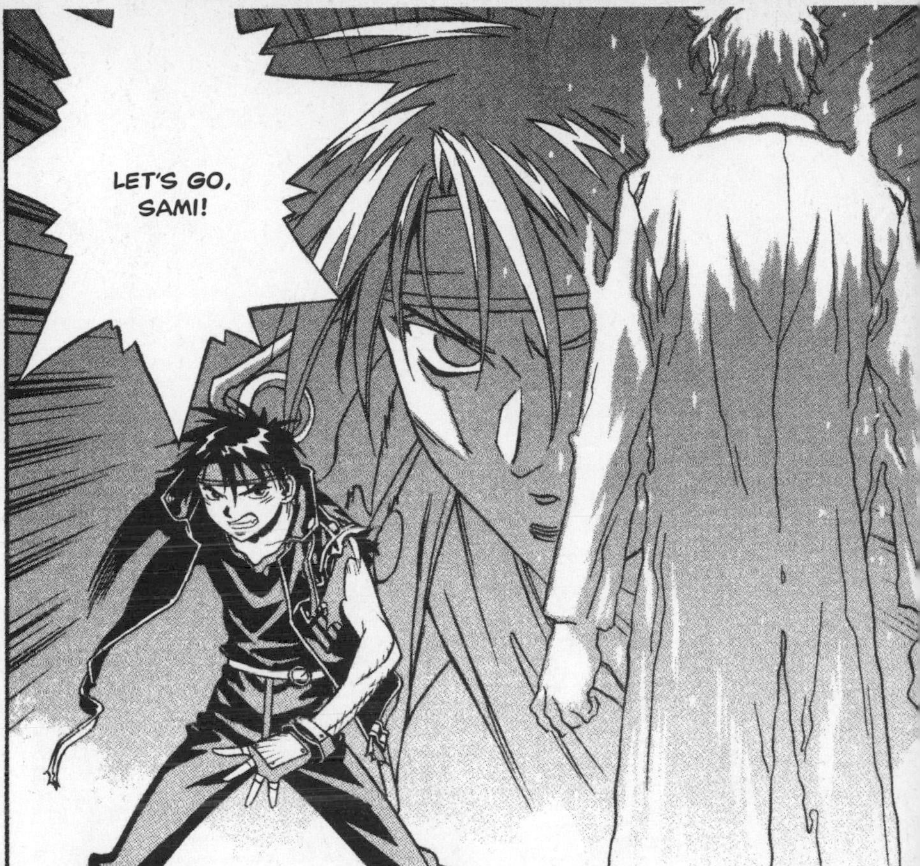
LET'S GO,
SAMI!
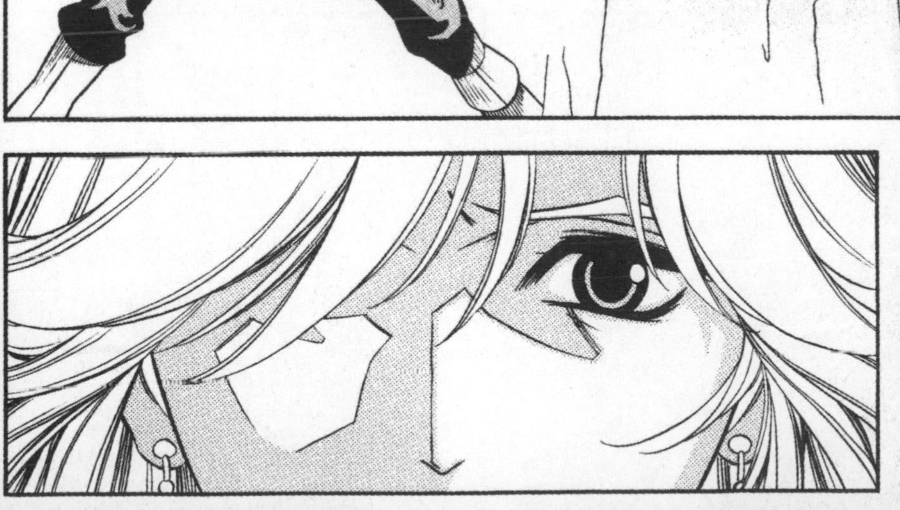

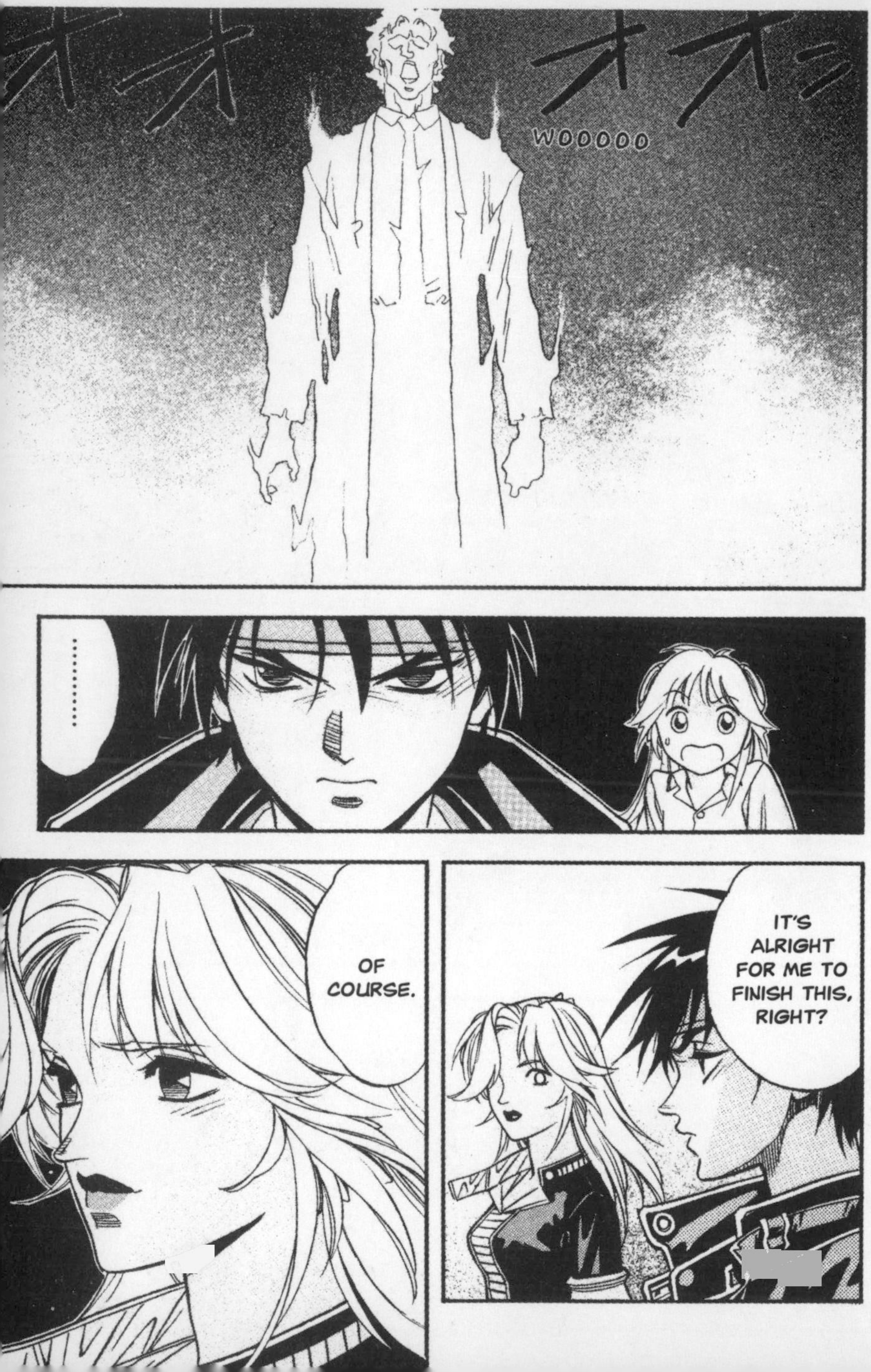
WOOOOO
......
IT'S ALRIGHT FOR ME TO FINISH THIS, RIGHT?
OF COURSE.

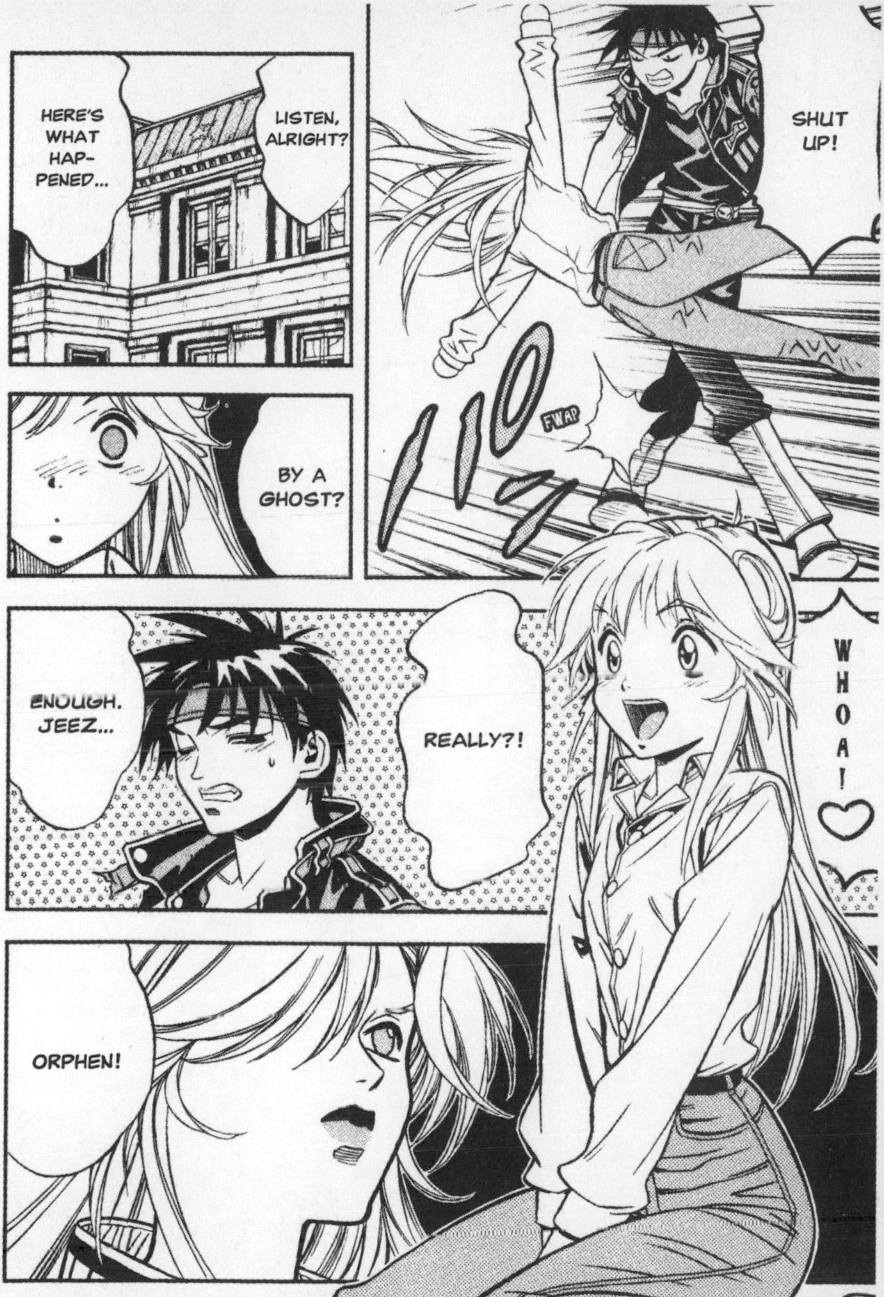
SHUT UP!
FWAP
LISTEN, ALRIGHT?
HERE'S WHAT HAP-PENED...
BY A GHOST?
WHOA! ♡
REALLY?!
ENOUGH. JEEZ...
ORPHEN!

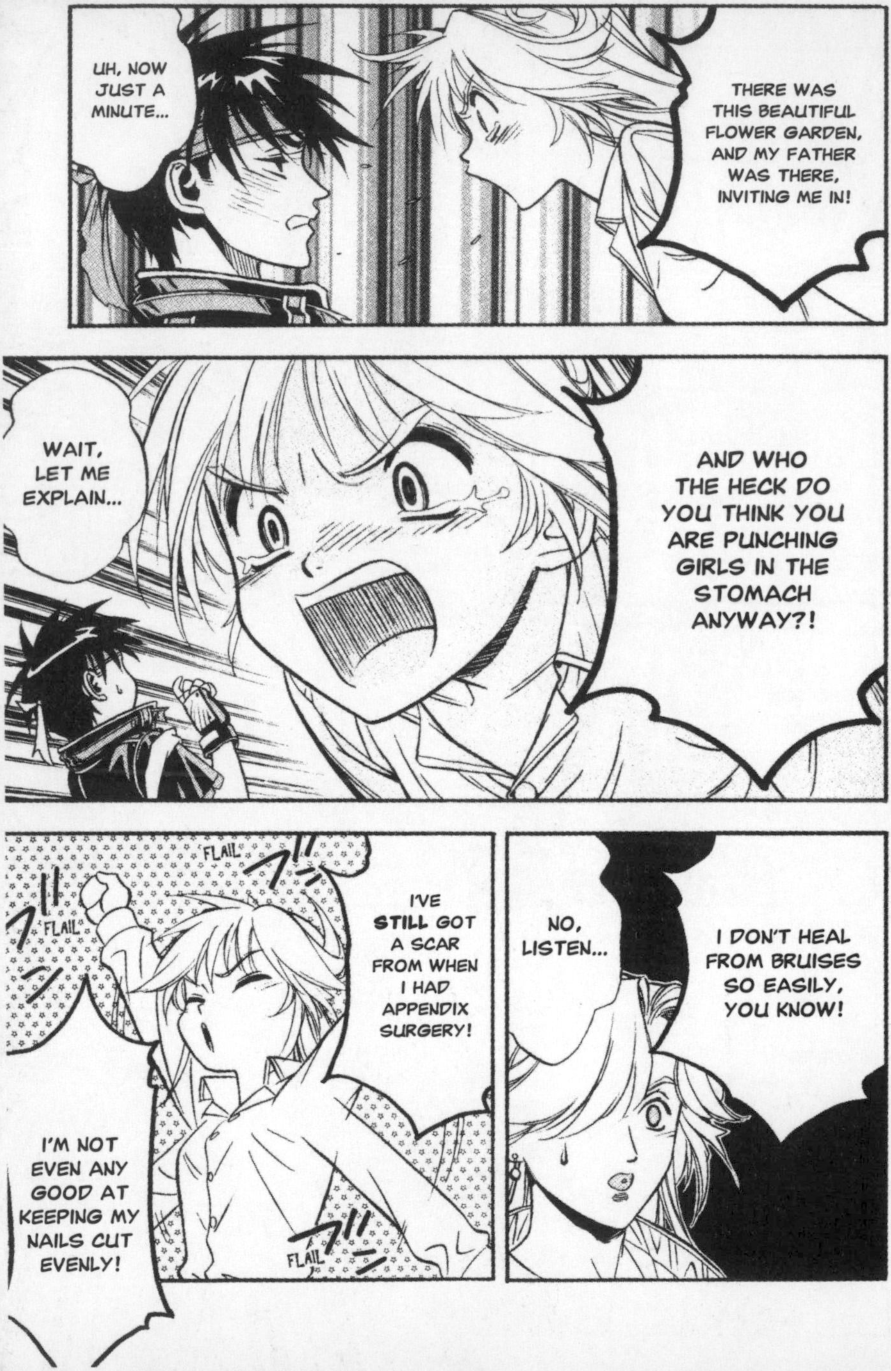
THERE WAS THIS BEAUTIFUL FLOWER GARDEN, AND MY FATHER WAS THERE, INVITING ME IN!
UH, NOW JUST A MINUTE...
AND WHO THE HECK DO YOU THINK YOU ARE PUNCHING GIRLS IN THE STOMACH ANYWAY?!
WAIT, LET ME EXPLAIN...
I DON'T HEAL FROM BRUISES SO EASILY, YOU KNOW!
NO, LISTEN...
I'VE **STILL** GOT A SCAR FROM WHEN I HAD APPENDIX SURGERY!
FLAIL
FLAIL
I'M NOT EVEN ANY GOOD AT KEEPING MY NAILS CUT EVENLY!
FLAIL

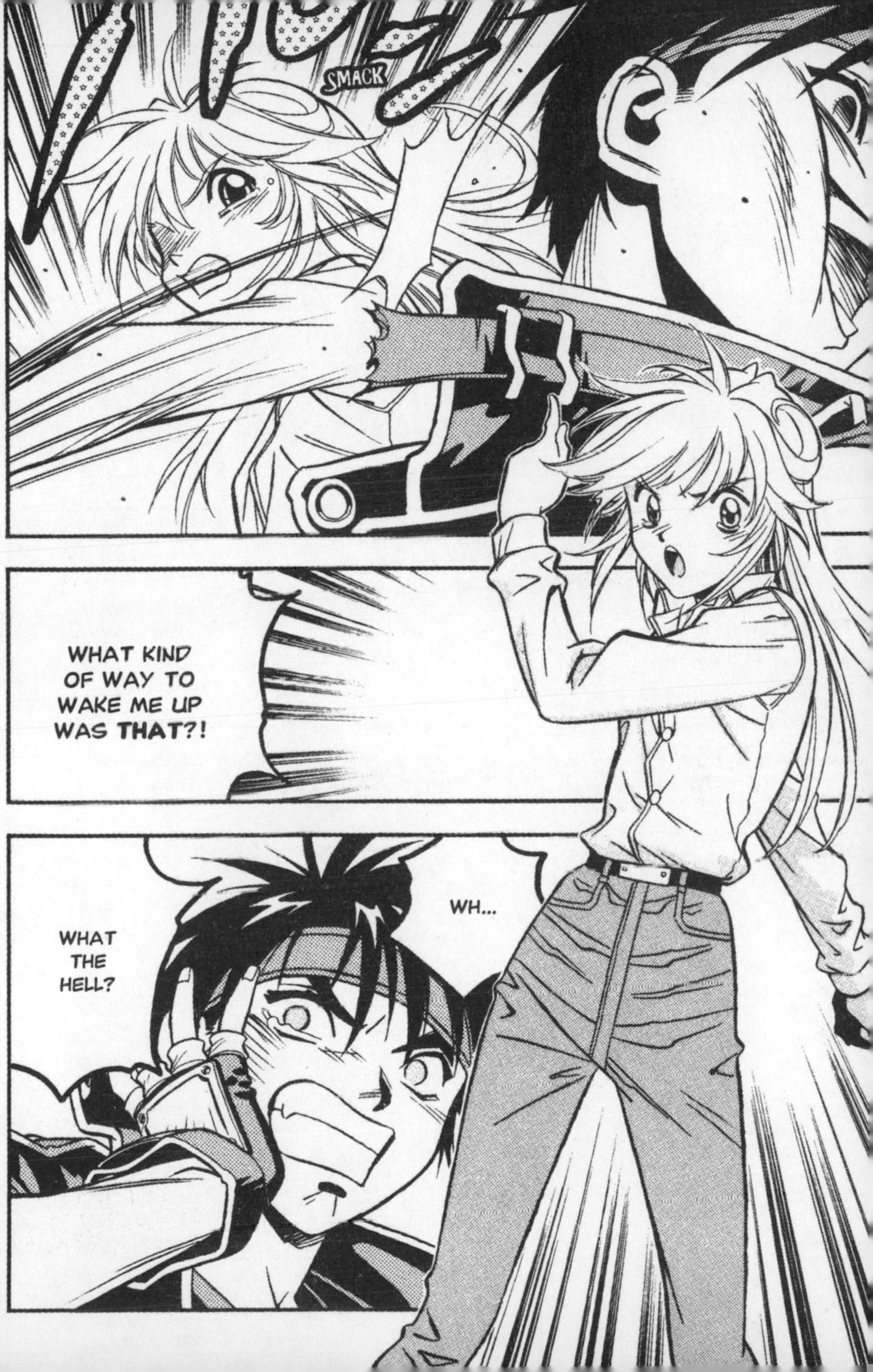
SMACK
WHAT KIND OF WAY TO WAKE ME UP WAS THAT?!
WH...
WHAT THE HELL?

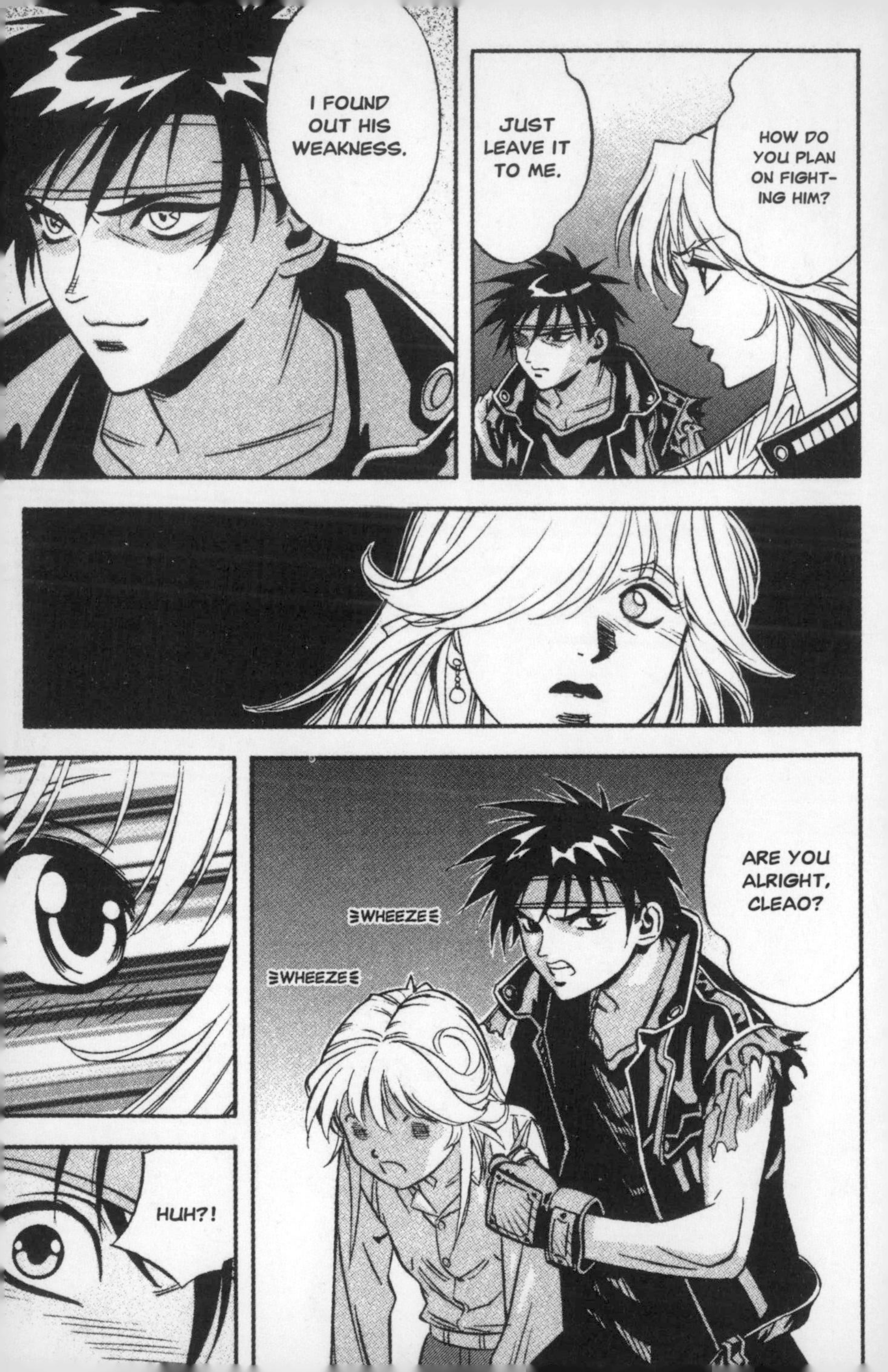
HOW DO YOU PLAN ON FIGHT-ING HIM?
JUST LEAVE IT TO ME.
I FOUND OUT HIS WEAKNESS.
ARE YOU ALRIGHT, CLEAO?
WHEEZE
WHEEZE
HUH?!

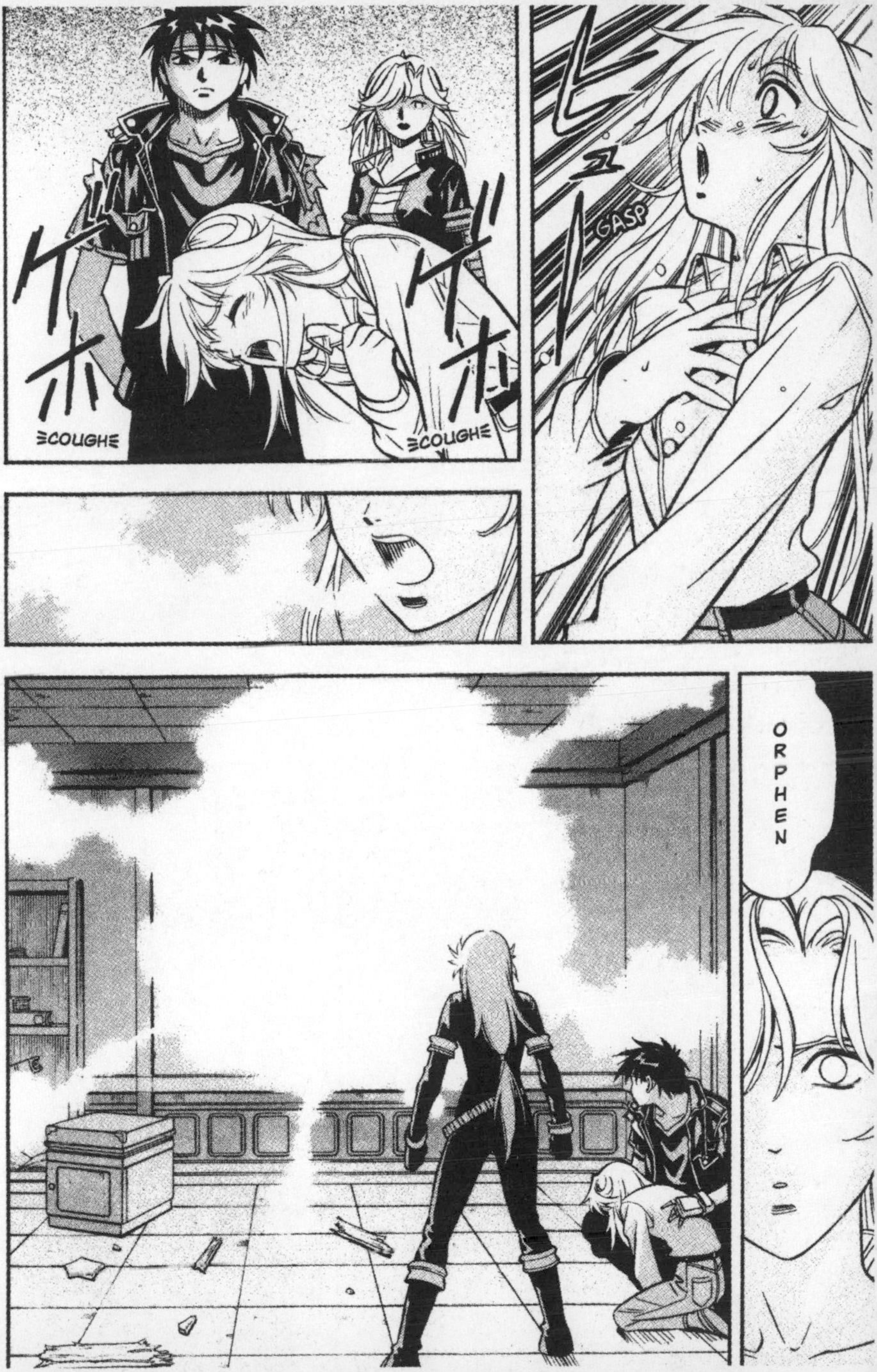
GASP
COUGH
COUGH
ORPHEN

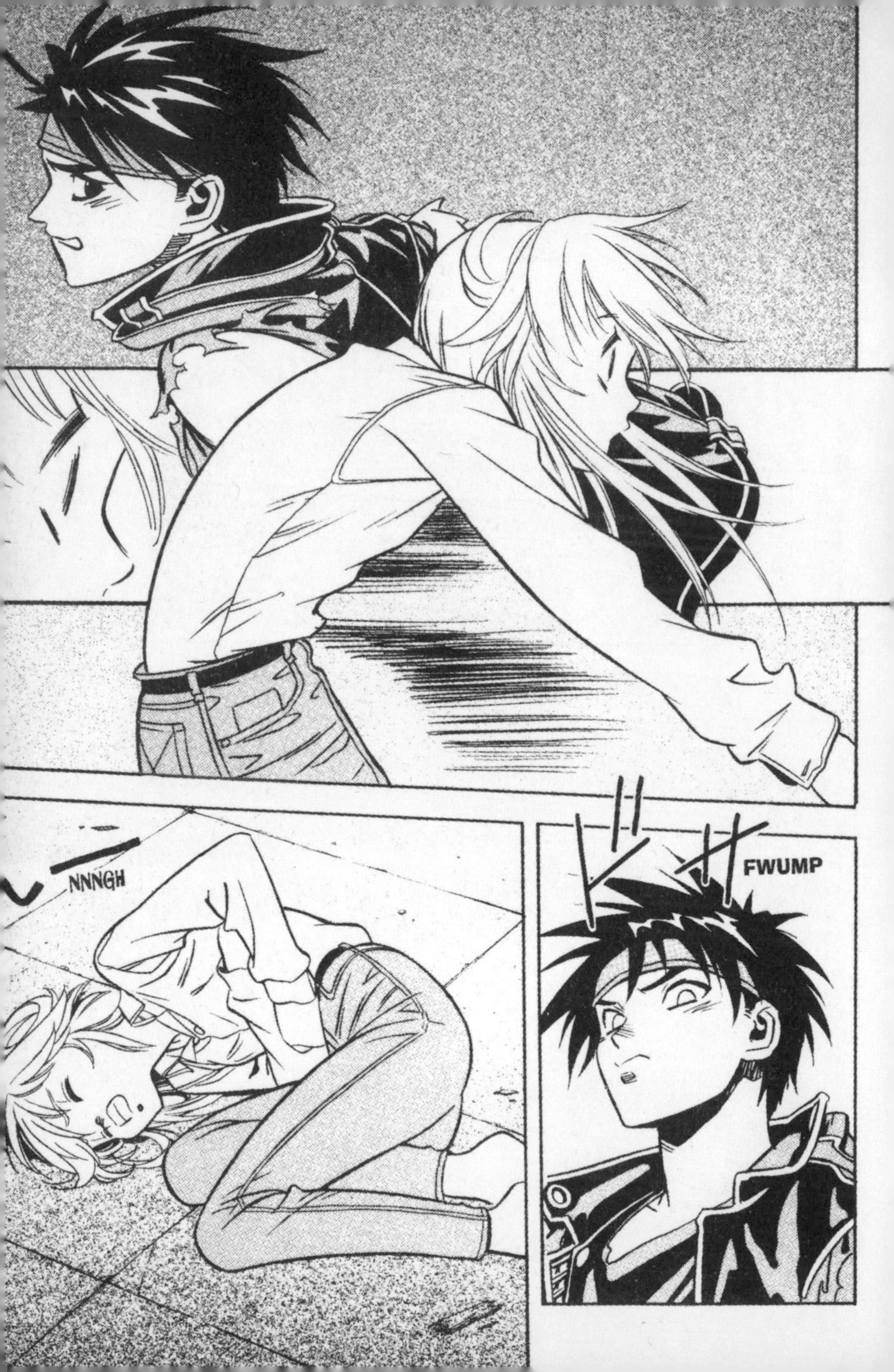
FWUMP
NNNGH

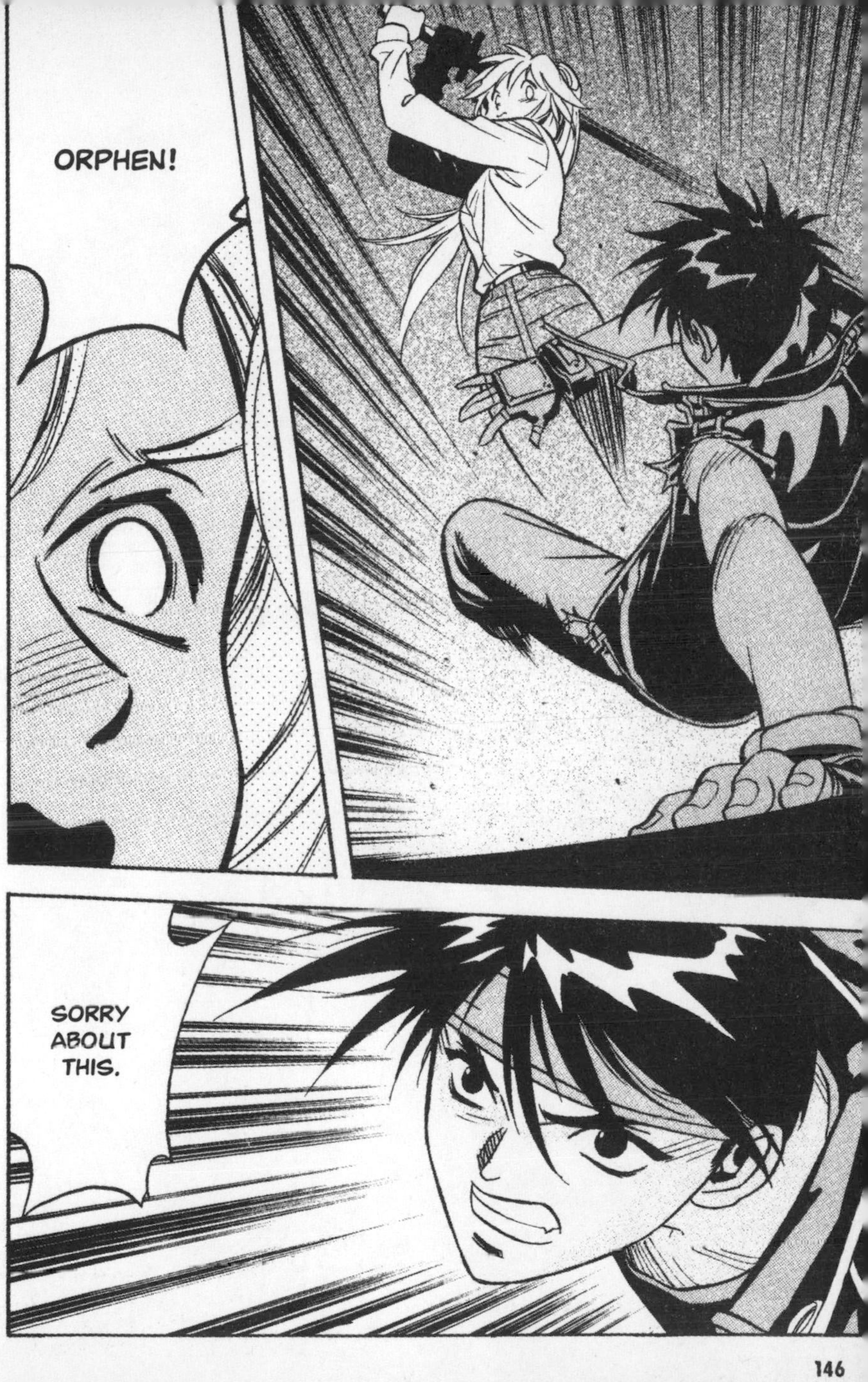
ORPHEN!
SORRY ABOUT THIS.

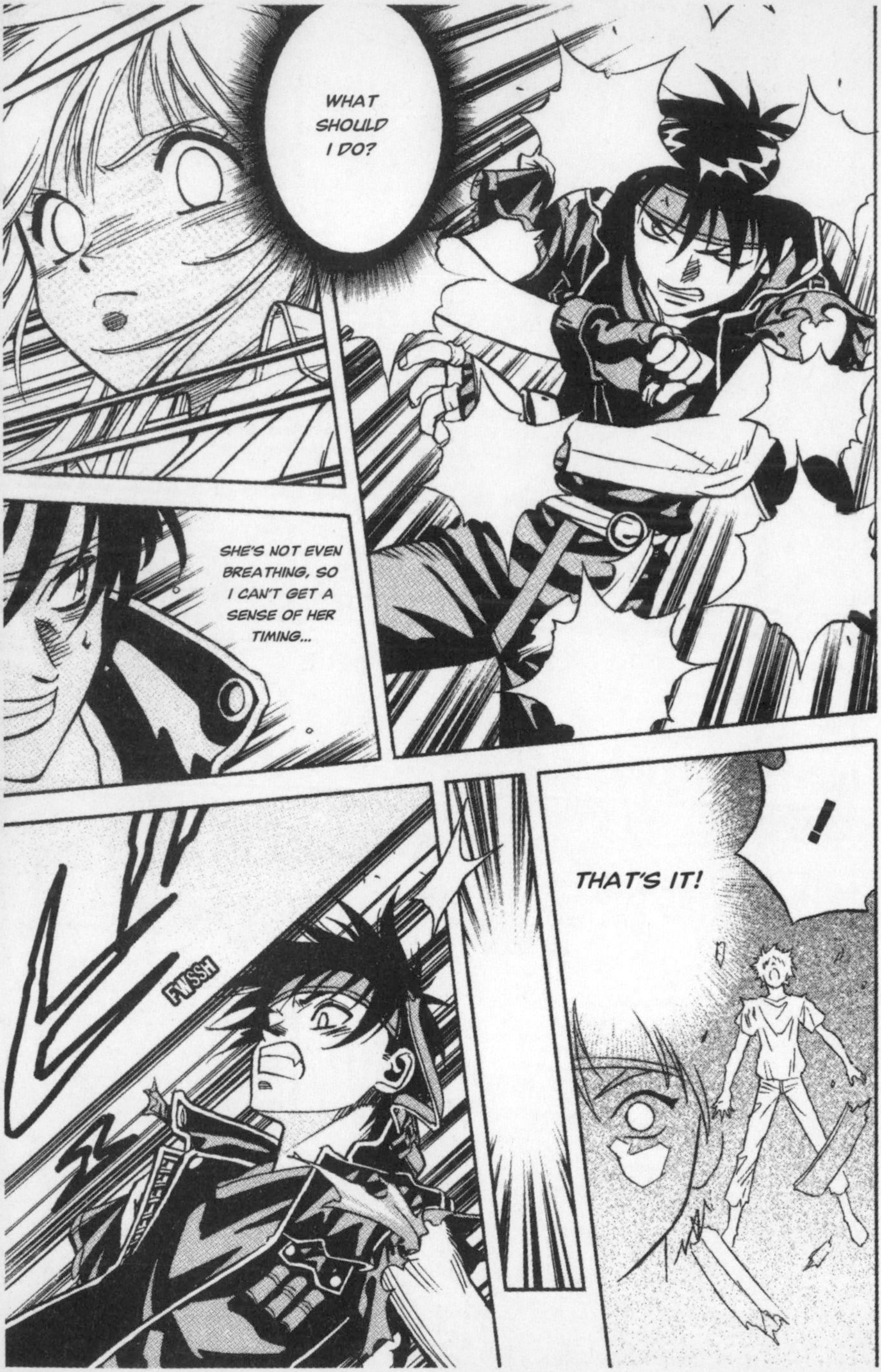
WHAT SHOULD I DO?
SHE'S NOT EVEN BREATHING, SO I CAN'T GET A SENSE OF HER TIMING...
!
THAT'S IT!
FWSSH

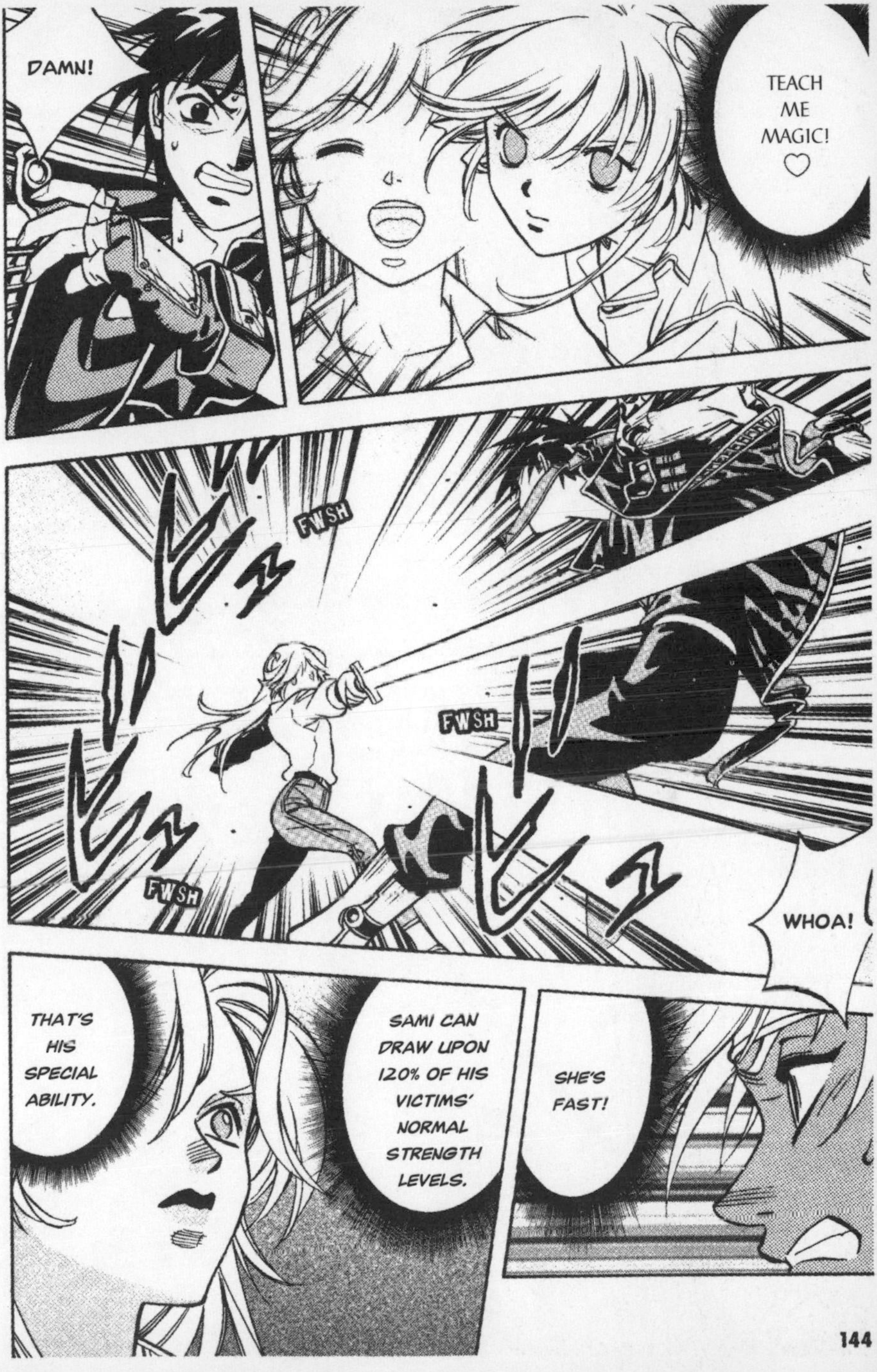
TEACH ME MAGIC! ♡
DAMN!
FWSH
FWSH
FWSH
WHOA!
SHE'S FAST!
SAMI CAN DRAW UPON 120% OF HIS VICTIMS' NORMAL STRENGTH LEVELS.
THAT'S HIS SPECIAL ABILITY.

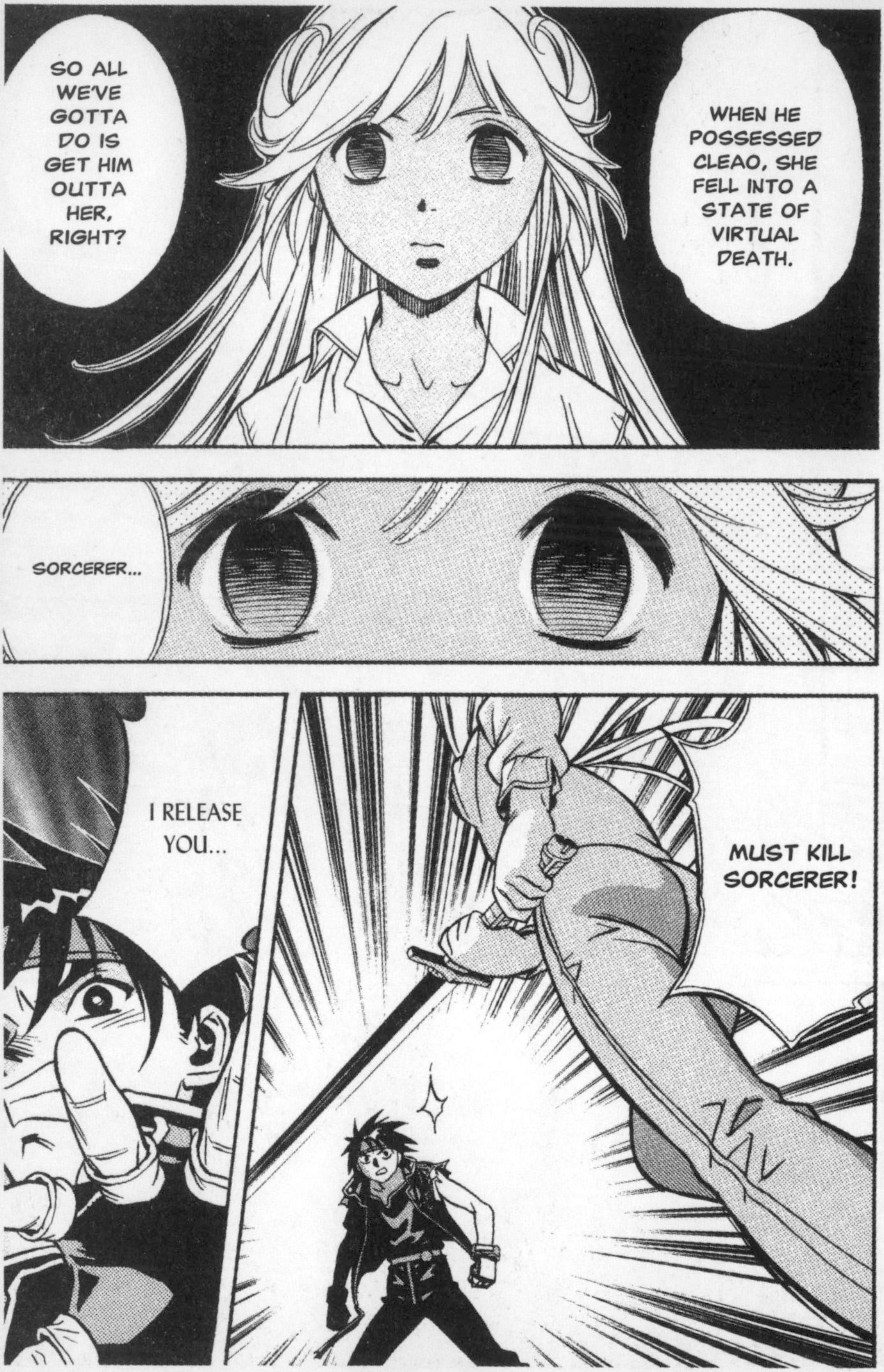
WHEN HE POSSESSED CLEAO, SHE FELL INTO A STATE OF VIRTUAL DEATH.
SO ALL WE'VE GOTTA DO IS GET HIM OUTTA HER, RIGHT?
SORCERER...
MUST KILL SORCERER!
I RELEASE YOU...

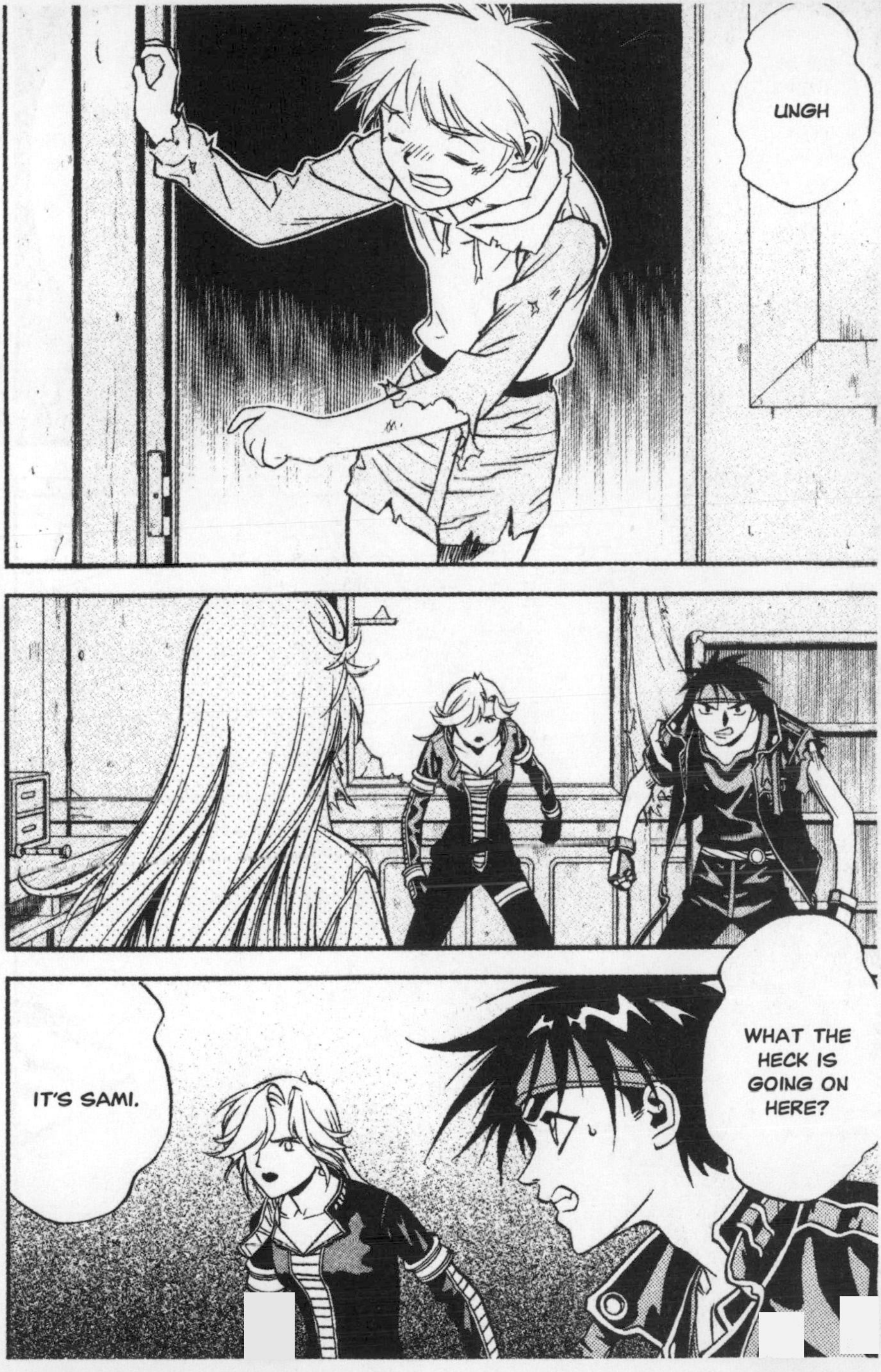
UNGH
WHAT THE HECK IS GOING ON HERE?
IT'S SAMI.

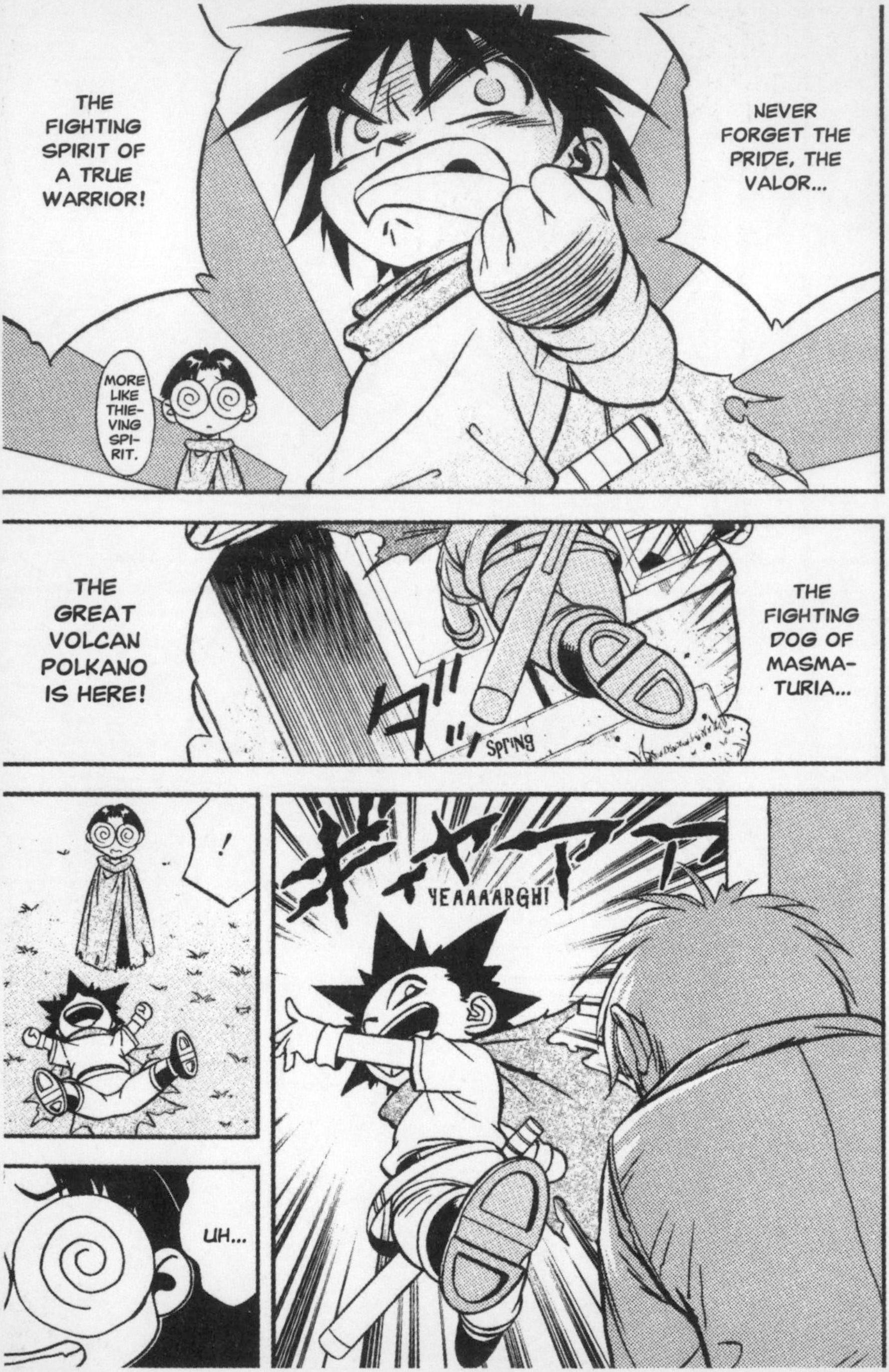
NEVER FORGET THE PRIDE, THE VALOR...
THE FIGHTING SPIRIT OF A TRUE WARRIOR!
MORE LIKE THIEVING SPIRIT.
THE FIGHTING DOG OF MASMATURIA...
THE GREAT VOLCAN POLKANO IS HERE!
SPRING
YEAAAARGH!
!
UH...

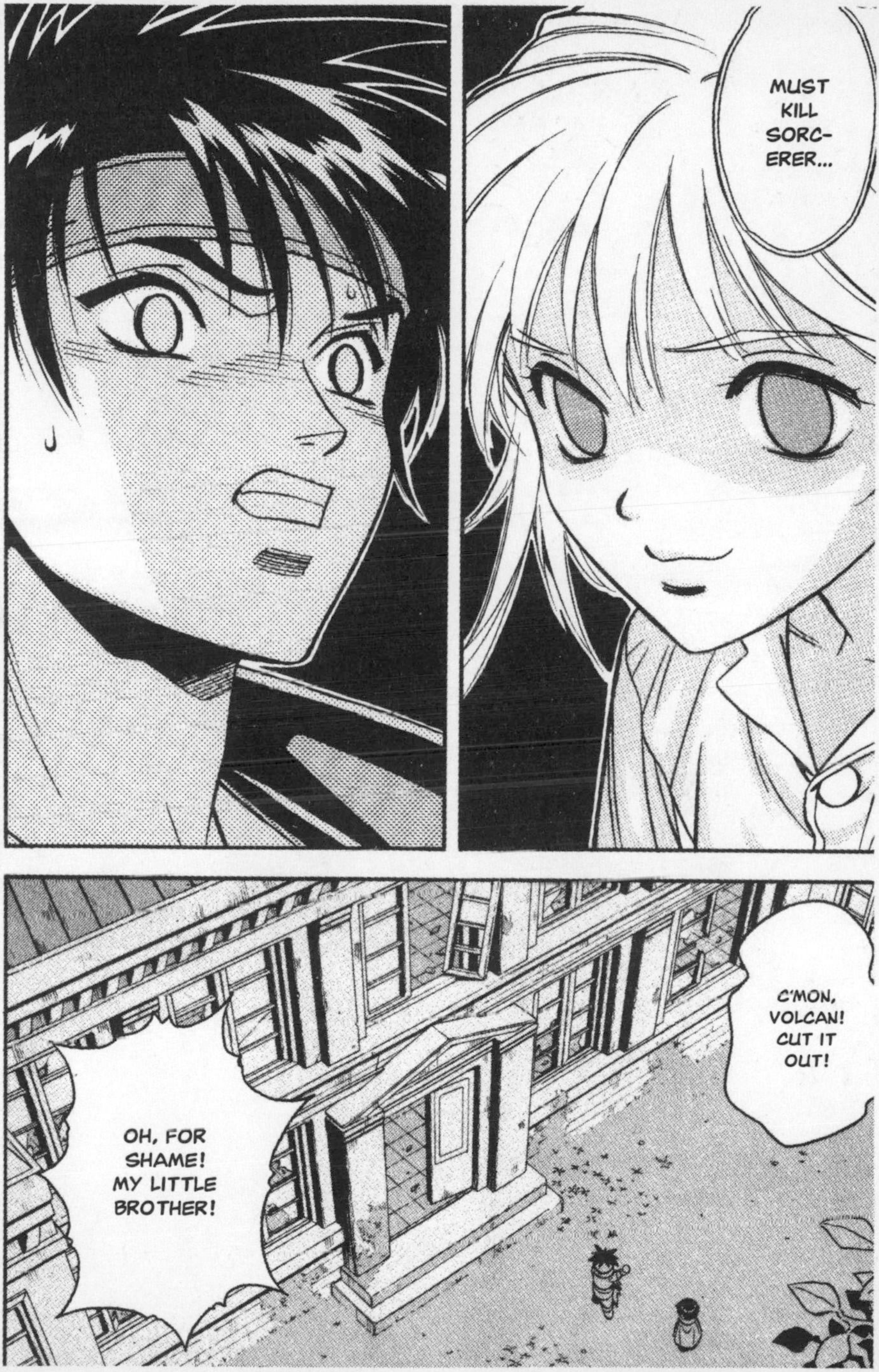
MUST KILL SORCERER...
C'MON, VOLCAN! CUT IT OUT!
OH, FOR SHAME! MY LITTLE BROTHER!

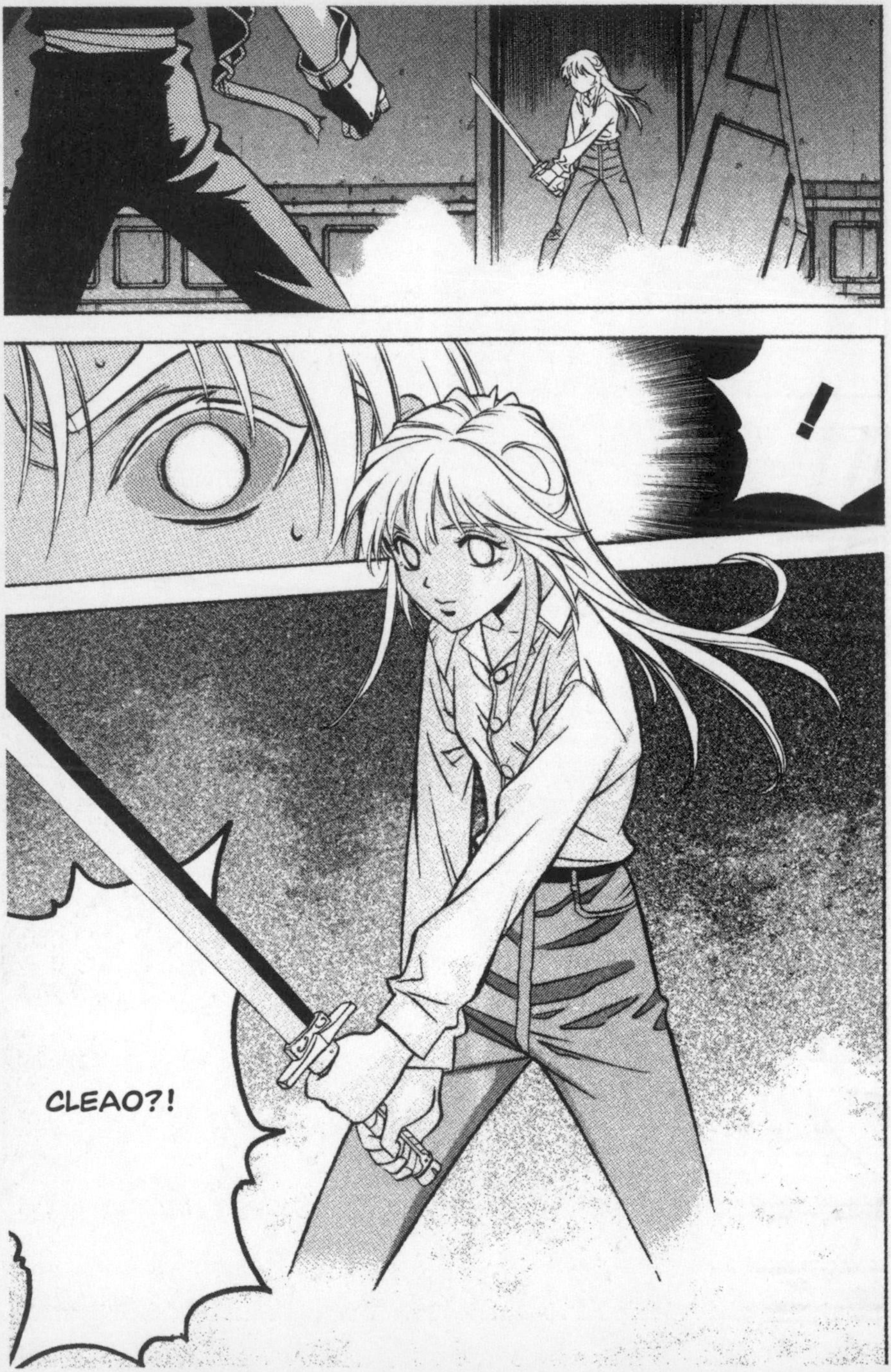
!
CLEAO?!

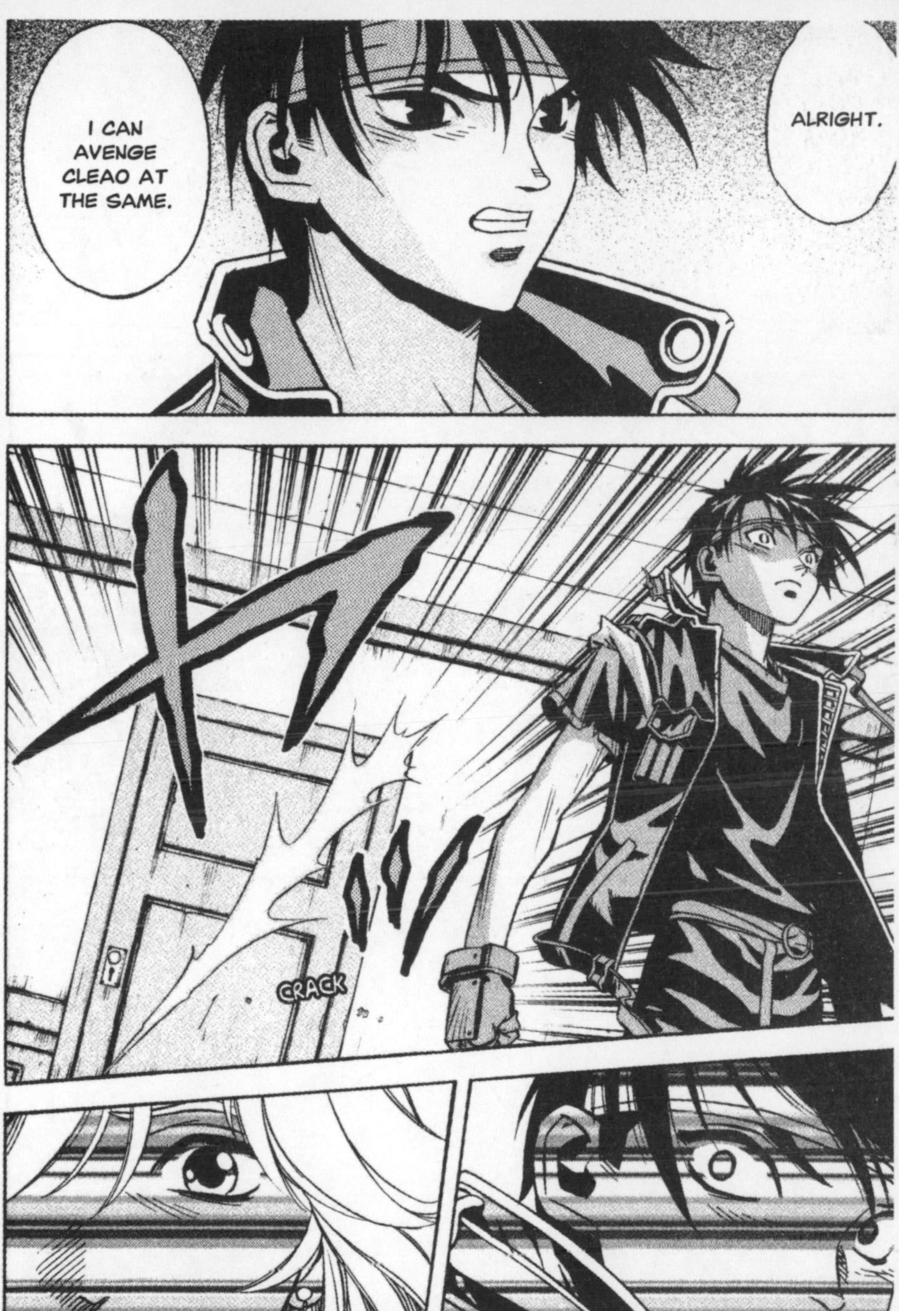
ALRIGHT.
I CAN AVENGE CLEAO AT THE SAME.
CRACK

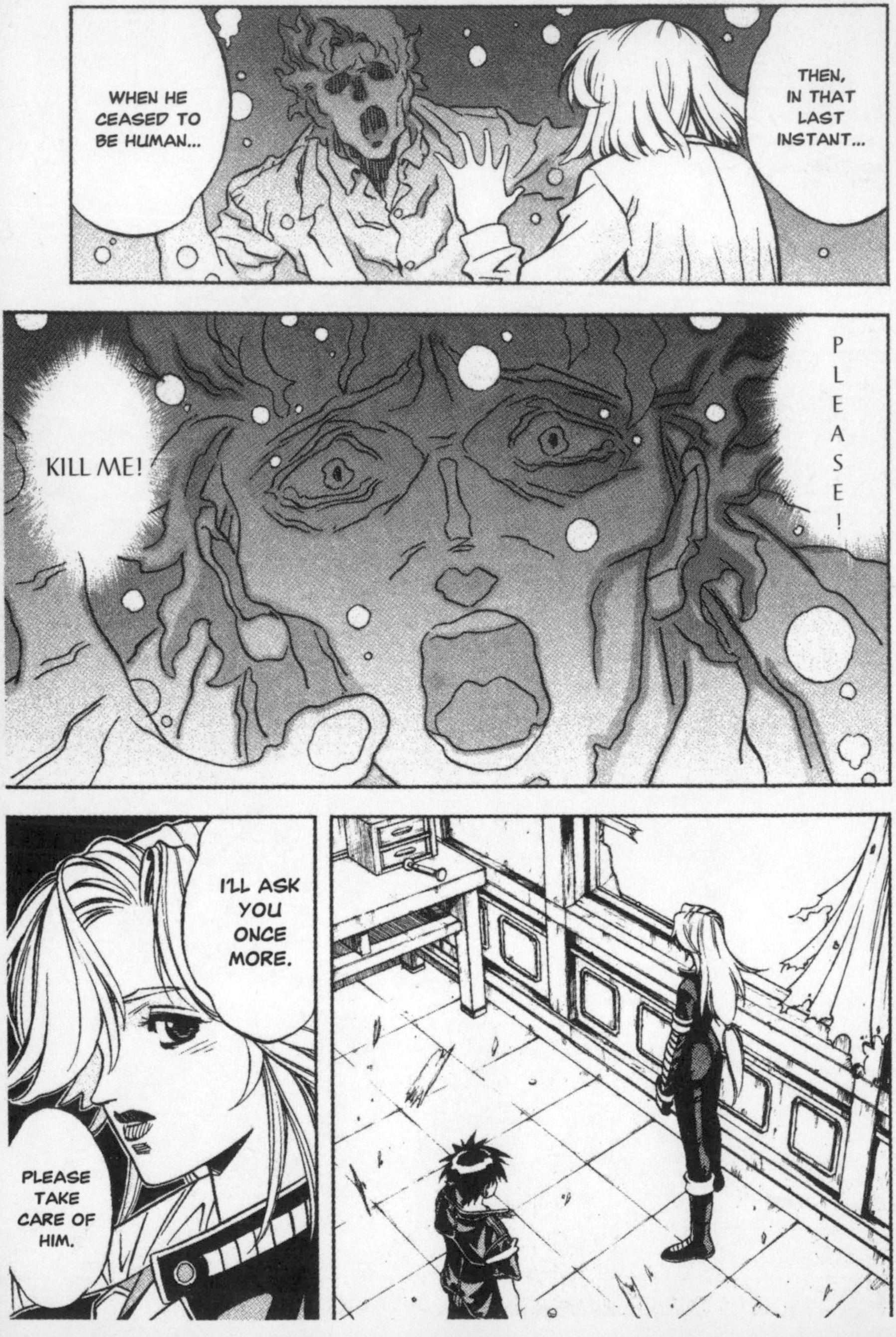
THEN, IN THAT LAST INSTANT...
WHEN HE CEASED TO BE HUMAN...
PLEASE!
KILL ME!
I'LL ASK YOU ONCE MORE.
PLEASE TAKE CARE OF HIM.

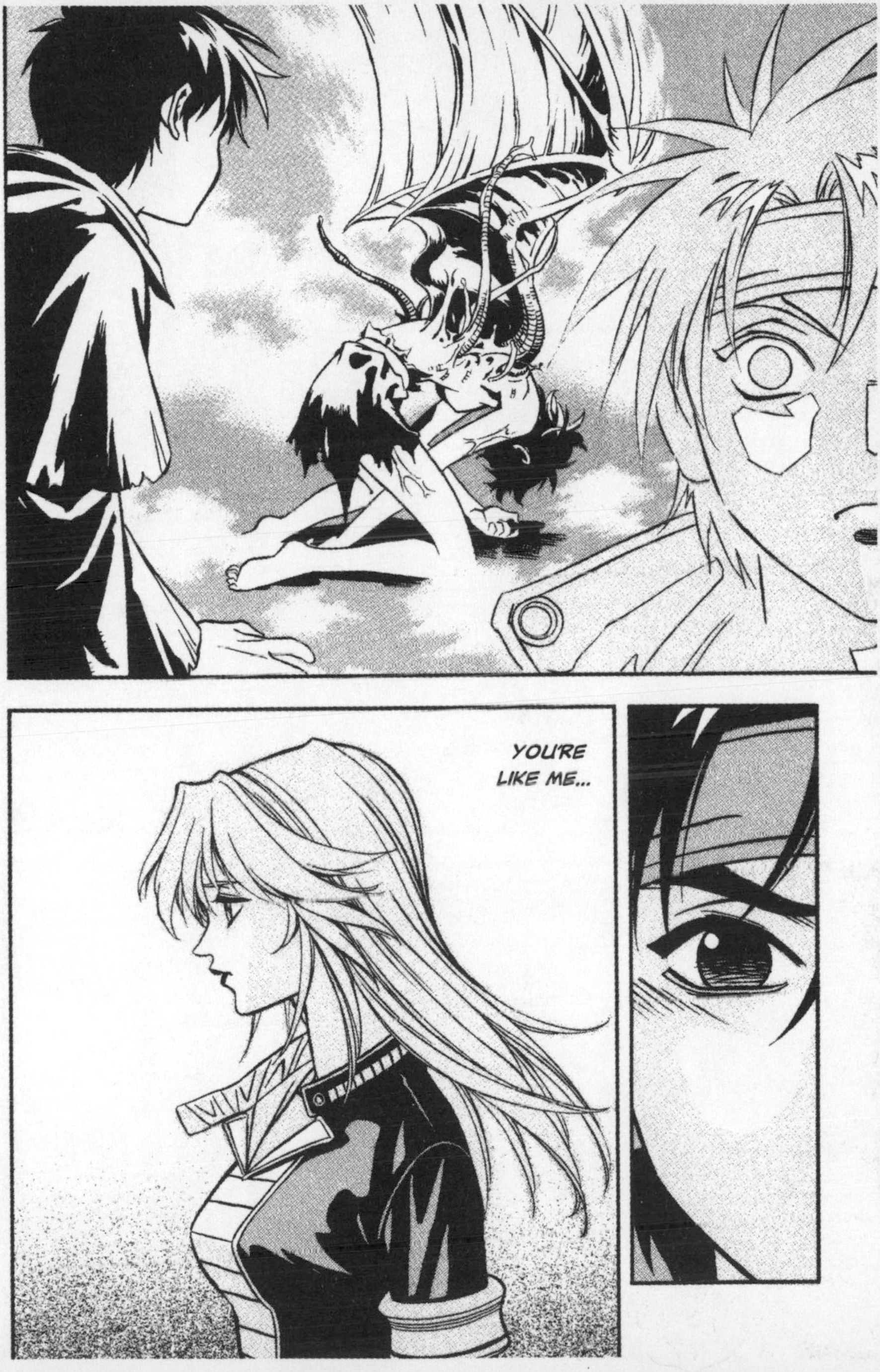
YOU'RE LIKE ME...

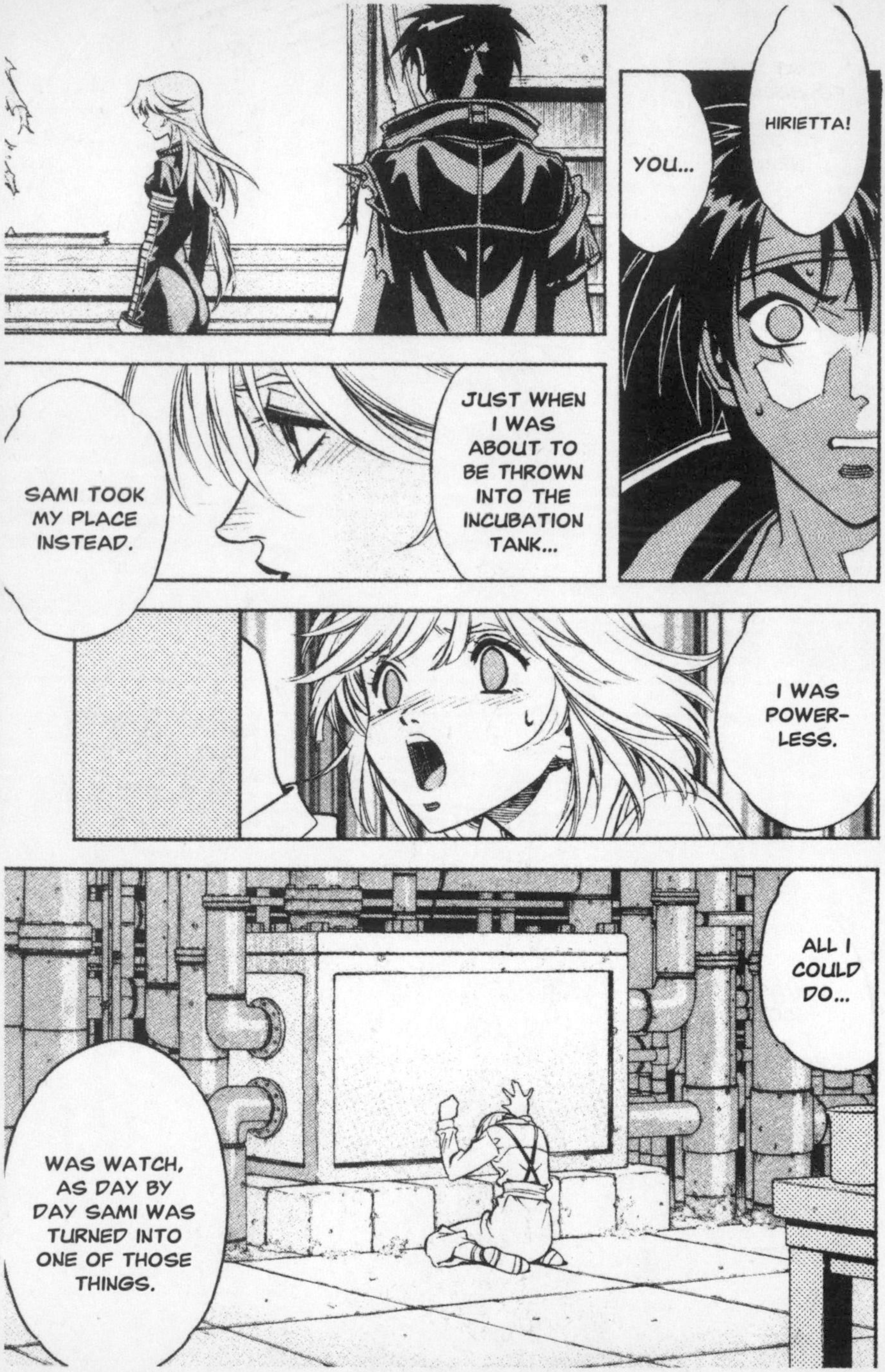
HIRIETTA!
YOU...
JUST WHEN I WAS ABOUT TO BE THROWN INTO THE INCUBATION TANK...
SAMI TOOK MY PLACE INSTEAD.
I WAS POWER-LESS.
ALL I COULD DO...
WAS WATCH, AS DAY BY DAY SAMI WAS TURNED INTO ONE OF THOSE THINGS.

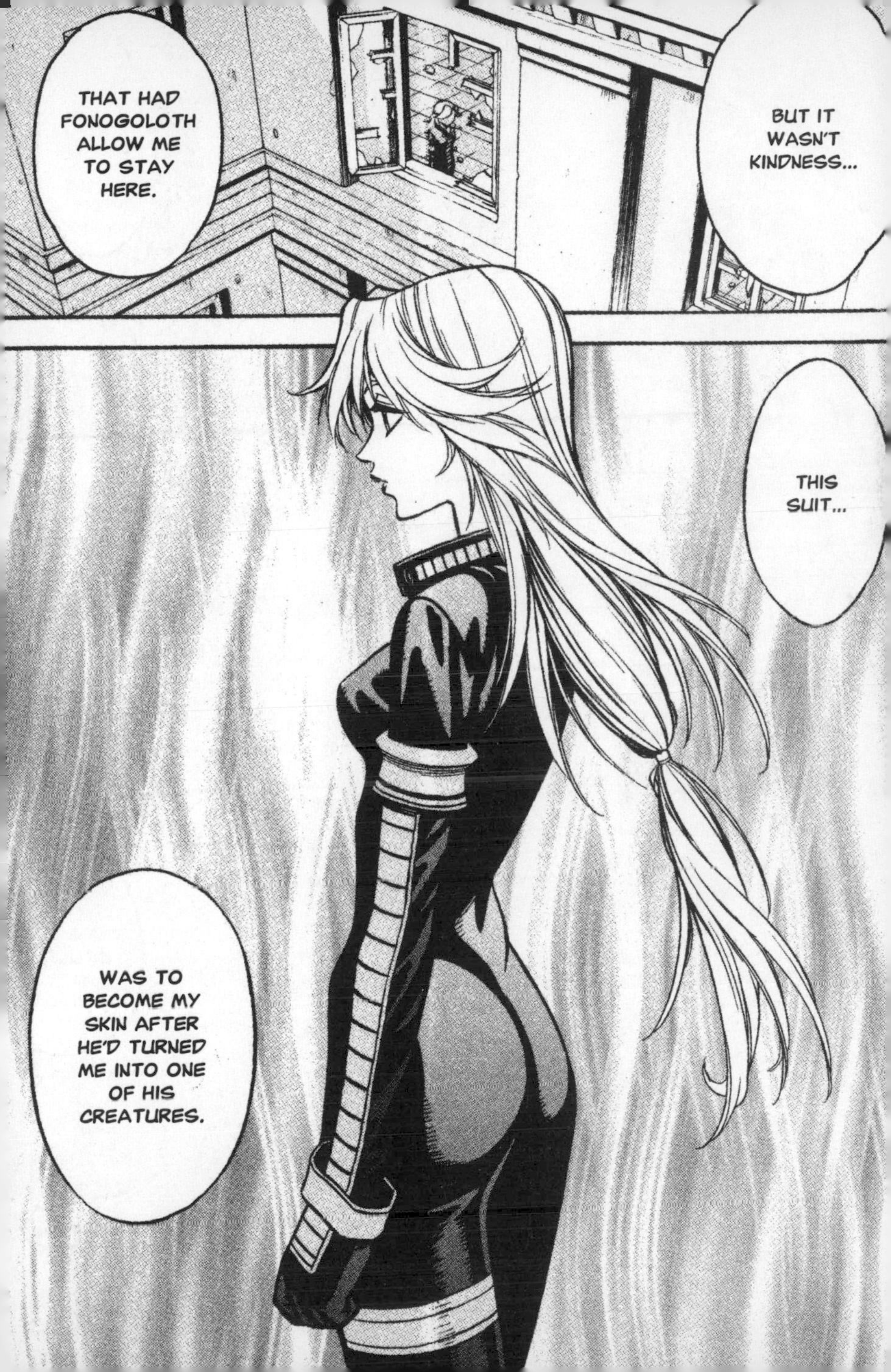
BUT IT WASN'T KINDNESS...
THAT HAD FONOGOLOTH ALLOW ME TO STAY HERE.
THIS SUIT...
WAS TO BECOME MY SKIN AFTER HE'D TURNED ME INTO ONE OF HIS CREATURES.

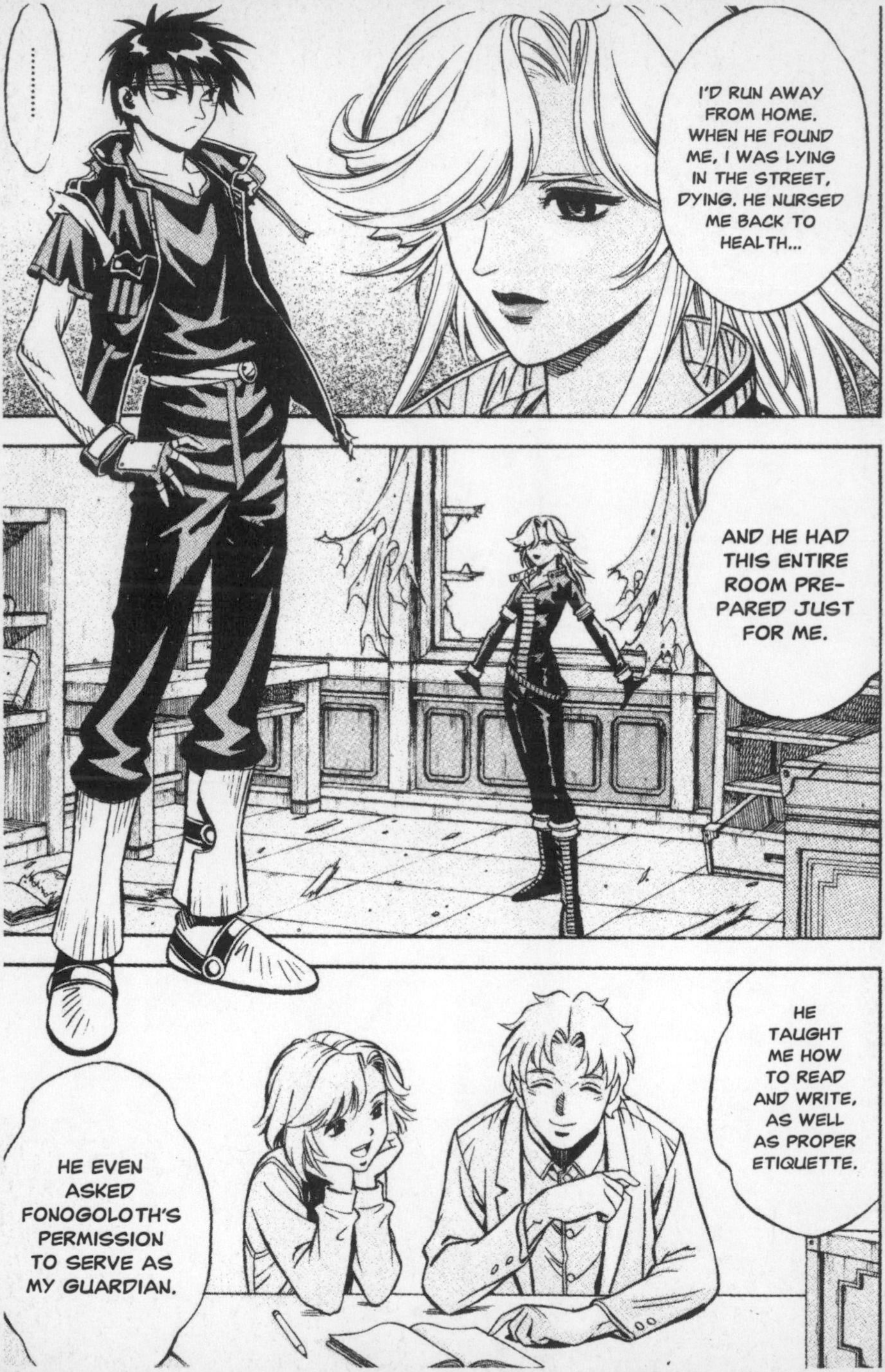
I'D RUN AWAY FROM HOME. WHEN HE FOUND ME, I WAS LYING IN THE STREET, DYING. HE NURSED ME BACK TO HEALTH...
......
AND HE HAD THIS ENTIRE ROOM PRE-PARED JUST FOR ME.
HE TAUGHT ME HOW TO READ AND WRITE, AS WELL AS PROPER ETIQUETTE.
HE EVEN ASKED FONOGOLOTH'S PERMISSION TO SERVE AS MY GUARDIAN.

Chapter 17: The Strongest Opponent

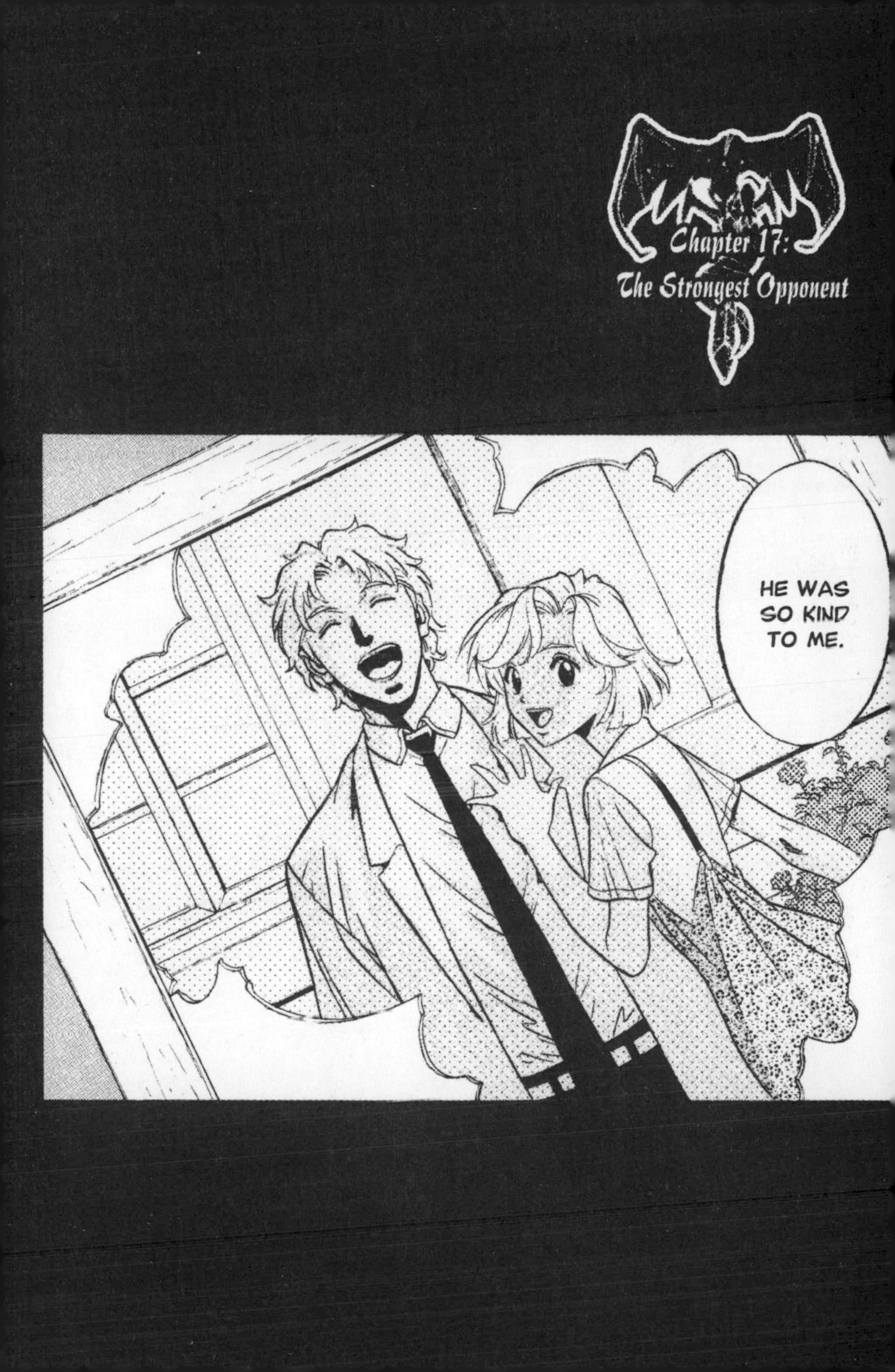
HE WAS SO KIND TO ME.

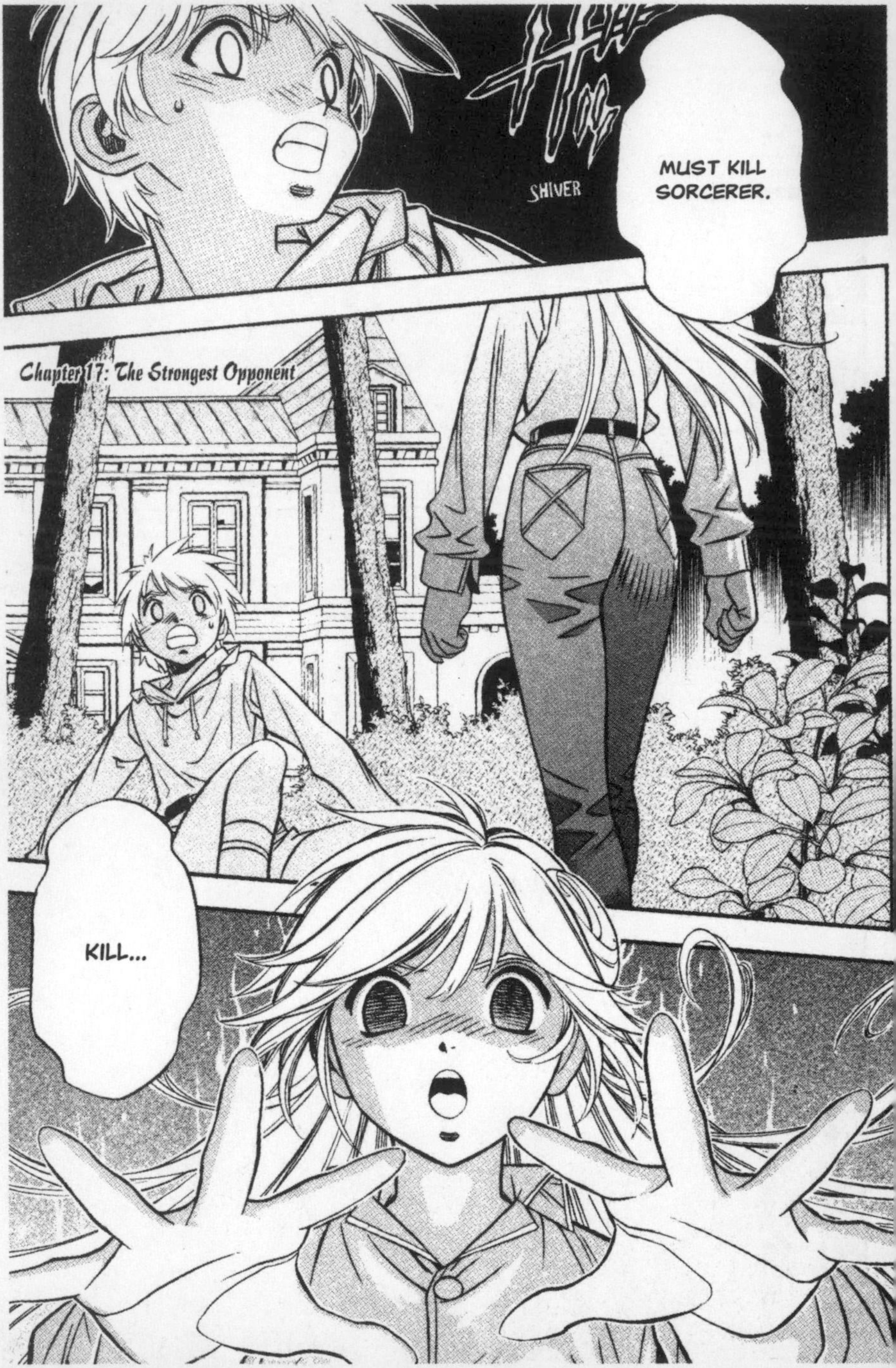
MUST KILL SORCERER.
SHIVER
Chapter 17: The Strongest Opponent
KILL...

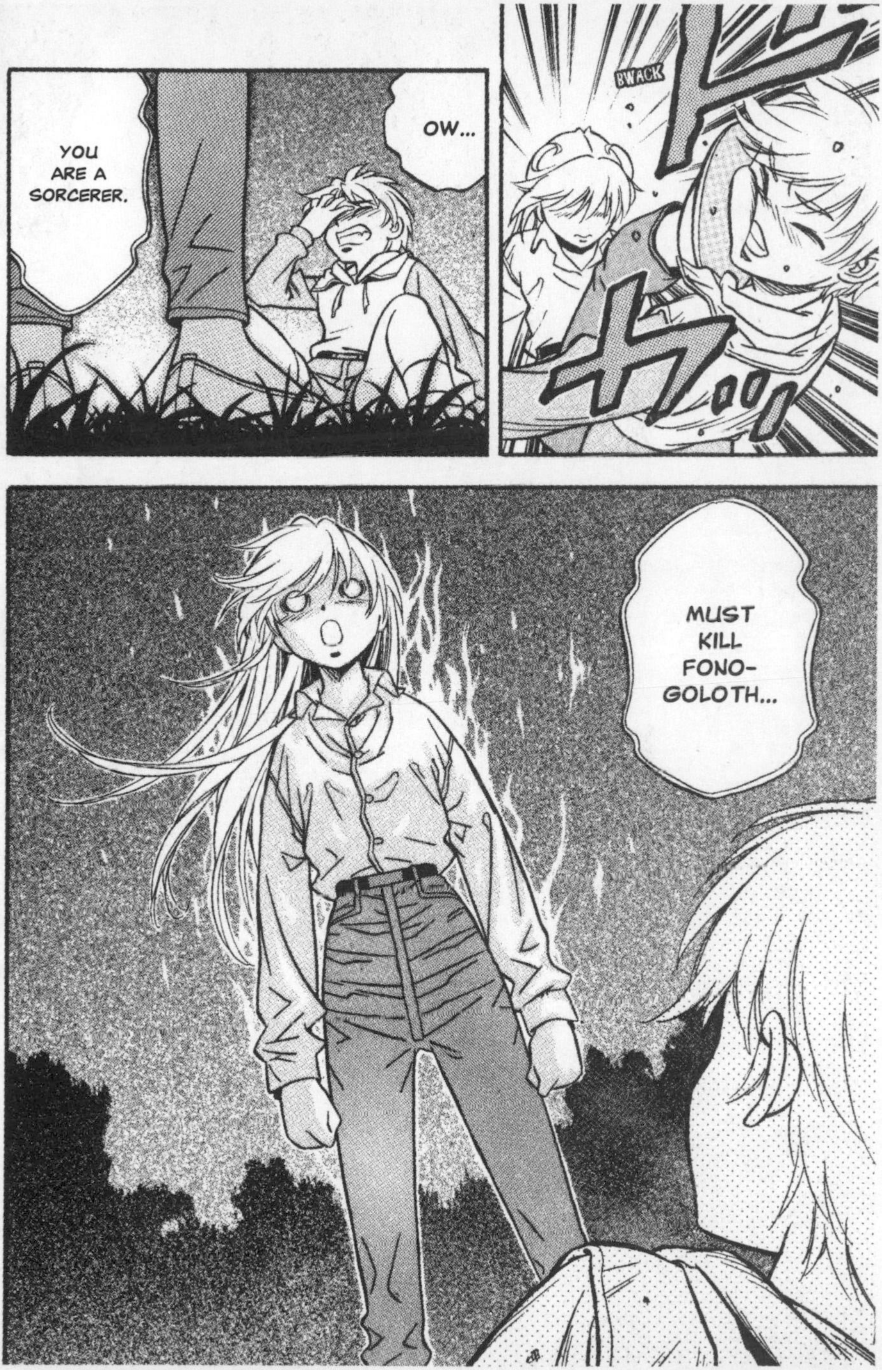
BWACK
OW...
YOU ARE A SORCERER.
MUST KILL FONO-GOLOTH...

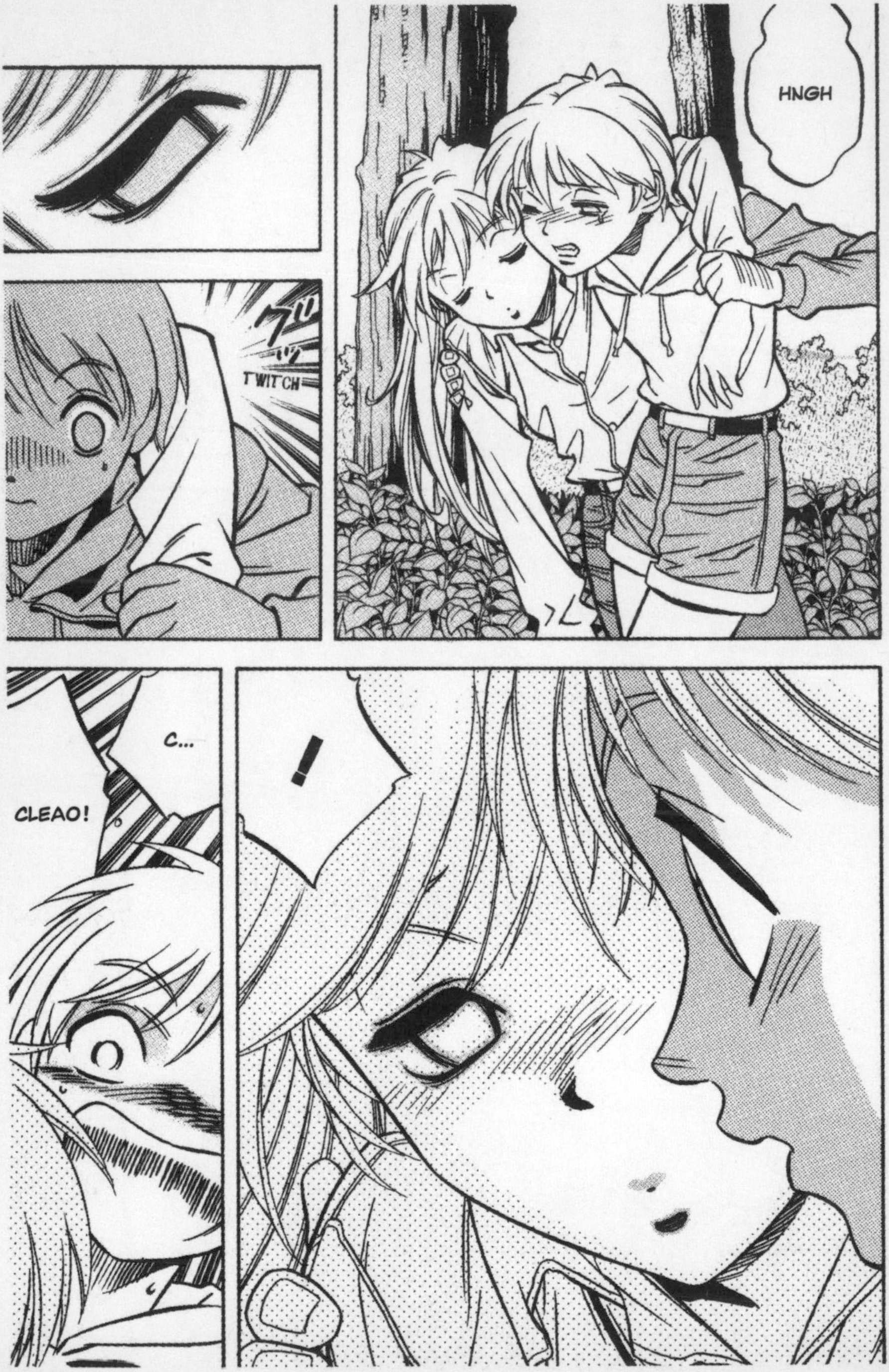

HNGH
TWITCH
!
C...
CLEAO!

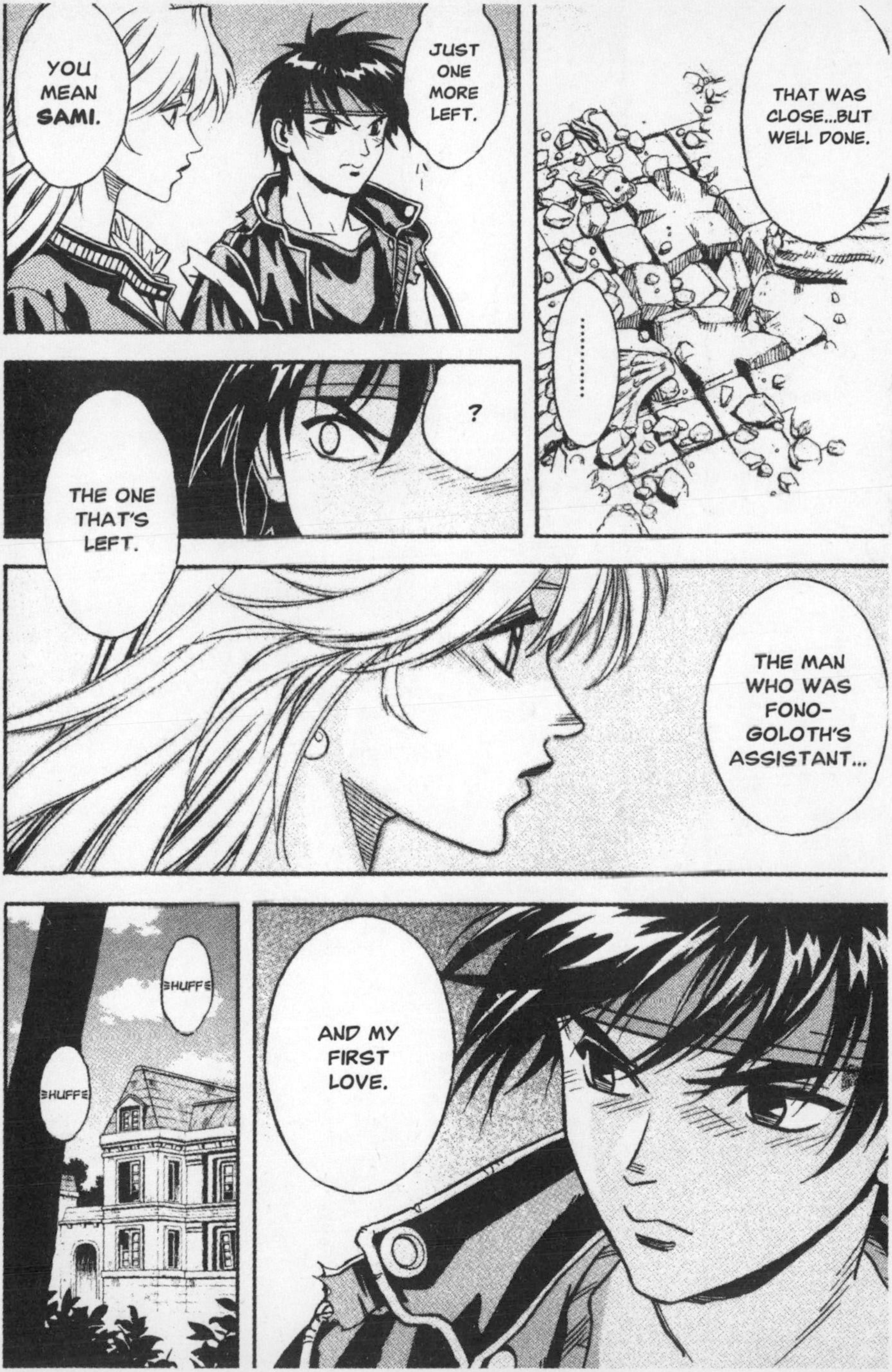
THAT WAS CLOSE...BUT WELL DONE.
....
JUST ONE MORE LEFT.
YOU MEAN SAMI.
?
THE ONE THAT'S LEFT.
THE MAN WHO WAS FONO-GOLOTH'S ASSISTANT...
AND MY FIRST LOVE.
HUFF
HUFF

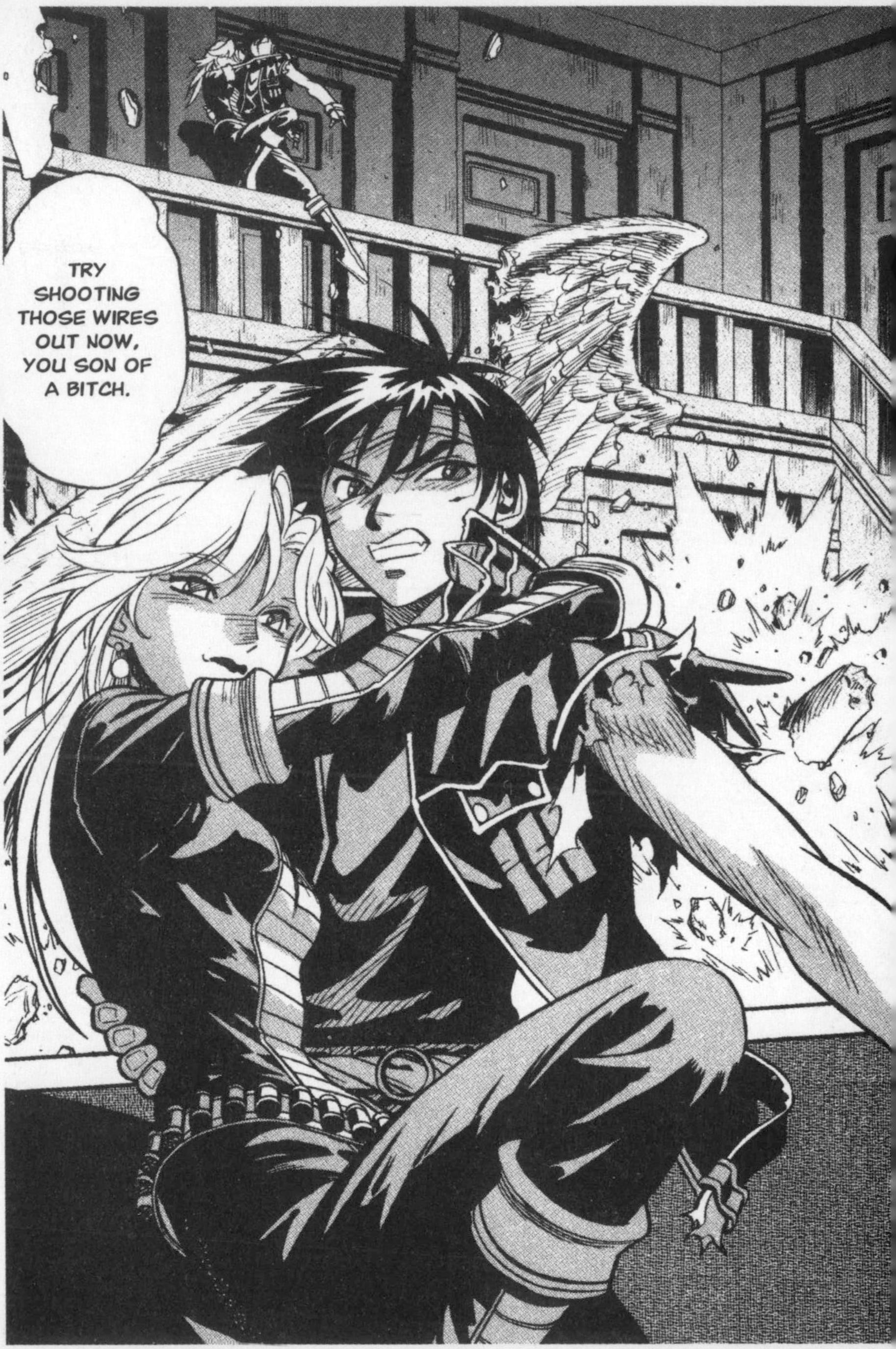
TRY SHOOTING THOSE WIRES OUT NOW, YOU SON OF A BITCH.

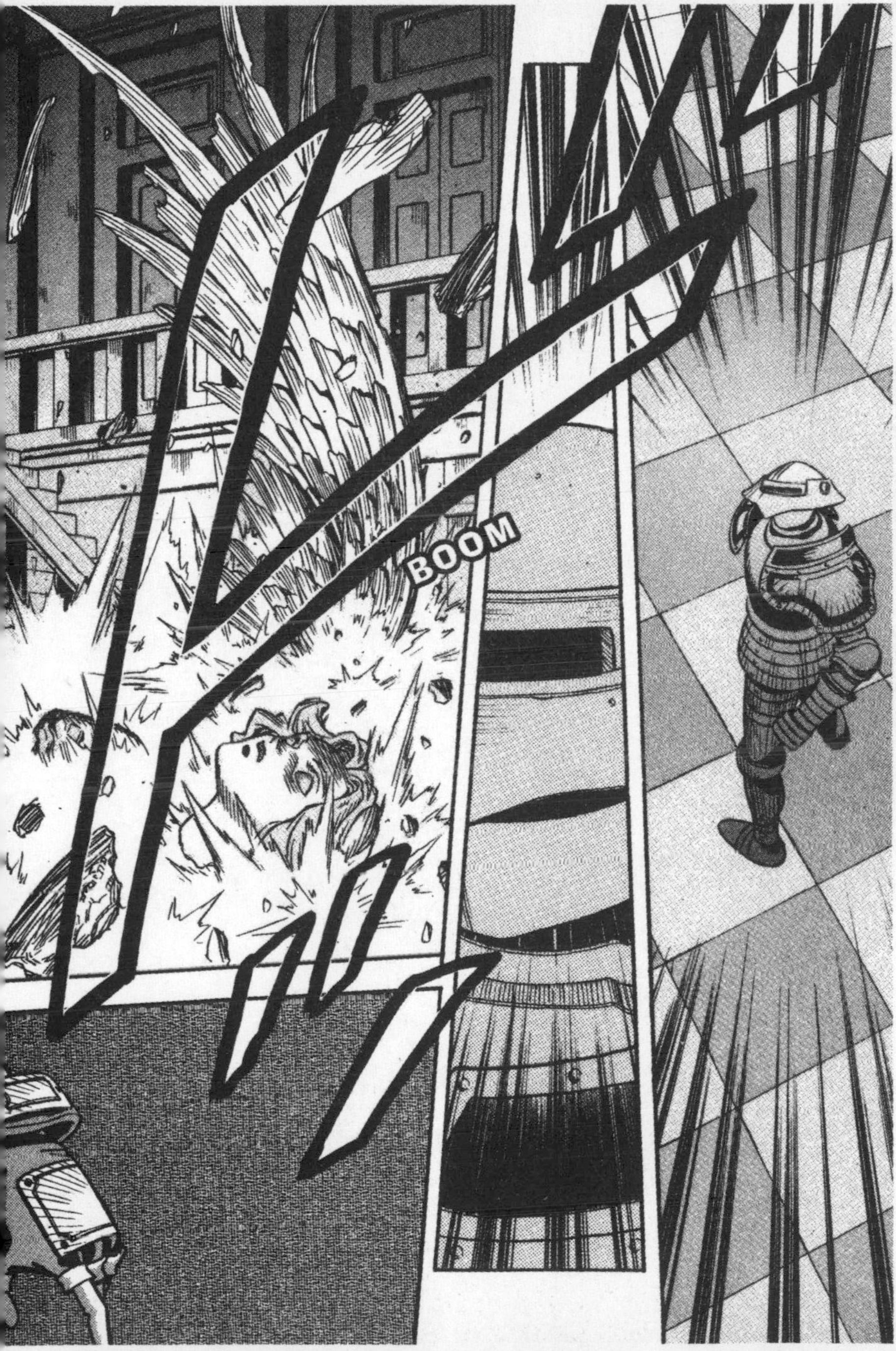
BOOM

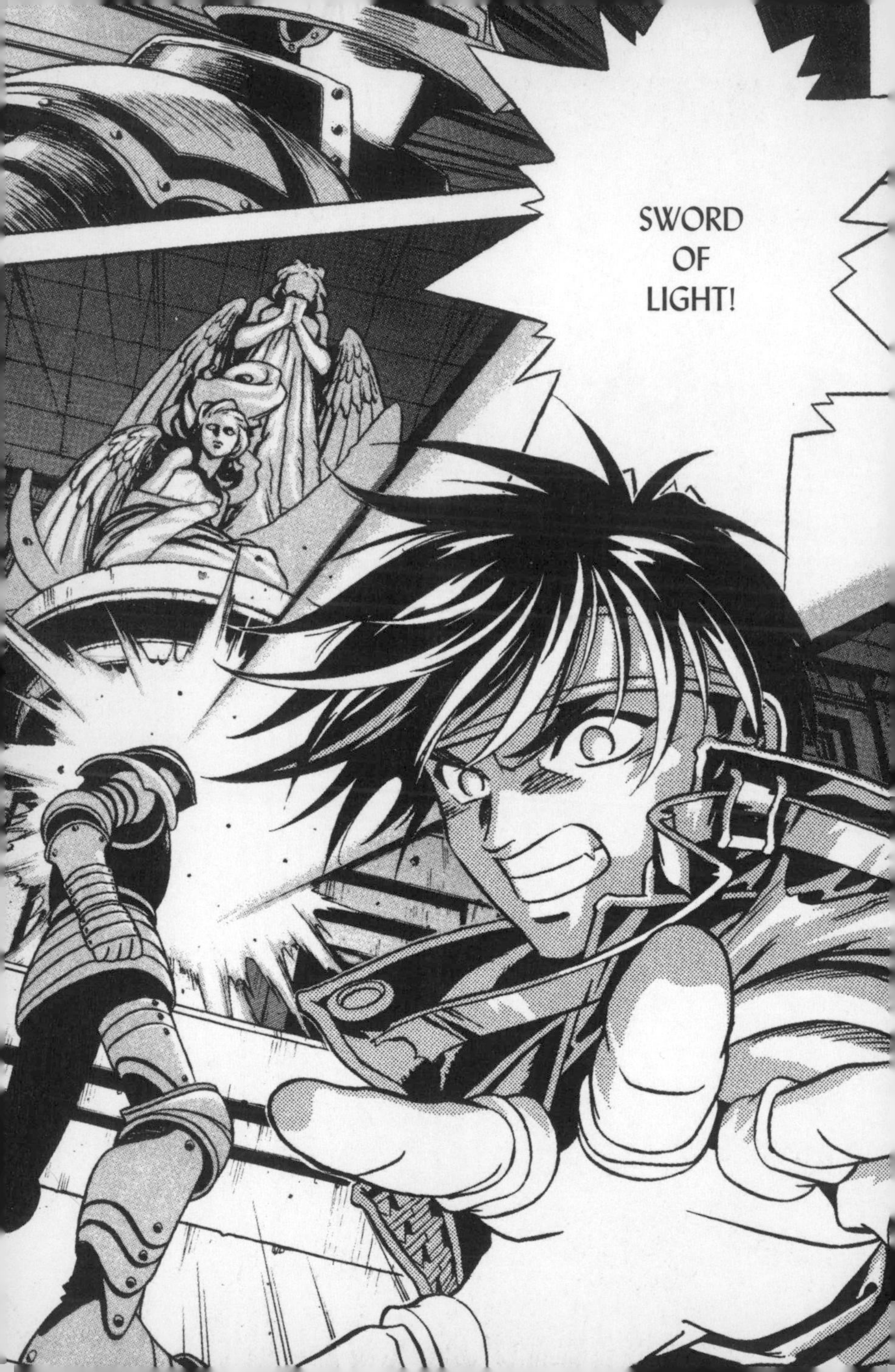
SWORD OF LIGHT!

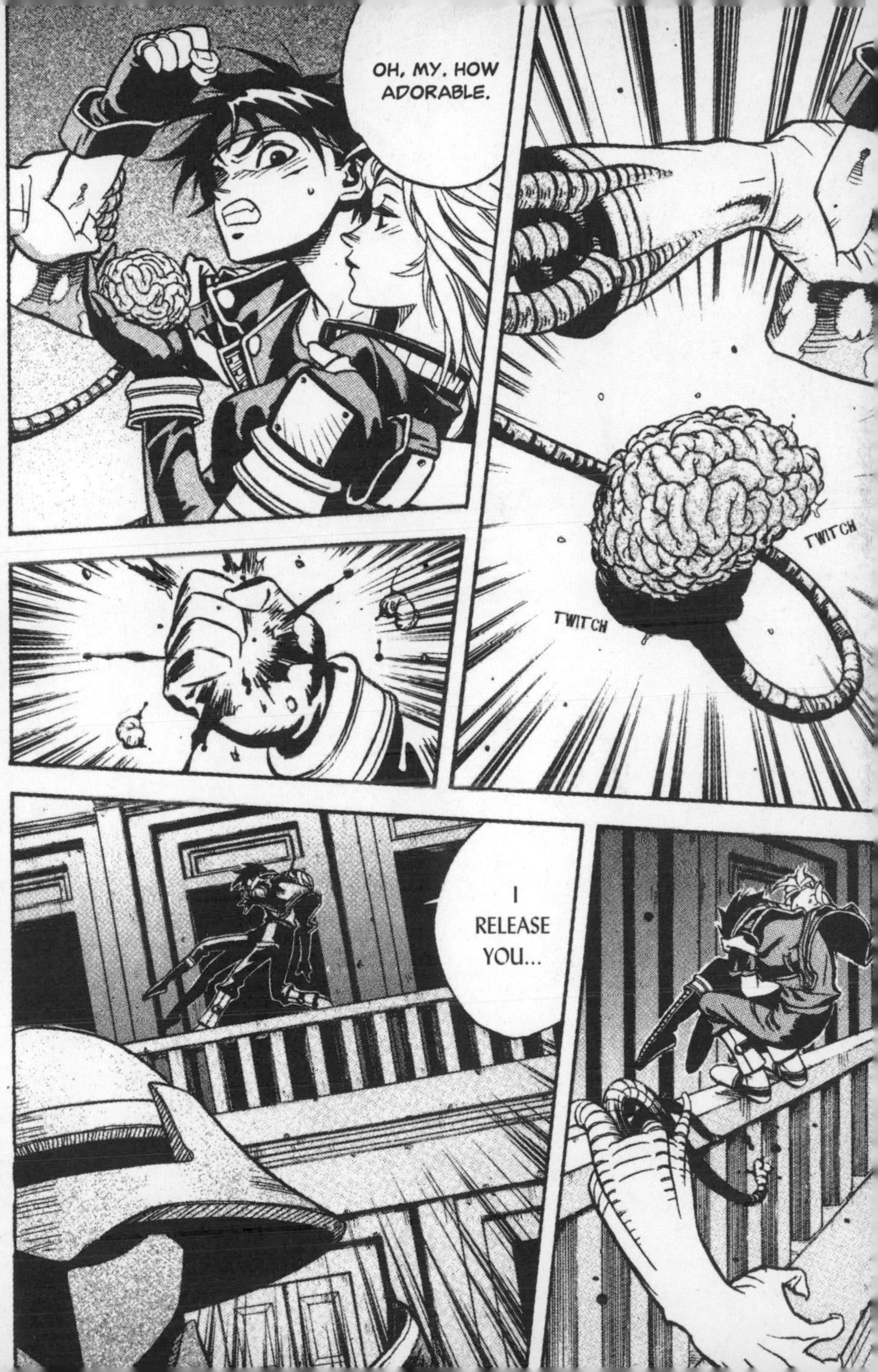
OH, MY. HOW ADORABLE.
TWITCH
TWITCH
I RELEASE YOU...

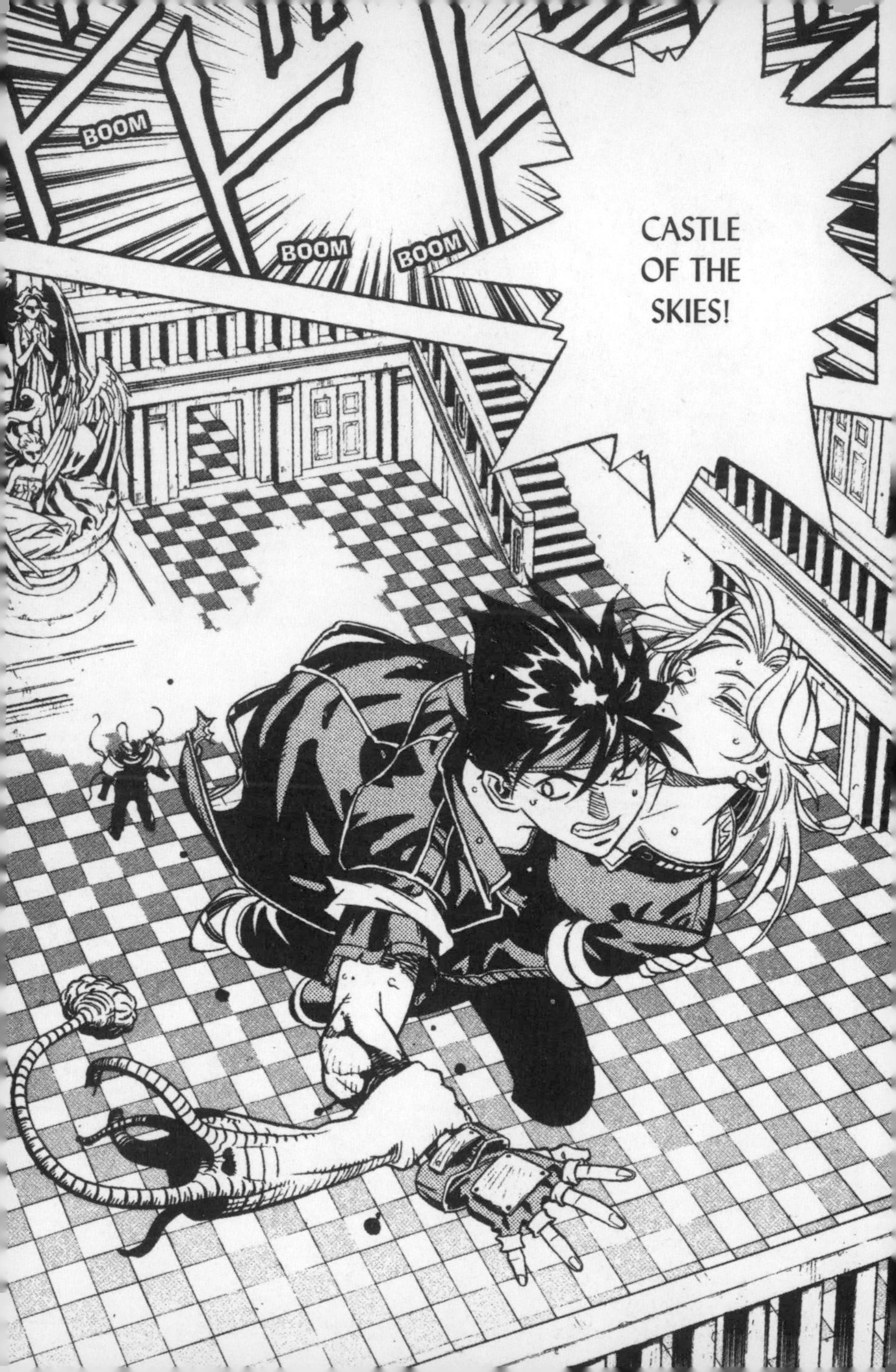
CASTLE OF THE SKIES!
BOOM
BOOM
BOOM

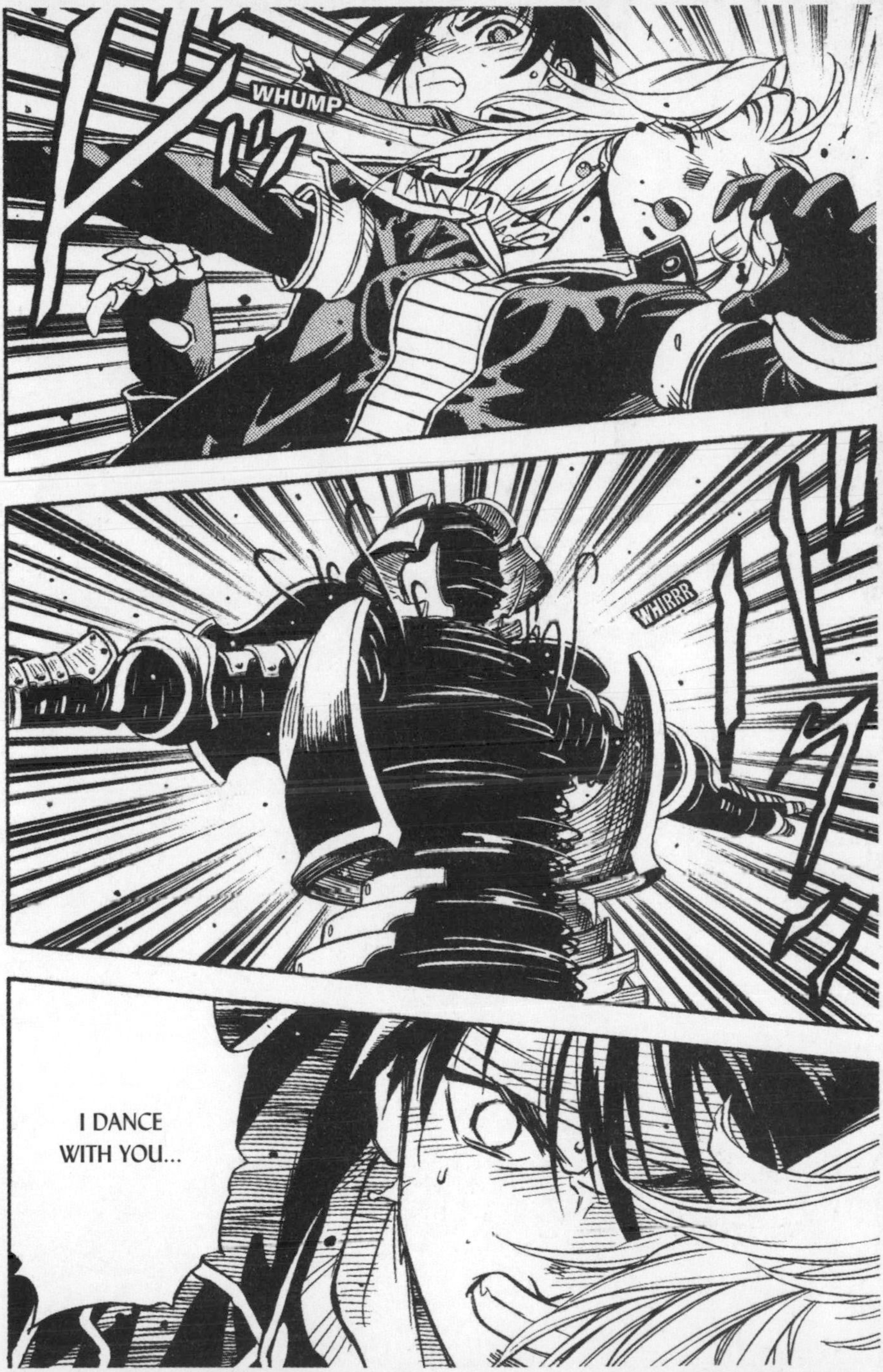
WHUMP
WHIRRR
I DANCE
WITH YOU...

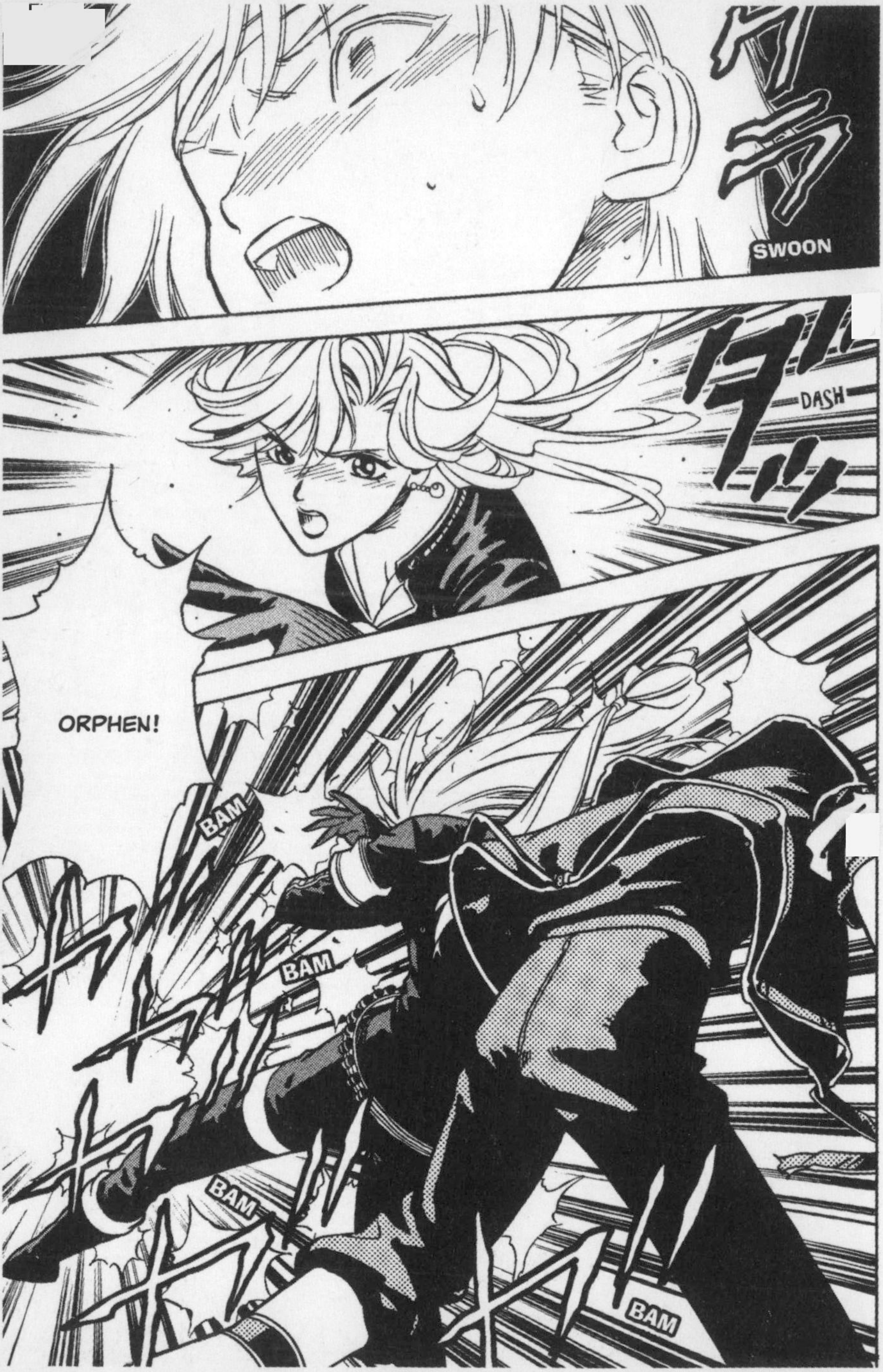
SWOON
DASH
ORPHEN!
BAM
BAM
BAM
BAM

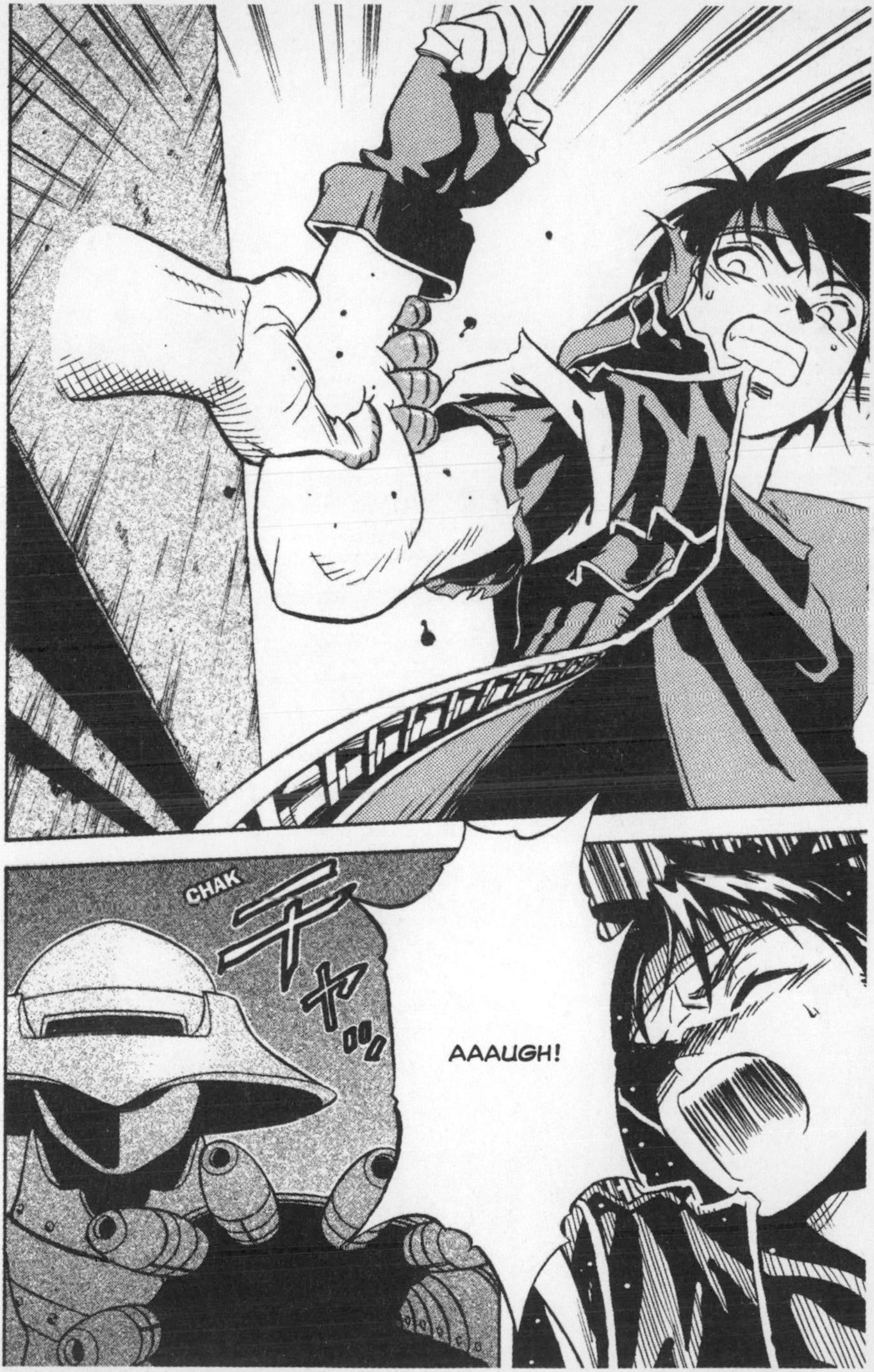
CHAK
チャッ
AAAUGH!

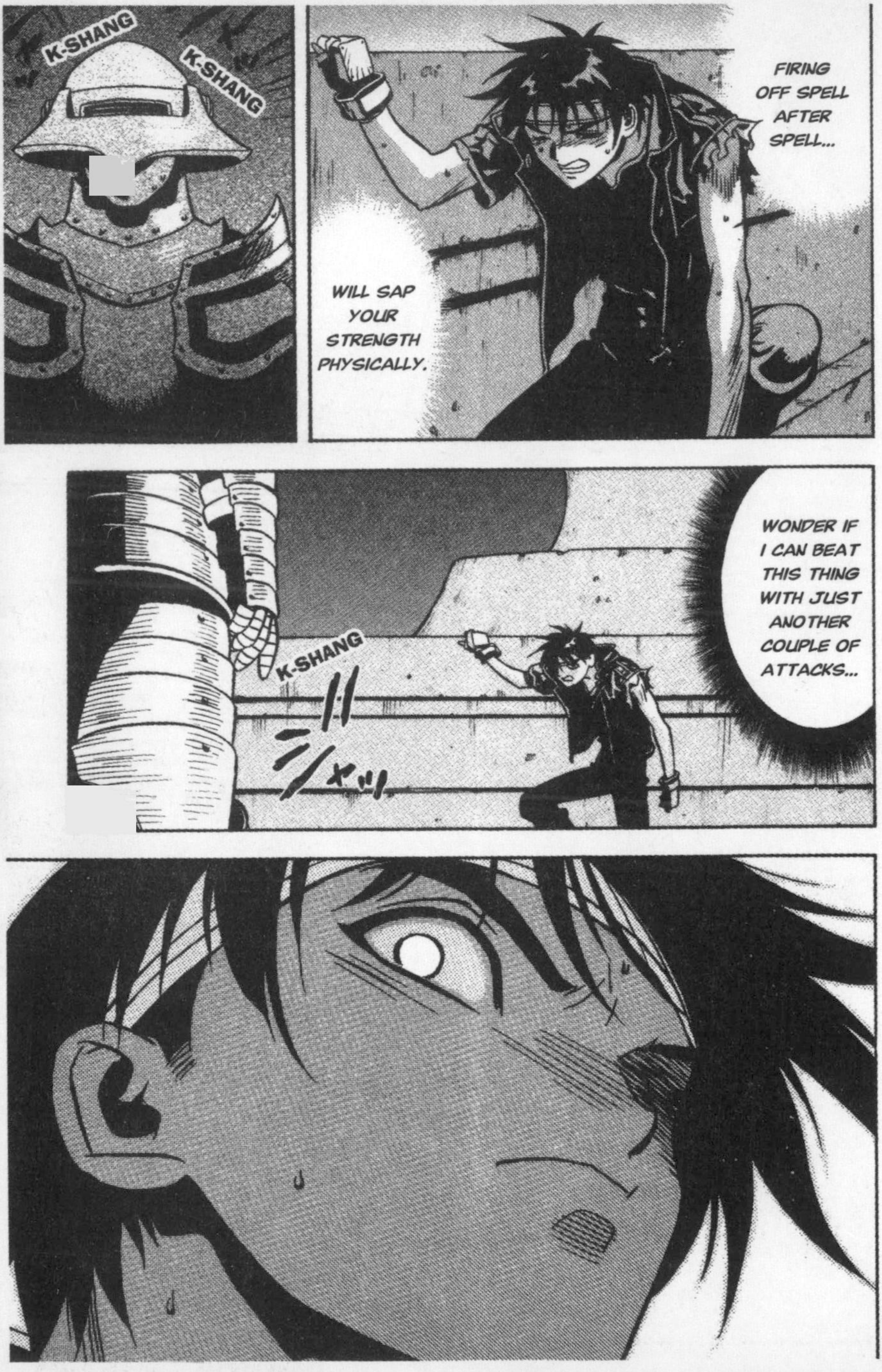
FIRING OFF SPELL AFTER SPELL...
WILL SAP YOUR STRENGTH PHYSICALLY.
K-SHANG
K-SHANG
WONDER IF I CAN BEAT THIS THING WITH JUST ANOTHER COUPLE OF ATTACKS...
K-SHANG

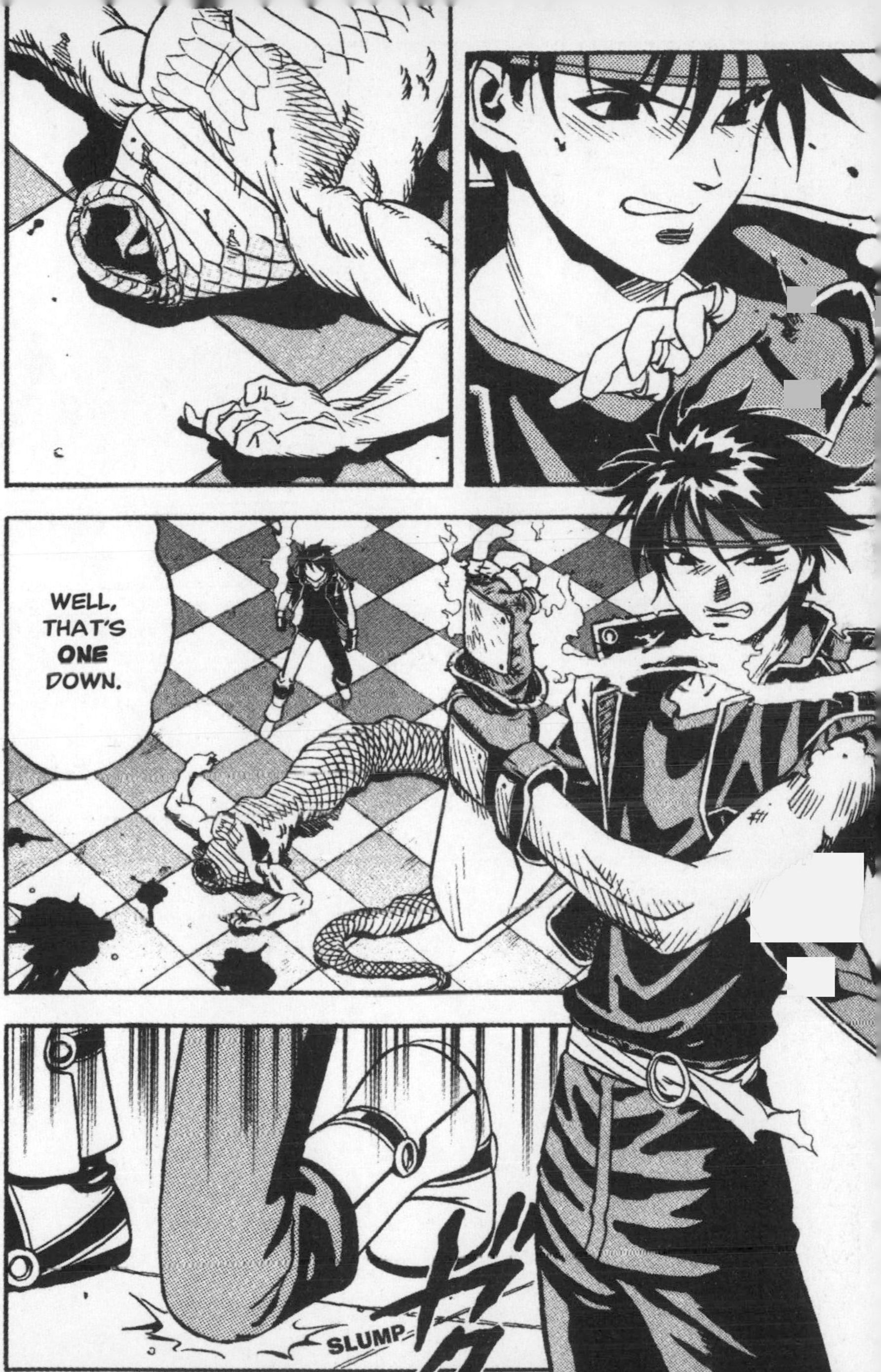
WELL, THAT'S ONE DOWN.
SLUMP

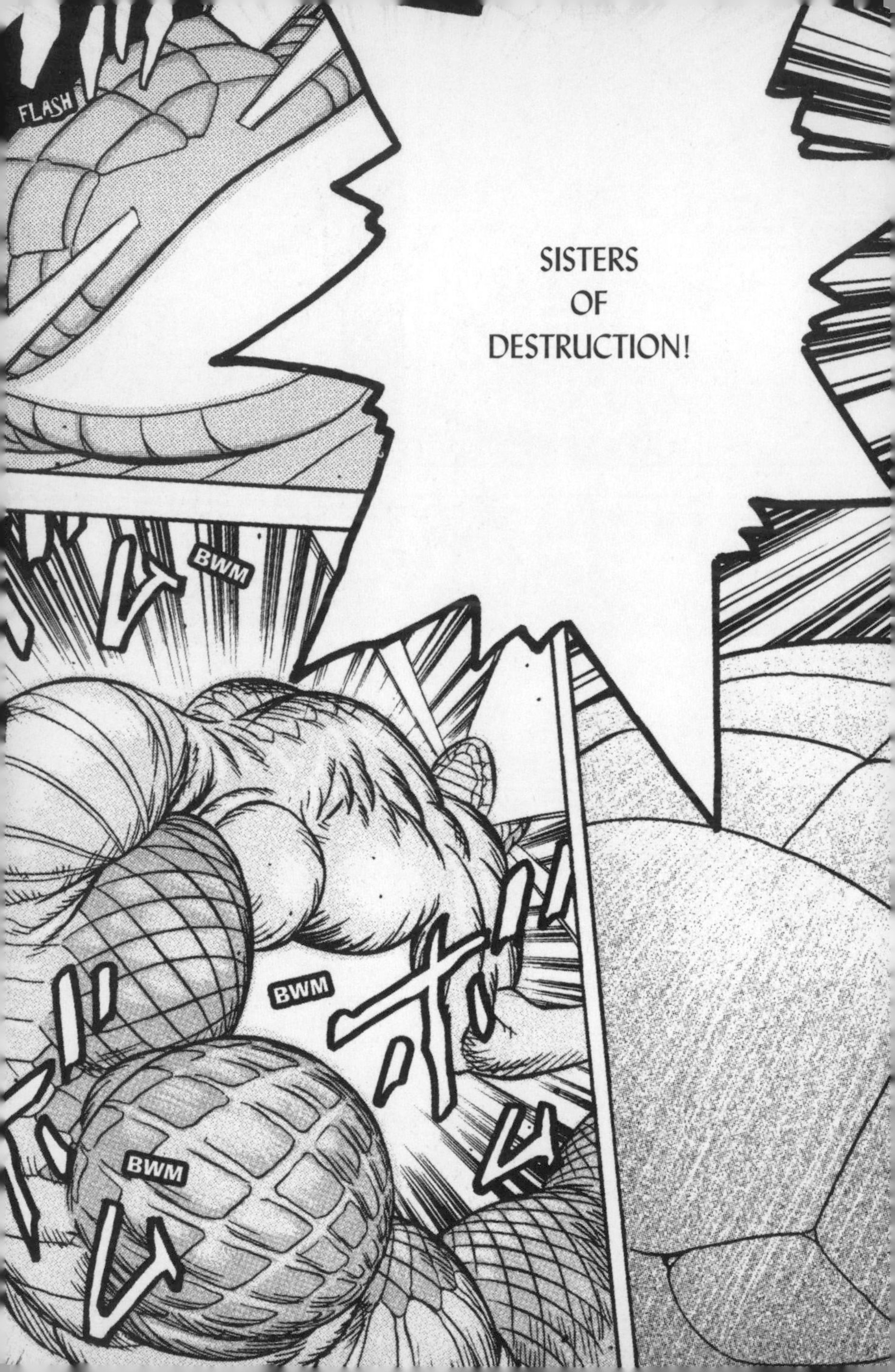

FLASH
SISTERS OF DESTRUCTION!
BWM
BWM
BWM

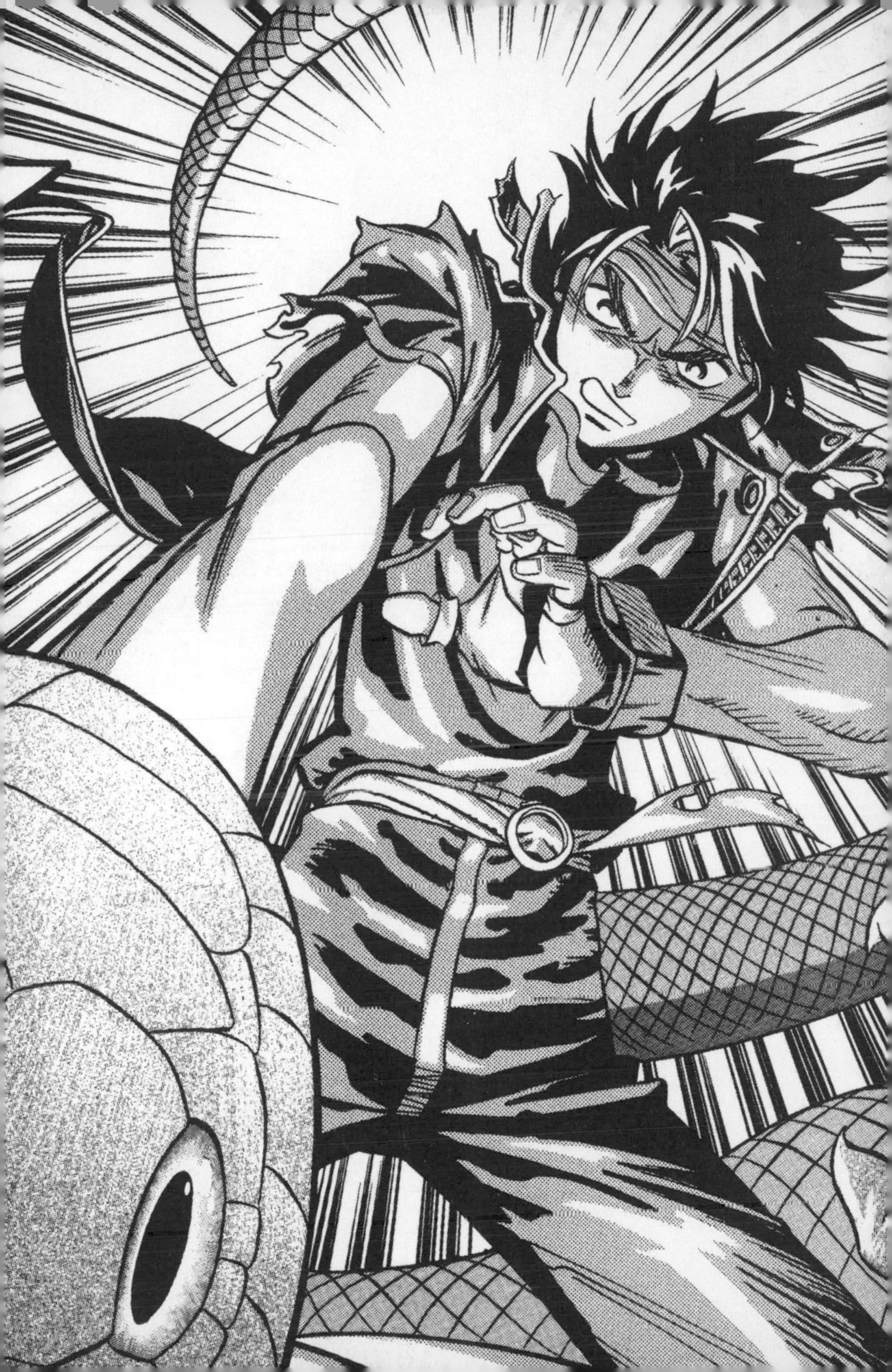

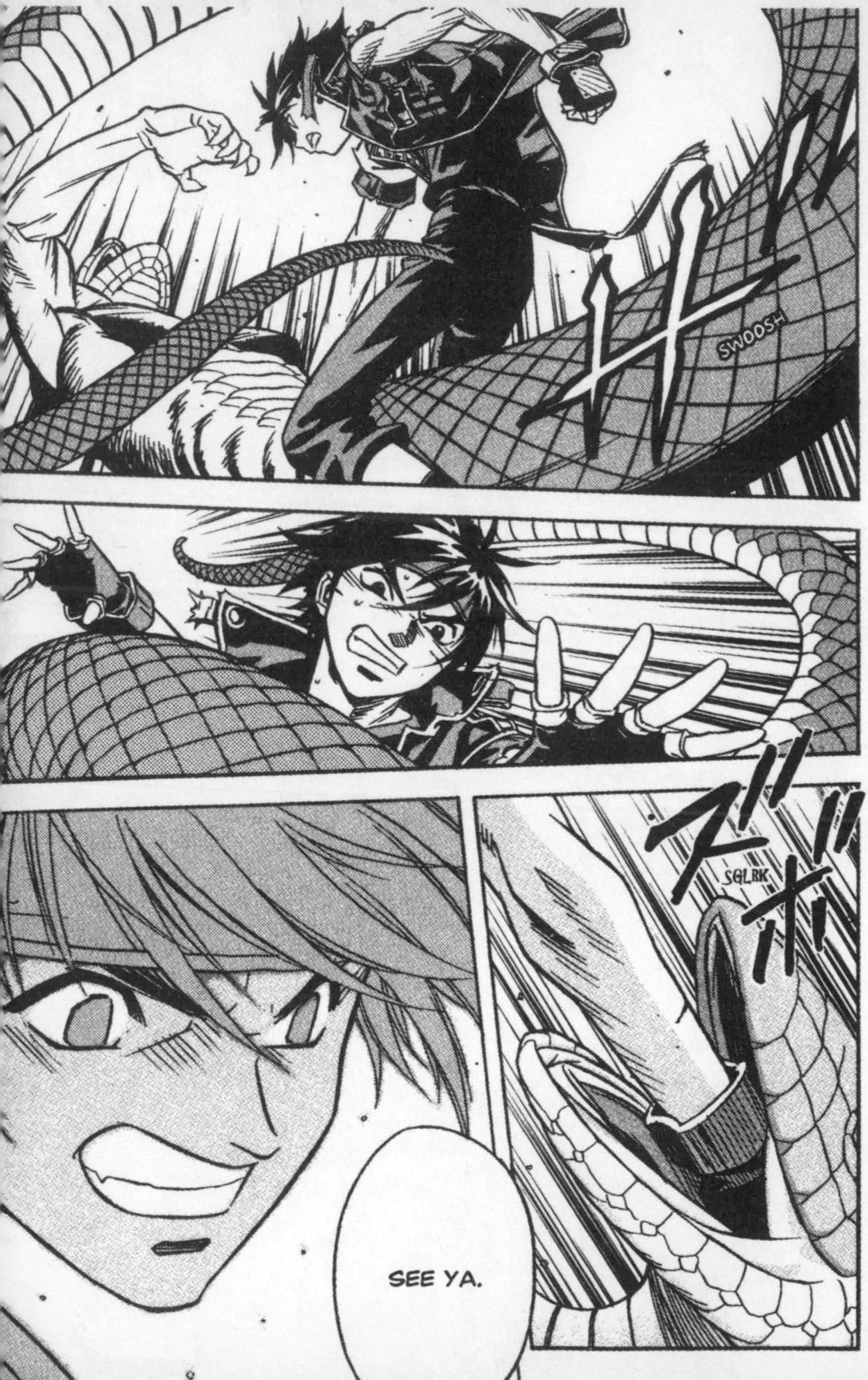
SWOOSH
SGLRK
SEE YA.

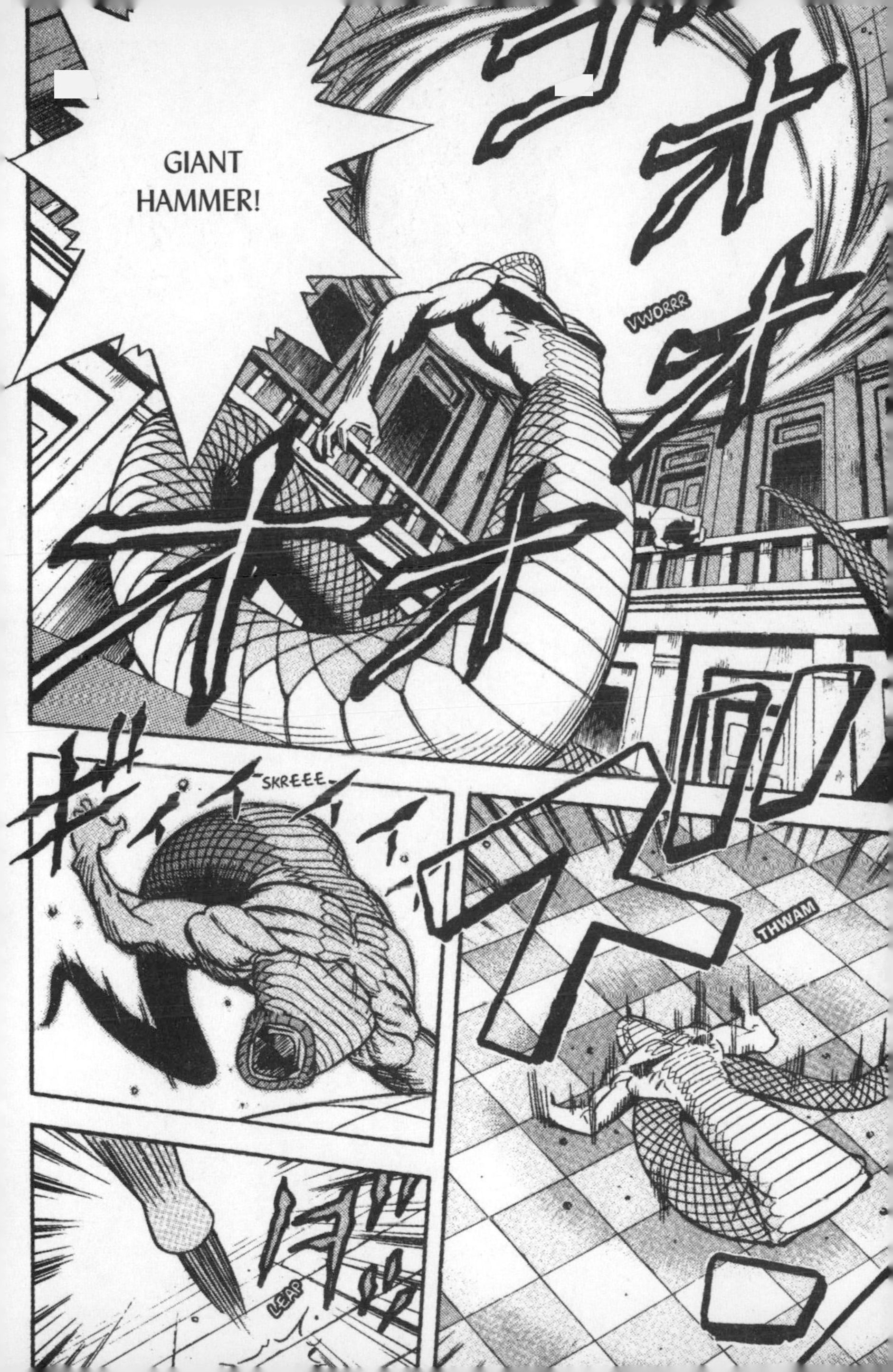
GIANT HAMMER!
VWORRR
SKREEE
THWAM
LEAP

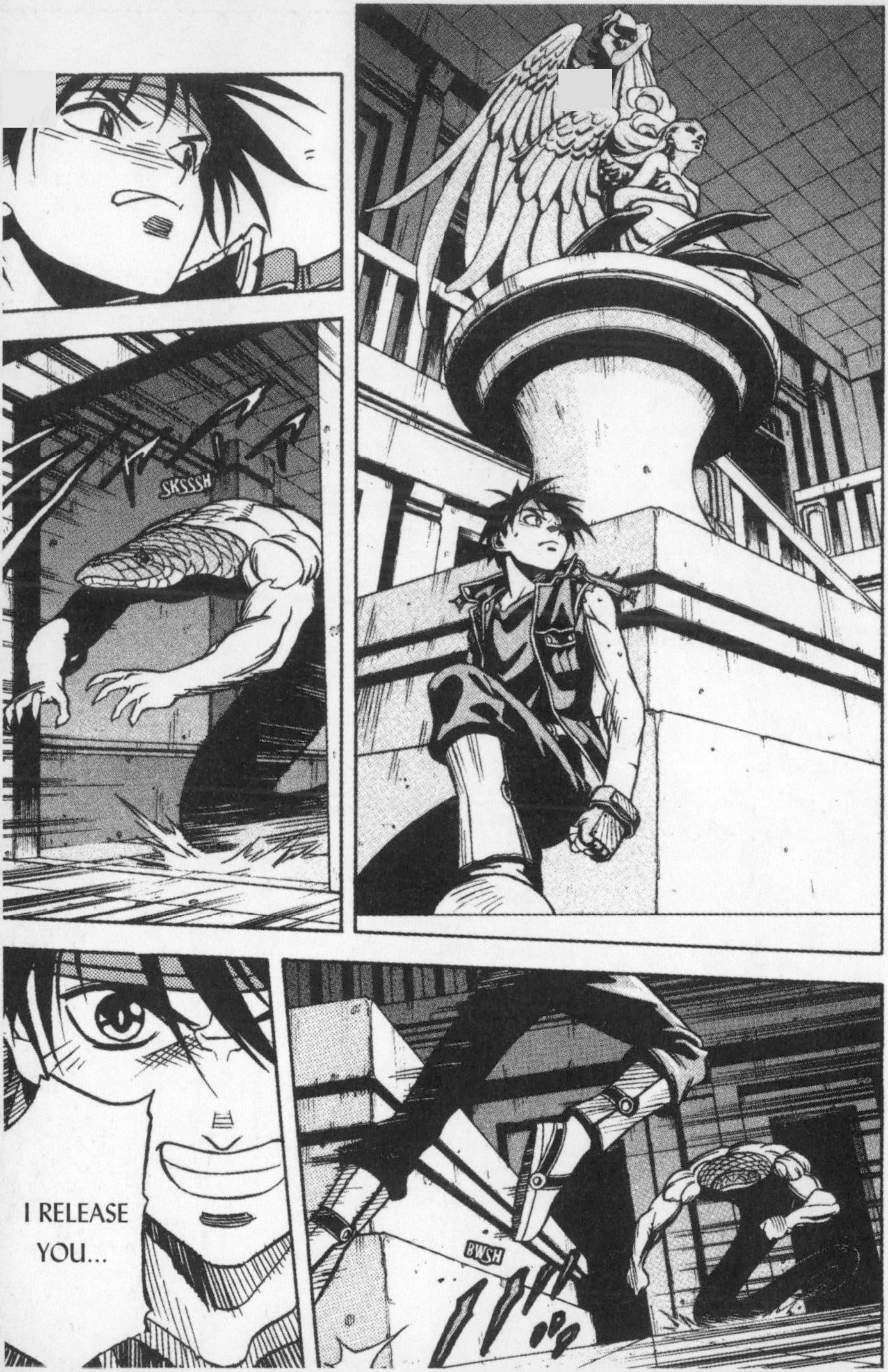
SKSSSH
I RELEASE YOU...
BWSH

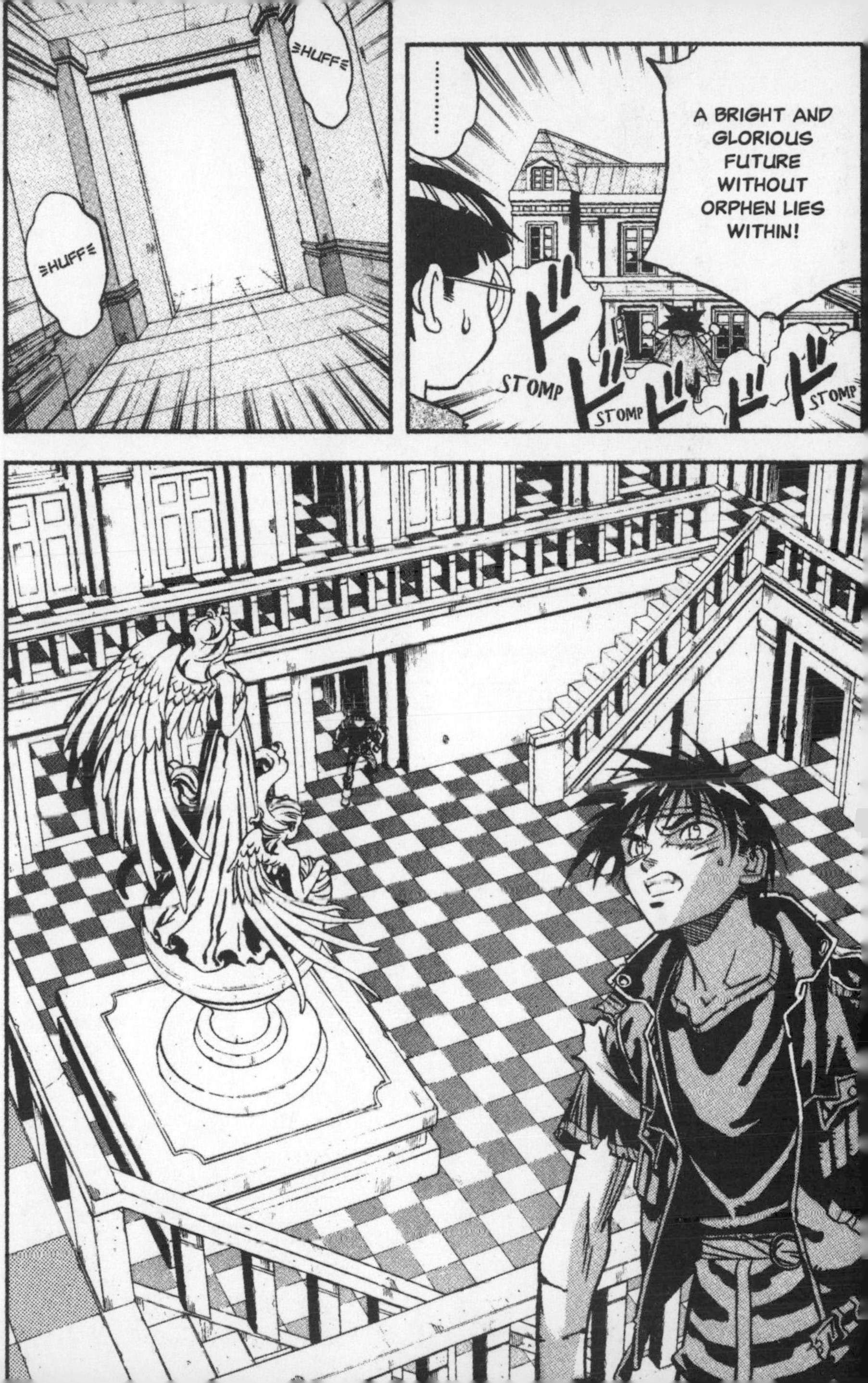
......
A BRIGHT AND GLORIOUS FUTURE WITHOUT ORPHEN LIES WITHIN!
STOMP
STOMP
STOMP
HUFF
HUFF

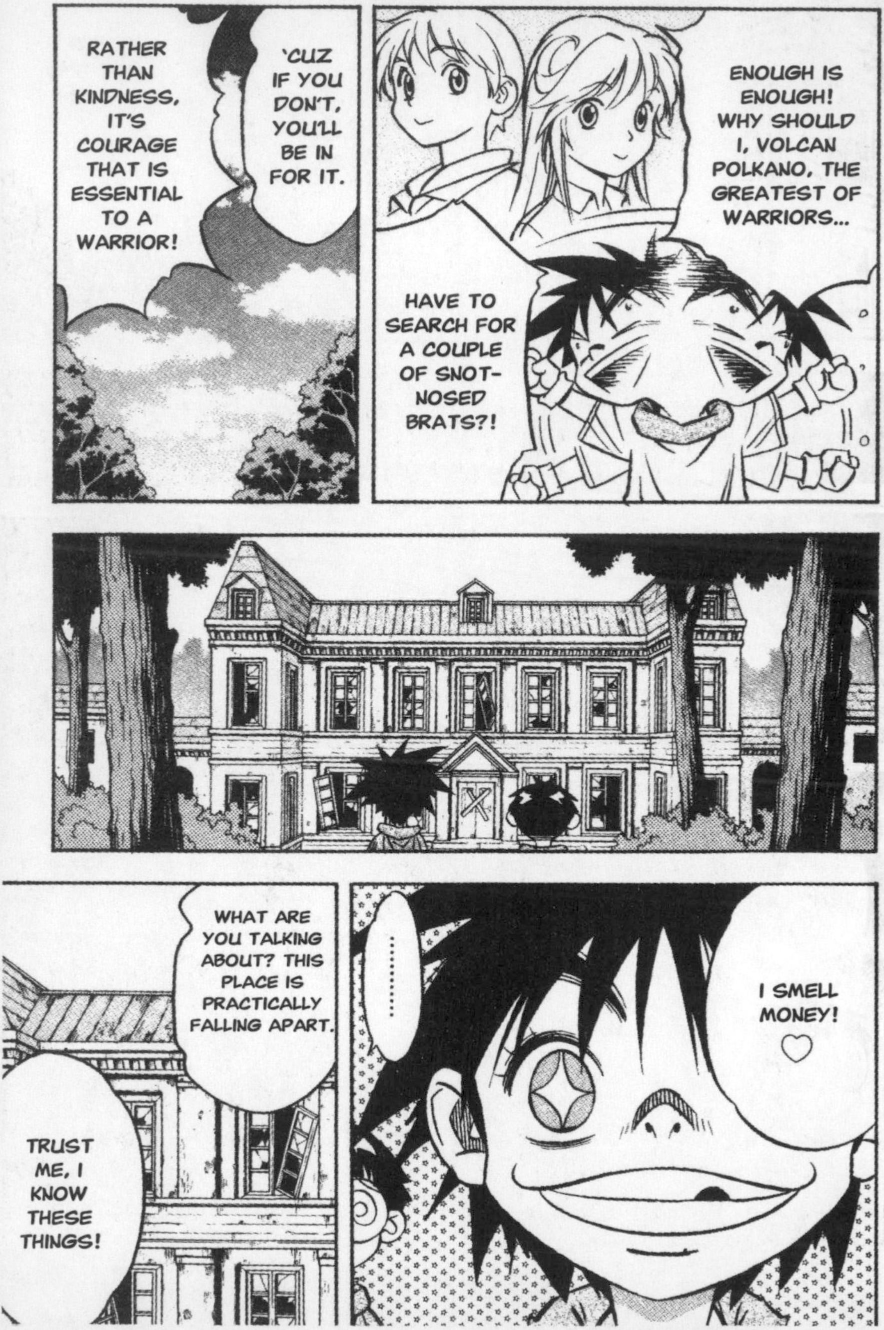
RATHER THAN KINDNESS, IT'S COURAGE THAT IS ESSENTIAL TO A WARRIOR!
'CUZ IF YOU DON'T, YOU'LL BE IN FOR IT.
ENOUGH IS ENOUGH! WHY SHOULD I, VOLCAN POLKANO, THE GREATEST OF WARRIORS...
HAVE TO SEARCH FOR A COUPLE OF SNOT-NOSED BRATS?!
WHAT ARE YOU TALKING ABOUT? THIS PLACE IS PRACTICALLY FALLING APART.
TRUST ME, I KNOW THESE THINGS!
....
I SMELL MONEY! ♡

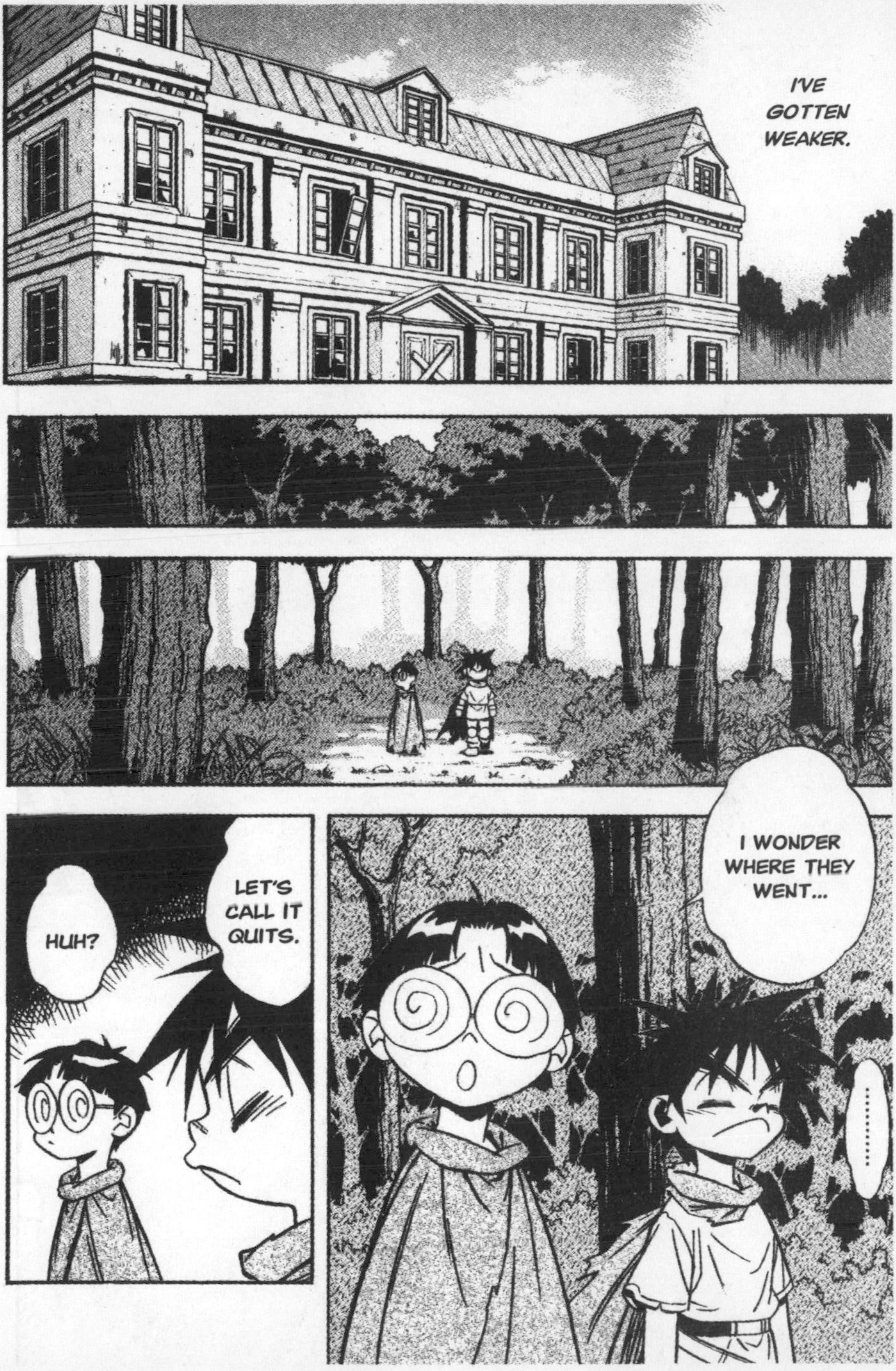
I'VE GOTTEN WEAKER.
I WONDER WHERE THEY WENT...
....
LET'S CALL IT QUITS.
HUH?

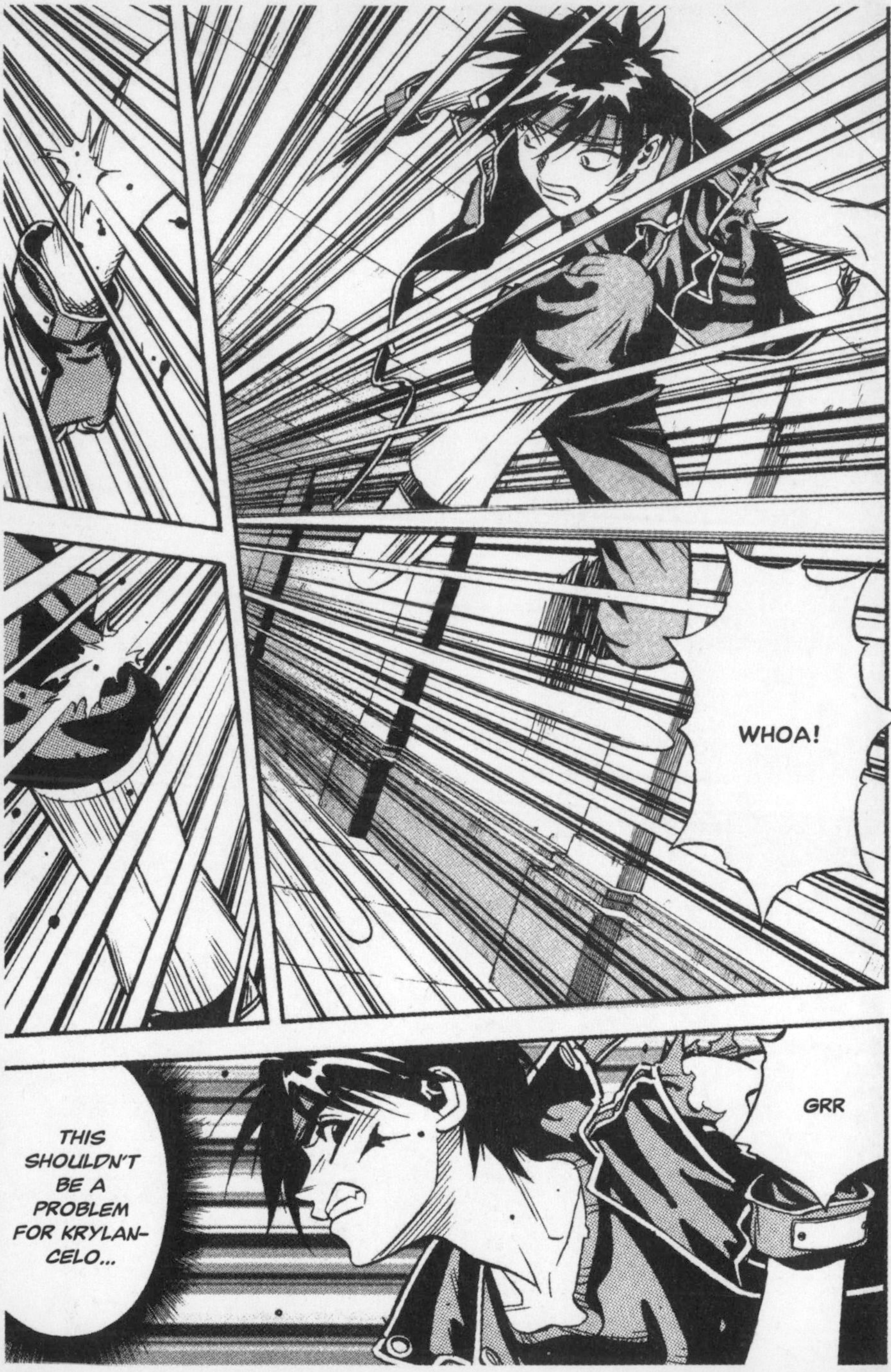
WHOA!
GRR
THIS SHOULDN'T BE A PROBLEM FOR KRYLAN-CELO...

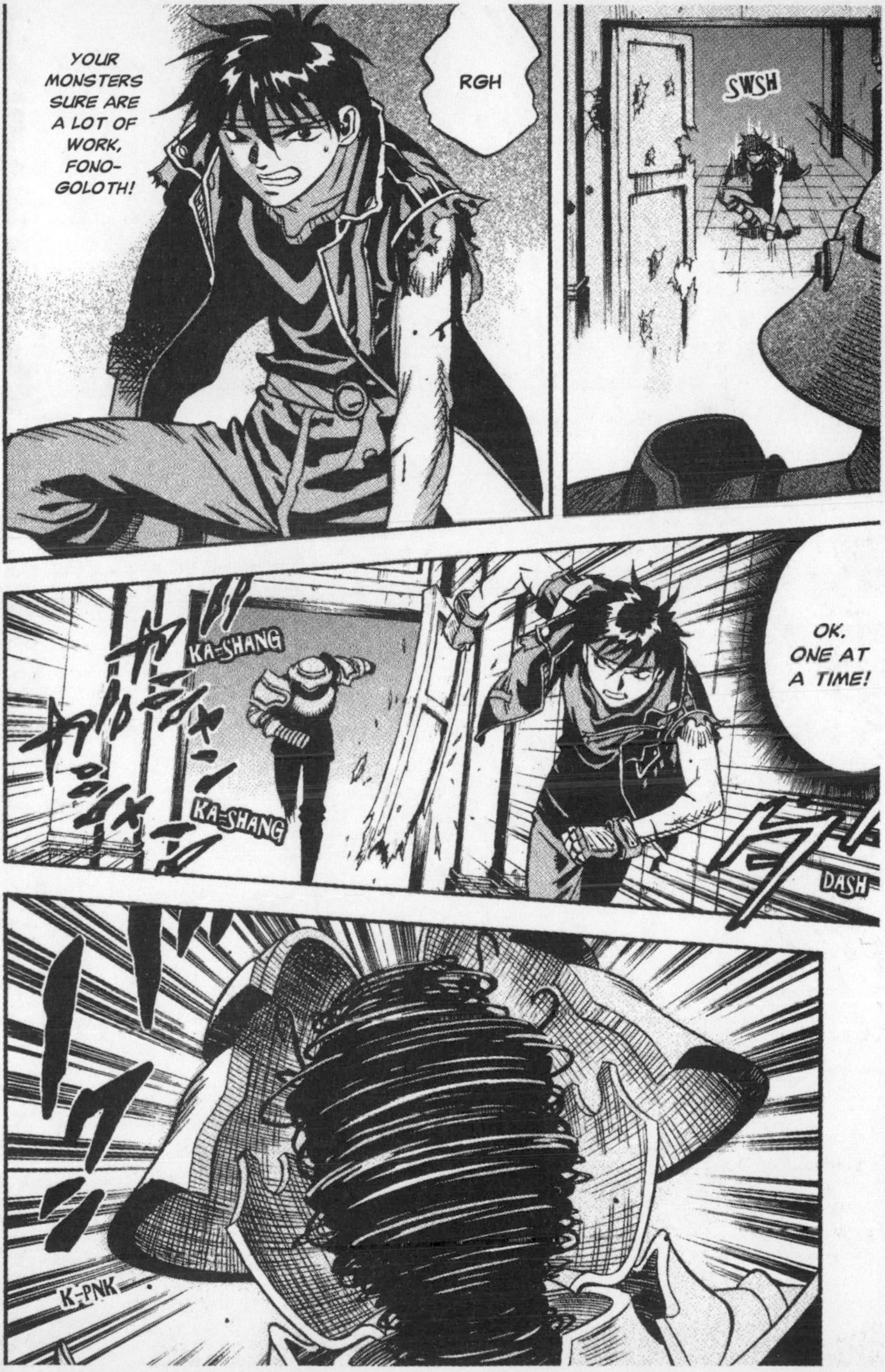
YOUR MONSTERS SURE ARE A LOT OF WORK, FONO-GOLOTH!
RGH
SWSH
KA-SHANG
KA-SHANG
OK. ONE AT A TIME!
DASH
K-PNK

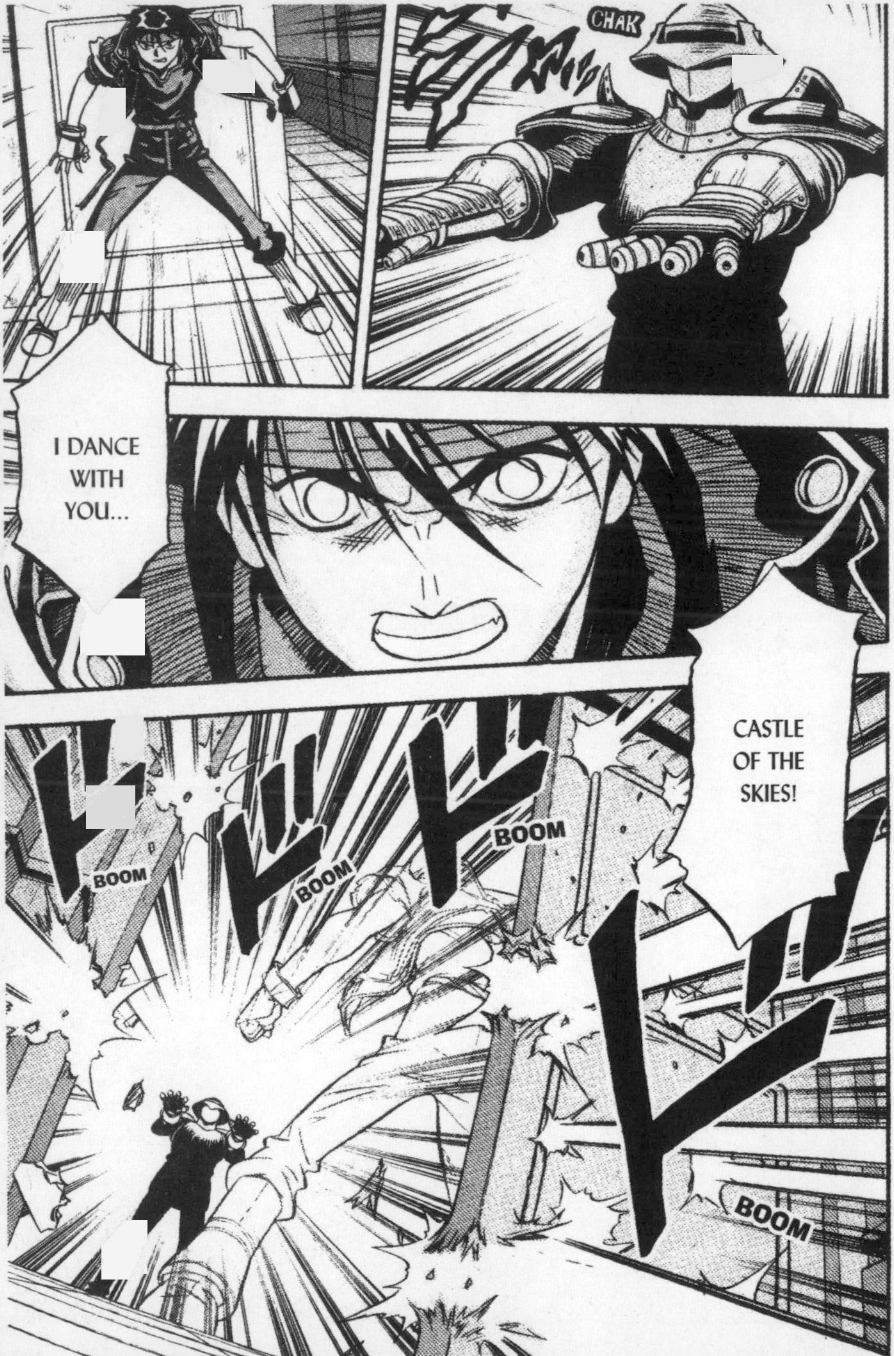
CHAK
I DANCE WITH YOU...
CASTLE OF THE SKIES!
BOOM
BOOM
BOOM
BOOM

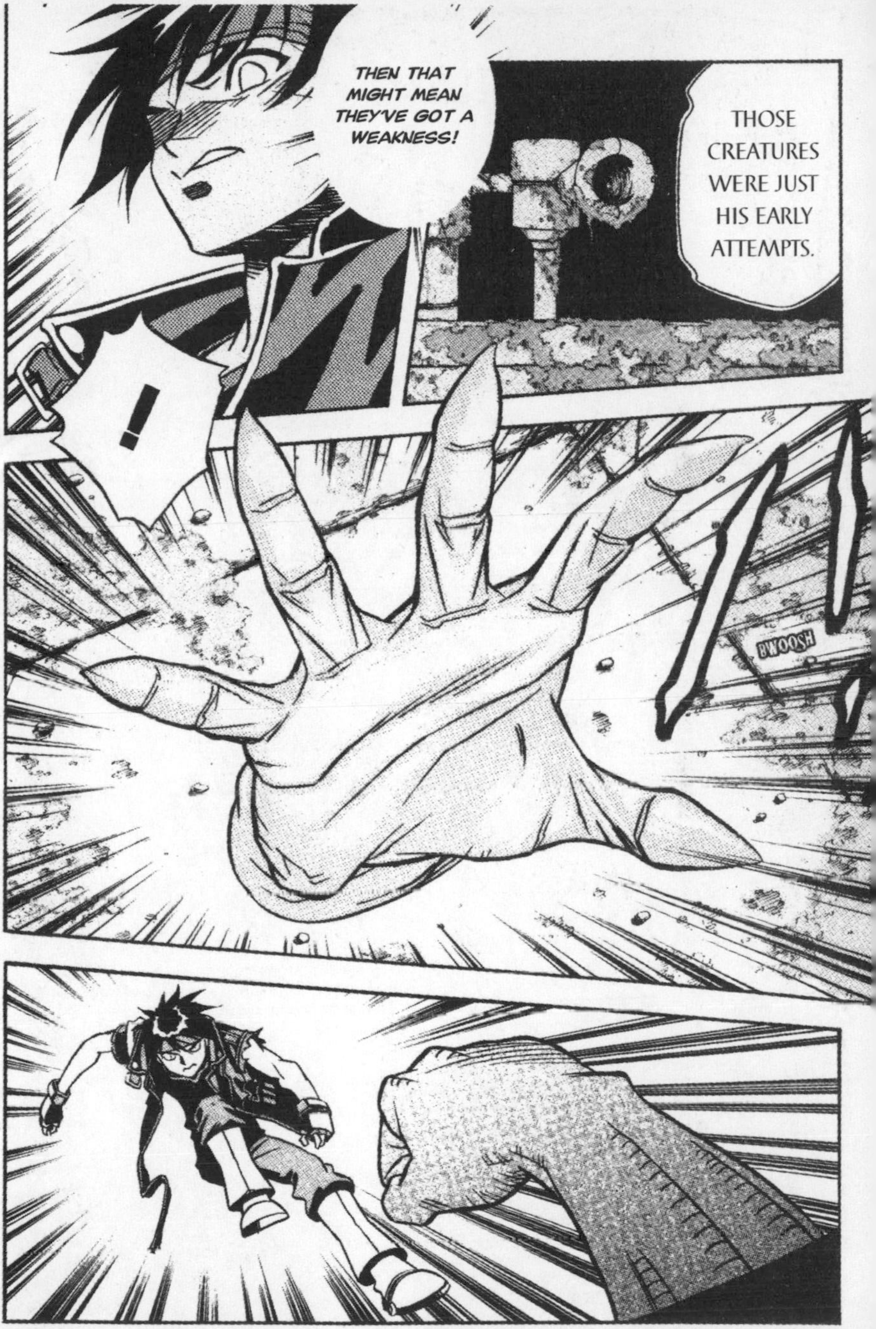
THOSE CREATURES WERE JUST HIS EARLY ATTEMPTS.
THEN THAT MIGHT MEAN THEY'VE GOT A WEAKNESS!
!
BWOOSH

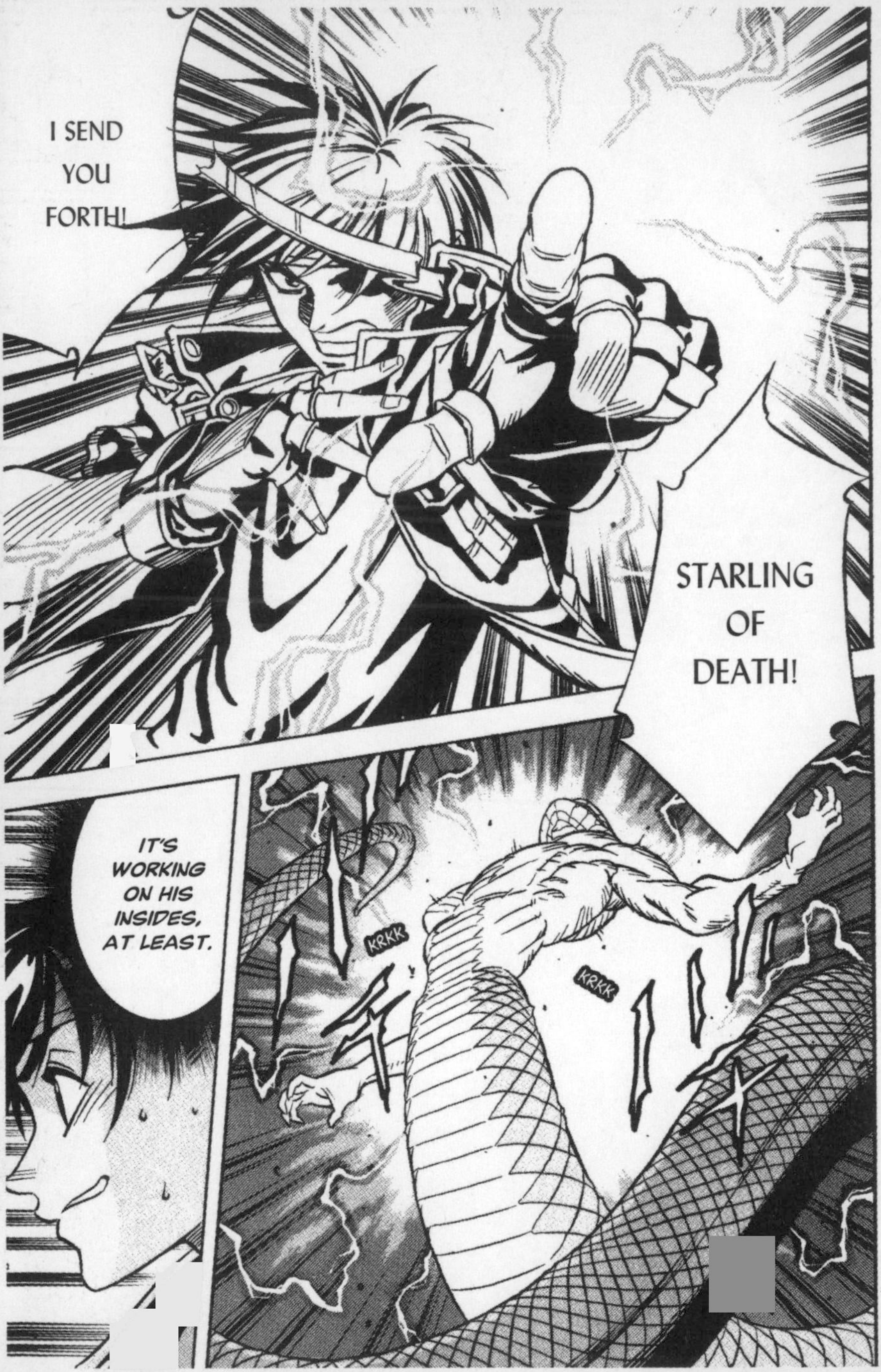

I SEND YOU FORTH!
STARLING OF DEATH!
KRKK
KRKK
IT'S WORKING ON HIS INSIDES, AT LEAST.

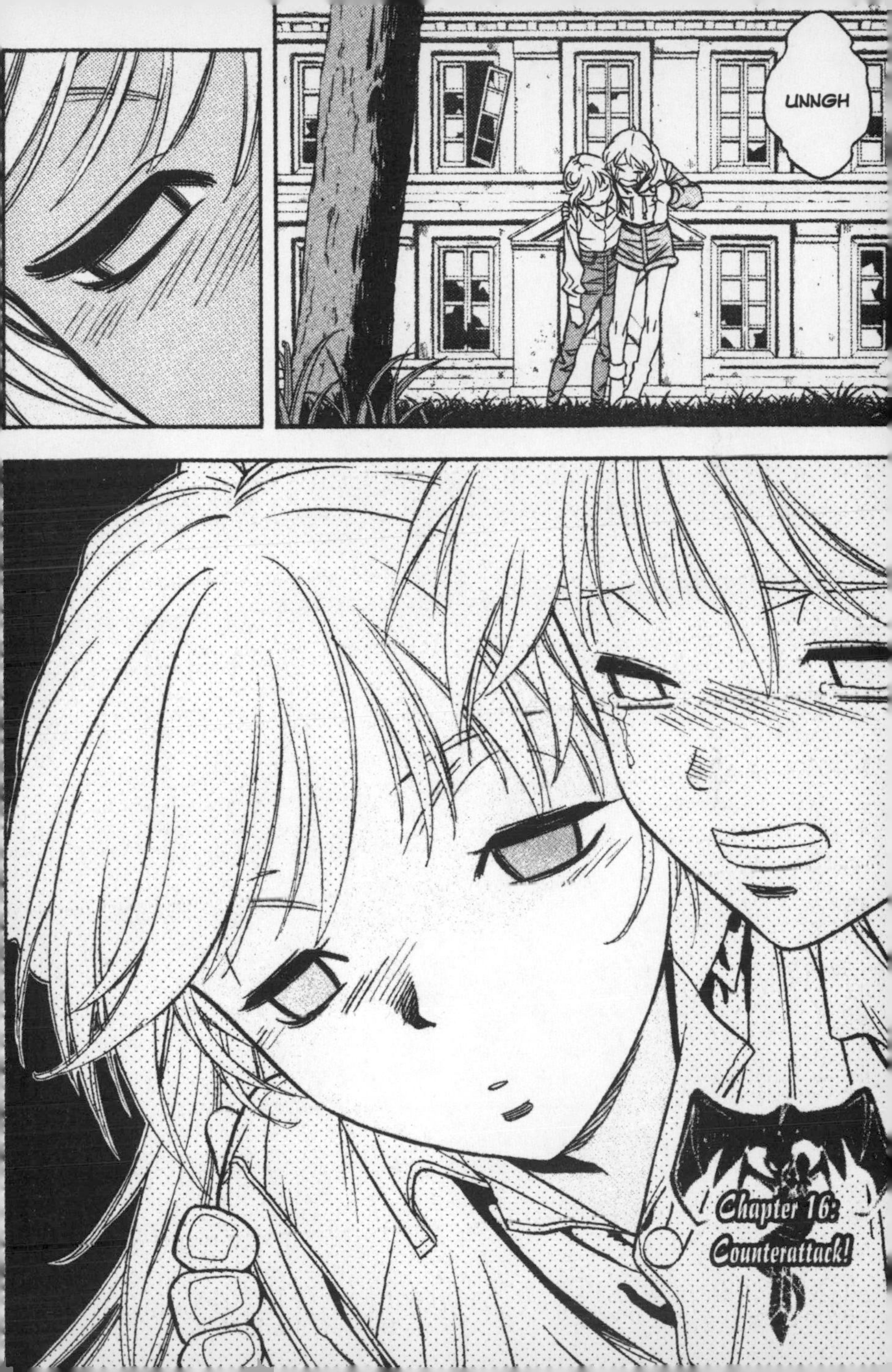
UNNGH
Chapter 16:
Counterattack!

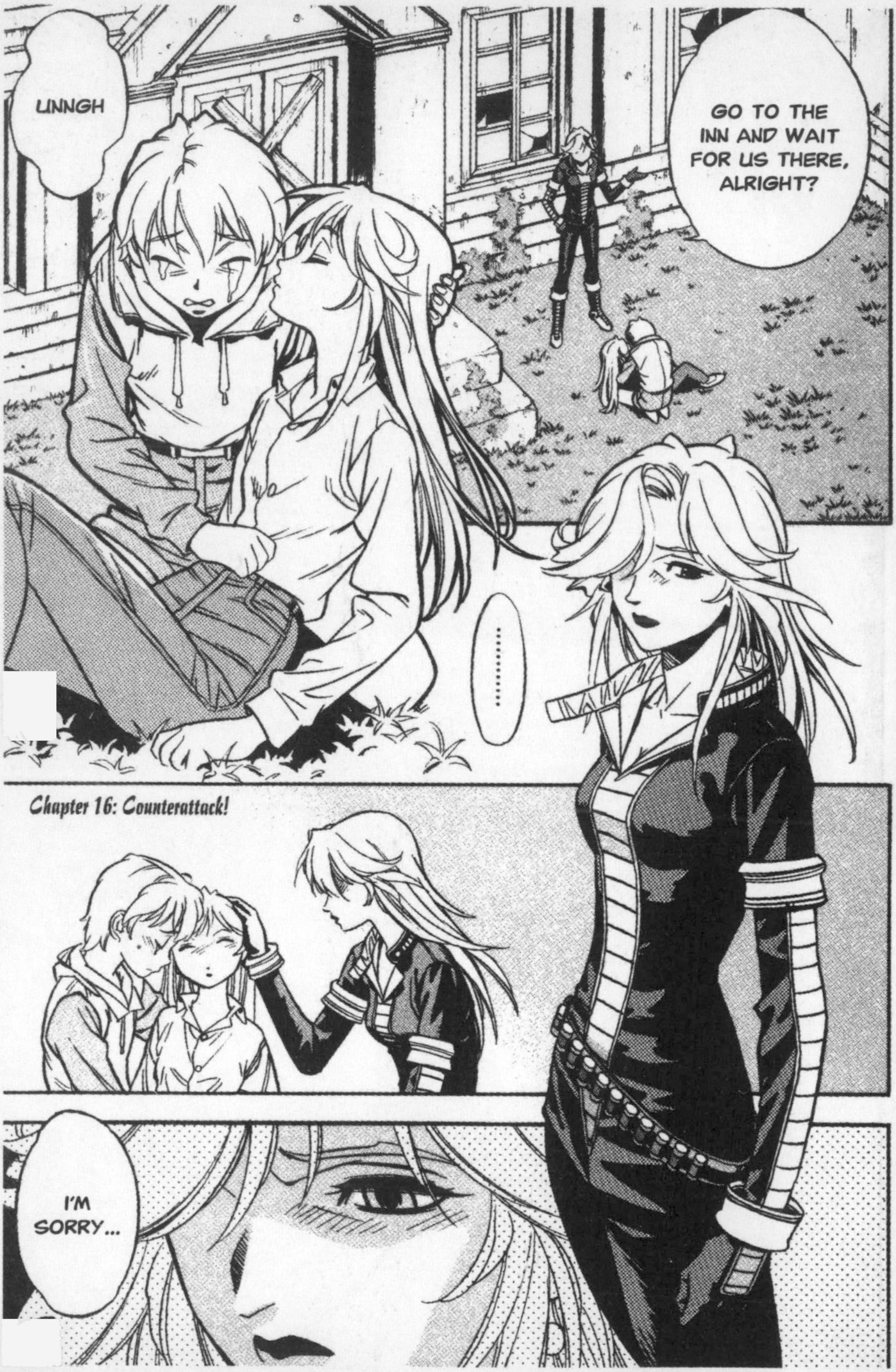
UNNGH
GO TO THE INN AND WAIT FOR US THERE, ALRIGHT?
....
Chapter 16: Counterattack!
I'M SORRY...

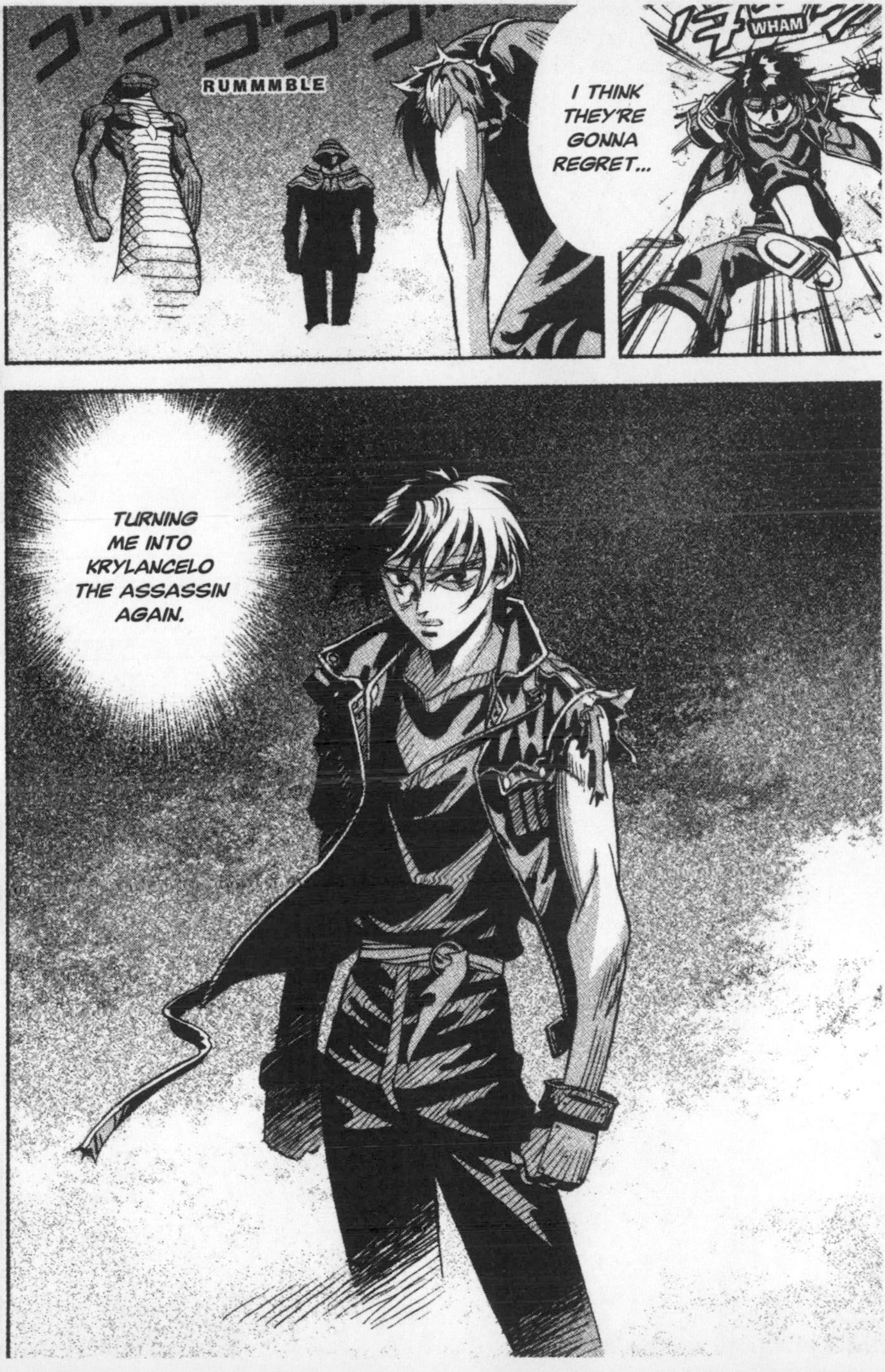

RUMMMBLE
WHAM
I THINK THEY'RE GONNA REGRET...
TURNING ME INTO KRYLANCELO THE ASSASSIN AGAIN.

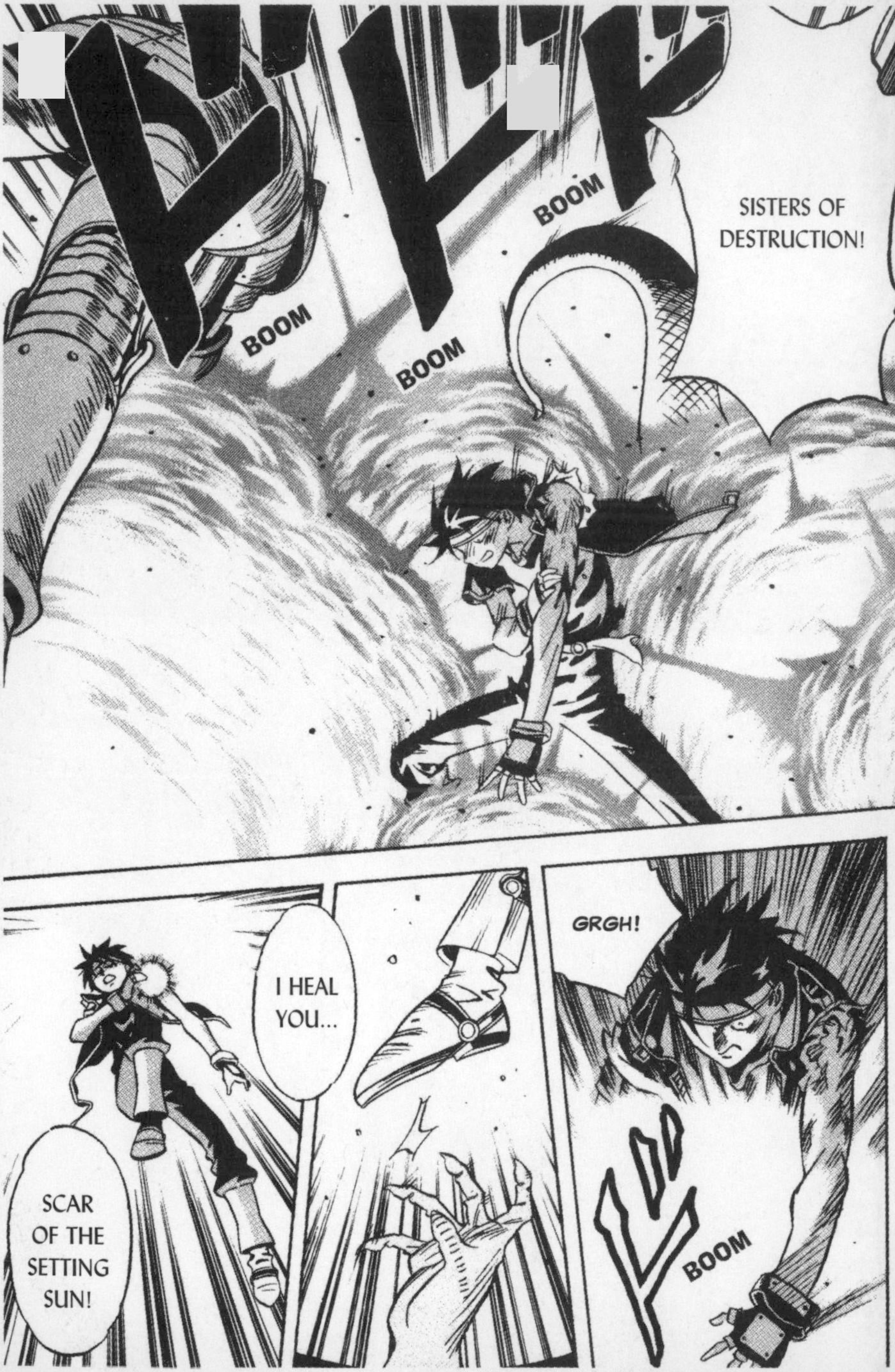
SISTERS OF DESTRUCTION!
BOOM
BOOM
BOOM
BOOM
GRGH!
BOOM
I HEAL YOU...
SCAR OF THE SETTING SUN!

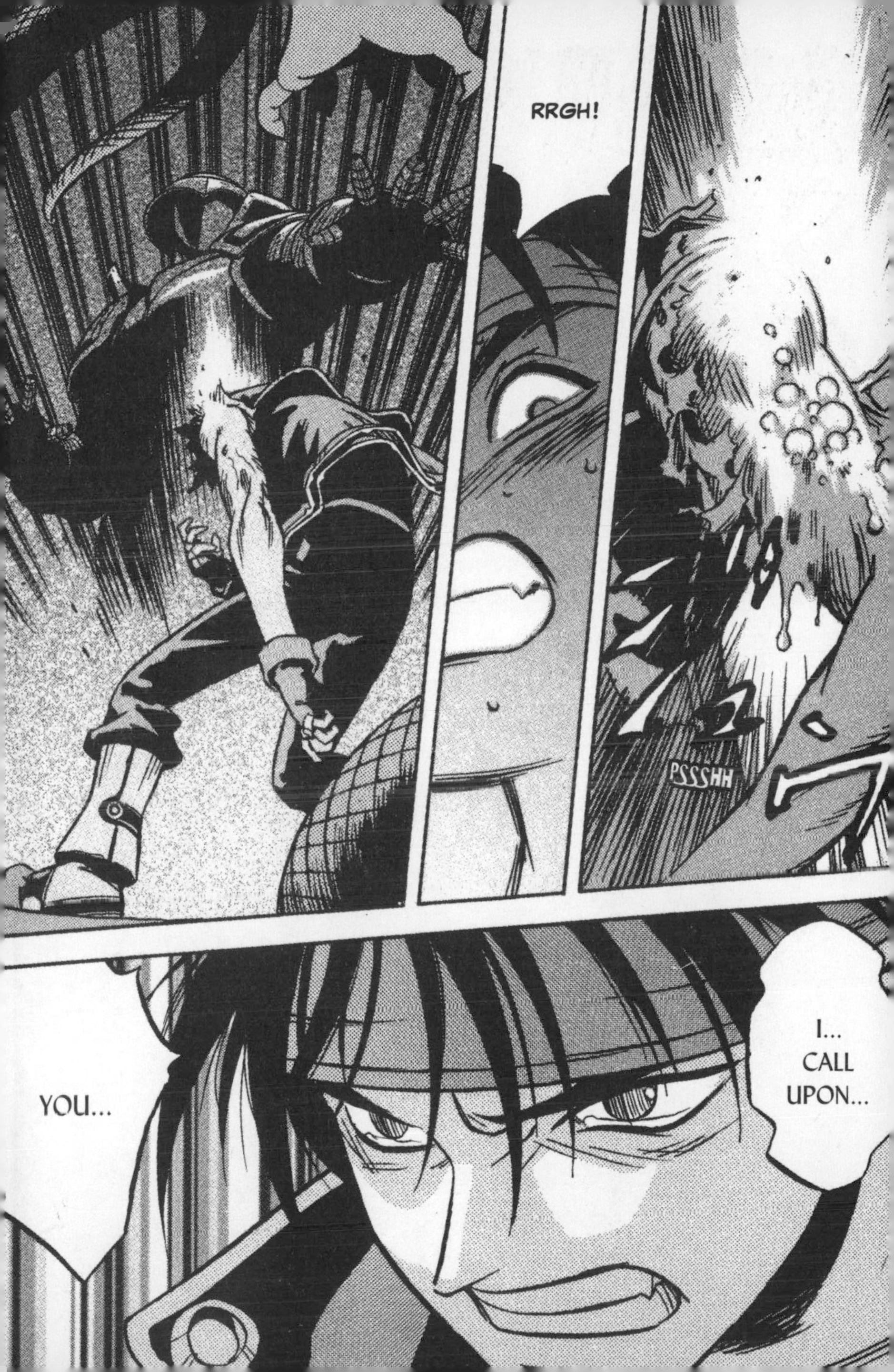
RRGH!
PSSSHH
I... CALL UPON...
YOU...

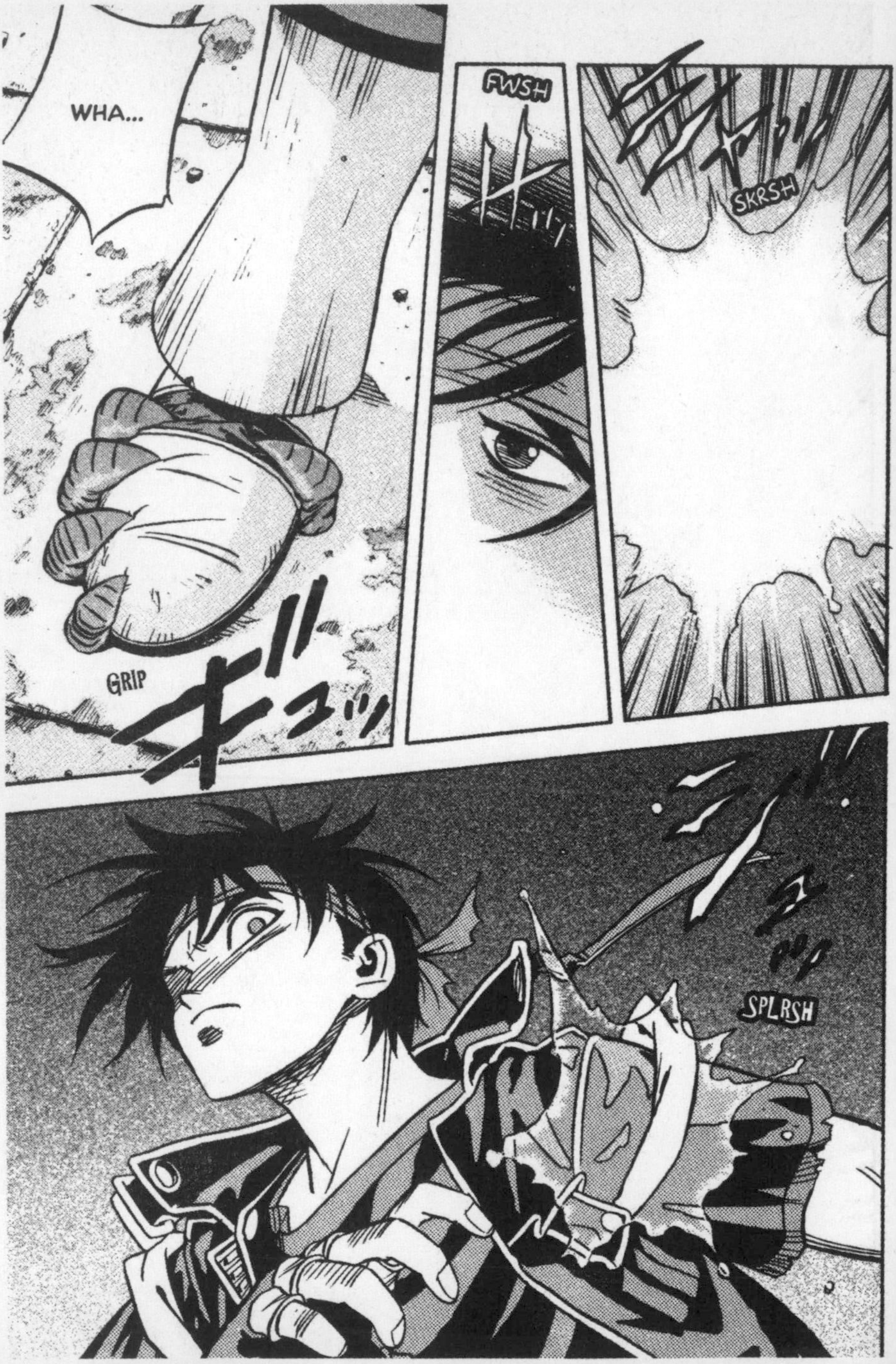
SKRSH
FWSH
WHA...
GRIP
SPLRSH

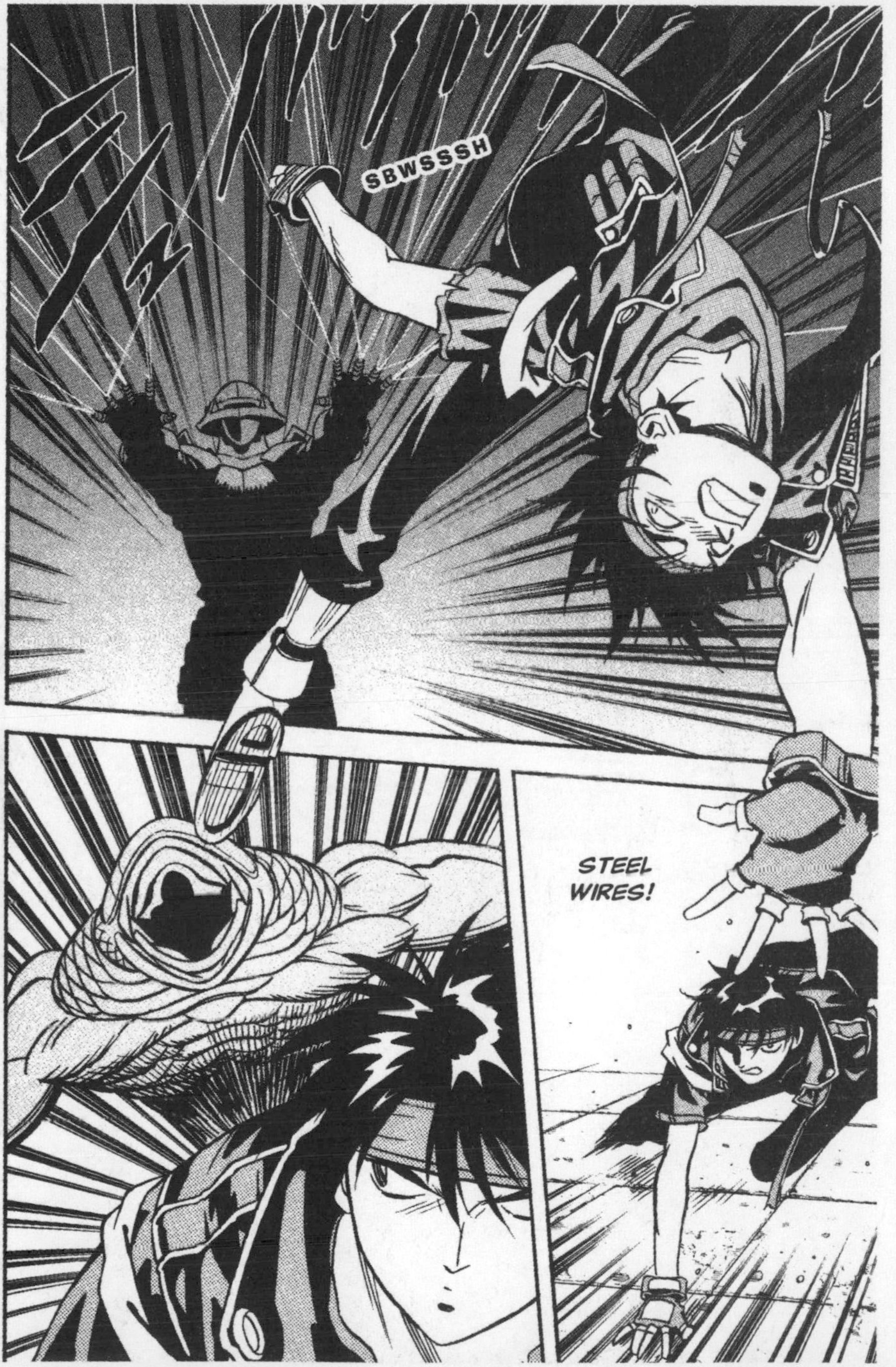
SBWSSSH
STEEL WIRES!

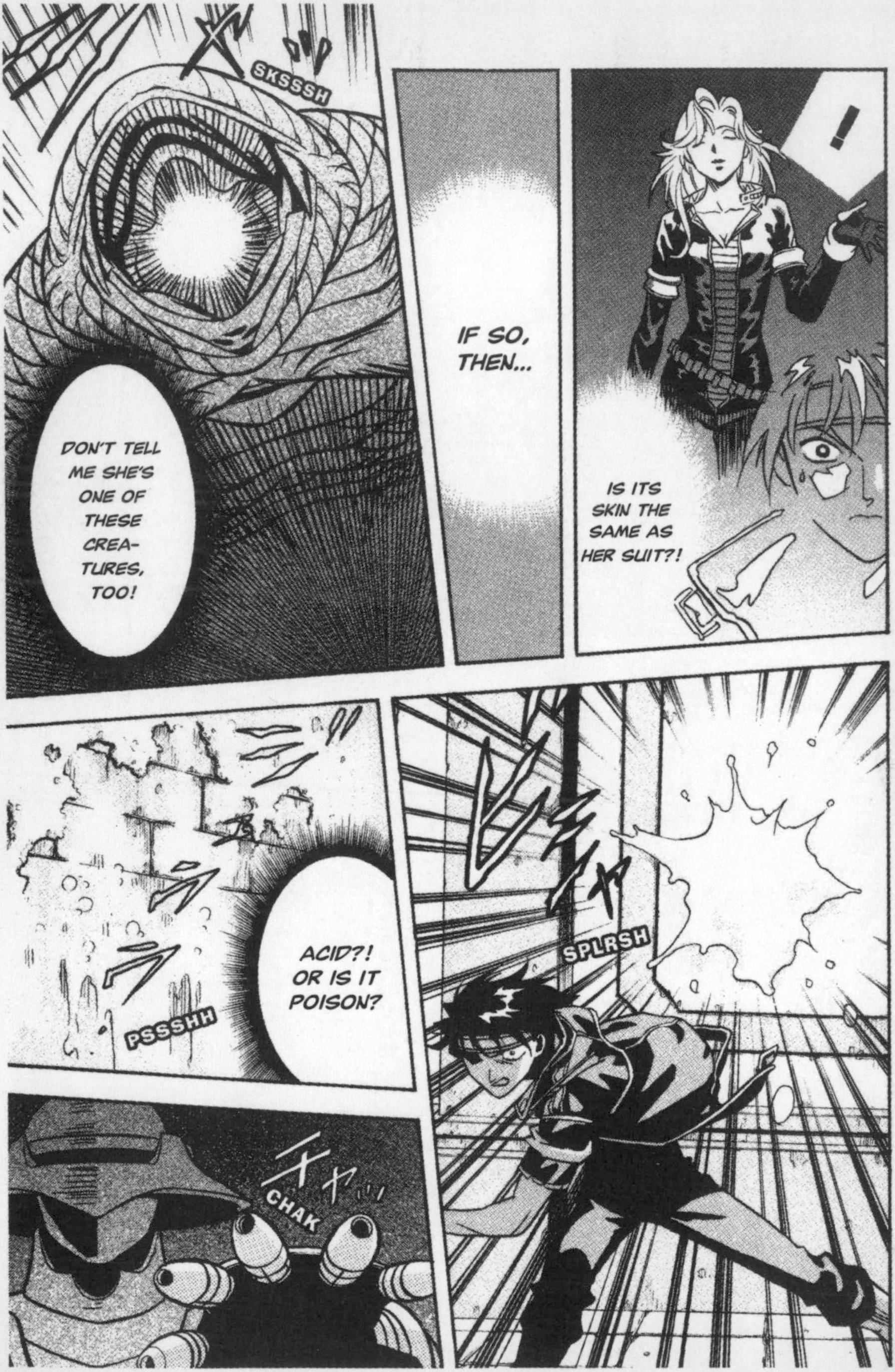
!
IS ITS SKIN THE SAME AS HER SUIT?!
IF SO, THEN...
SKSSSH
DON'T TELL ME SHE'S ONE OF THESE CREA- TURES, TOO!
SPLRSH
ACID?! OR IS IT POISON?
PSSSHH
CHAK

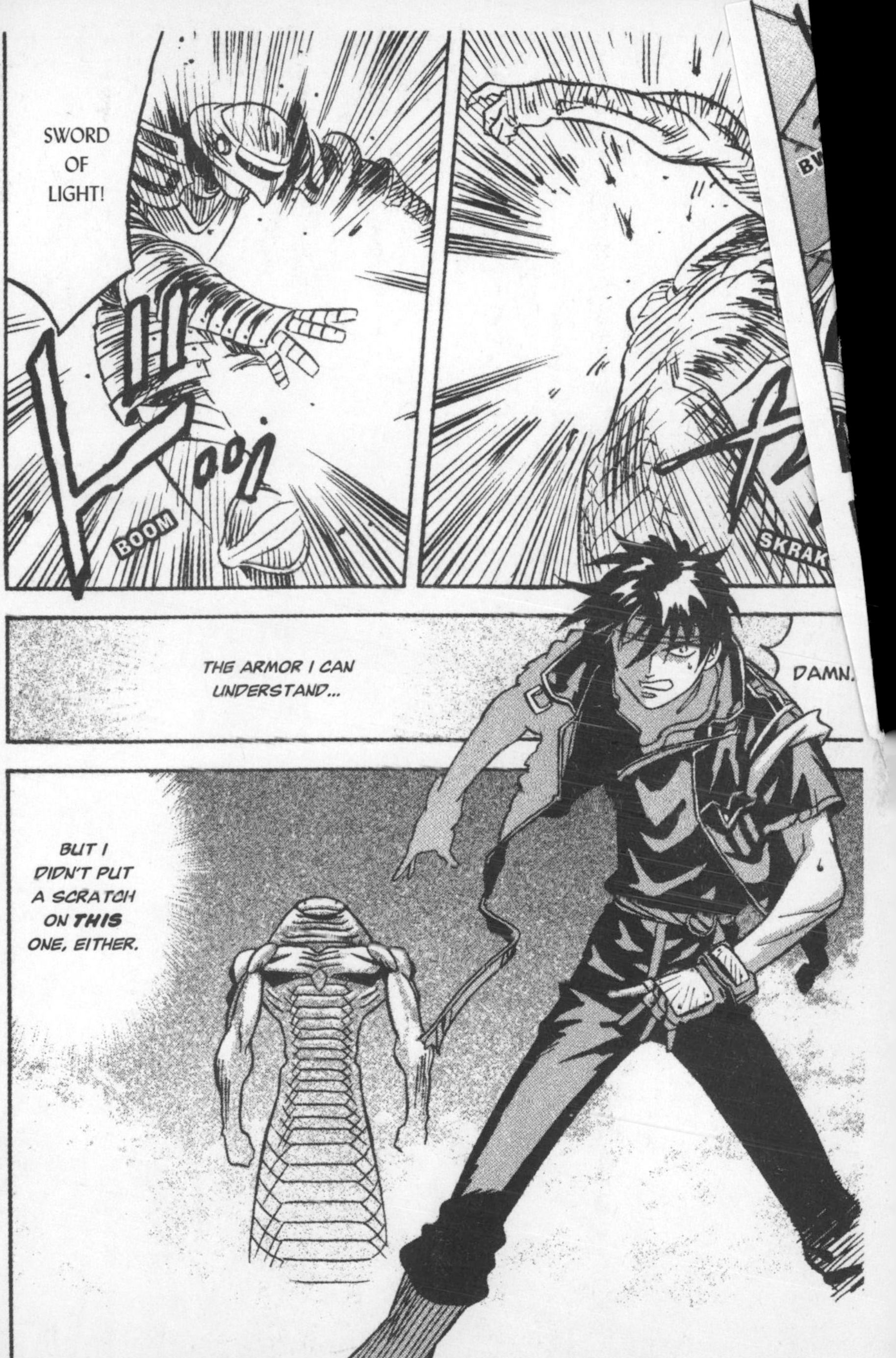
SWORD OF LIGHT!
BOOM
SKRAK
BW
THE ARMOR I CAN UNDERSTAND...
DAMN.
BUT I DIDN'T PUT A SCRATCH ON THIS ONE, EITHER.

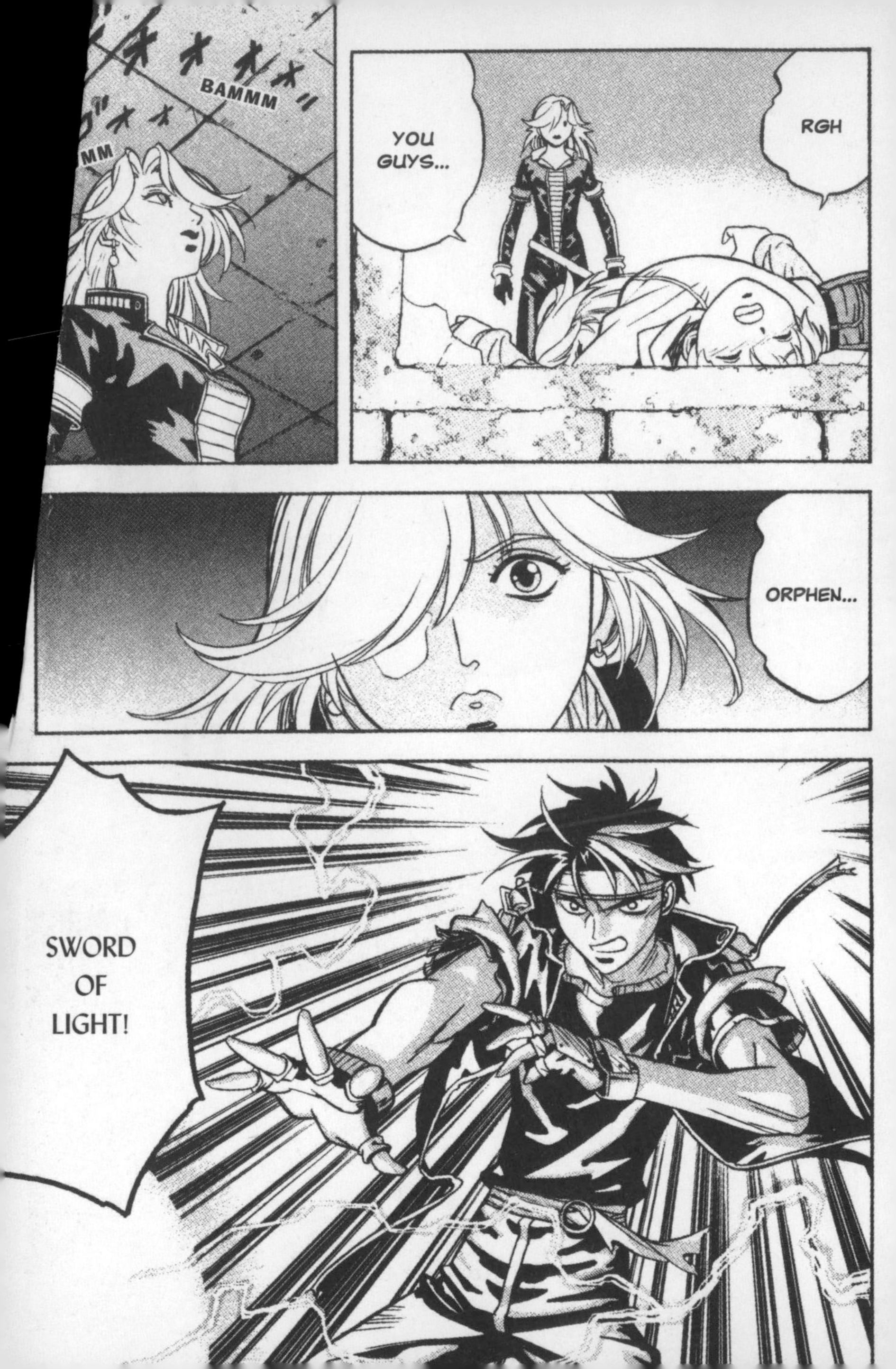
BAMMMM
MM
YOU GUYS...
RGH
ORPHEN...
SWORD OF LIGHT!

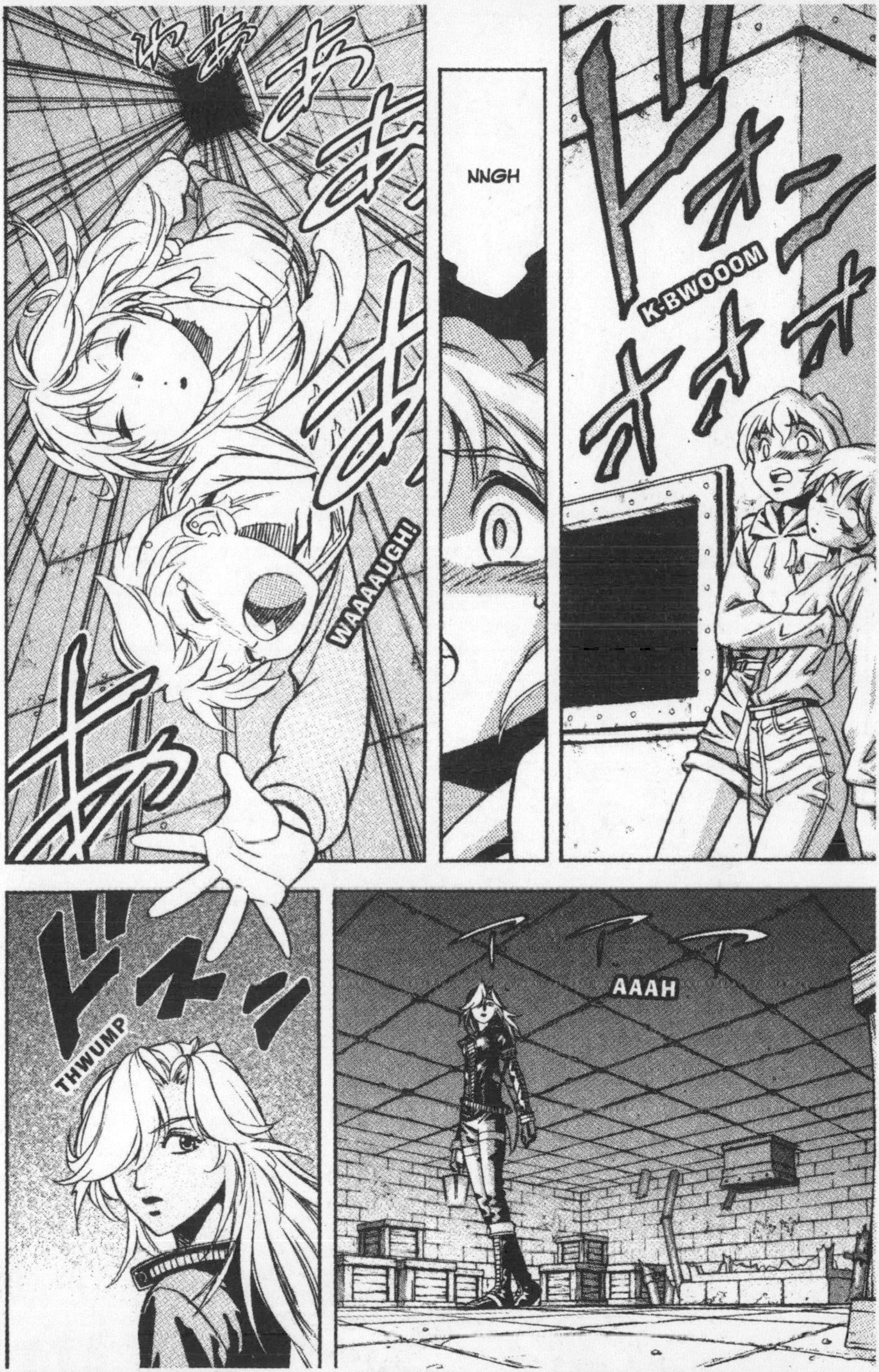
K-BWOOOM
NNGH
WAAAAUGH!
AAAH
THWUMP

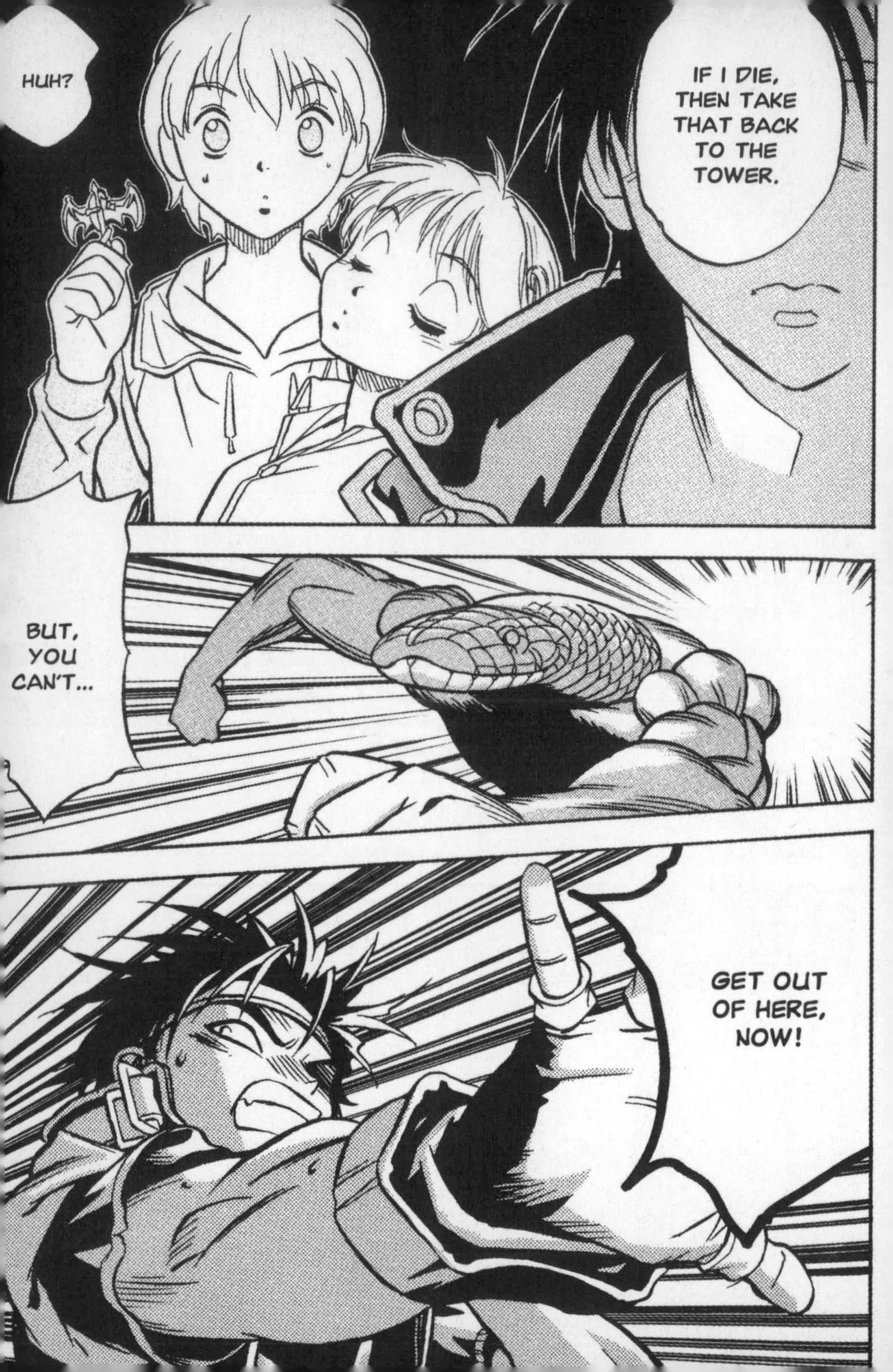
IF I DIE, THEN TAKE THAT BACK TO THE TOWER.
HUH?
BUT, YOU CAN'T...
GET OUT OF HERE, NOW!

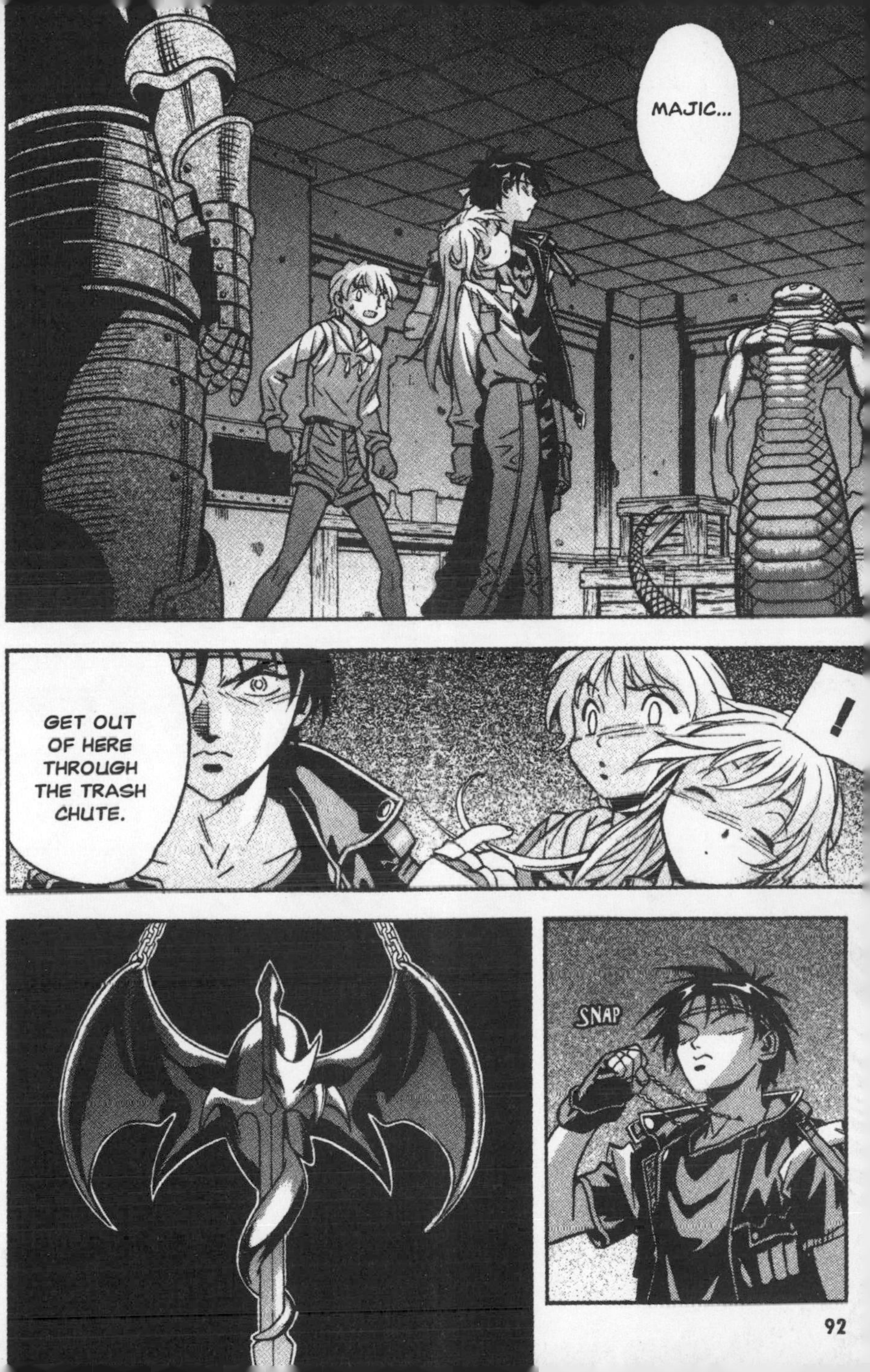
MAJIC...
GET OUT OF HERE THROUGH THE TRASH CHUTE.
!
SNAP

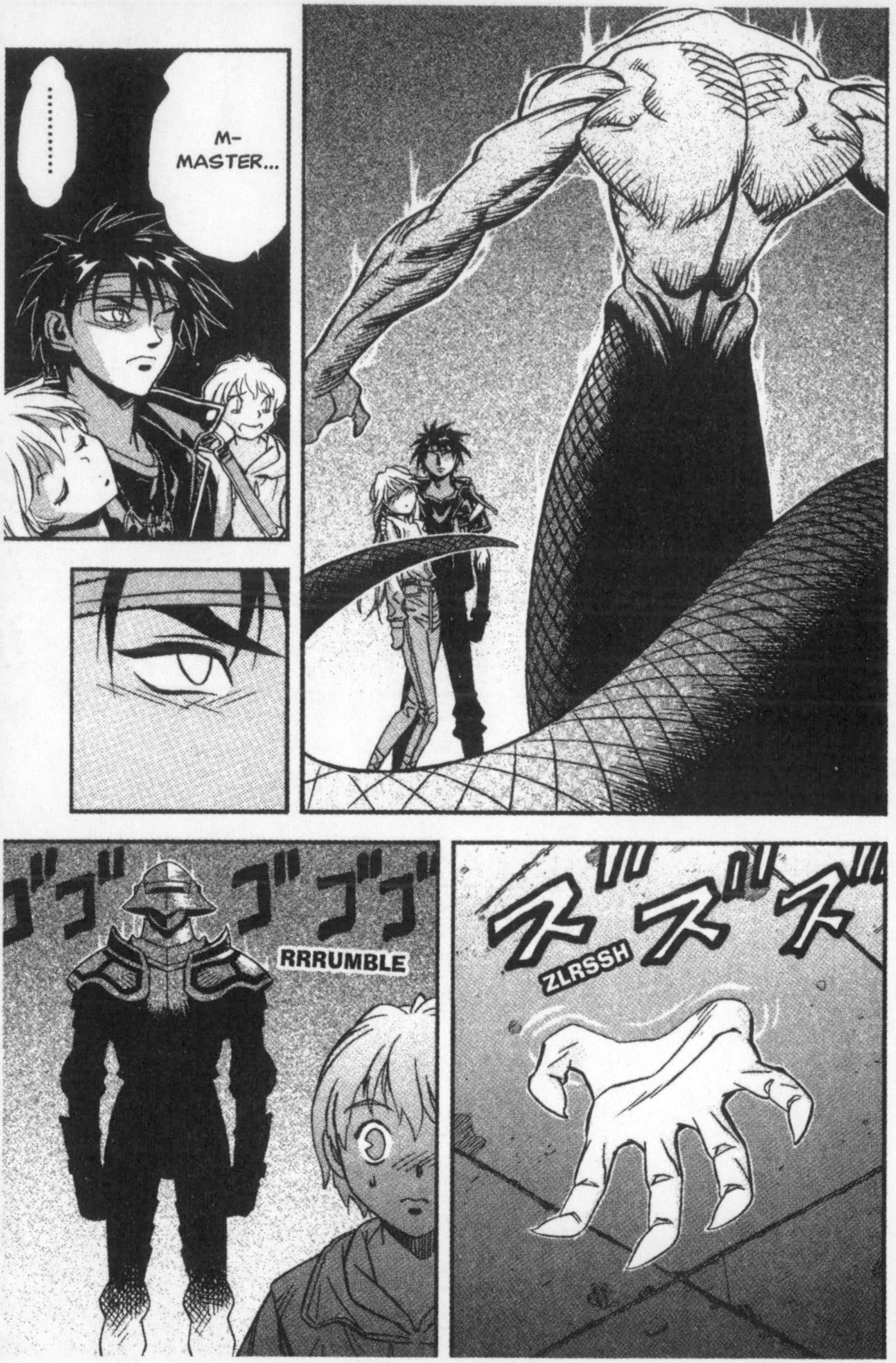

M-
MASTER...
RRRUMBLE
ZLRSSH

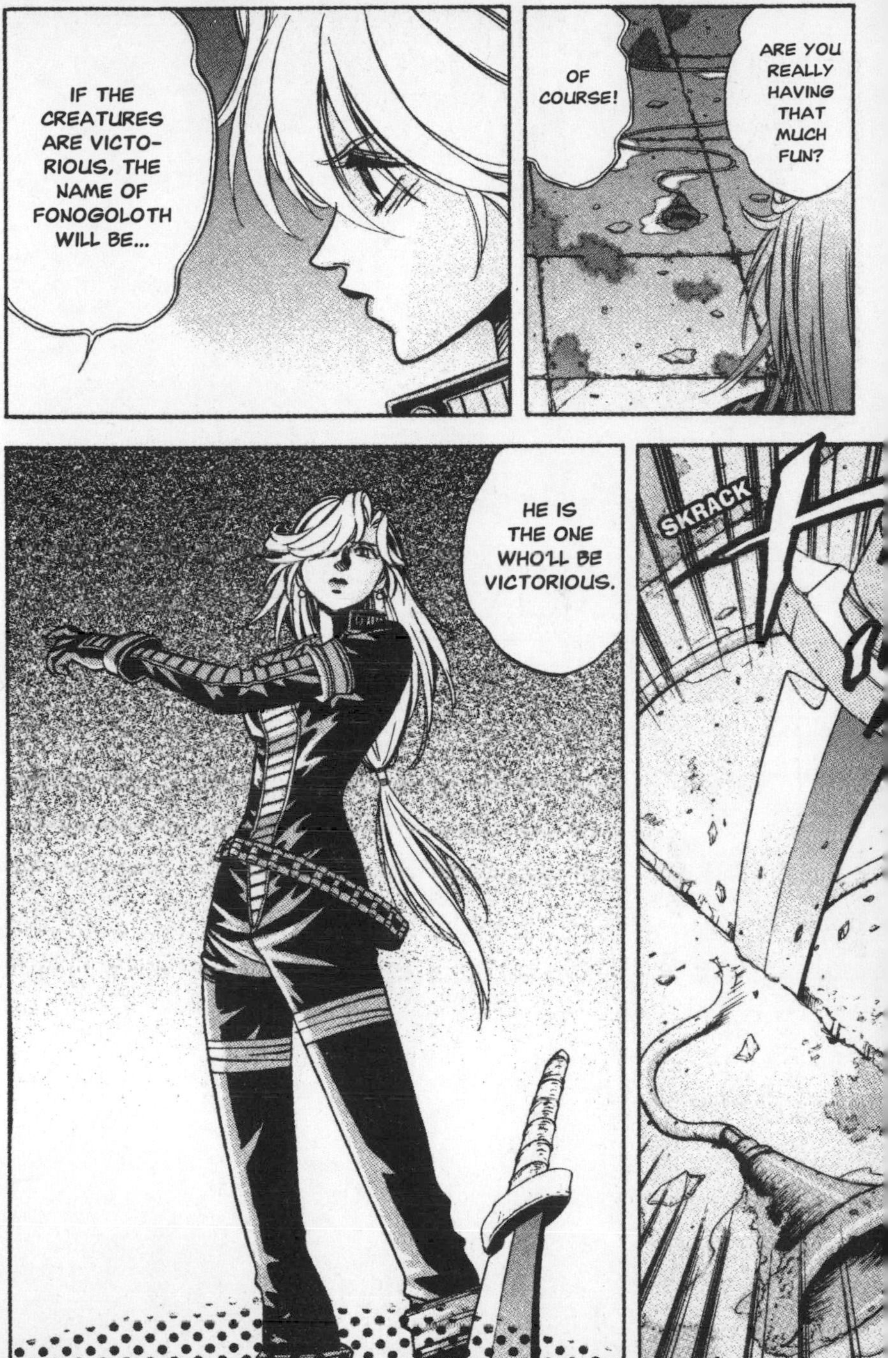
IF THE CREATURES ARE VICTO- RIOUS, THE NAME OF FONOGOLOTH WILL BE...
ARE YOU REALLY HAVING THAT MUCH FUN?
OF COURSE!
HE IS THE ONE WHO'LL BE VICTORIOUS.
SKRACK

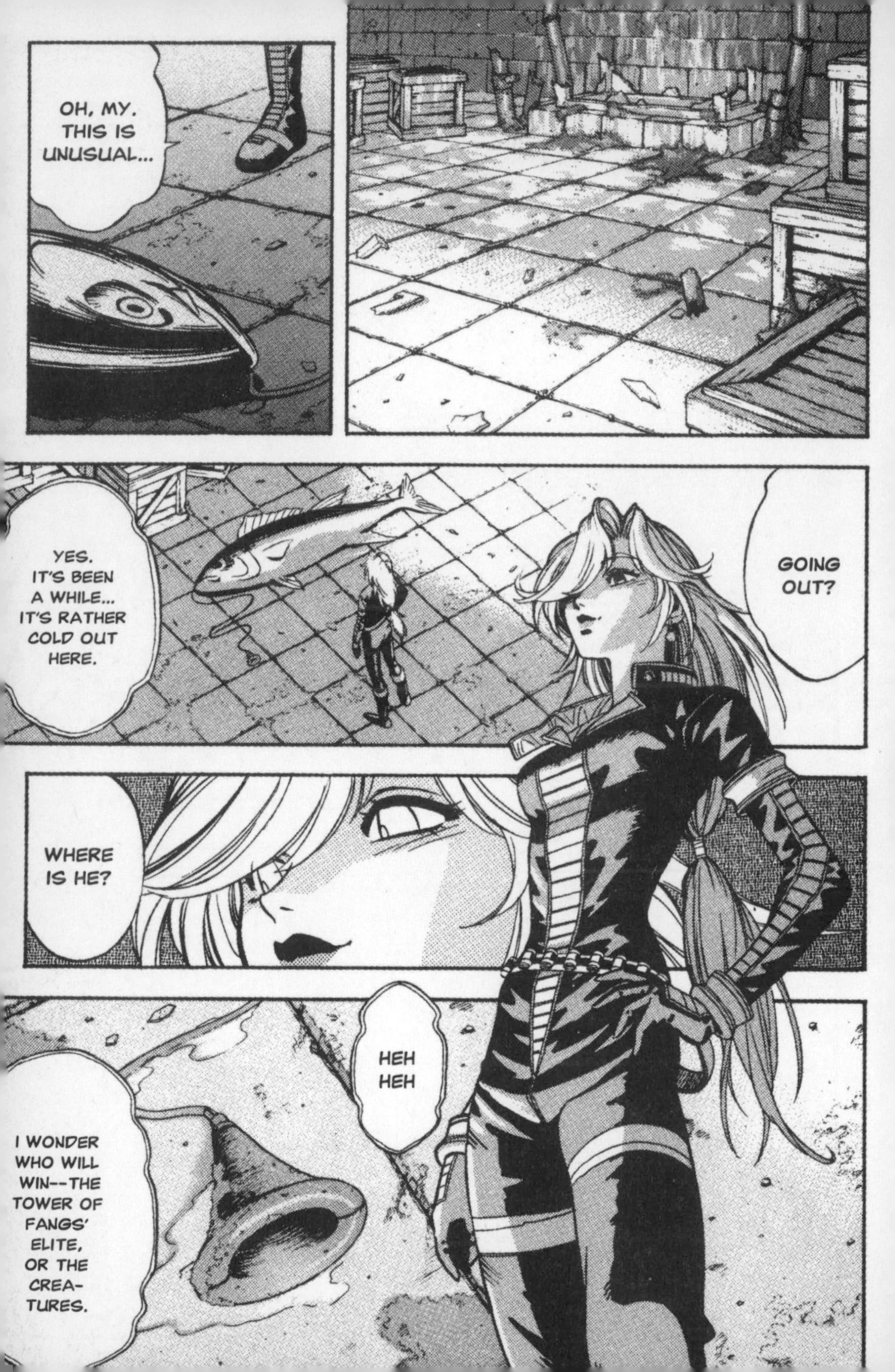
OH, MY. THIS IS UNUSUAL...
GOING OUT?
YES. IT'S BEEN A WHILE... IT'S RATHER COLD OUT HERE.
WHERE IS HE?
HEH HEH
I WONDER WHO WILL WIN--THE TOWER OF FANGS' ELITE, OR THE CREA-TURES.

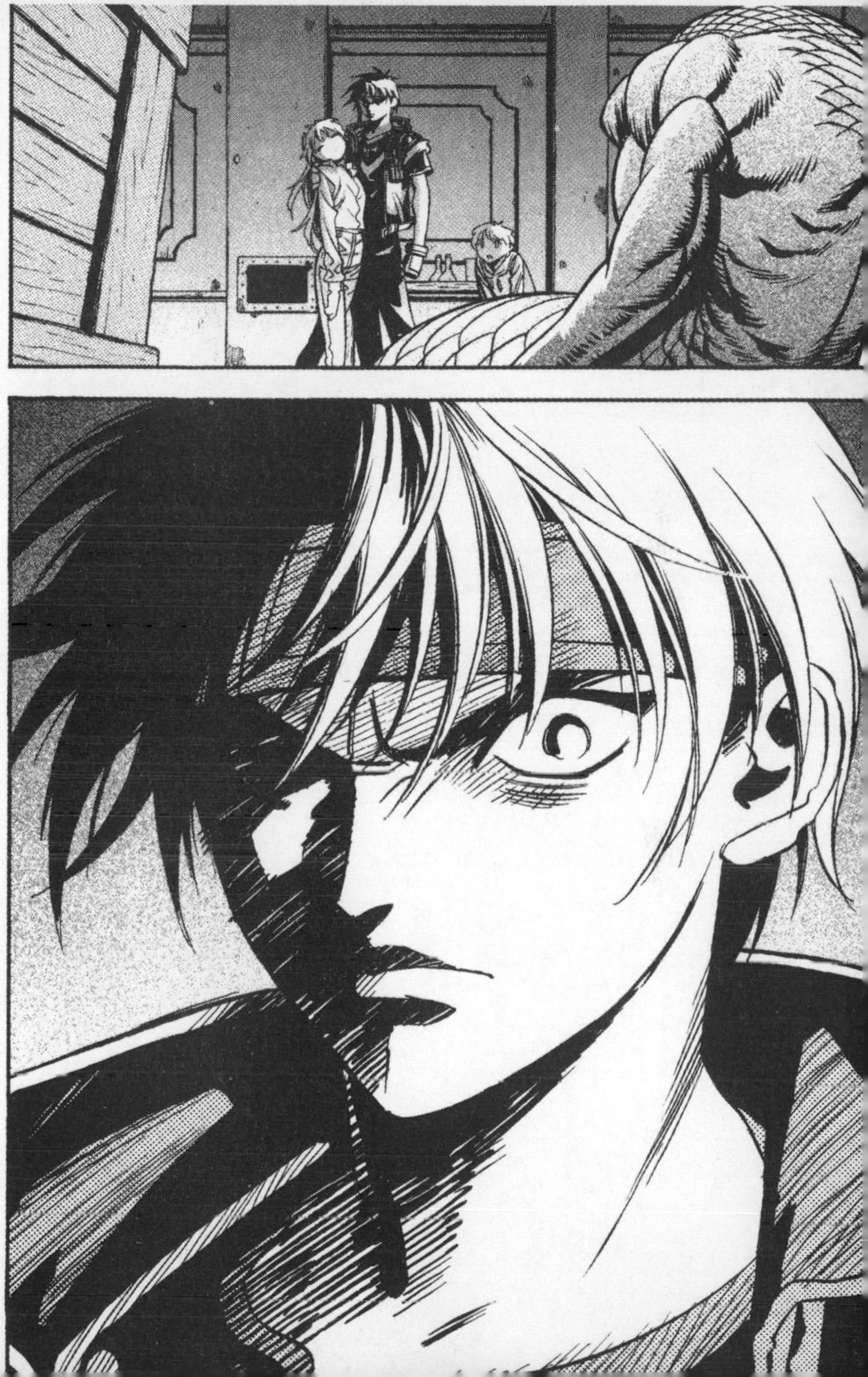

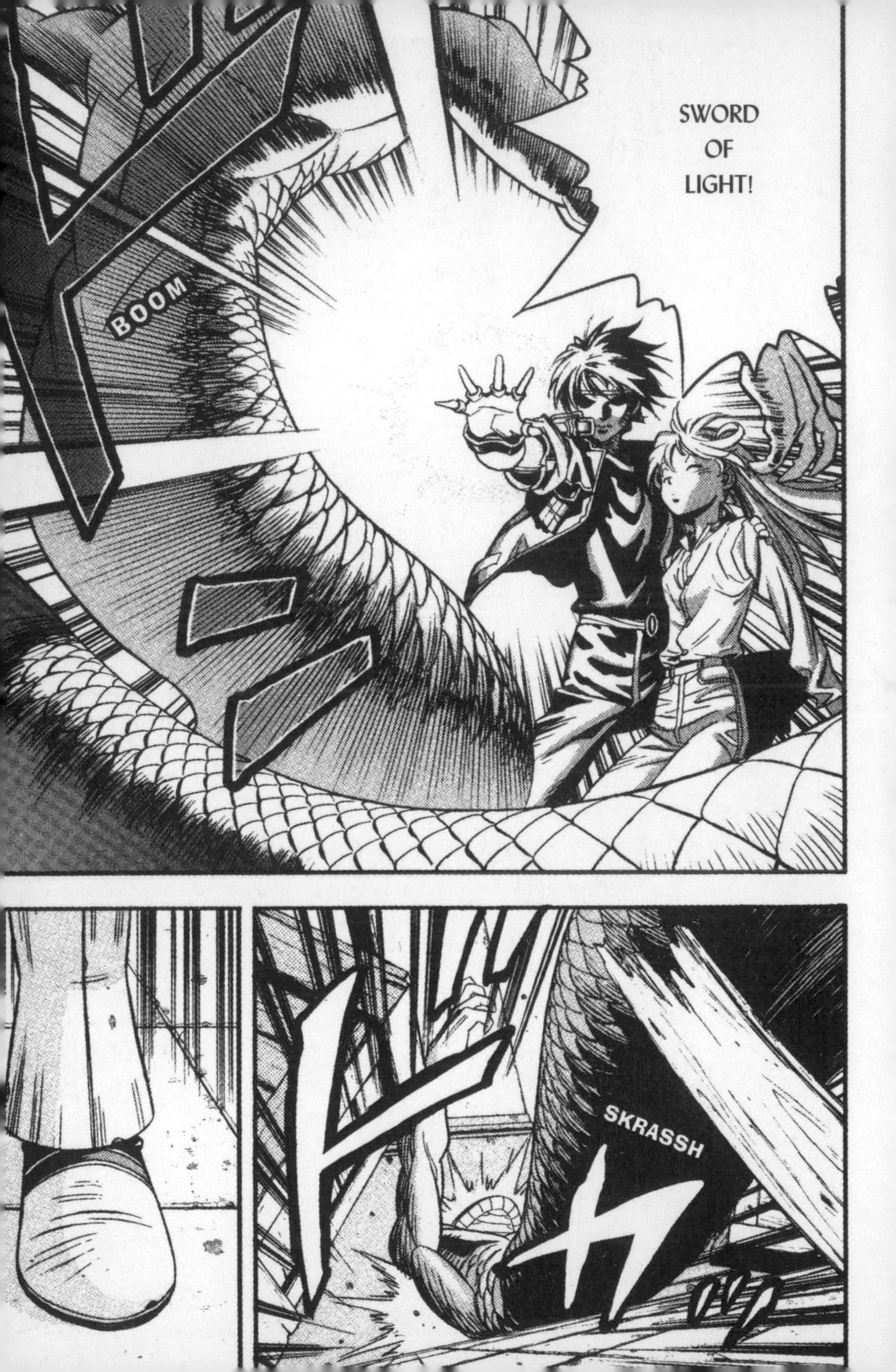
SWORD OF LIGHT!
BOOM
SKRASSH

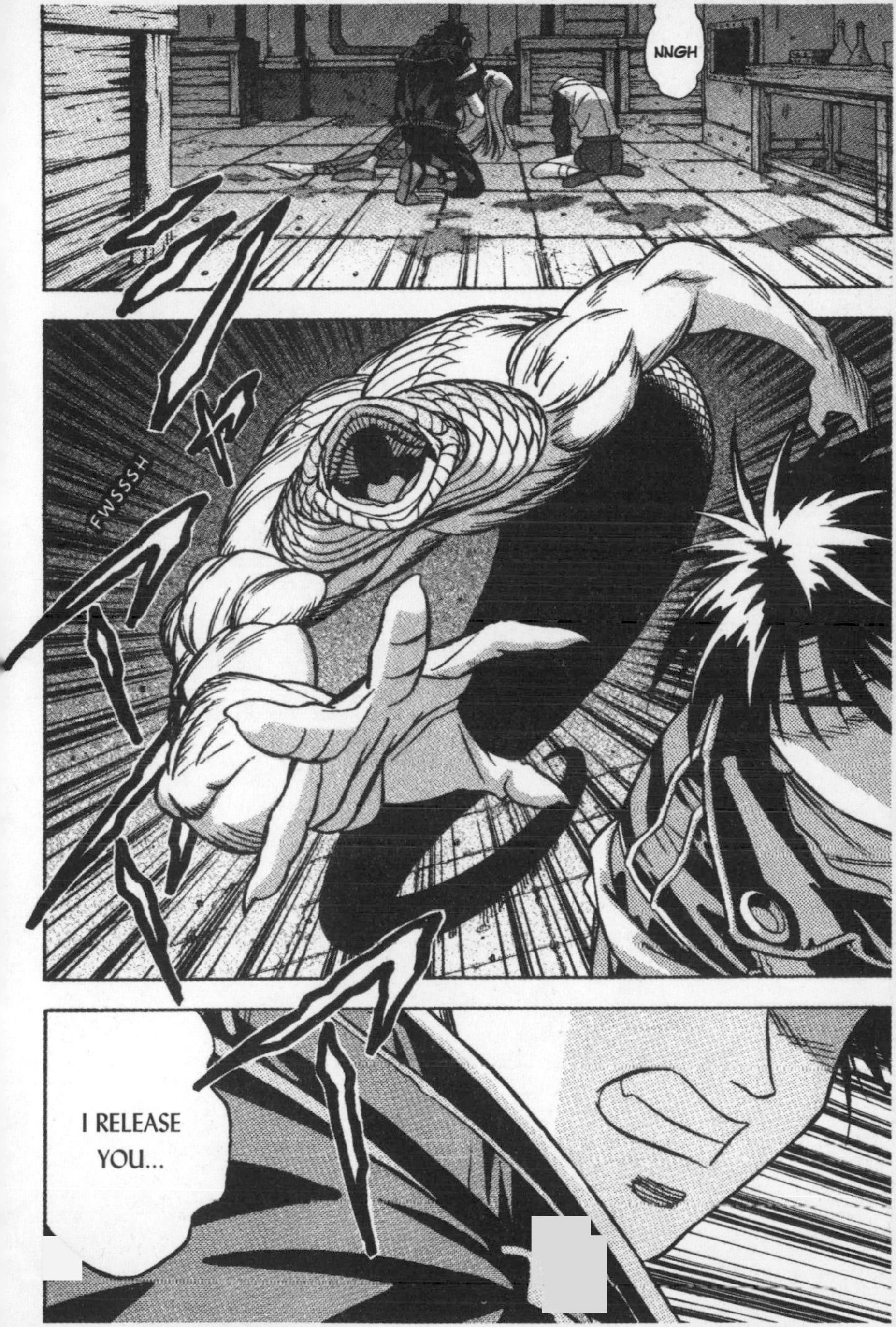
NNGH
FWSSSH
I RELEASE YOU...

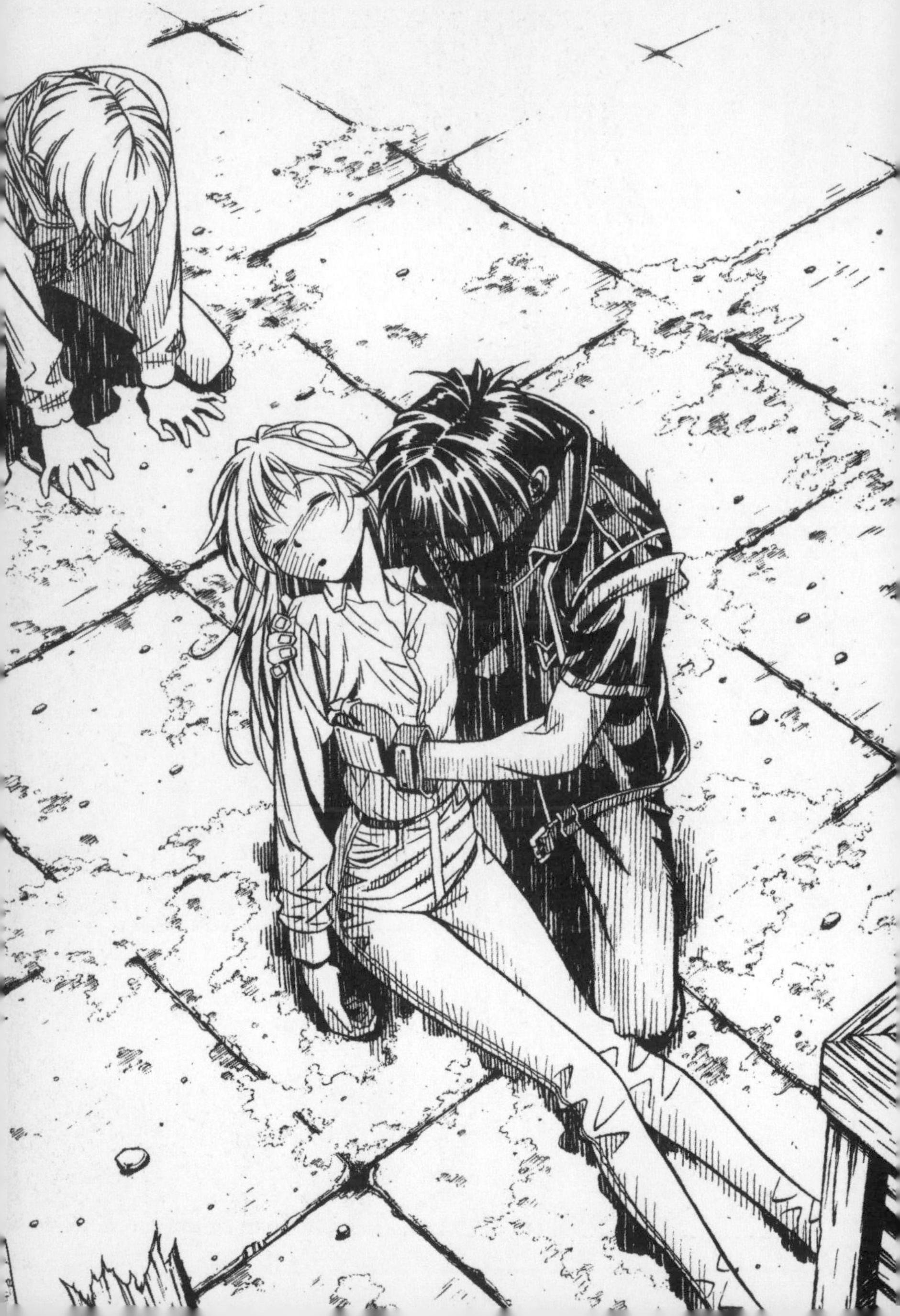

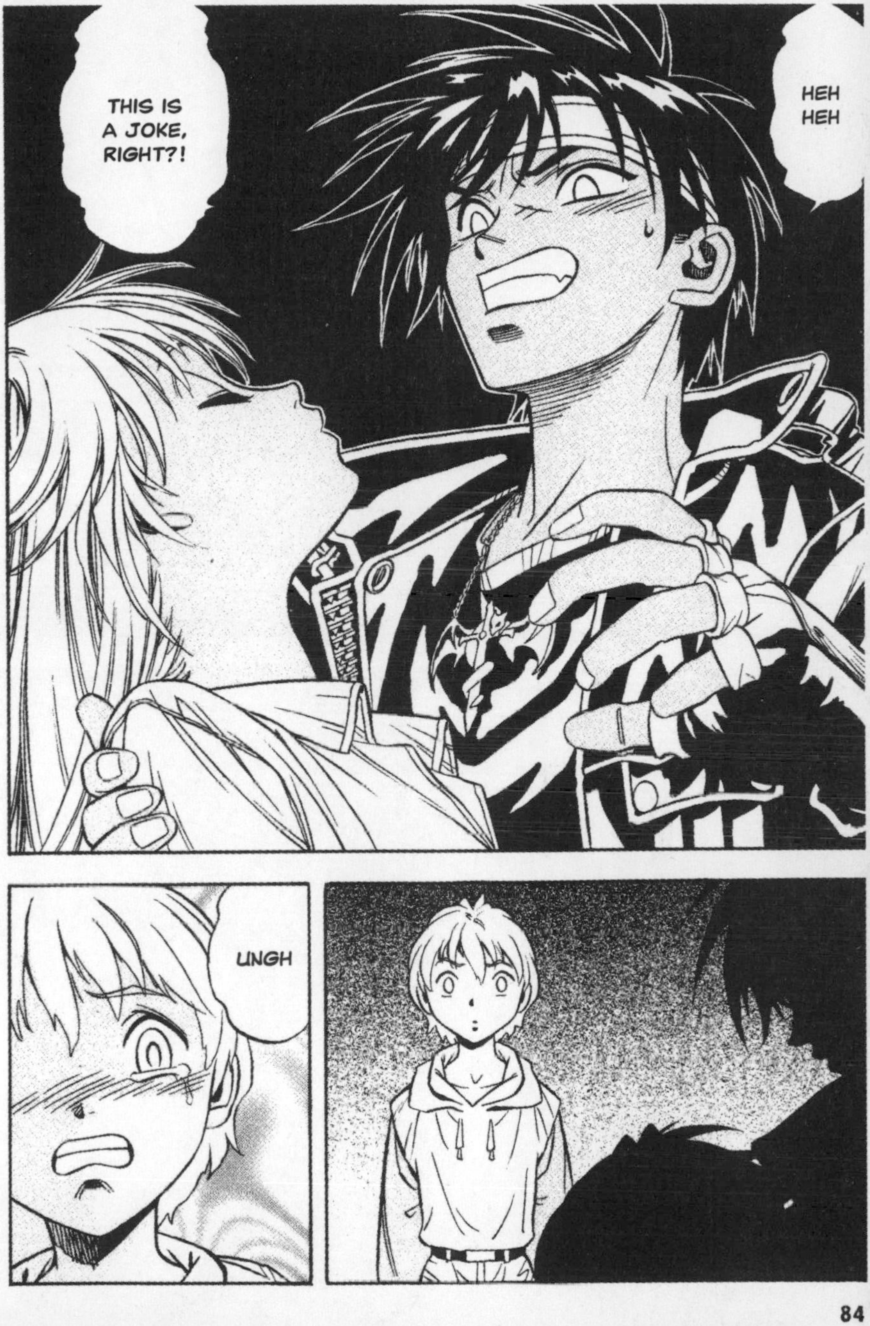
HEH HEH
THIS IS A JOKE, RIGHT?!
UNGH

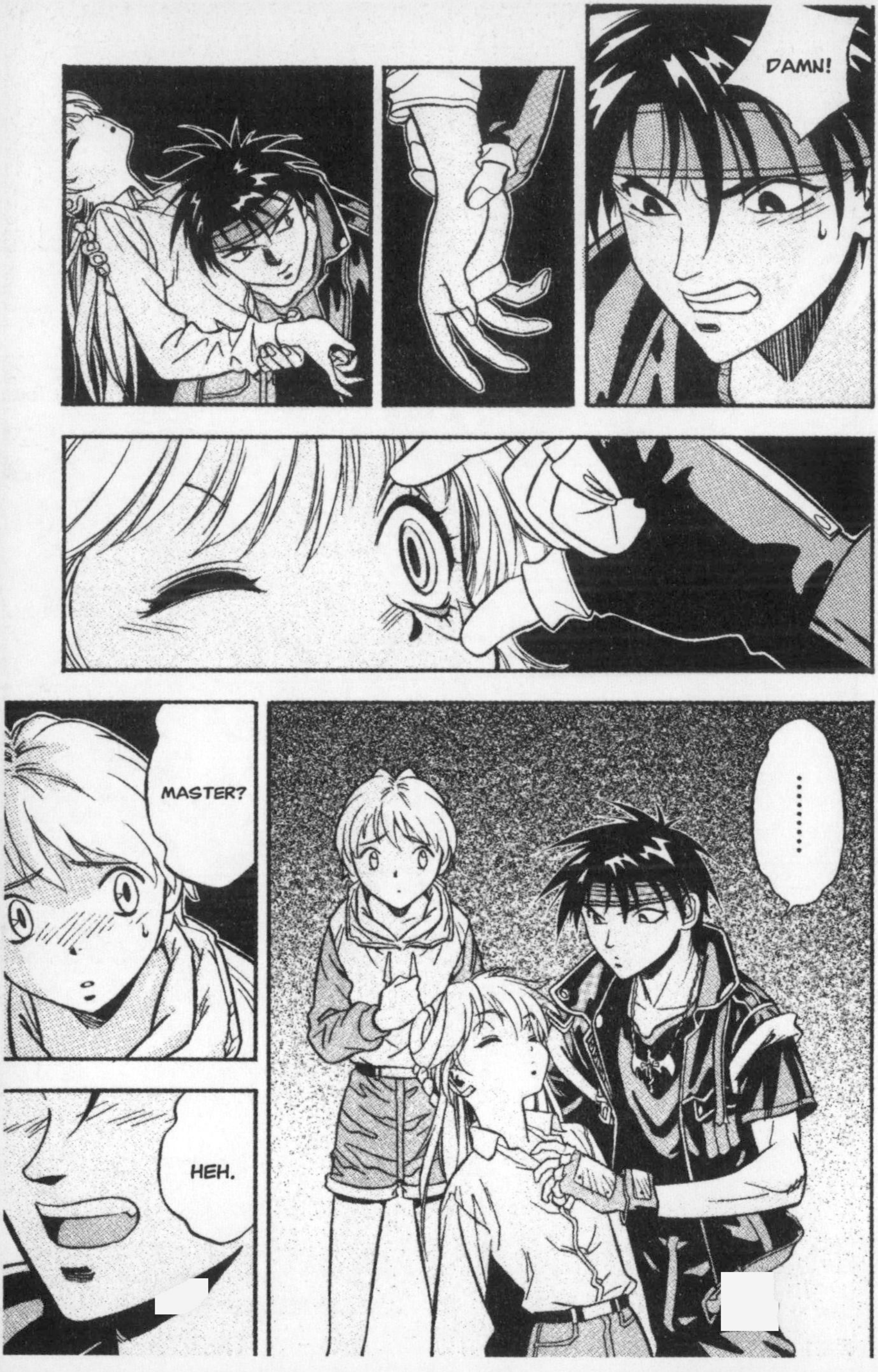
DAMN!
......
MASTER?
HEH.

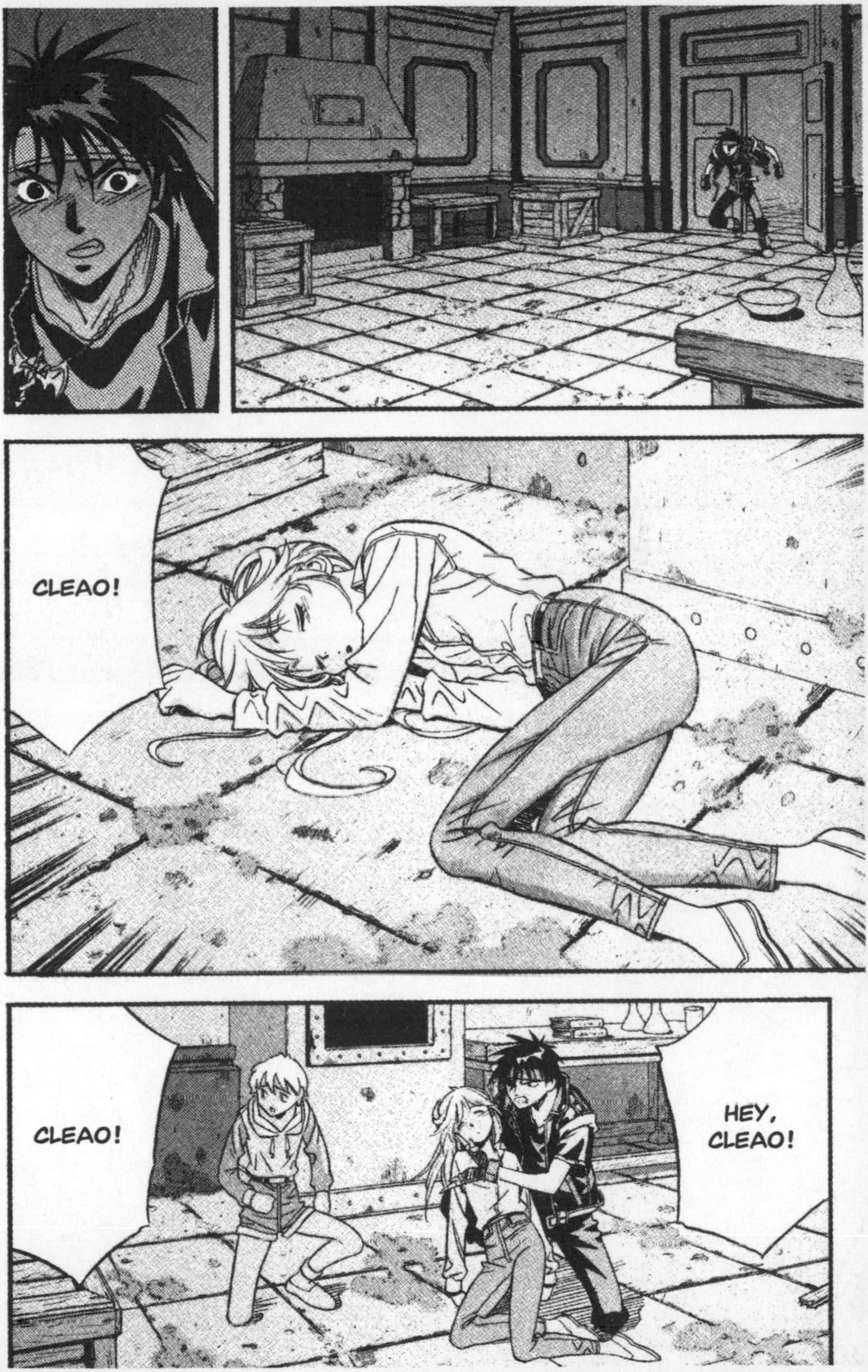
CLEAO!
CLEAO!
HEY, CLEAO!

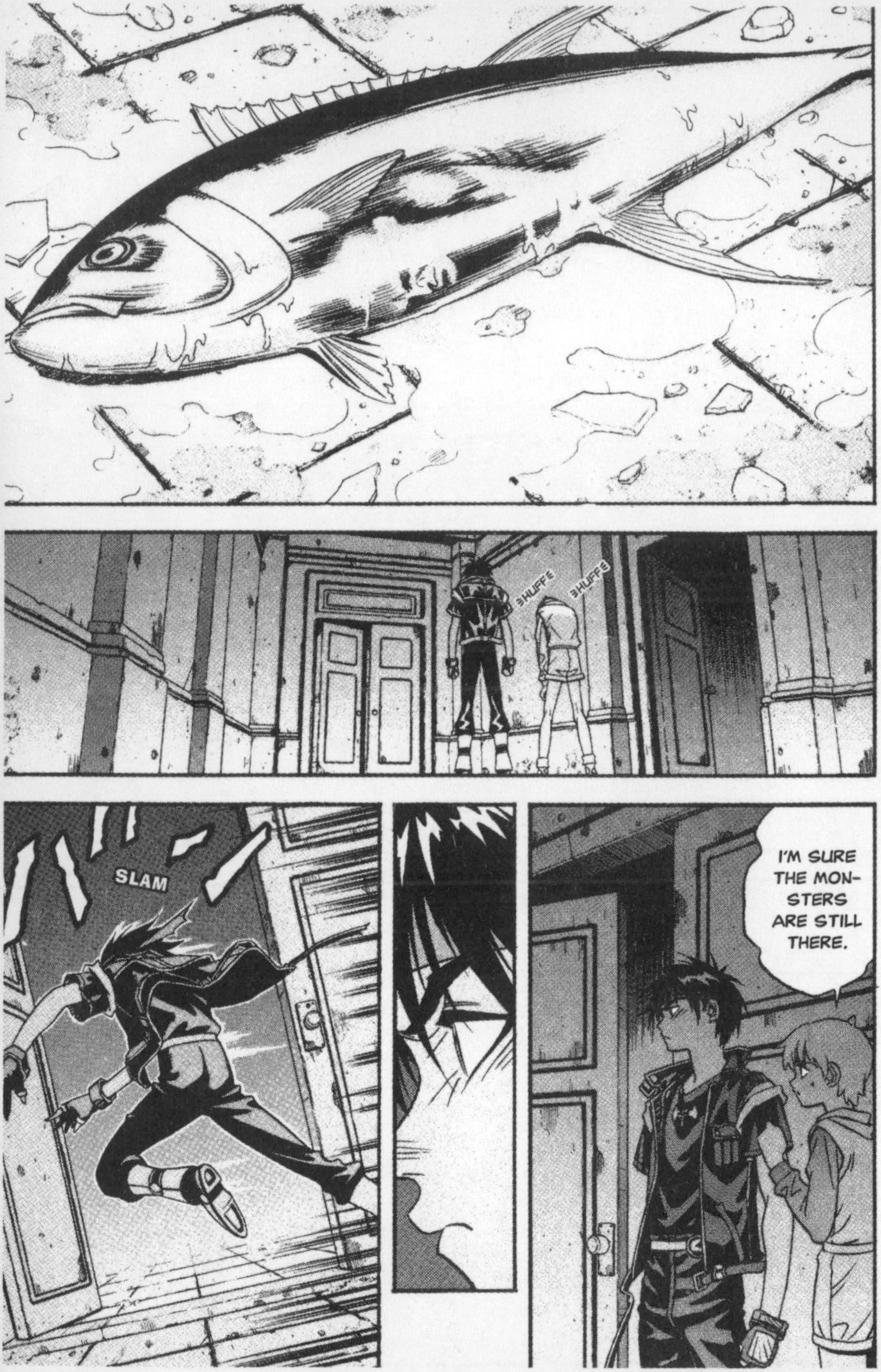
HUFF
HUFF
SLAM
I'M SURE THE MON-STERS ARE STILL THERE.

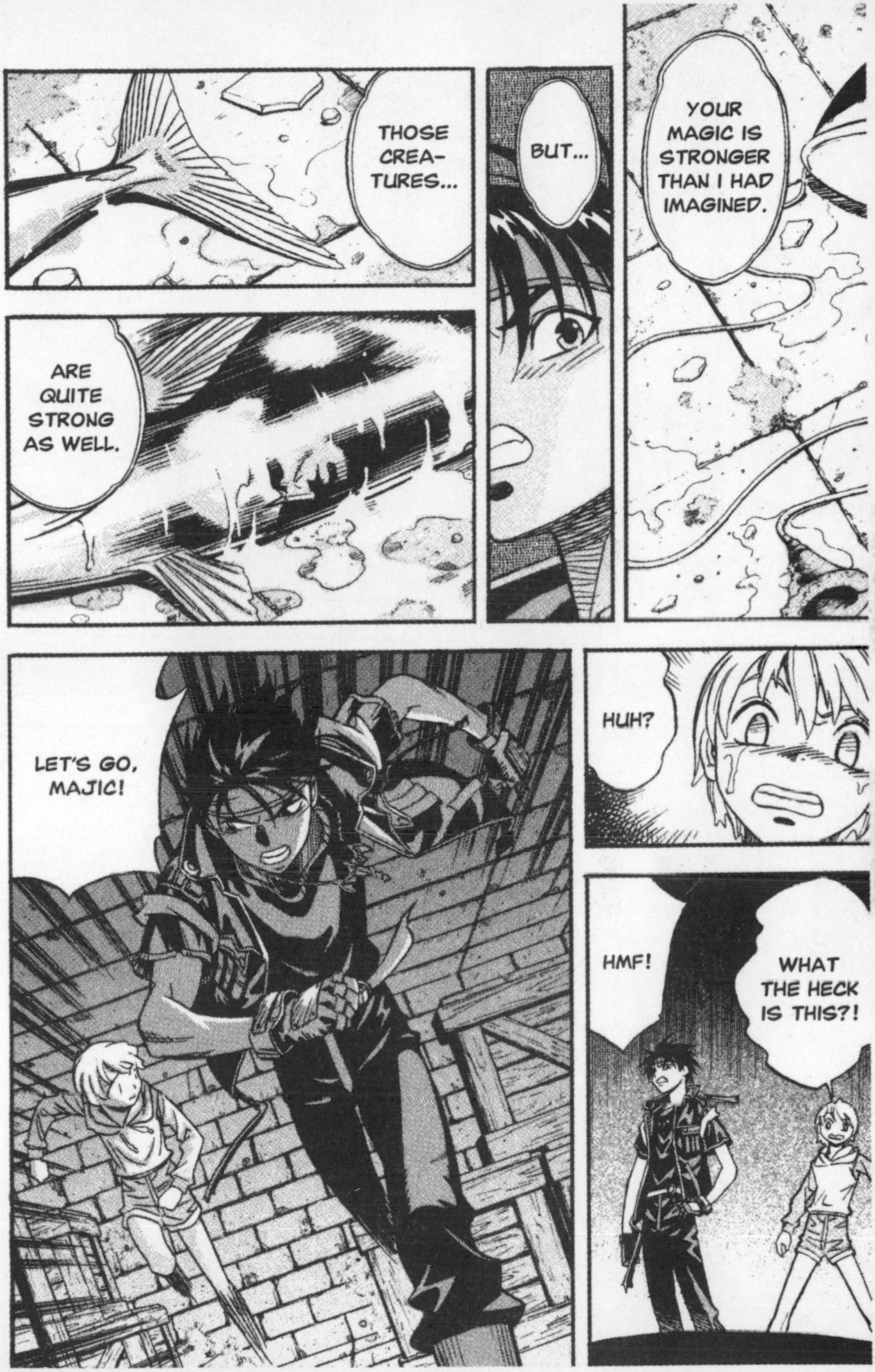

YOUR MAGIC IS STRONGER THAN I HAD IMAGINED.
BUT...
THOSE CREA-TURES...
ARE QUITE STRONG AS WELL.
HUH?
WHAT THE HECK IS THIS?!
HMF!
LET'S GO, MAJIC!

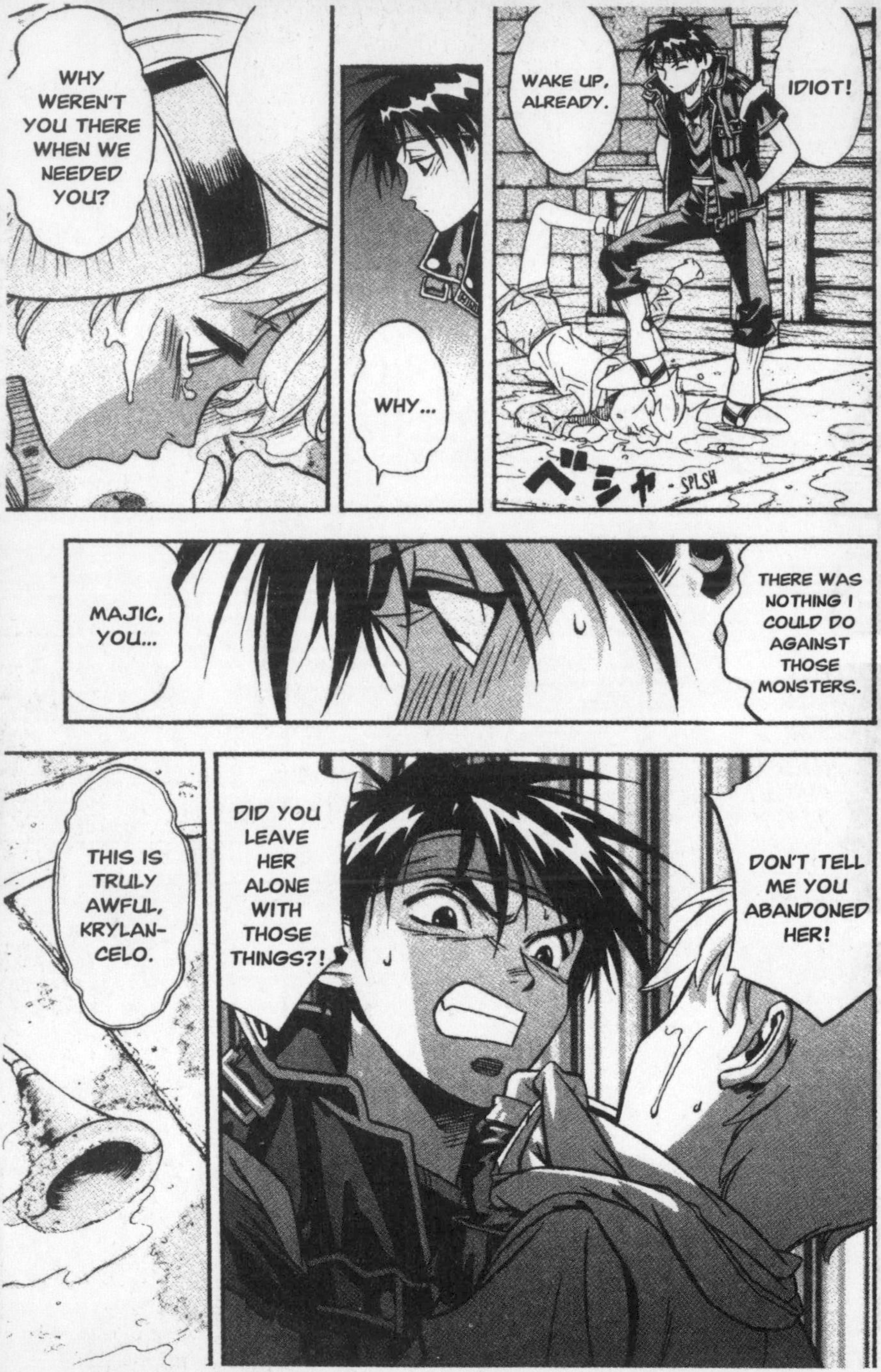

IDIOT!
WAKE UP, ALREADY.
ベシャ
SPLSH
WHY...
WHY WEREN'T YOU THERE WHEN WE NEEDED YOU?
THERE WAS NOTHING I COULD DO AGAINST THOSE MONSTERS.
MAJIC, YOU...
DON'T TELL ME YOU ABANDONED HER!
DID YOU LEAVE HER ALONE WITH THOSE THINGS?!
THIS IS TRULY AWFUL, KRYLANCELO.

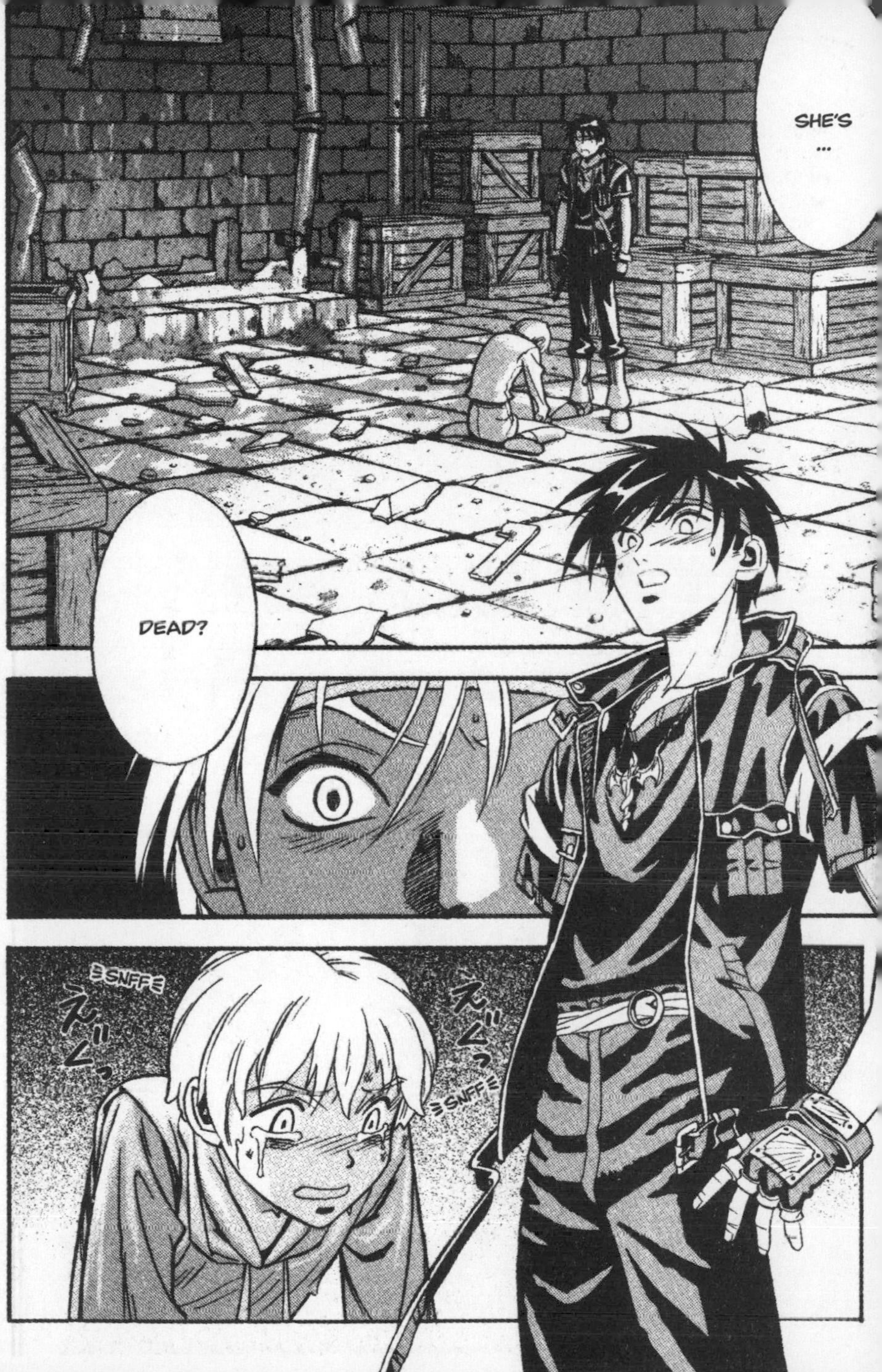
SHE'S ...
DEAD?
SNFF
SNFF

Chapter 15: Cleao's Dead!

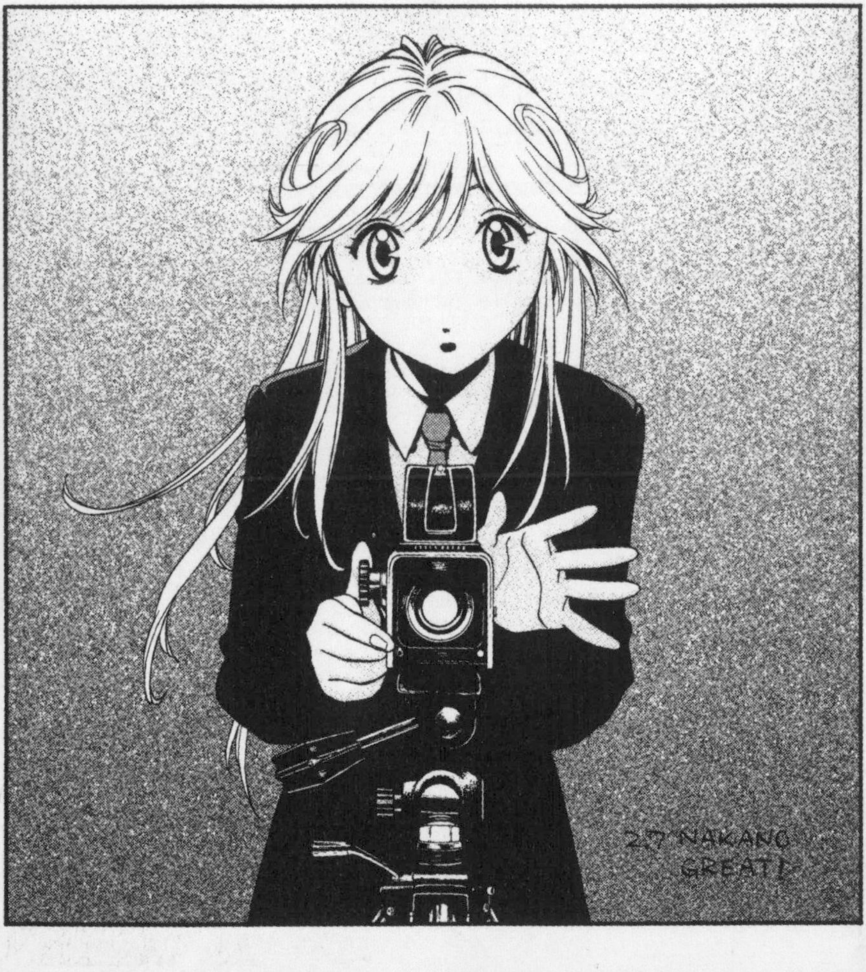
27 NAKANO
GREAT!

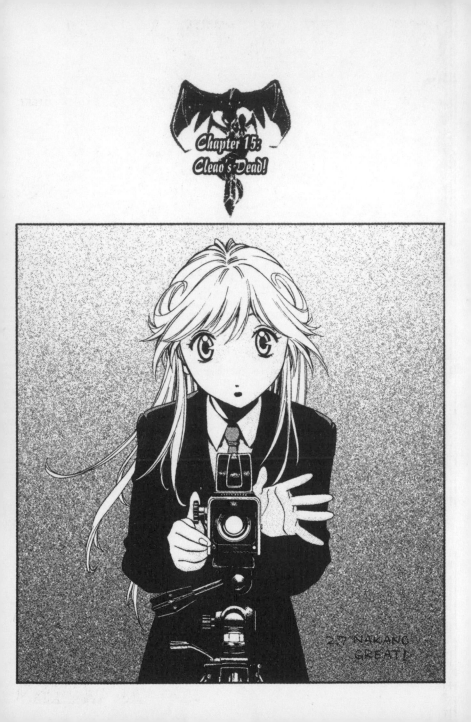

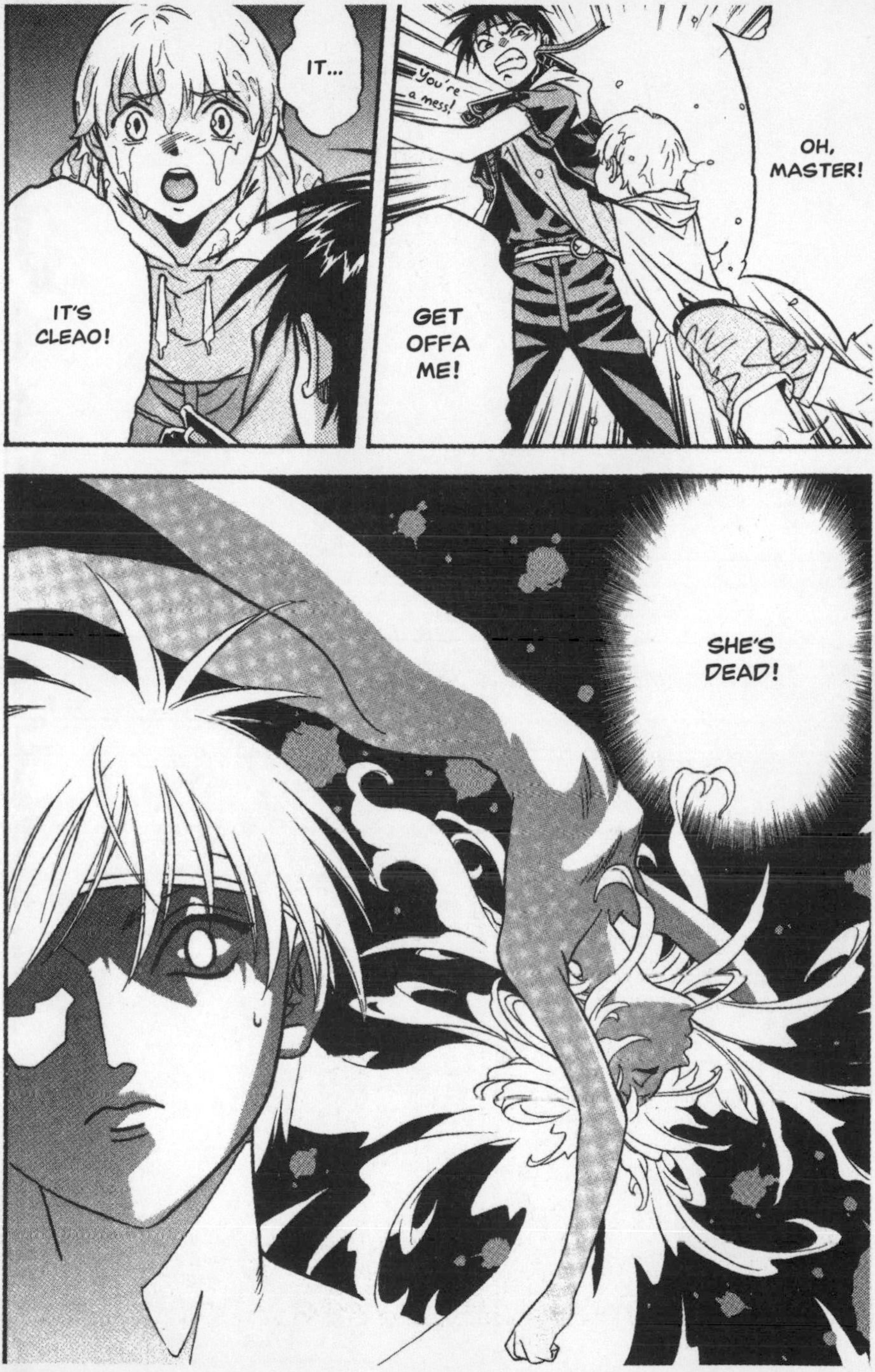
OH, MASTER!
You're a mess!
GET OFFA ME!
IT...
IT'S CLEAO!
SHE'S DEAD!

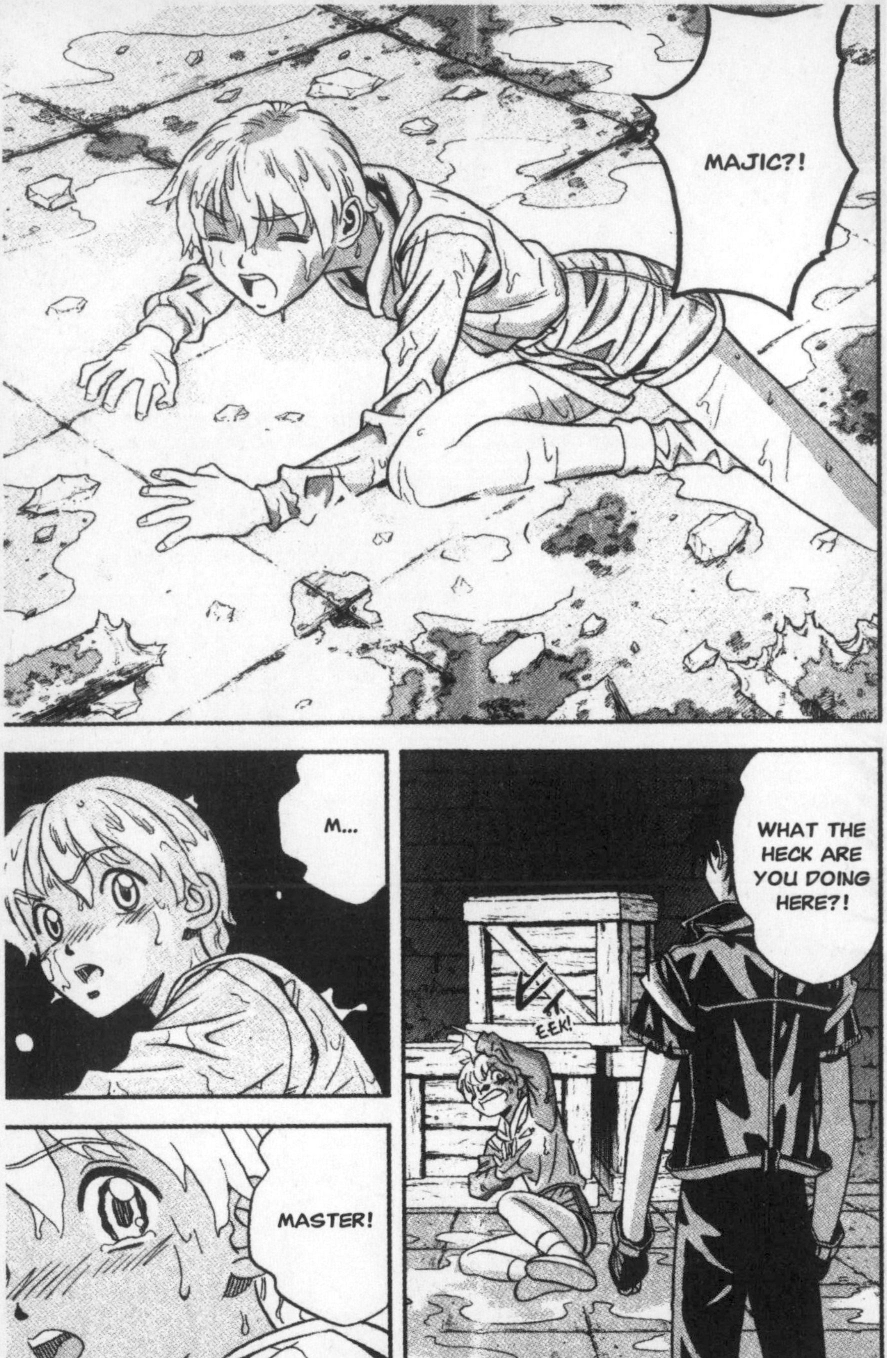
MAJIC?!
WHAT THE HECK ARE YOU DOING HERE?!
EEK!
M...
MASTER!

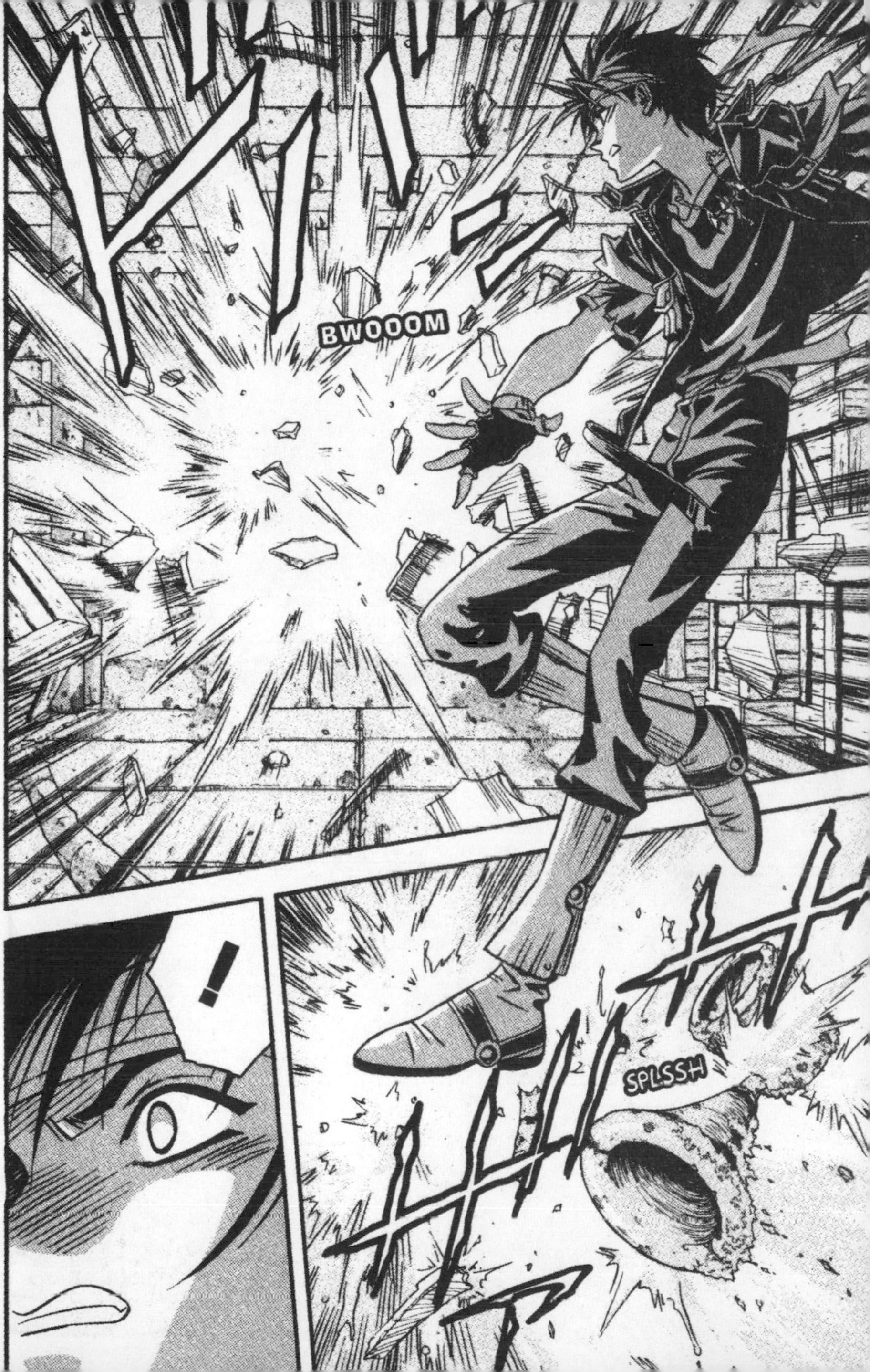
BWOOOM
!
SPLSSH

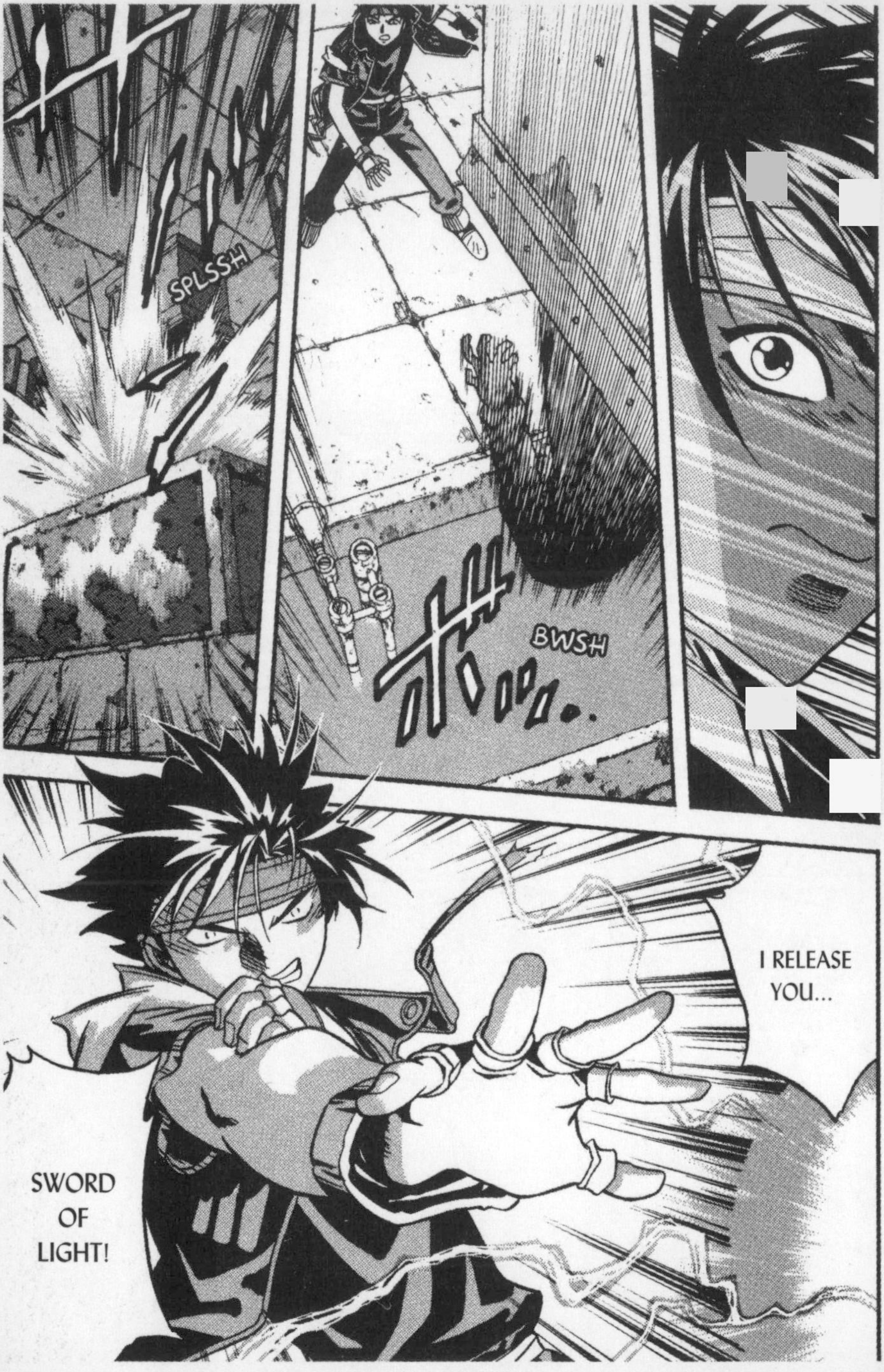
SPLSSH
BWSH
I RELEASE YOU...
SWORD OF LIGHT!

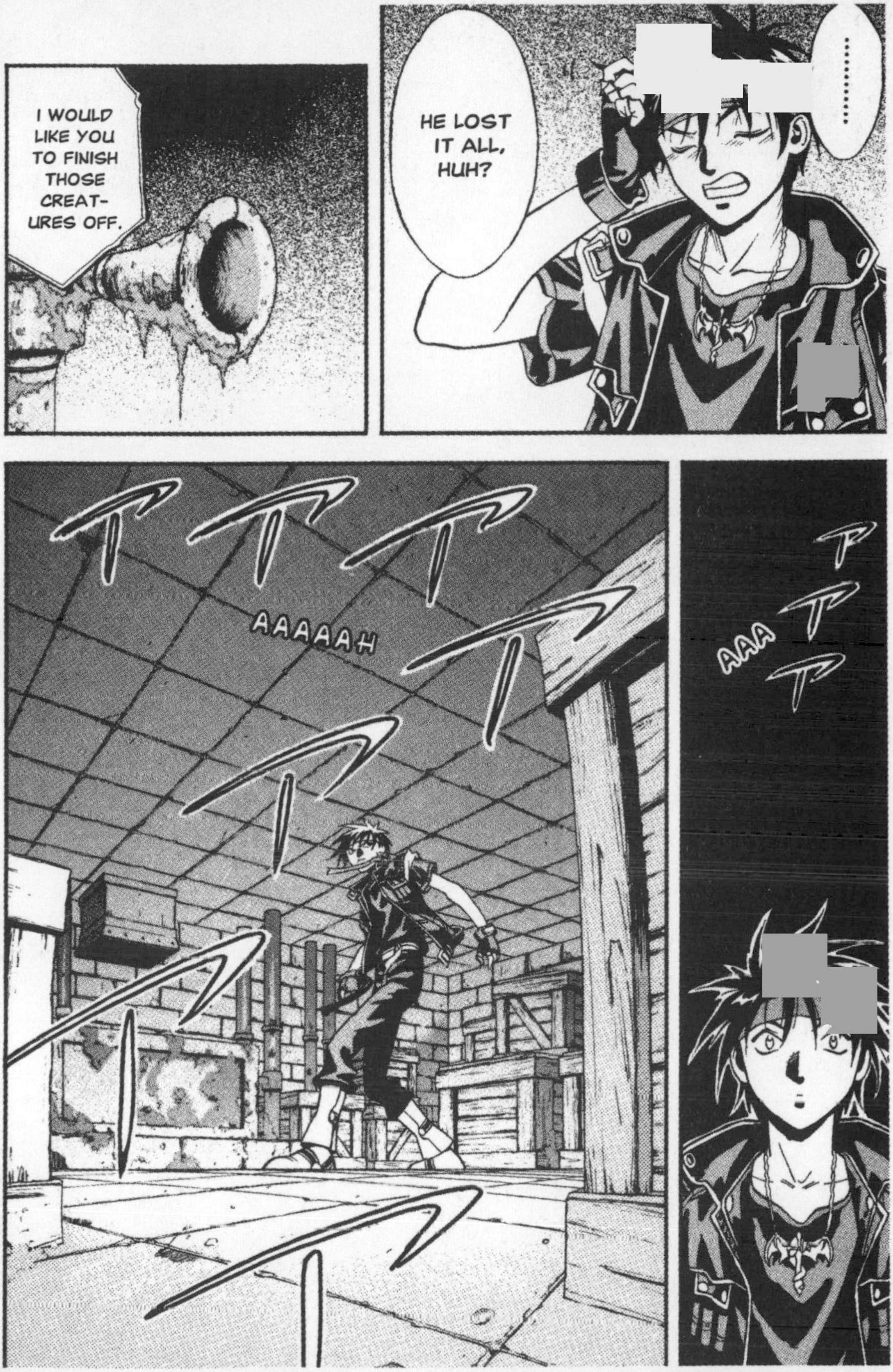

......
HE LOST IT ALL, HUH?
I WOULD LIKE YOU TO FINISH THOSE CREAT-URES OFF.
AAA
AAAAAH

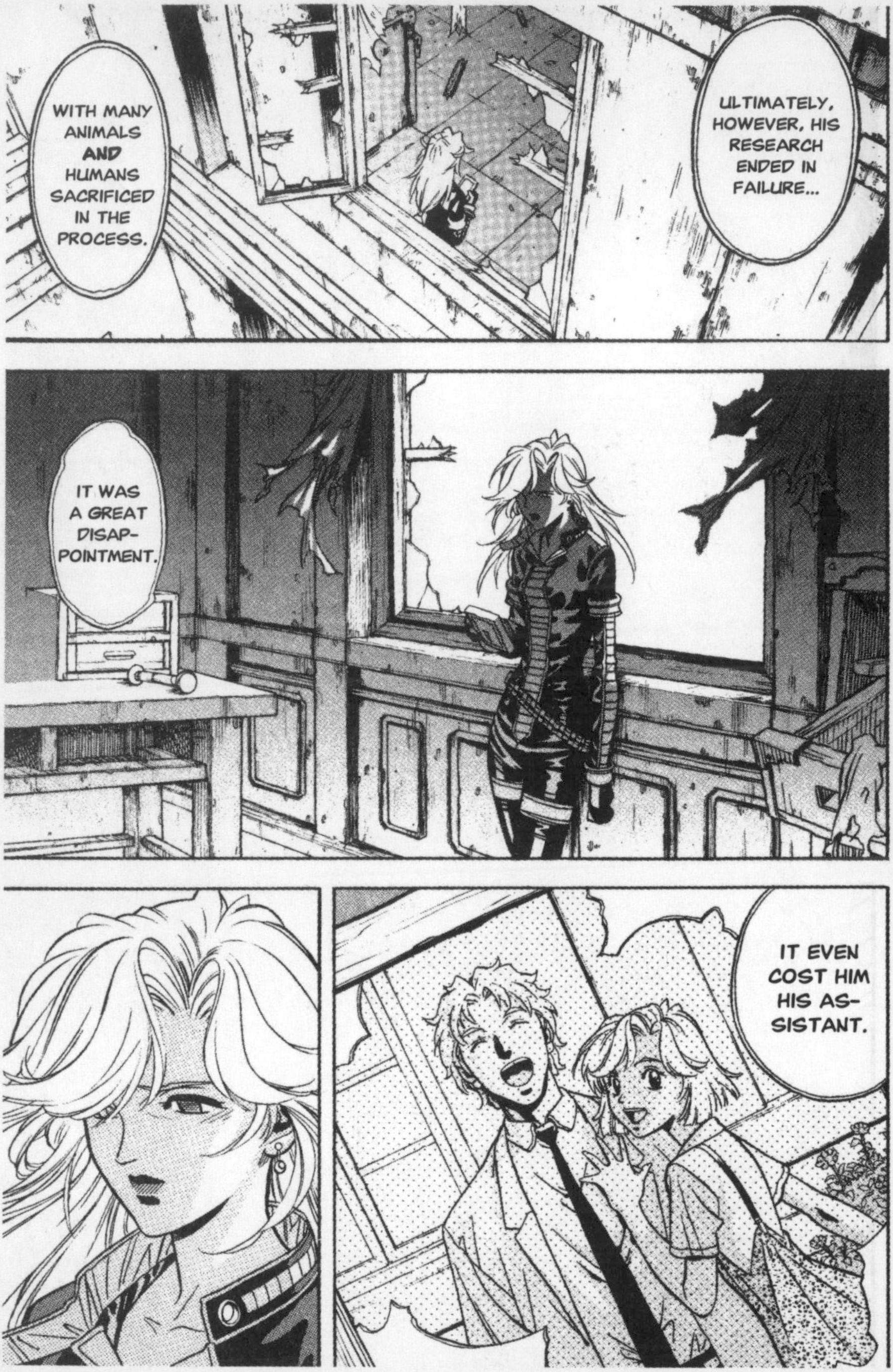
ULTIMATELY, HOWEVER, HIS RESEARCH ENDED IN FAILURE...
WITH MANY ANIMALS AND HUMANS SACRIFICED IN THE PROCESS.
IT WAS A GREAT DISAP-POINTMENT.
IT EVEN COST HIM HIS AS-SISTANT.

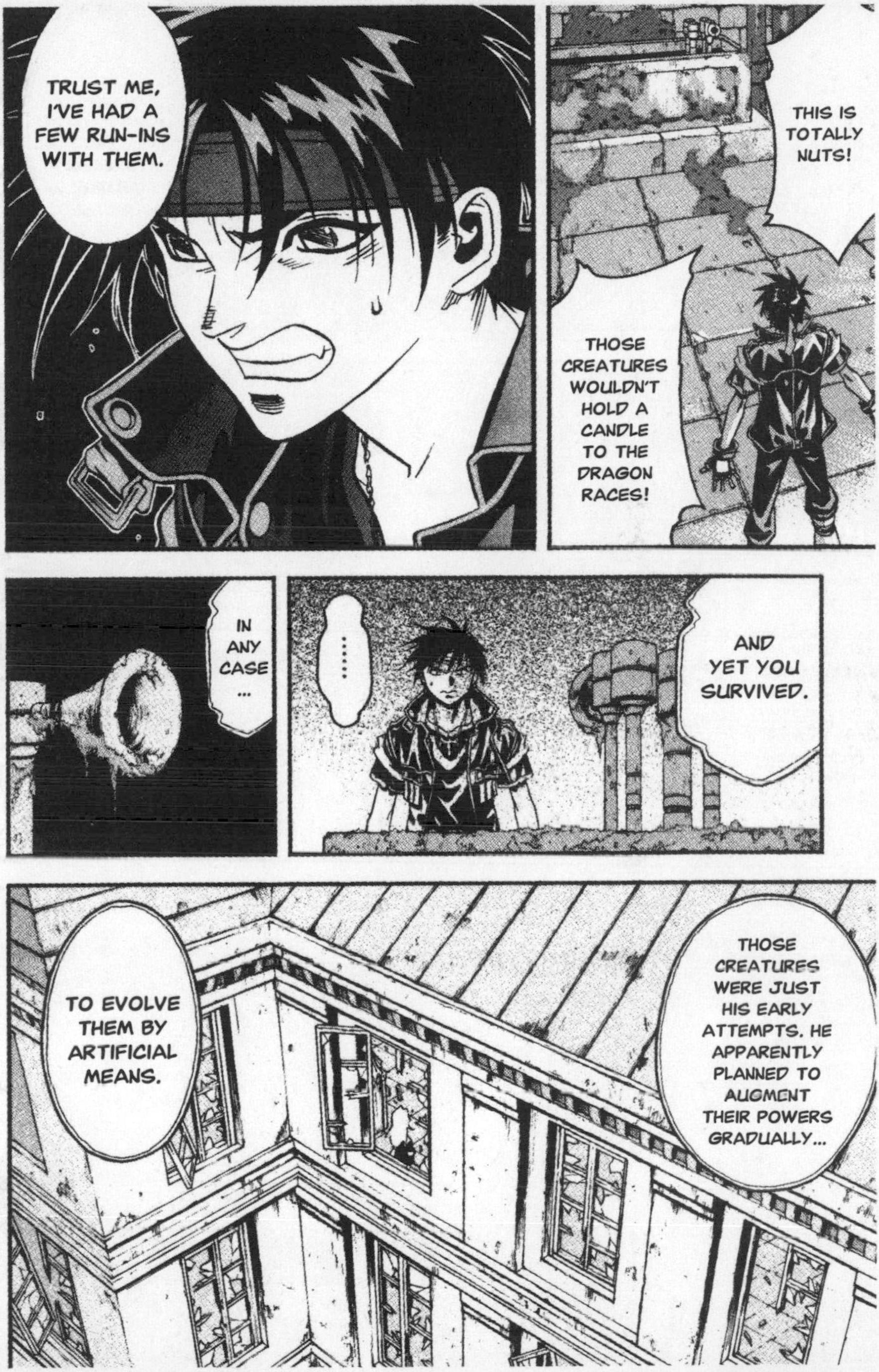
THIS IS TOTALLY NUTS!
THOSE CREATURES WOULDN'T HOLD A CANDLE TO THE DRAGON RACES!
TRUST ME, I'VE HAD A FEW RUN-INS WITH THEM.
AND YET YOU SURVIVED.
......
IN ANY CASE ...
THOSE CREATURES WERE JUST HIS EARLY ATTEMPTS. HE APPARENTLY PLANNED TO AUGMENT THEIR POWERS GRADUALLY...
TO EVOLVE THEM BY ARTIFICIAL MEANS.

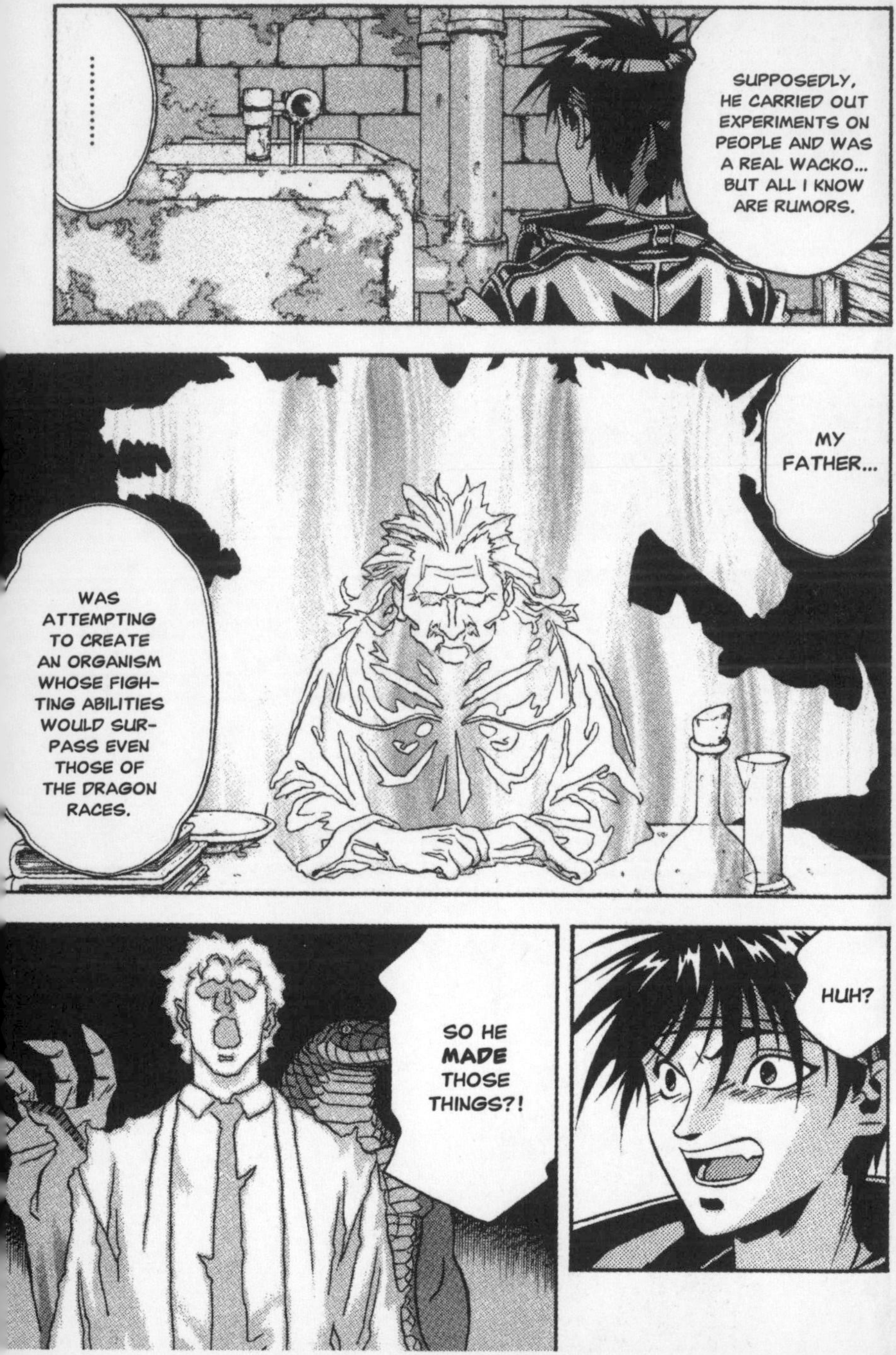

......
SUPPOSEDLY, HE CARRIED OUT EXPERIMENTS ON PEOPLE AND WAS A REAL WACKO... BUT ALL I KNOW ARE RUMORS.
MY FATHER...
WAS ATTEMPTING TO CREATE AN ORGANISM WHOSE FIGHTING ABILITIES WOULD SURPASS EVEN THOSE OF THE DRAGON RACES.
SO HE **MADE** THOSE THINGS?!
HUH?

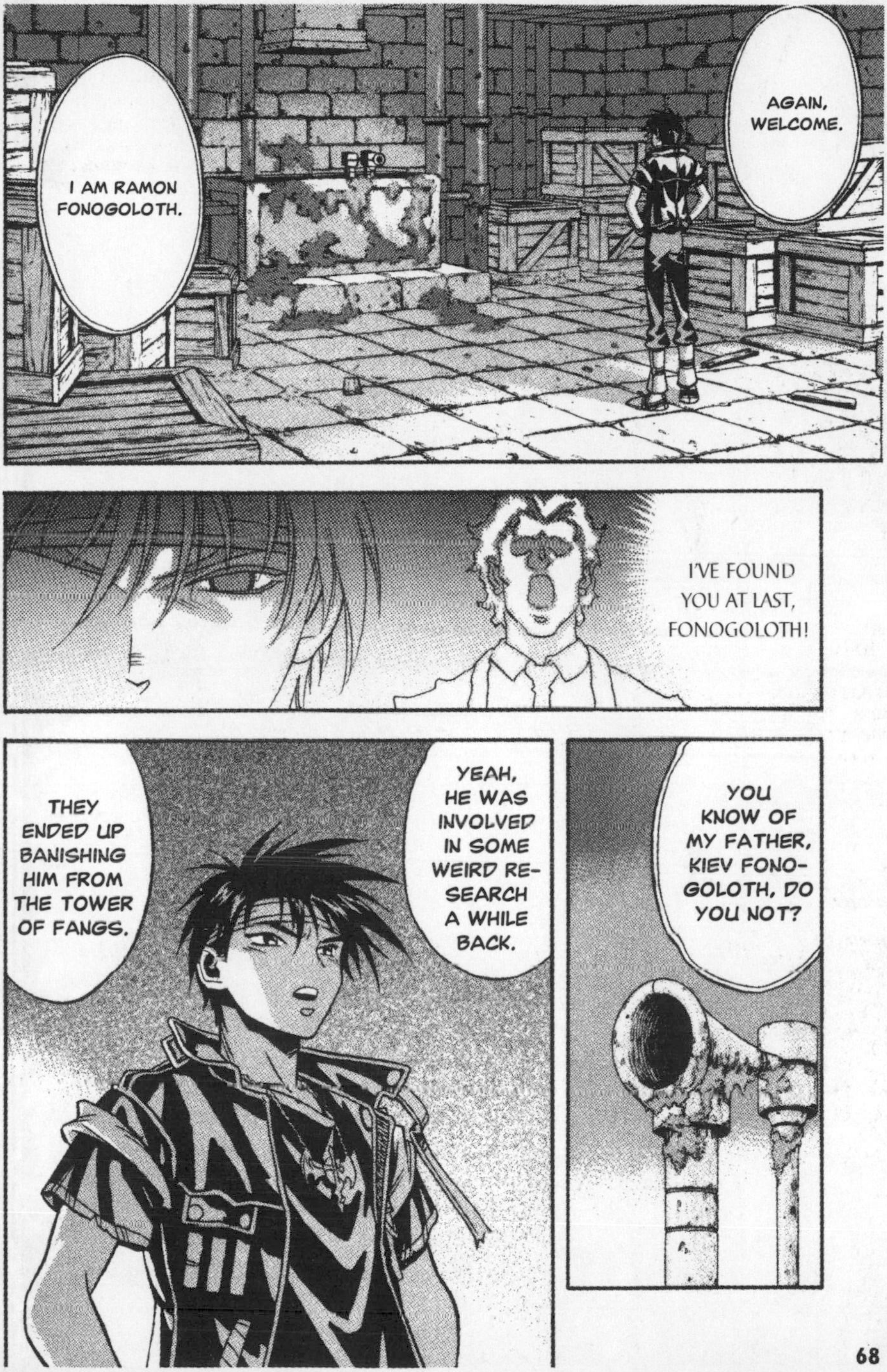
AGAIN, WELCOME.
I AM RAMON FONOGOLOTH.
I'VE FOUND YOU AT LAST, FONOGOLOTH!
YOU KNOW OF MY FATHER, KIEV FONO-GOLOTH, DO YOU NOT?
YEAH, HE WAS INVOLVED IN SOME WEIRD RE-SEARCH A WHILE BACK.
THEY ENDED UP BANISHING HIM FROM THE TOWER OF FANGS.

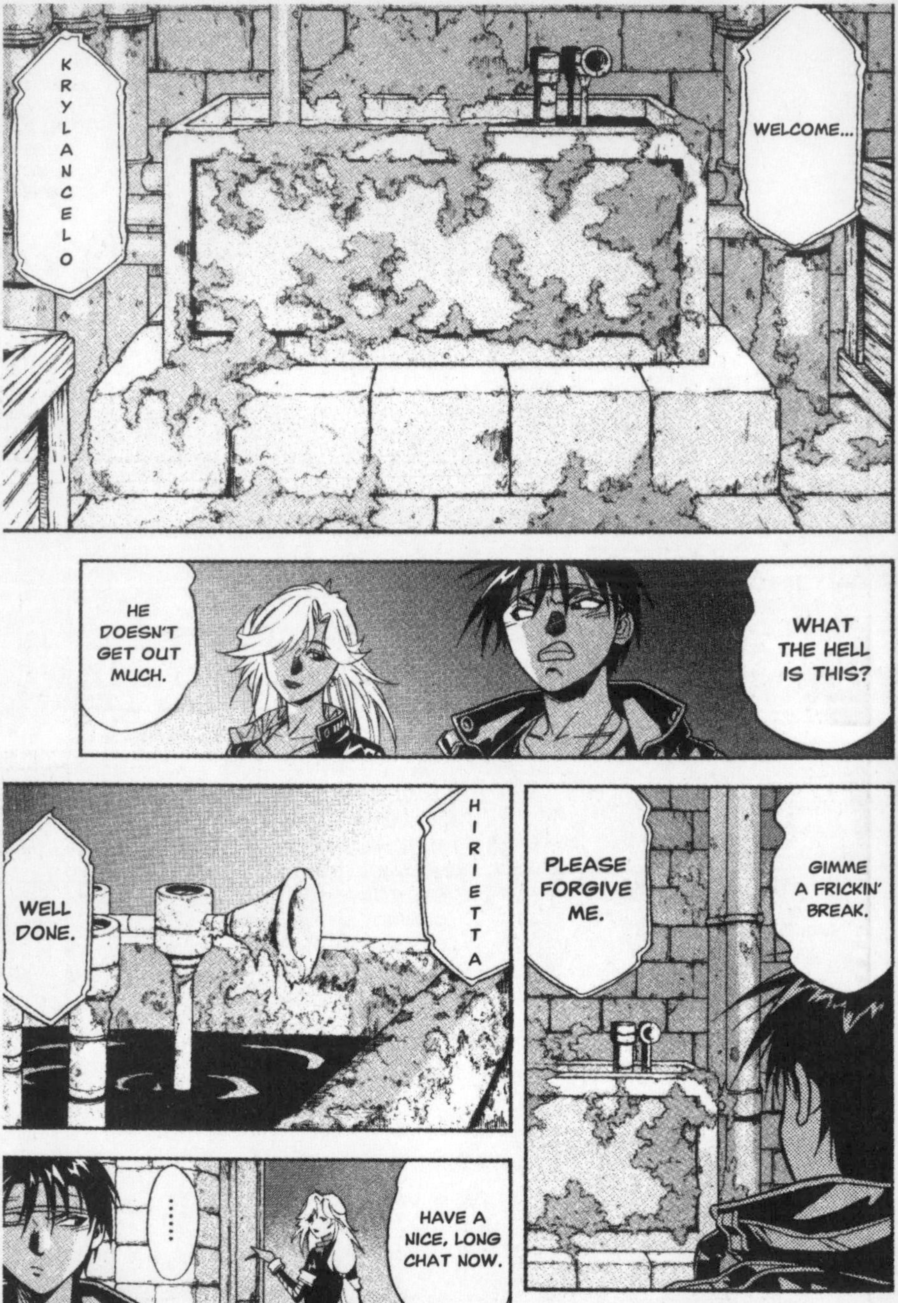
WELCOME...
KRYLANCELO
WHAT THE HELL IS THIS?
HE DOESN'T GET OUT MUCH.
GIMME A FRICKIN' BREAK.
PLEASE FORGIVE ME.
HIRIETTA
WELL DONE.
HAVE A NICE, LONG CHAT NOW.
......

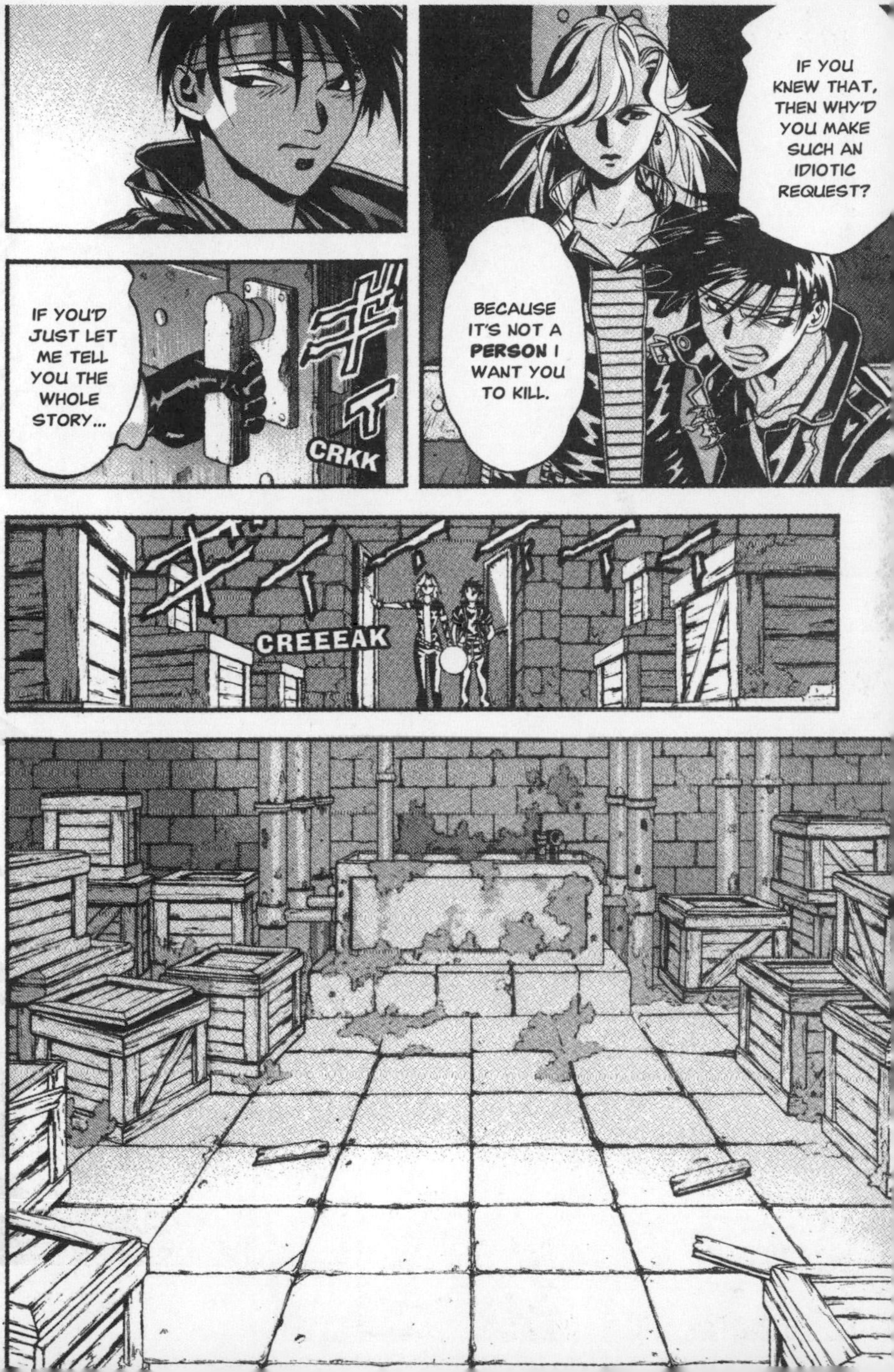
IF YOU KNEW THAT, THEN WHY'D YOU MAKE SUCH AN IDIOTIC REQUEST?
BECAUSE IT'S NOT A PERSON I WANT YOU TO KILL.
IF YOU'D JUST LET ME TELL YOU THE WHOLE STORY...
CRKK
CREEEAK

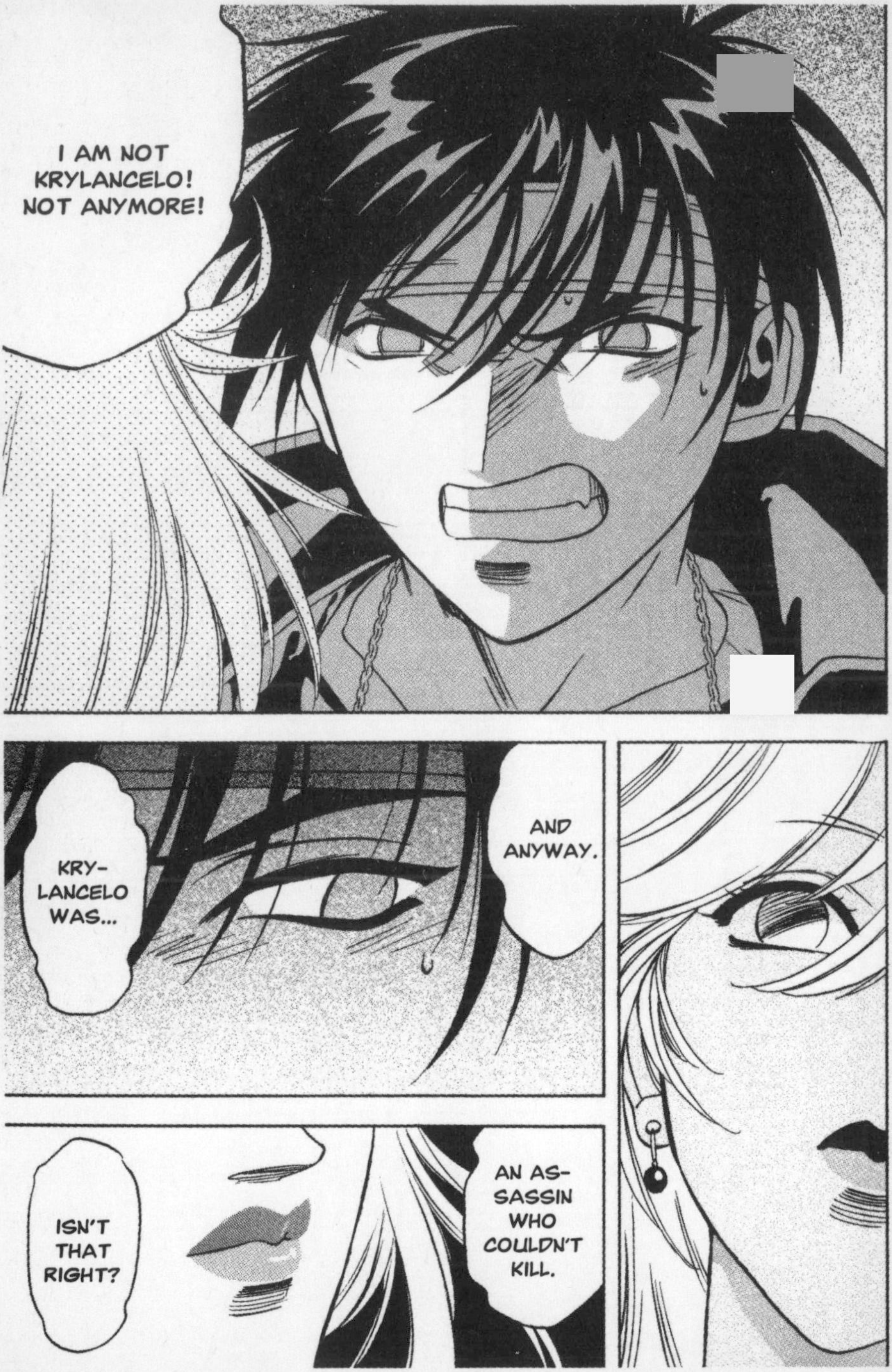
I AM NOT KRYLANCELO! NOT ANYMORE!
AND ANYWAY.
KRY-LANCELO WAS...
AN AS-SASSIN WHO COULDN'T KILL.
ISN'T THAT RIGHT?

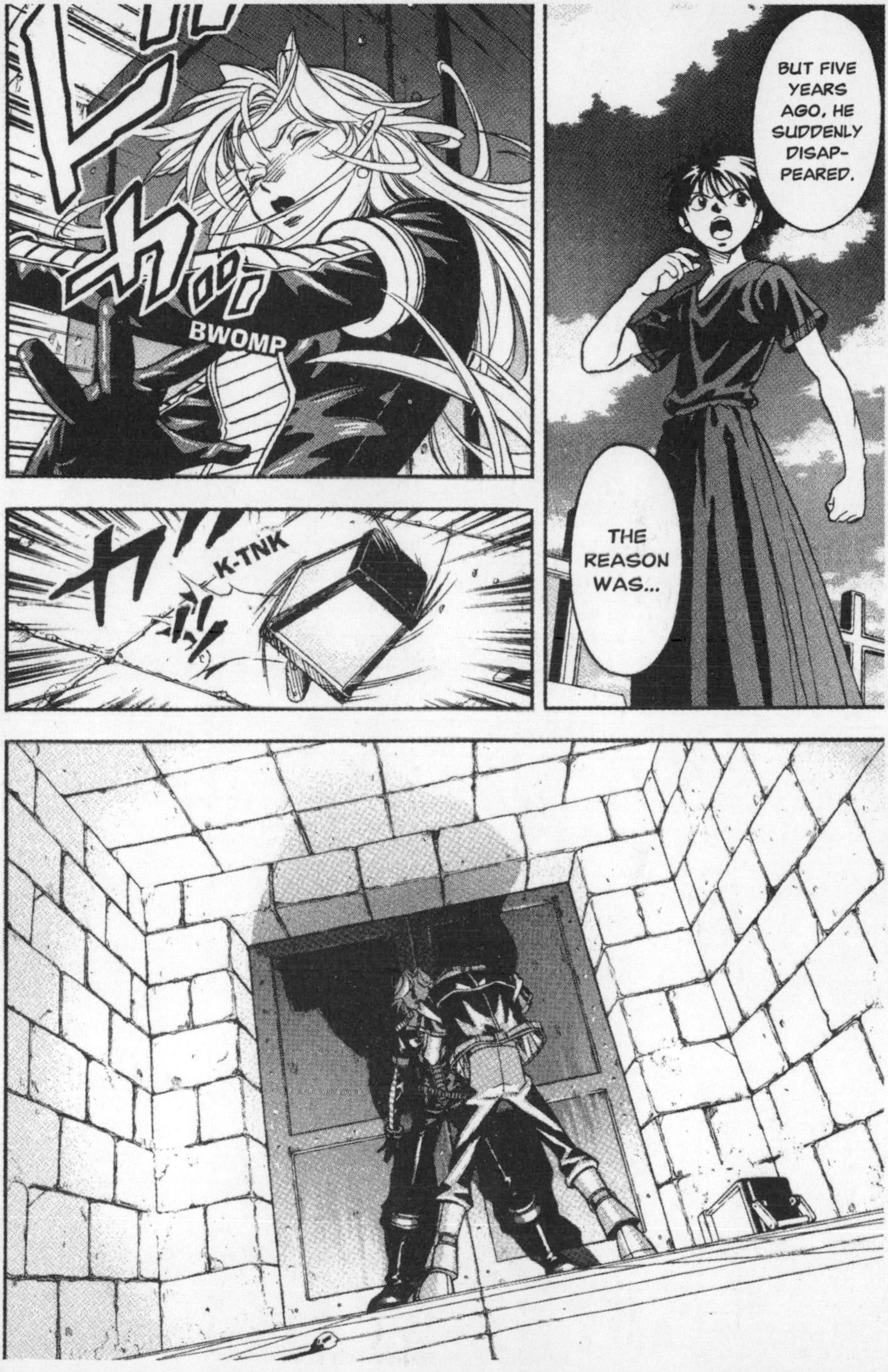
BUT FIVE YEARS AGO, HE SUDDENLY DISAP-PEARED.
BWOMP
THE REASON WAS...
K-TNK

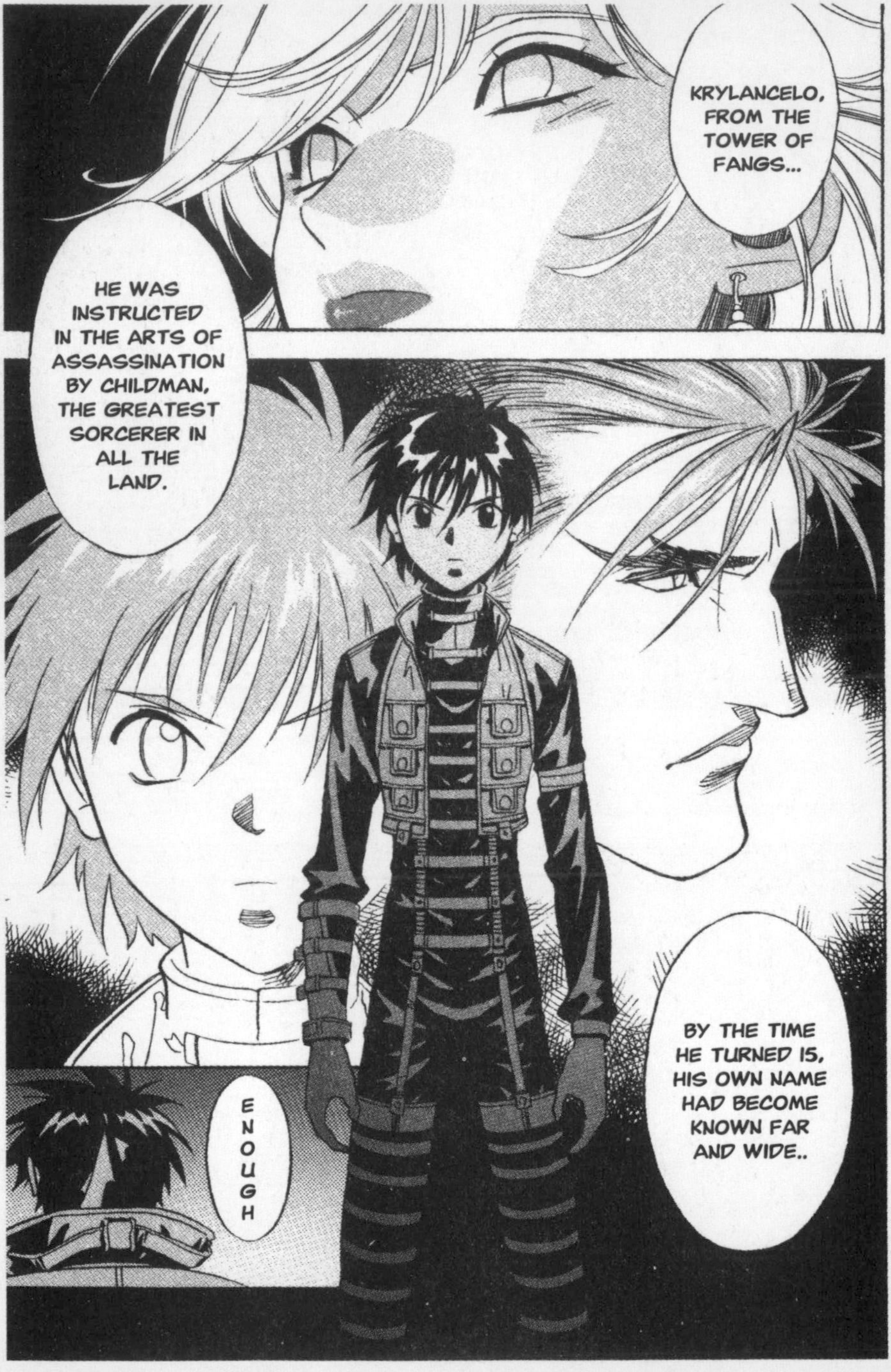
KRYLANCELO, FROM THE TOWER OF FANGS...
HE WAS INSTRUCTED IN THE ARTS OF ASSASSINATION BY CHILDMAN, THE GREATEST SORCERER IN ALL THE LAND.
BY THE TIME HE TURNED 15, HIS OWN NAME HAD BECOME KNOWN FAR AND WIDE..
ENOUGH

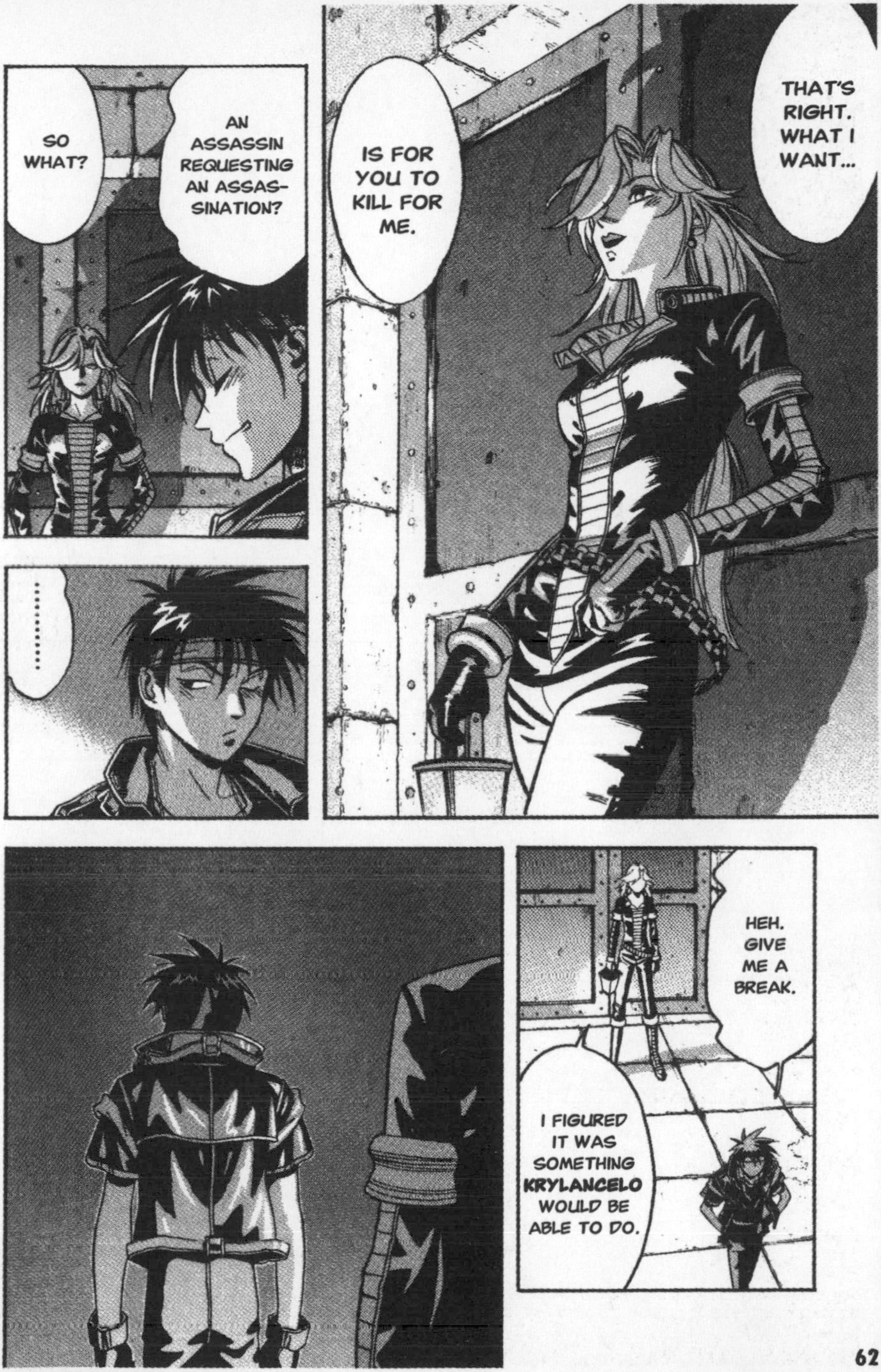
THAT'S RIGHT. WHAT I WANT...
IS FOR YOU TO KILL FOR ME.
AN ASSASSIN REQUESTING AN ASSAS-SINATION?
SO WHAT?
....
HEH. GIVE ME A BREAK.
I FIGURED IT WAS SOMETHING KRYLANCELO WOULD BE ABLE TO DO.

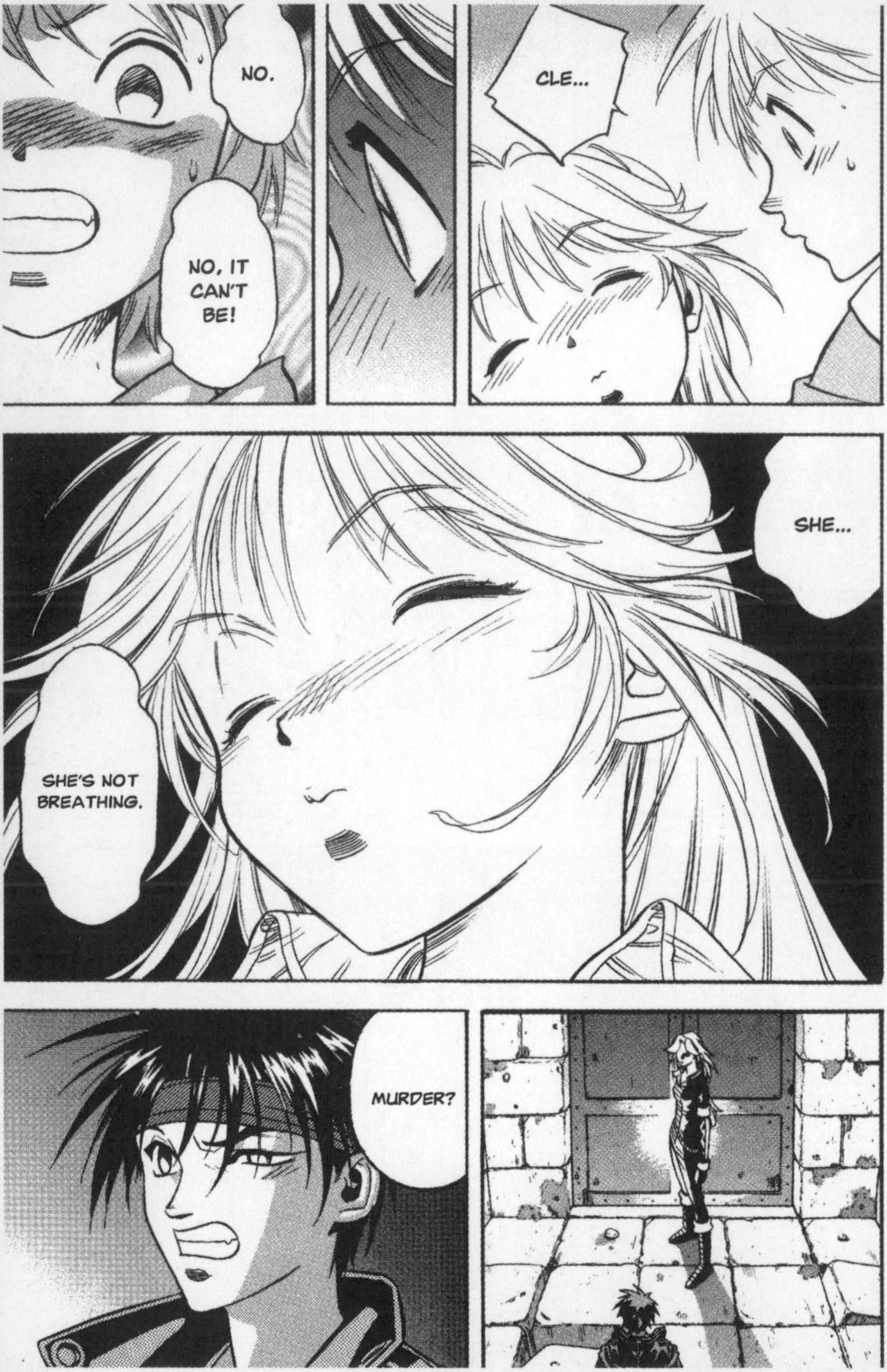
CLE...
NO.
NO, IT CAN'T BE!
SHE...
SHE'S NOT BREATHING.
MURDER?

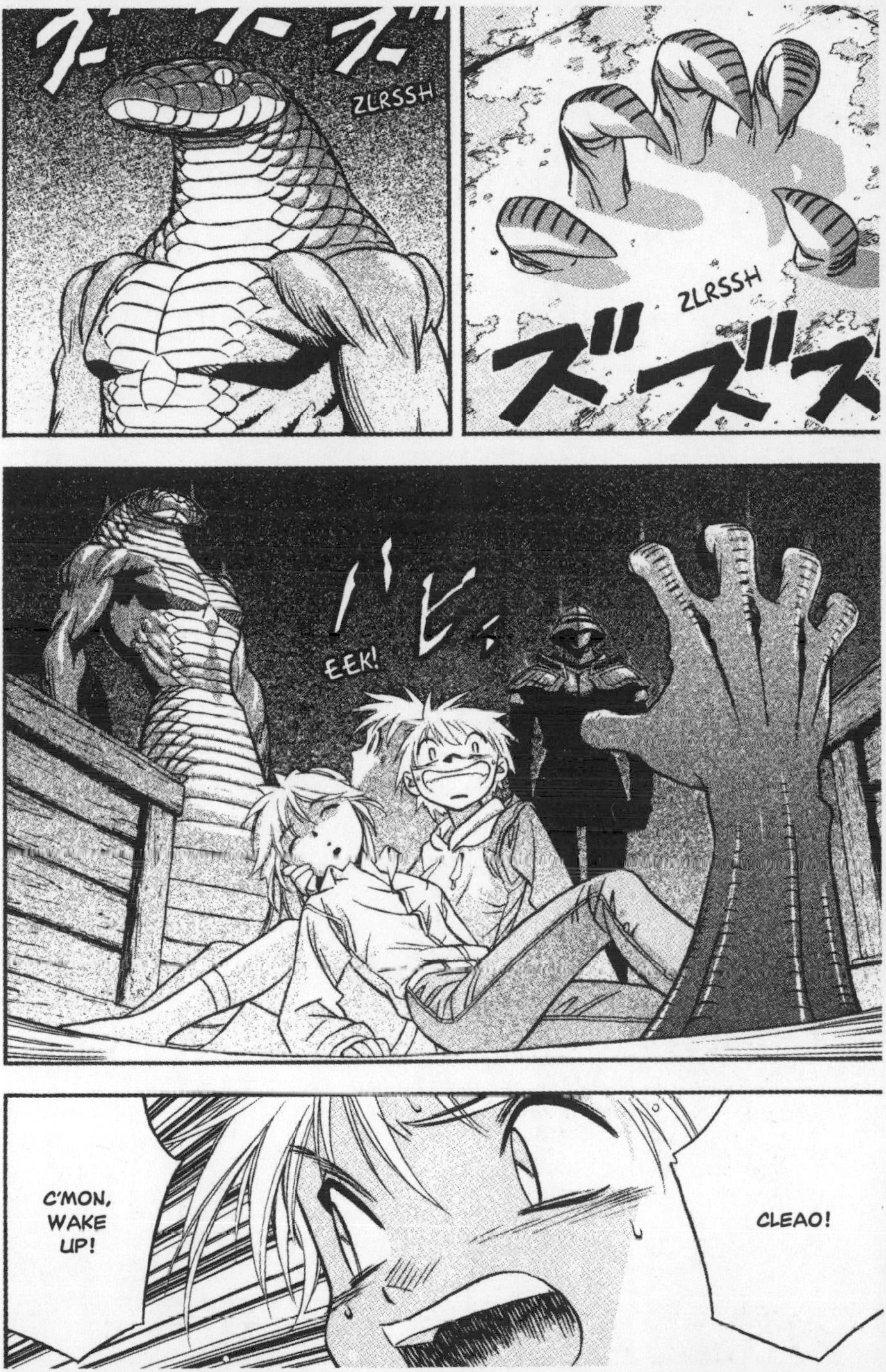
ズーズーズ
ZLRSSH
ZLRSSH
ズズズ
ハヒ
EEK!
CLEAO!
C'MON, WAKE UP!

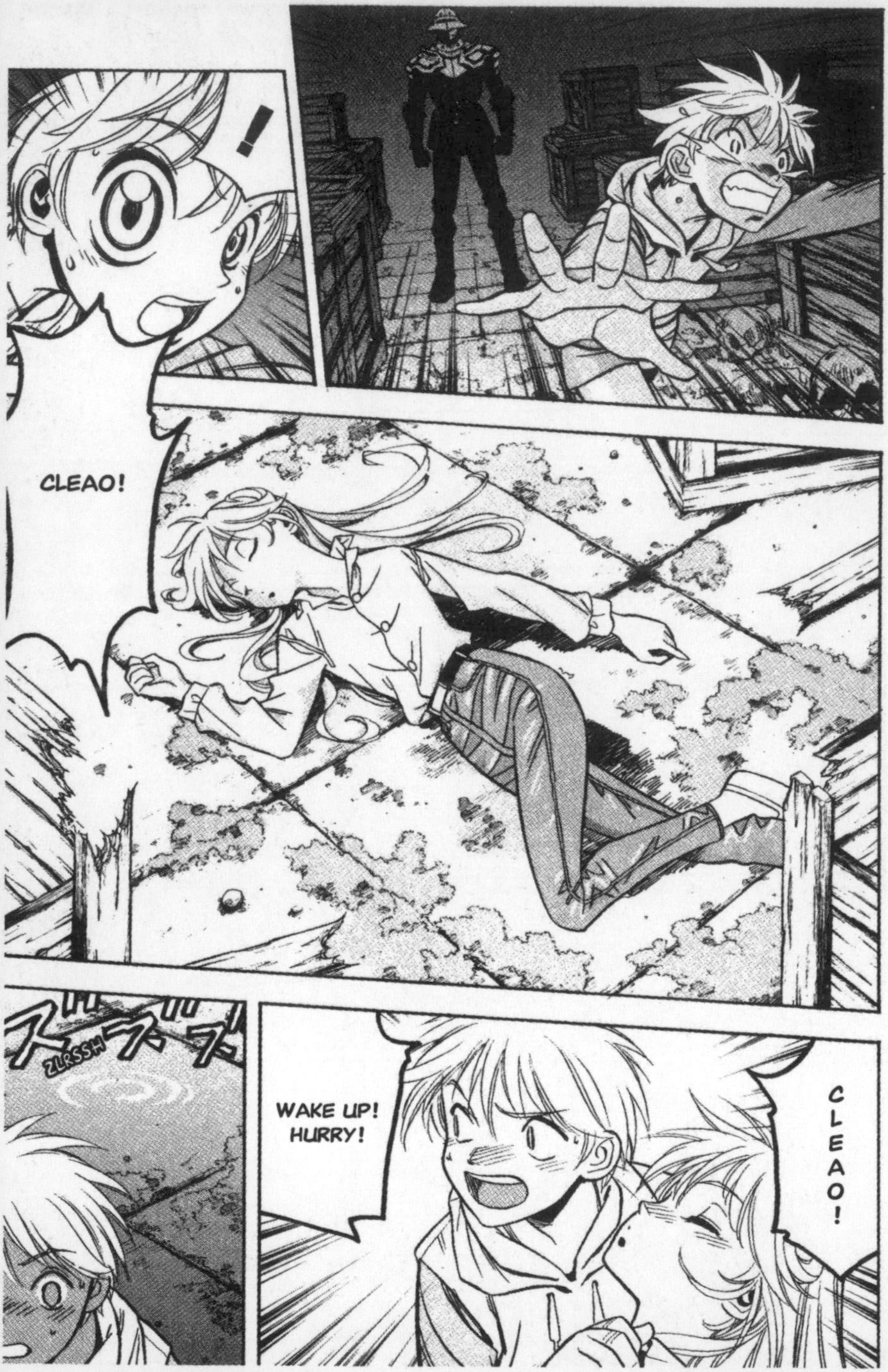
!
CLEAO!
ZLRSSH
WAKE UP! HURRY!
CLEAO!

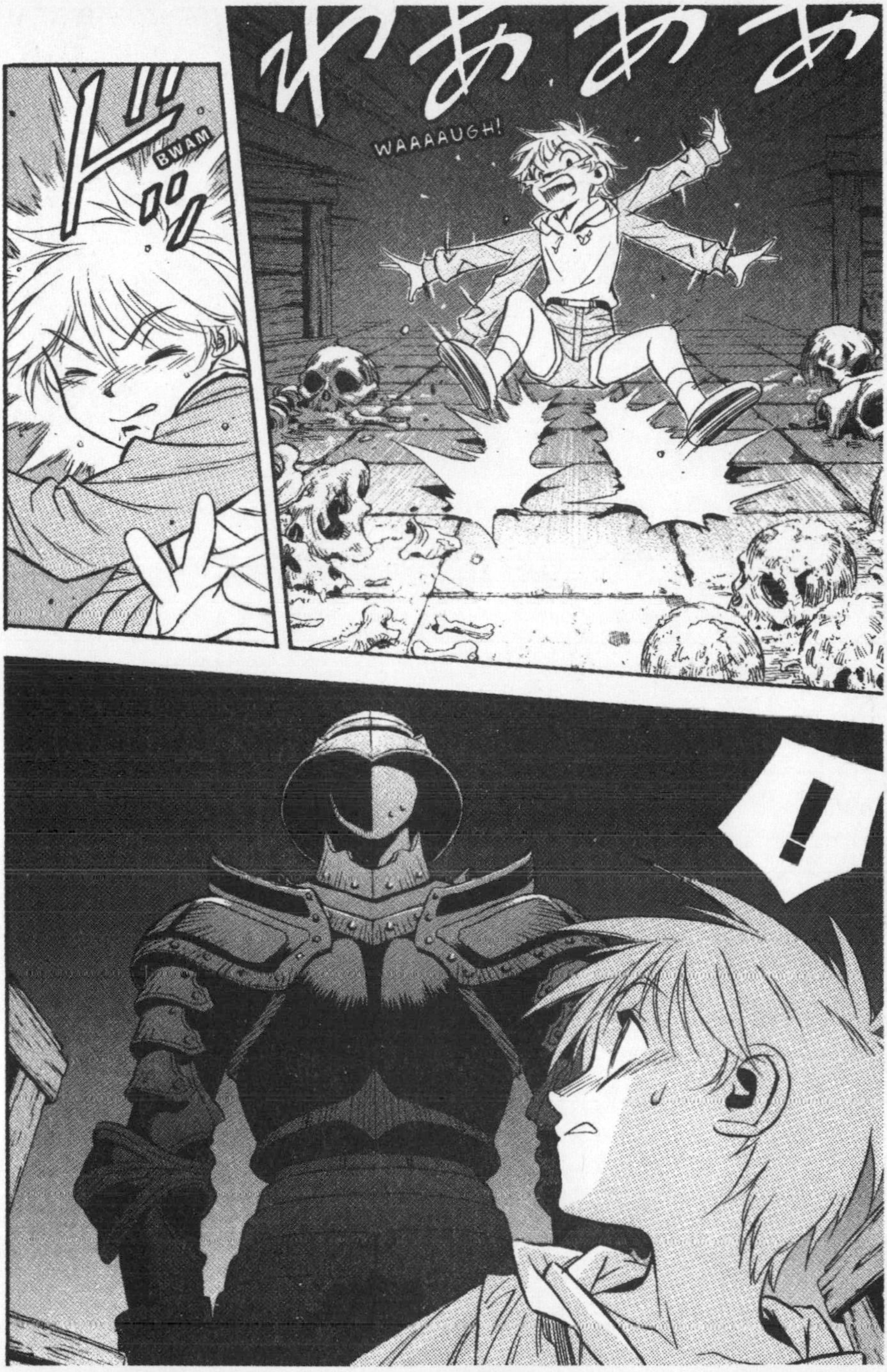
わあああ
WAAAAUGH!
ドッ
BWAM
!

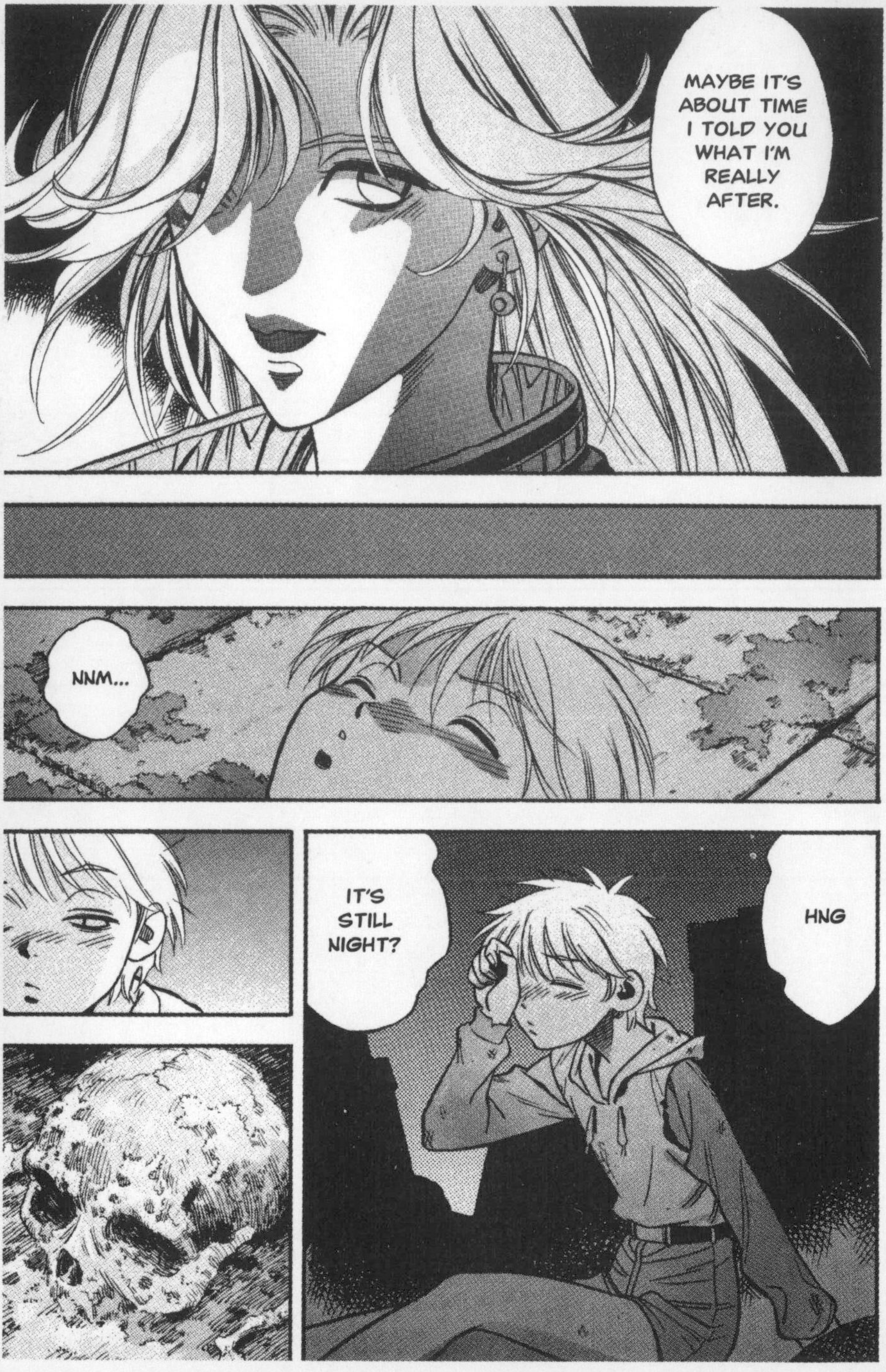
MAYBE IT'S ABOUT TIME I TOLD YOU WHAT I'M REALLY AFTER.
NNM...
HNG
IT'S STILL NIGHT?

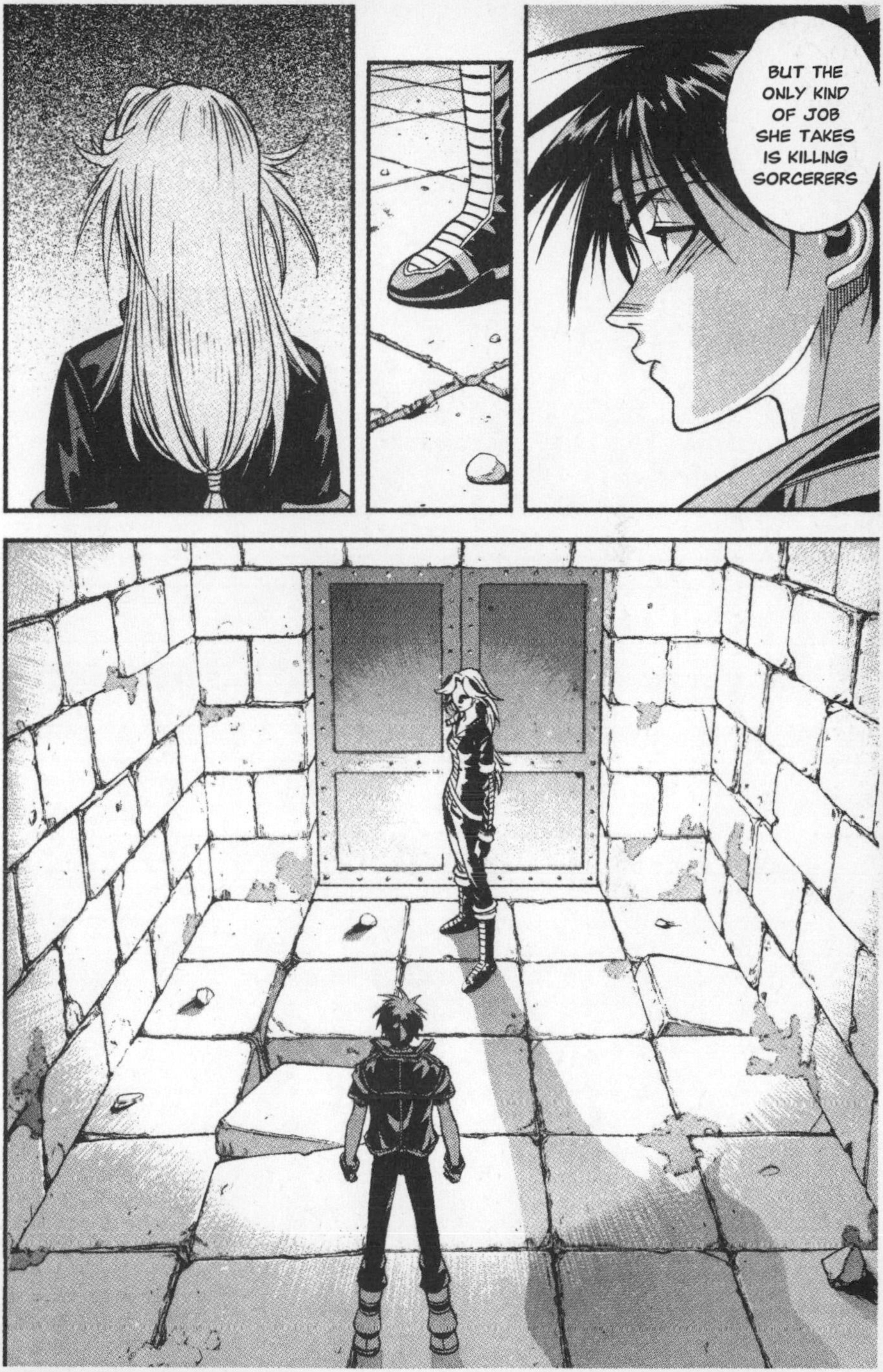
BUT THE ONLY KIND OF JOB SHE TAKES IS KILLING SORCERERS

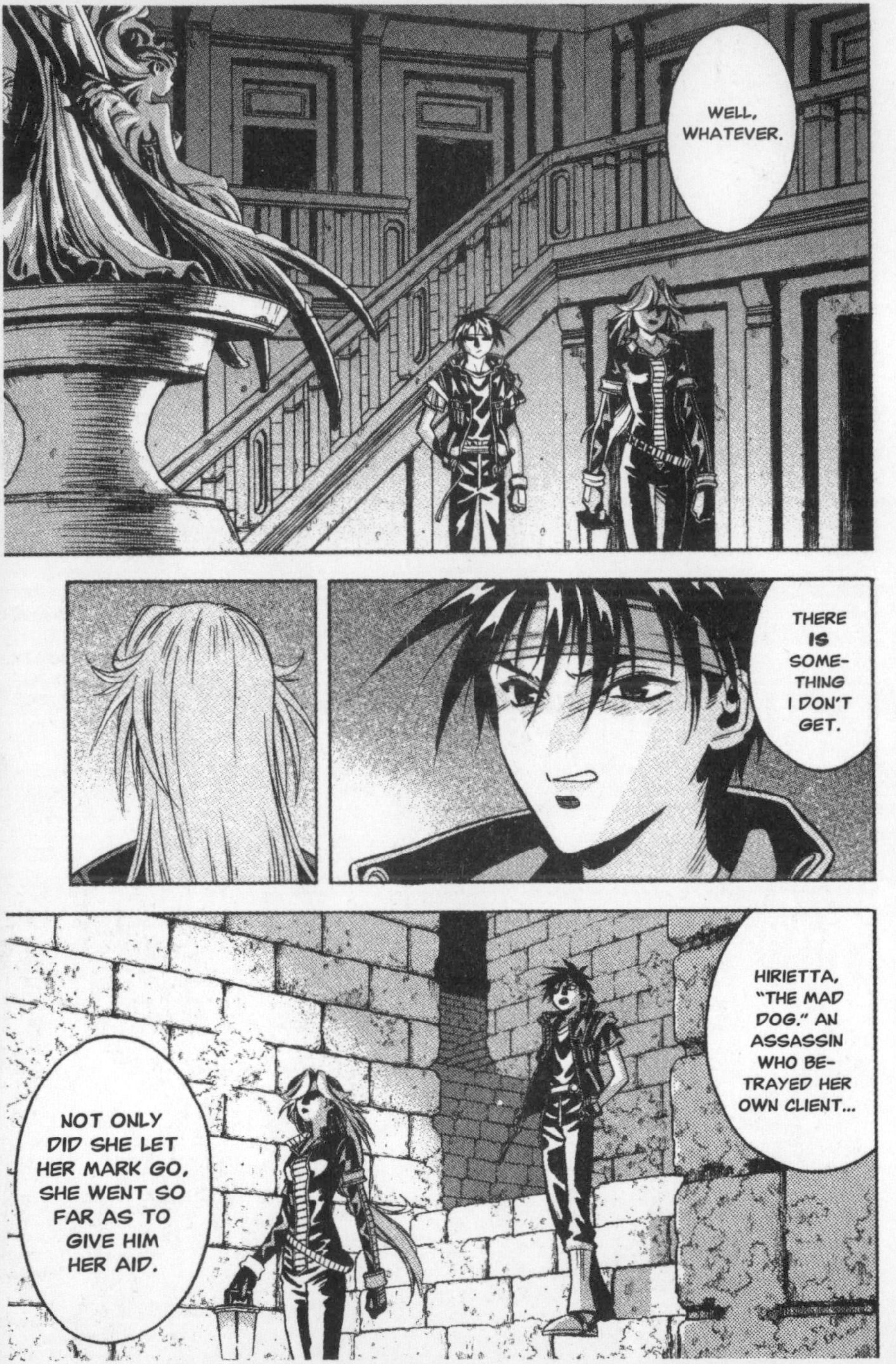
WELL, WHATEVER.
THERE IS SOMETHING I DON'T GET.
HIRIETTA, "THE MAD DOG." AN ASSASSIN WHO BETRAYED HER OWN CLIENT...
NOT ONLY DID SHE LET HER MARK GO, SHE WENT SO FAR AS TO GIVE HIM HER AID.

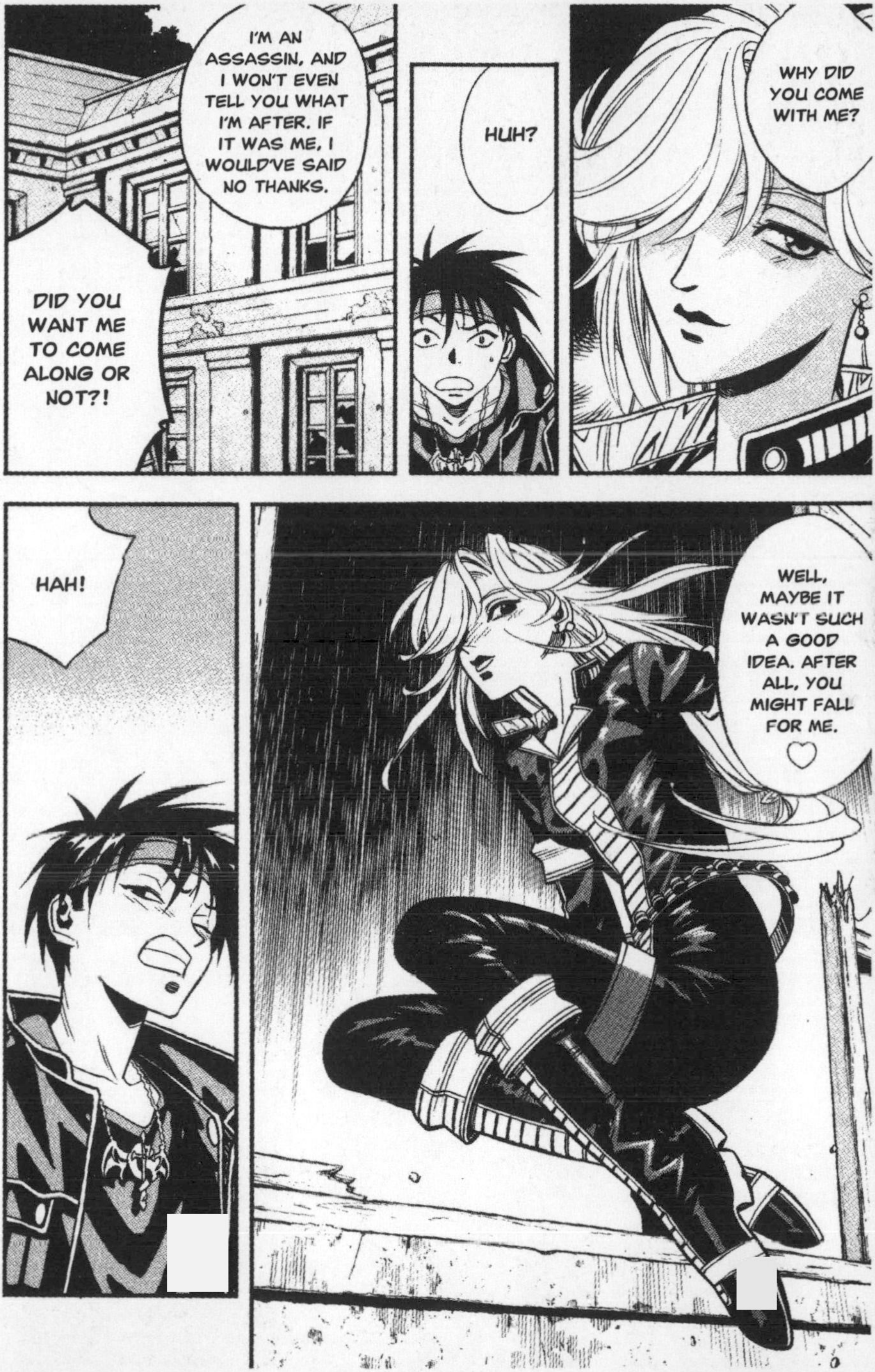
WHY DID YOU COME WITH ME?
HUH?
I'M AN ASSASSIN, AND I WON'T EVEN TELL YOU WHAT I'M AFTER. IF IT WAS ME, I WOULD'VE SAID NO THANKS.
DID YOU WANT ME TO COME ALONG OR NOT?!
WELL, MAYBE IT WASN'T SUCH A GOOD IDEA. AFTER ALL, YOU MIGHT FALL FOR ME. ♡
HAH!

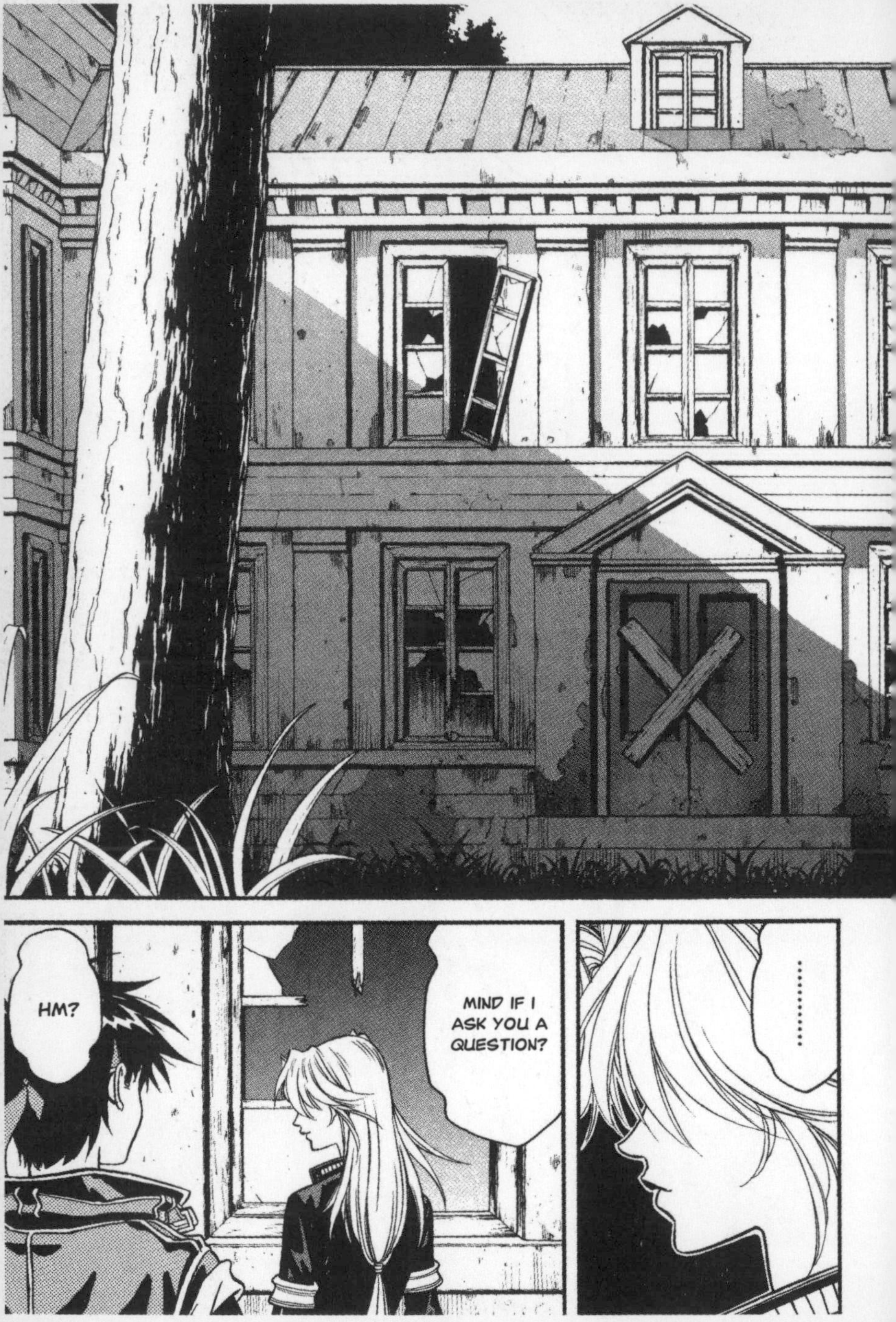
......
MIND IF I ASK YOU A QUESTION?
HM?

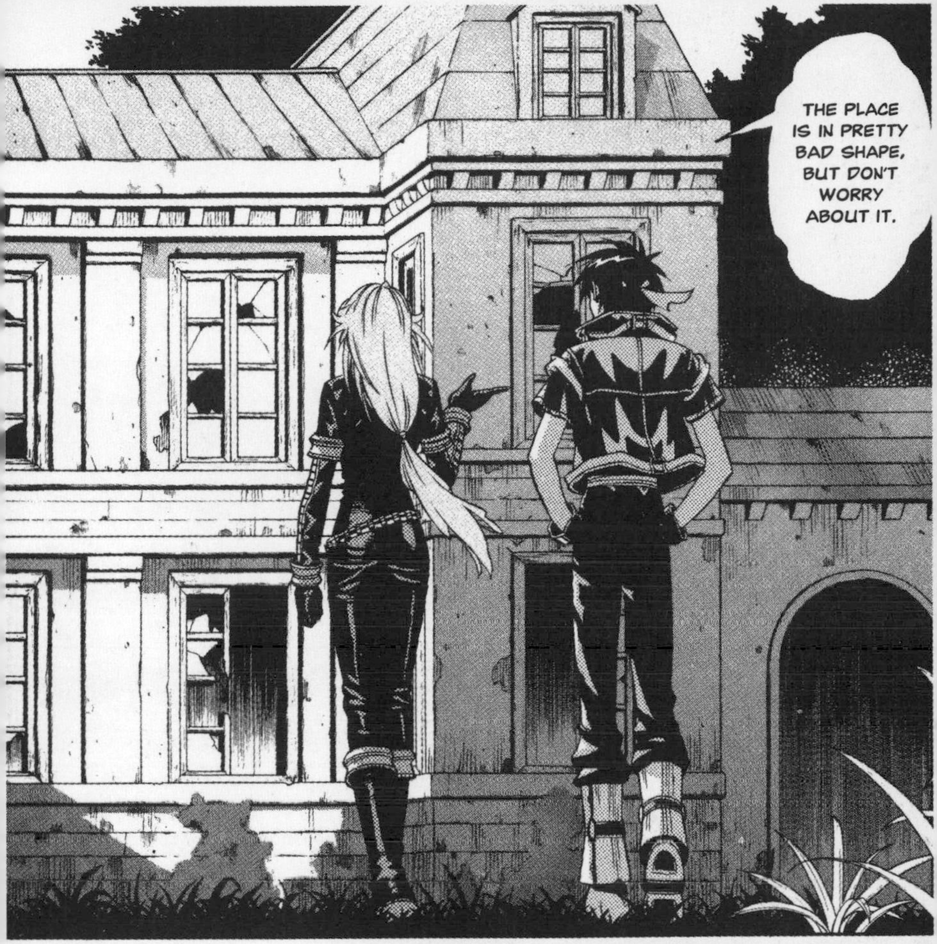
THE PLACE IS IN PRETTY BAD SHAPE, BUT DON'T WORRY ABOUT IT.

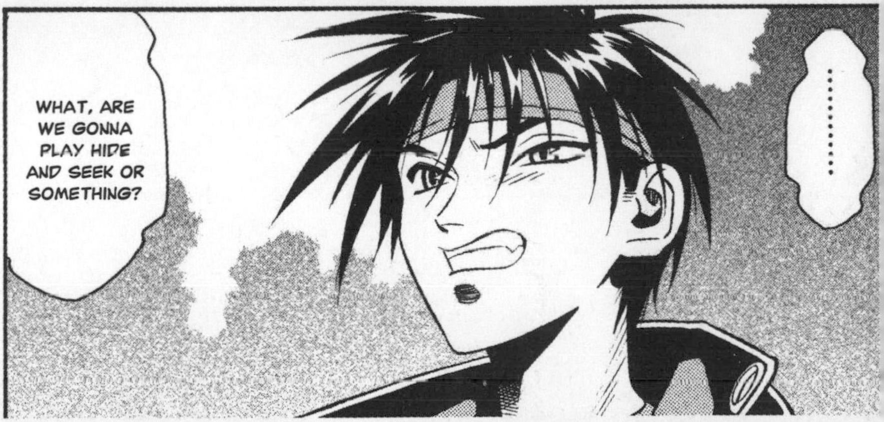
....
WHAT, ARE WE GONNA PLAY HIDE AND SEEK OR SOMETHING?

Chapter 14: Fonogoloth

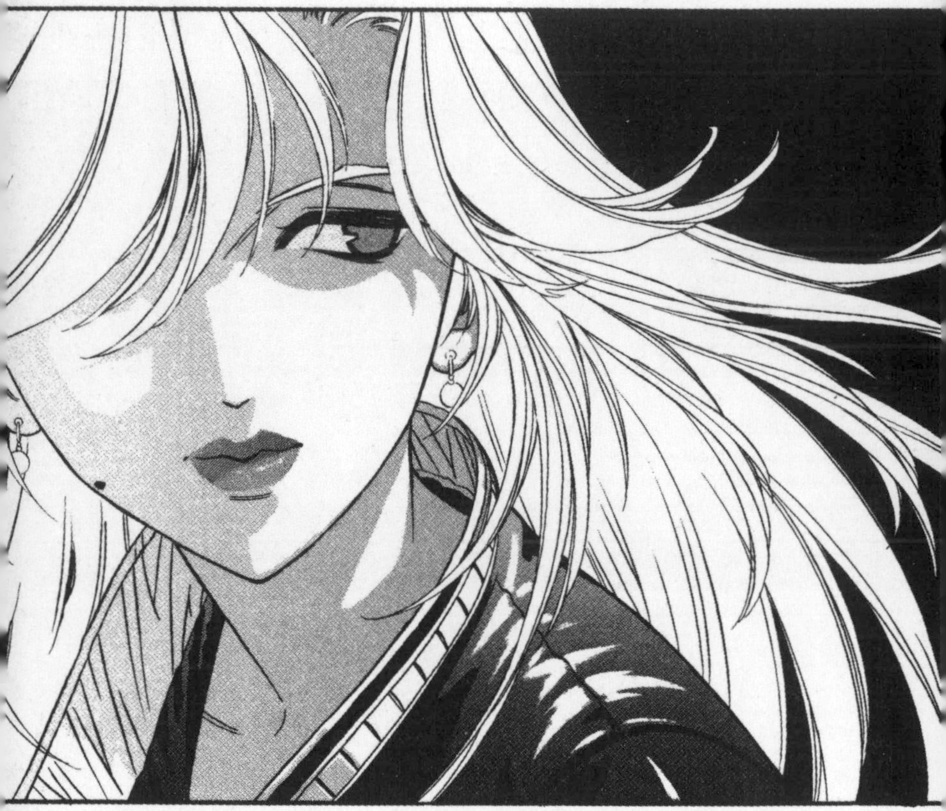

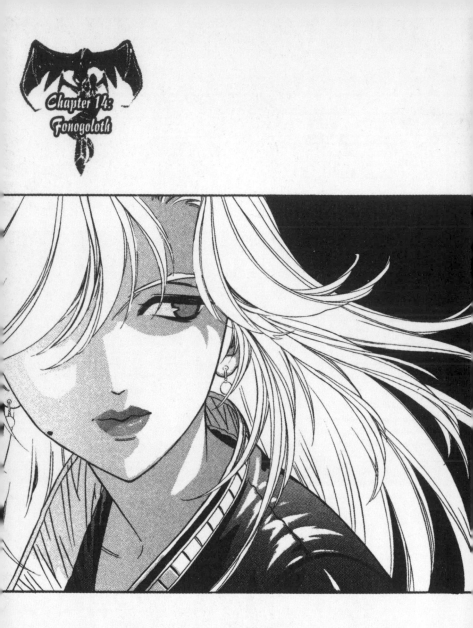

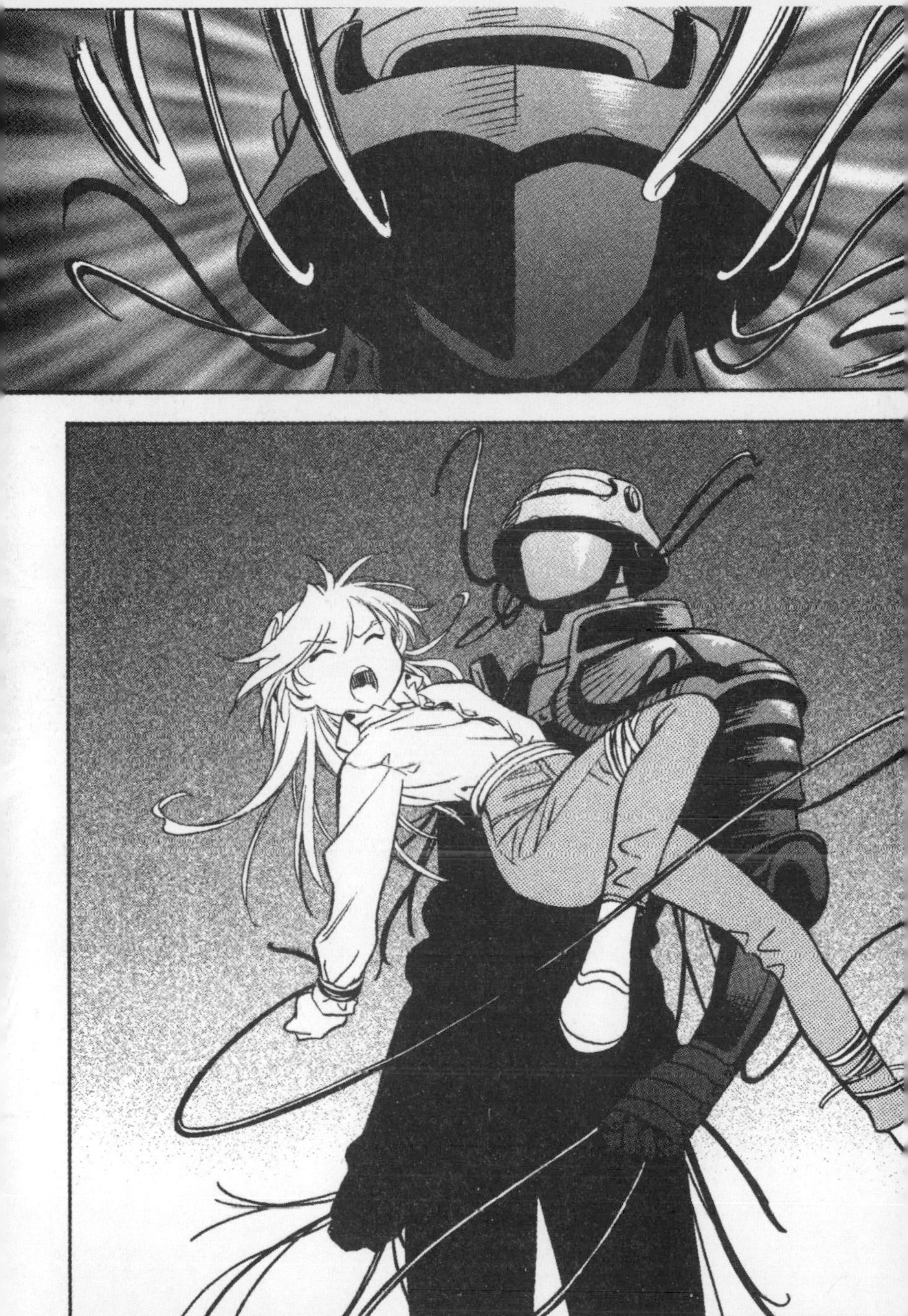

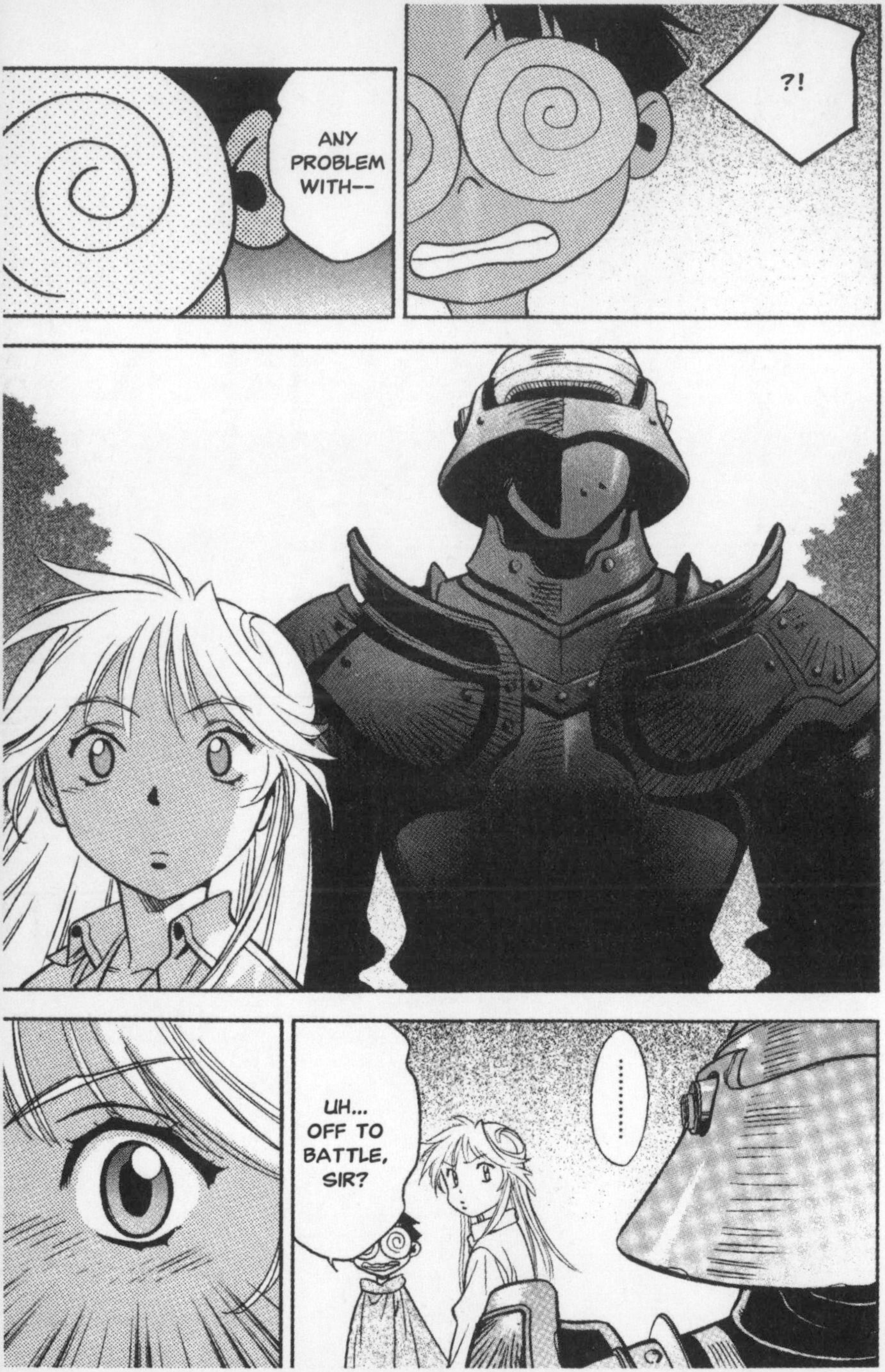
ANY PROBLEM WITH--
?!
UH... OFF TO BATTLE, SIR?
......

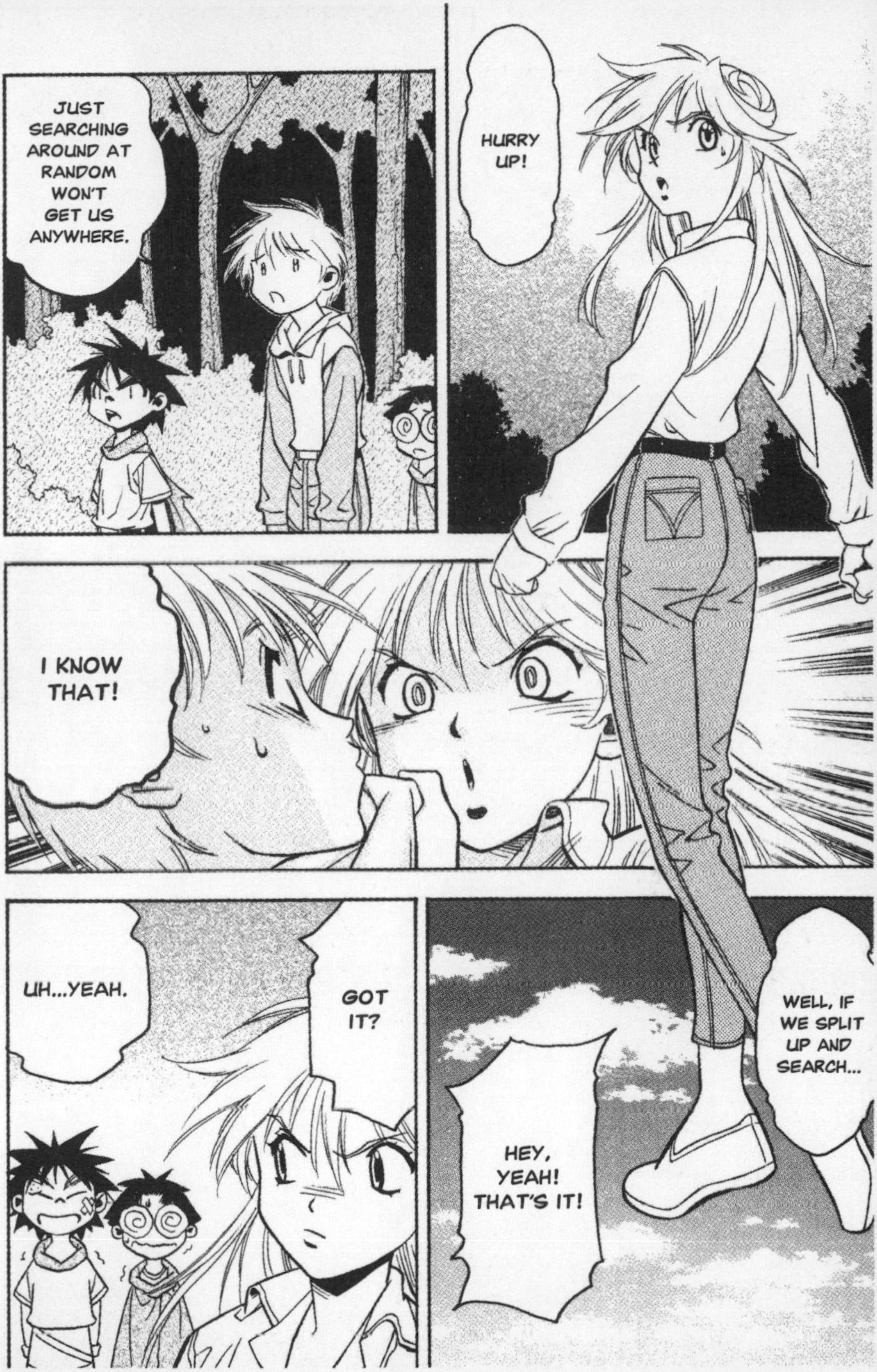
HURRY UP!
JUST SEARCHING AROUND AT RANDOM WON'T GET US ANYWHERE.
I KNOW THAT!
WELL, IF WE SPLIT UP AND SEARCH...
HEY, YEAH! THAT'S IT!
GOT IT?
UH...YEAH.

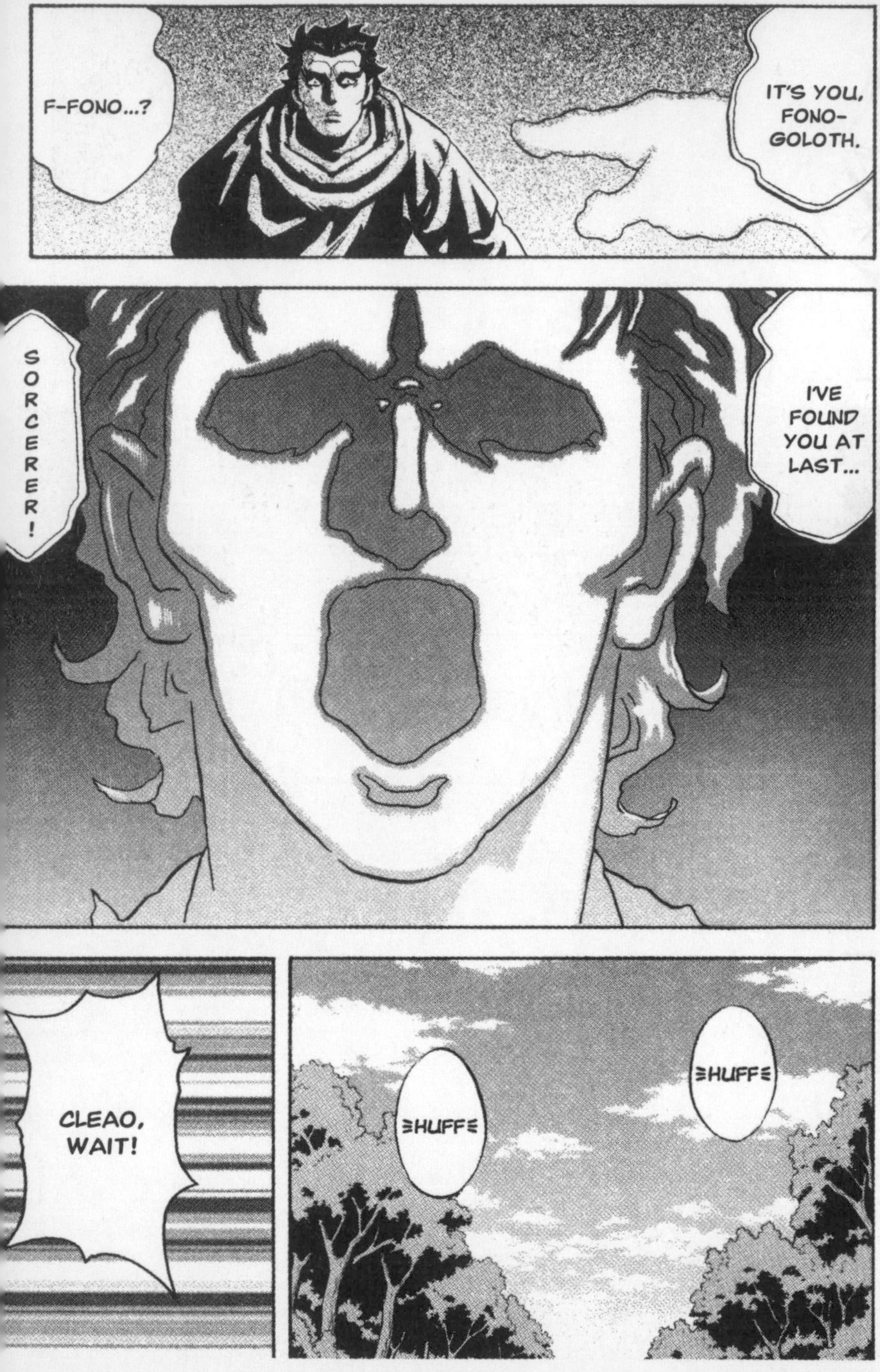
IT'S YOU, FONO-GOLOTH.
F-FONO...?
I'VE FOUND YOU AT LAST...
SORCERER!
≡HUFF≡
≡HUFF≡
CLEAO, WAIT!

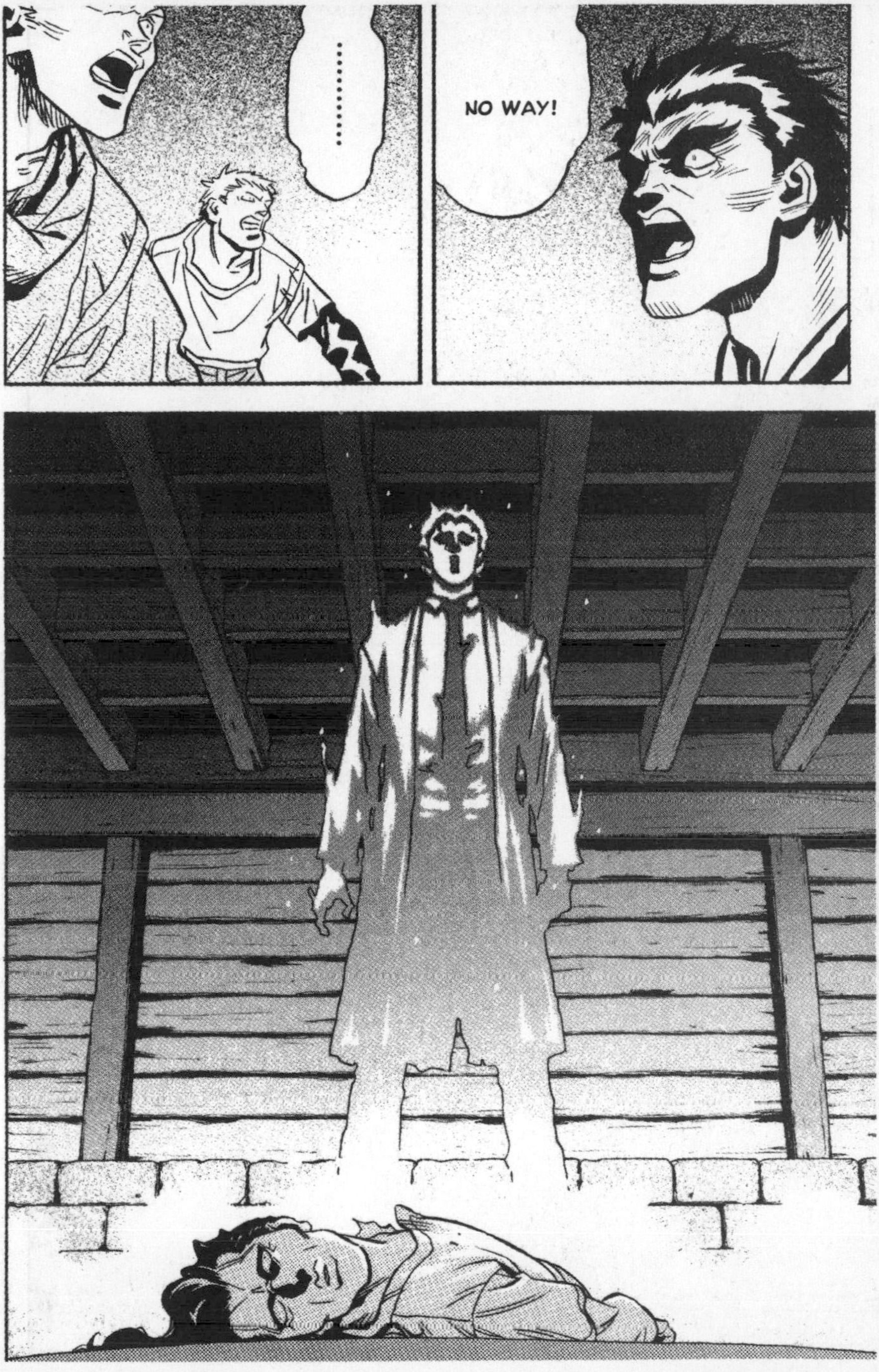

....
NO WAY!

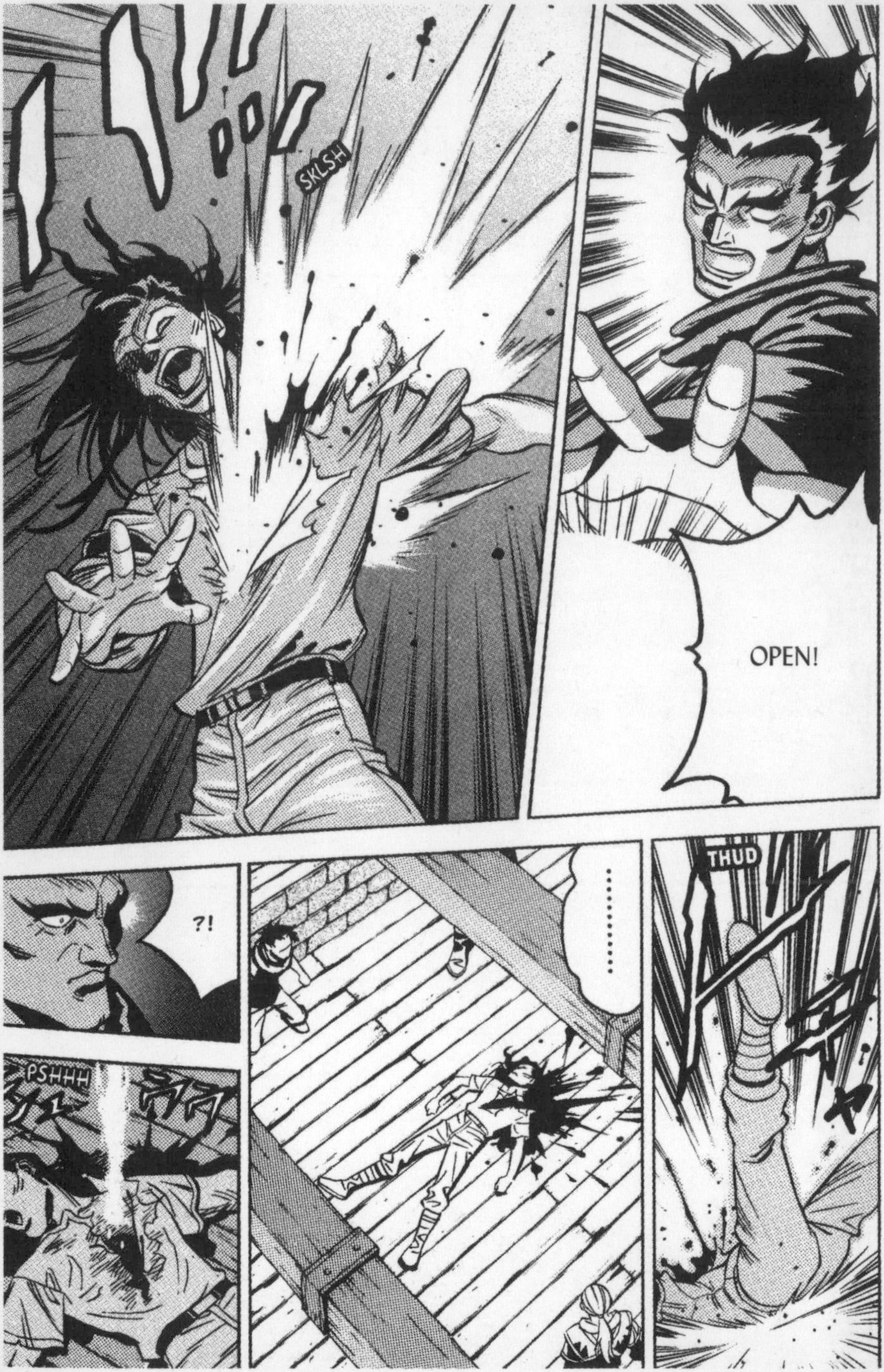
SKLSH
OPEN!
?!
......
THUD
PSHHH

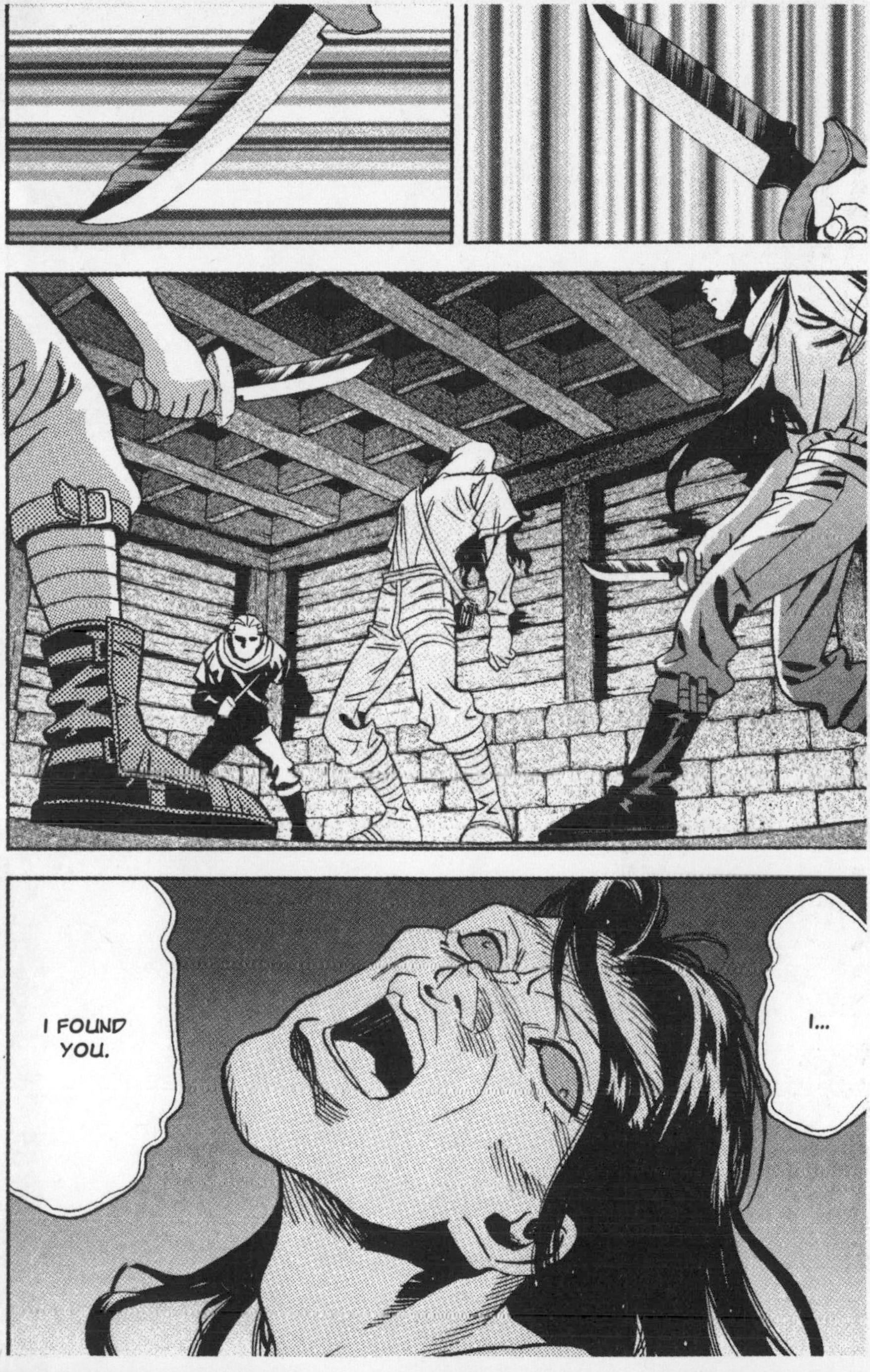
I...
I FOUND YOU.

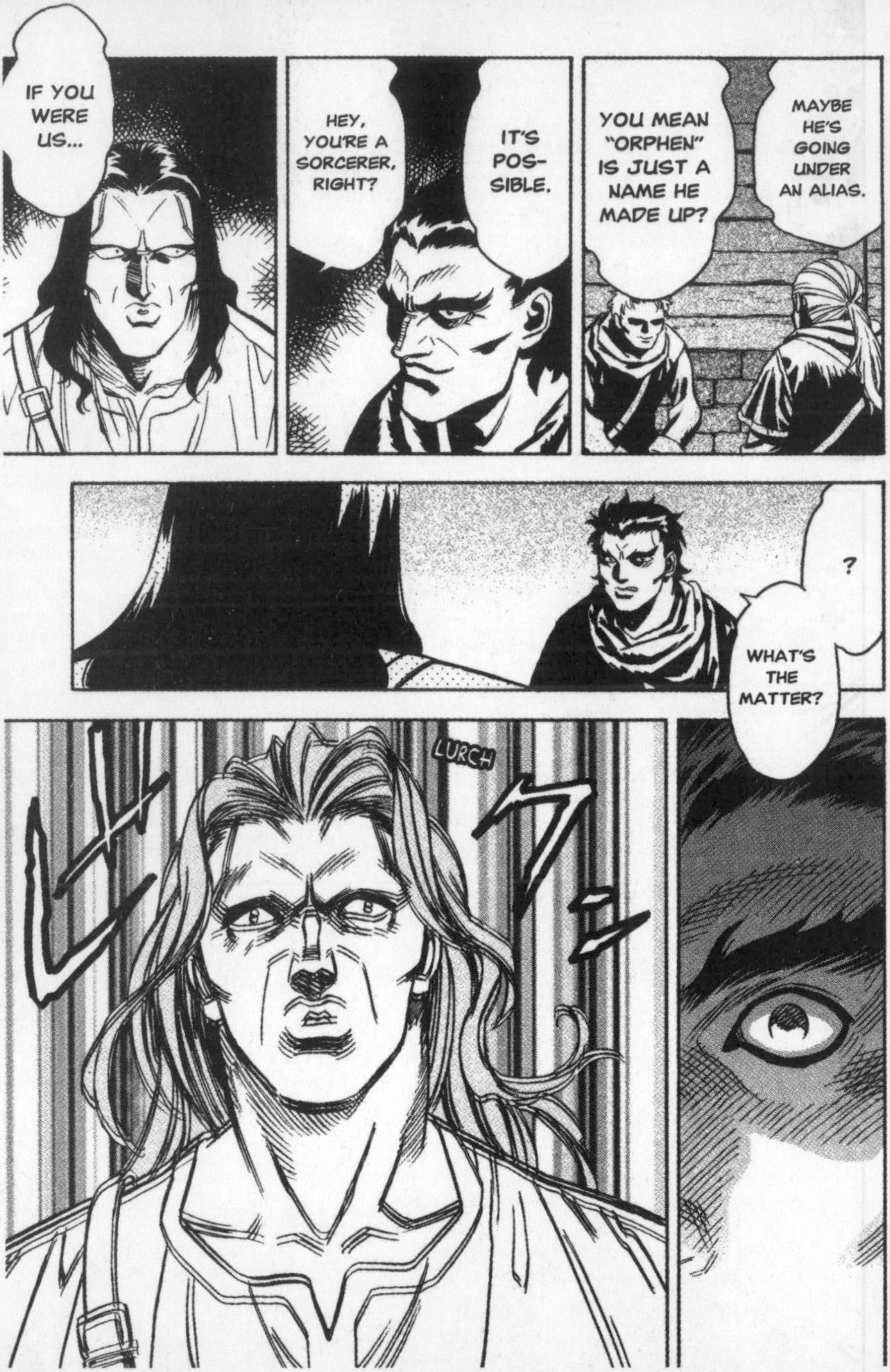
IF YOU WERE US...
HEY, YOU'RE A SORCERER, RIGHT?
IT'S POS-SIBLE.
YOU MEAN "ORPHEN" IS JUST A NAME HE MADE UP?
MAYBE HE'S GOING UNDER AN ALIAS.
?
WHAT'S THE MATTER?
LURCH

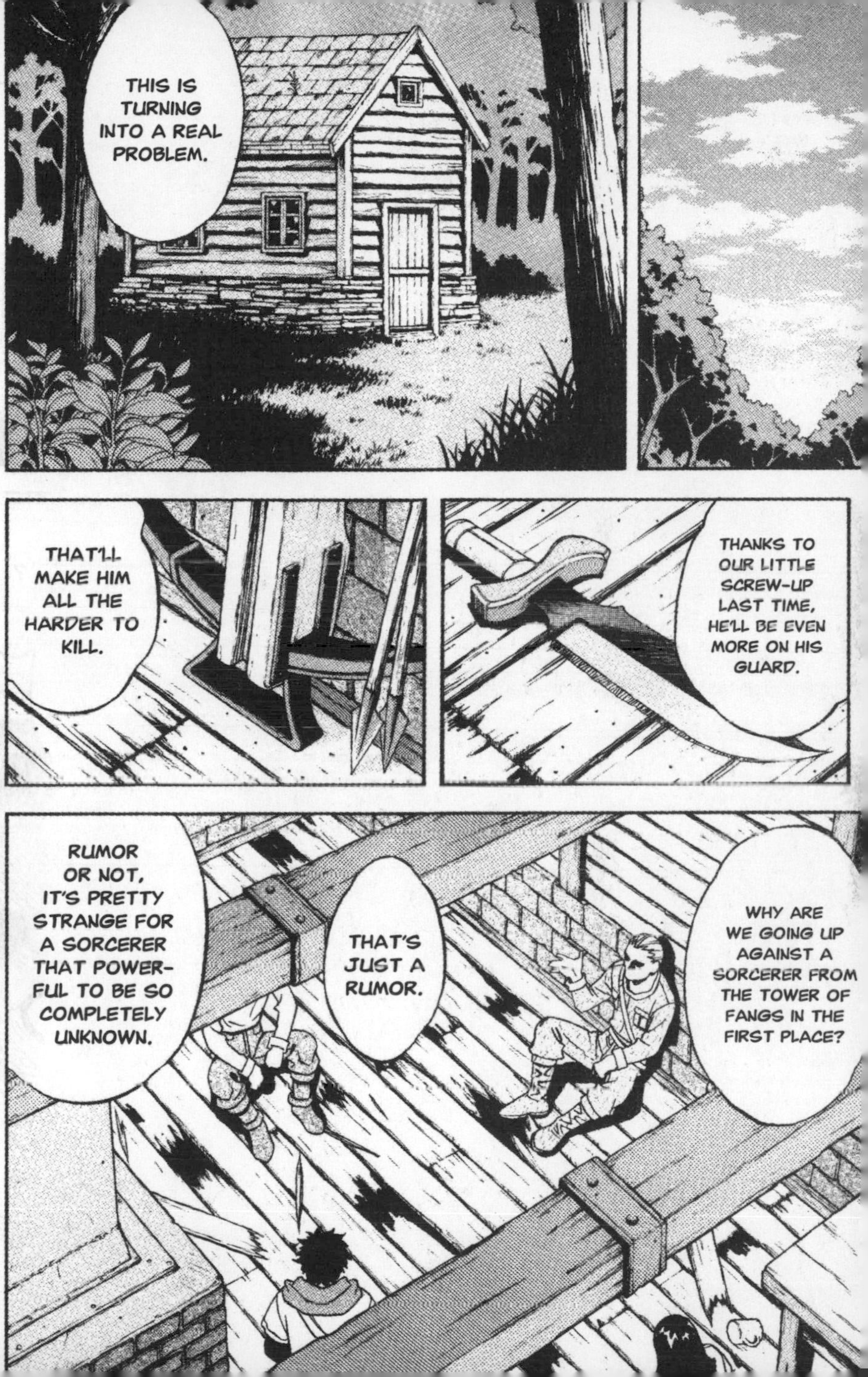
THIS IS TURNING INTO A REAL PROBLEM.
THANKS TO OUR LITTLE SCREW-UP LAST TIME, HE'LL BE EVEN MORE ON HIS GUARD.
THAT'LL MAKE HIM ALL THE HARDER TO KILL.
WHY ARE WE GOING UP AGAINST A SORCERER FROM THE TOWER OF FANGS IN THE FIRST PLACE?
THAT'S JUST A RUMOR.
RUMOR OR NOT, IT'S PRETTY STRANGE FOR A SORCERER THAT POWER-FUL TO BE SO COMPLETELY UNKNOWN.

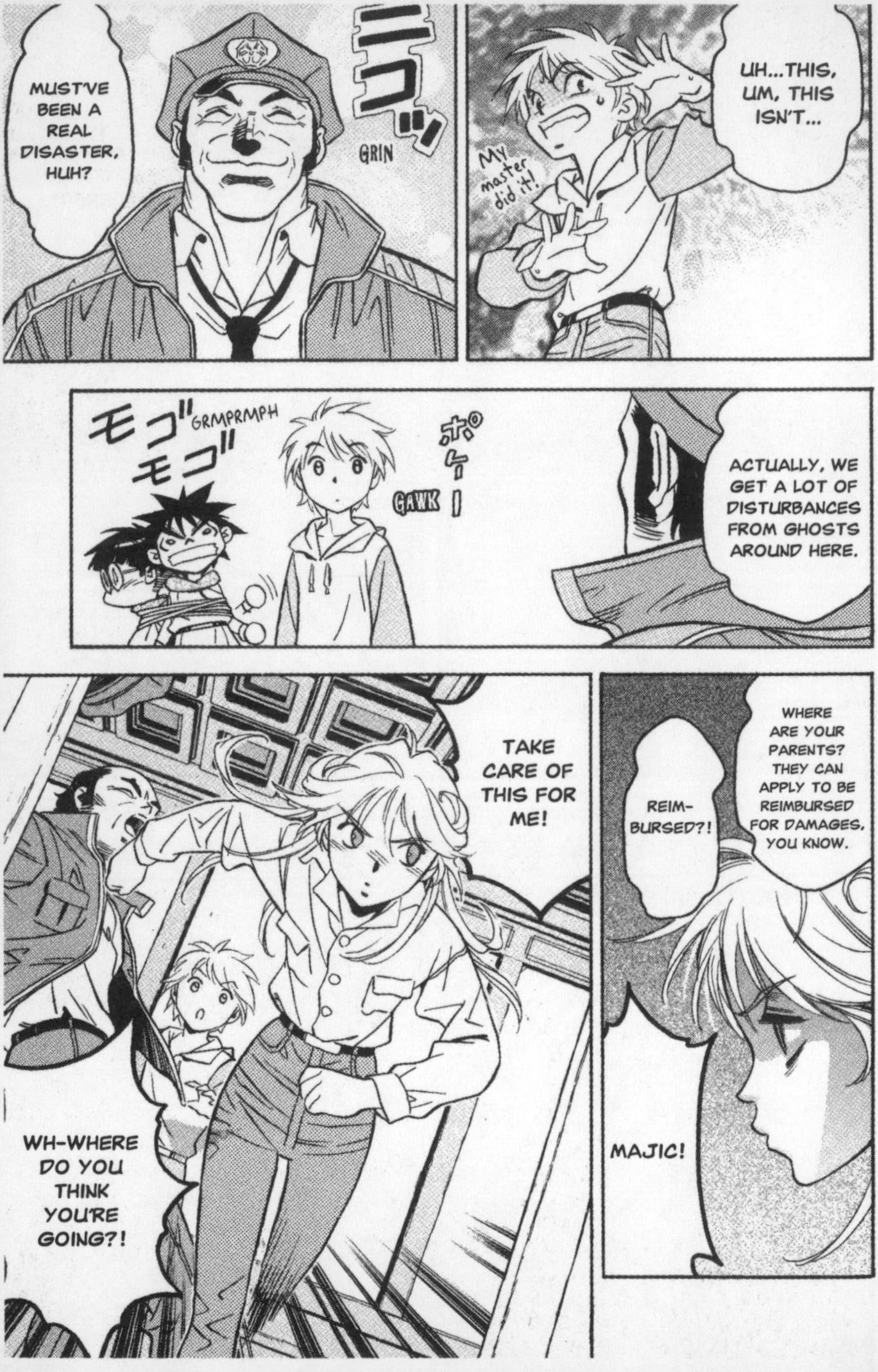
UH...THIS, UM, THIS ISN'T...
My master did it!
MUST'VE BEEN A REAL DISASTER, HUH?
ニコッ
GRIN
ACTUALLY, WE GET A LOT OF DISTURBANCES FROM GHOSTS AROUND HERE.
ポイ
GAWK
モゴ モゴ
GRMPRMPH
WHERE ARE YOUR PARENTS? THEY CAN APPLY TO BE REIMBURSED FOR DAMAGES, YOU KNOW.
REIM-BURSED?!
MAJIC!
TAKE CARE OF THIS FOR ME!
WH-WHERE DO YOU THINK YOU'RE GOING?!

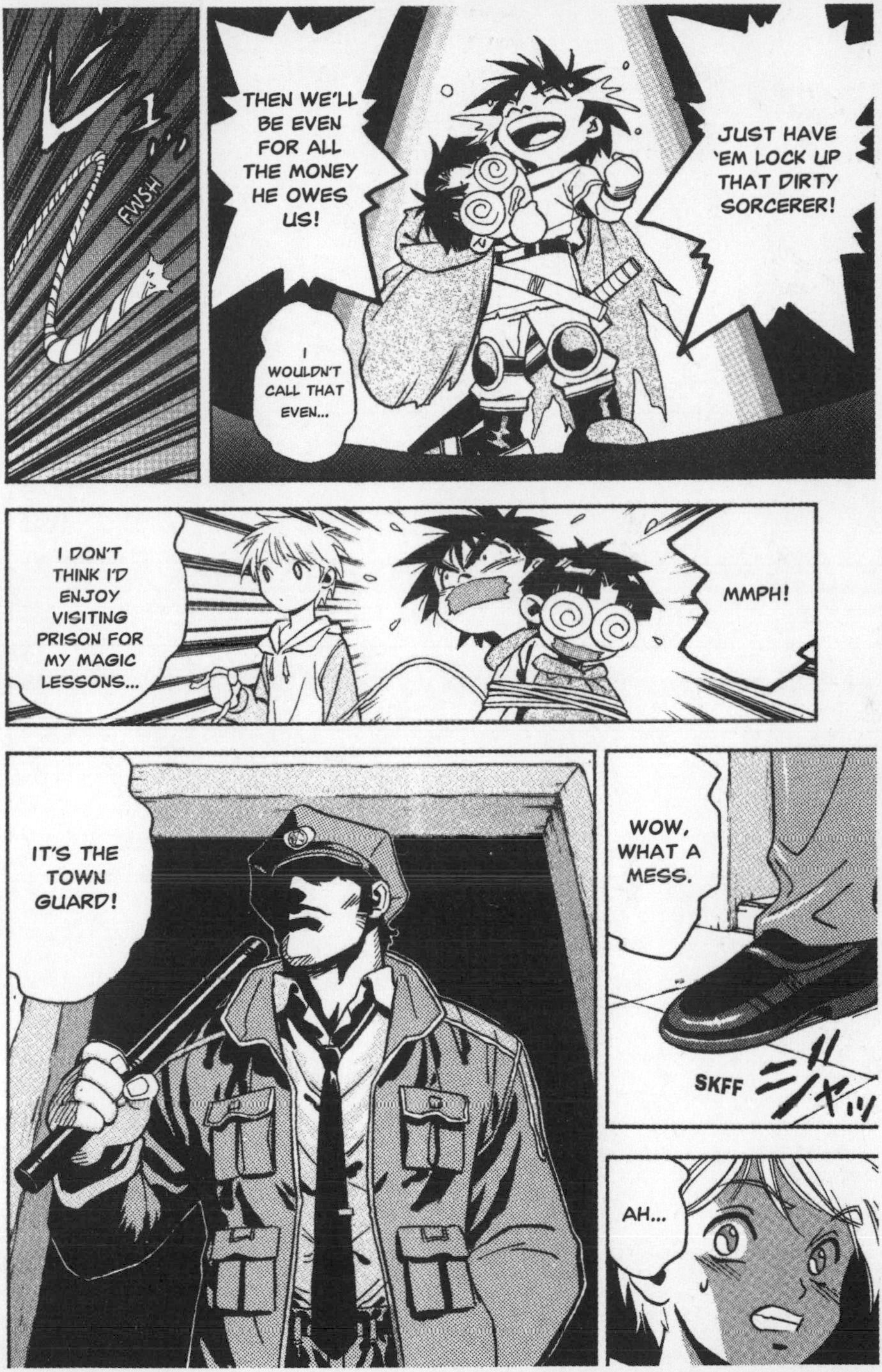
FWSH
JUST HAVE 'EM LOCK UP THAT DIRTY SORCERER!
THEN WE'LL BE EVEN FOR ALL THE MONEY HE OWES US!
I WOULDN'T CALL THAT EVEN...
MMPH!
I DON'T THINK I'D ENJOY VISITING PRISON FOR MY MAGIC LESSONS...
WOW, WHAT A MESS.
SKFF
IT'S THE TOWN GUARD!
AH...

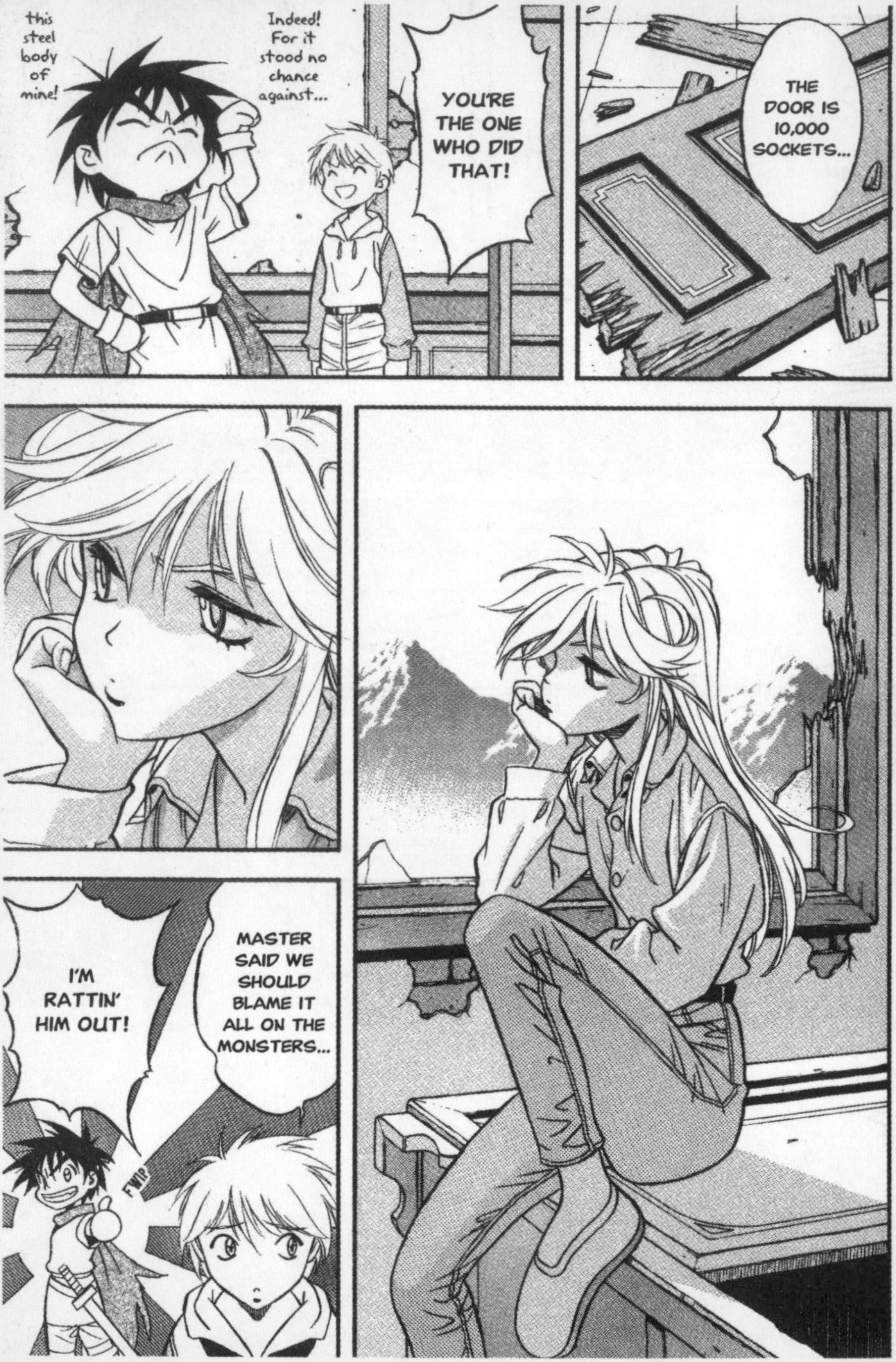
THE DOOR IS 10,000 SOCKETS...
YOU'RE THE ONE WHO DID THAT!
Indeed! For it stood no chance against...
this steel body of mine!
MASTER SAID WE SHOULD BLAME IT ALL ON THE MONSTERS...
I'M RATTIN' HIM OUT!
FWIP

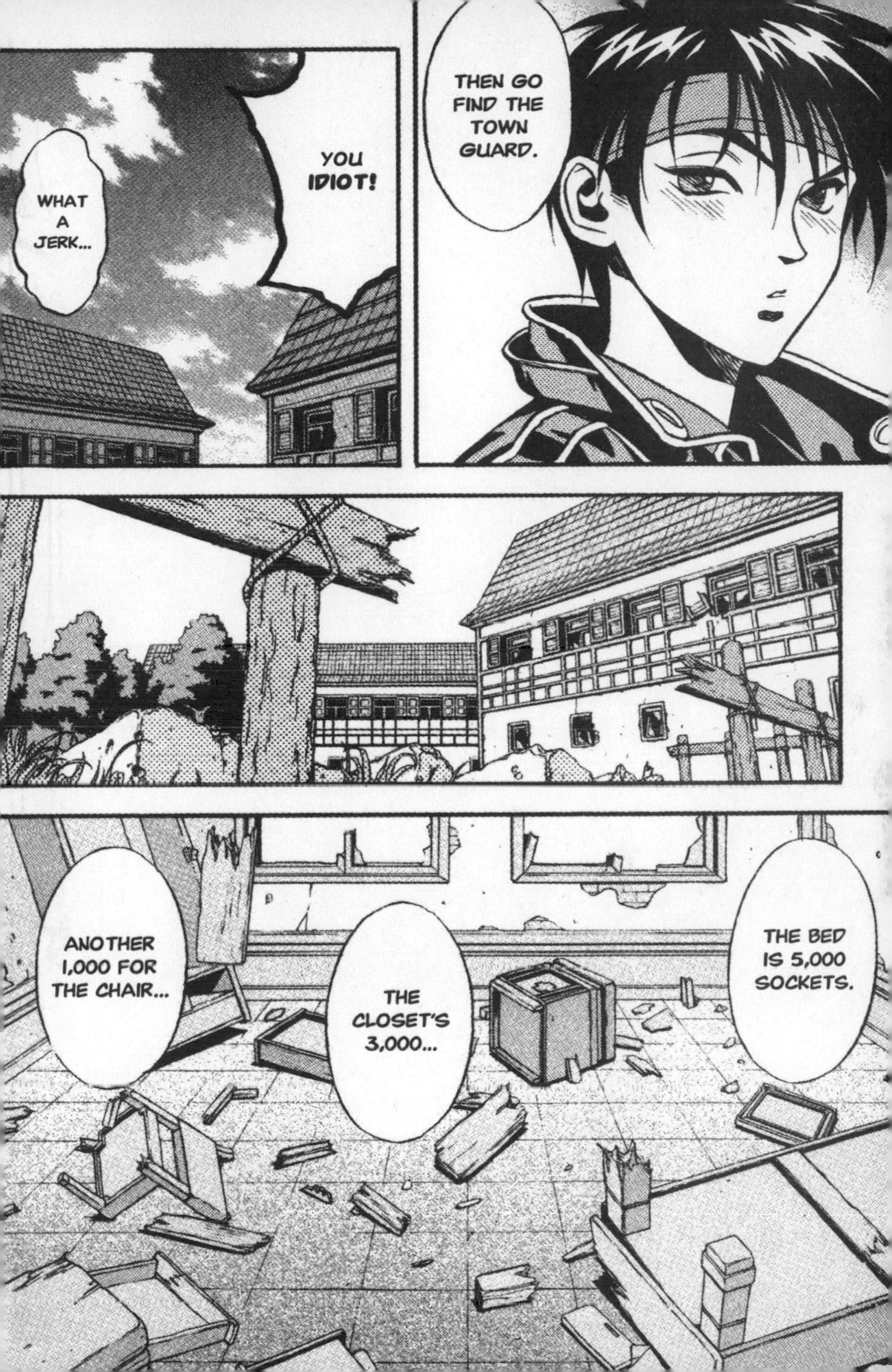
THEN GO FIND THE TOWN GUARD.
YOU IDIOT!
WHAT A JERK...
THE BED IS 5,000 SOCKETS.
THE CLOSET'S 3,000...
ANOTHER 1,000 FOR THE CHAIR...

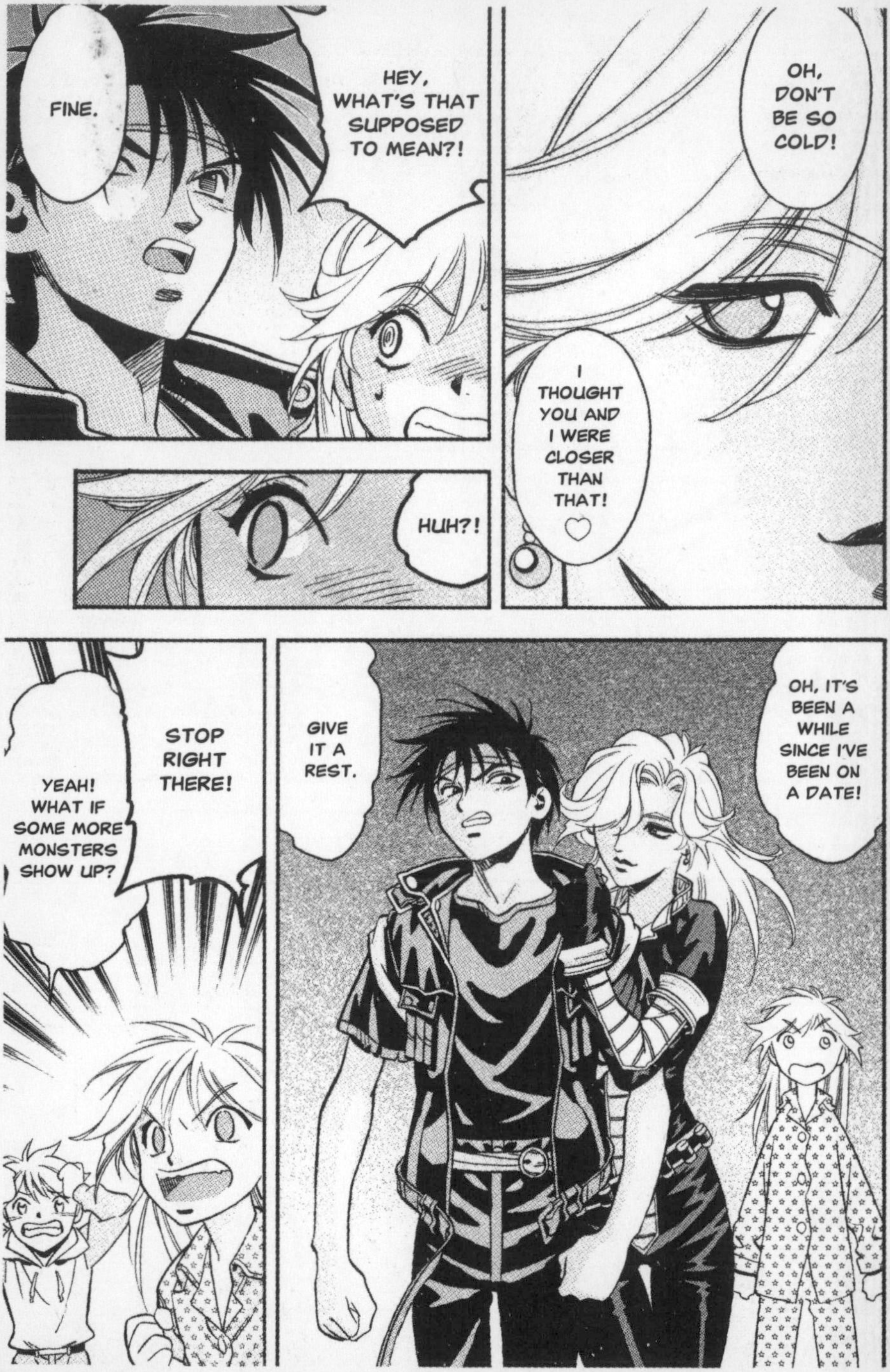
FINE.
HEY, WHAT'S THAT SUPPOSED TO MEAN?!
OH, DON'T BE SO COLD!
I THOUGHT YOU AND I WERE CLOSER THAN THAT! ♡
HUH?!
STOP RIGHT THERE!
YEAH! WHAT IF SOME MORE MONSTERS SHOW UP?
GIVE IT A REST.
OH, IT'S BEEN A WHILE SINCE I'VE BEEN ON A DATE!

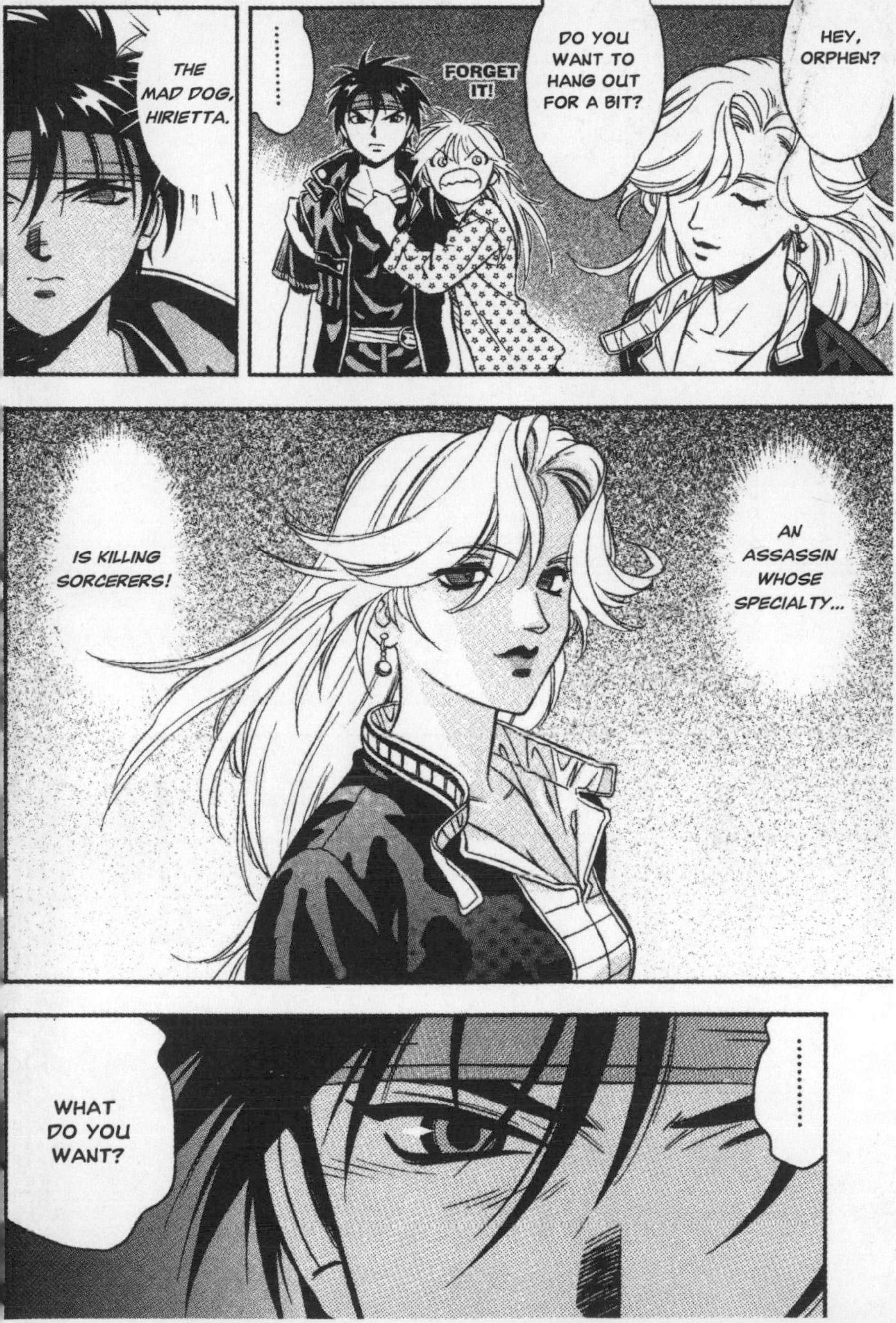
HEY, ORPHEN?
DO YOU WANT TO HANG OUT FOR A BIT?
FORGET IT!
......
THE MAD DOG, HIRIETTA.
AN ASSASSIN WHOSE SPECIALTY...
IS KILLING SORCERERS!
....
WHAT DO YOU WANT?

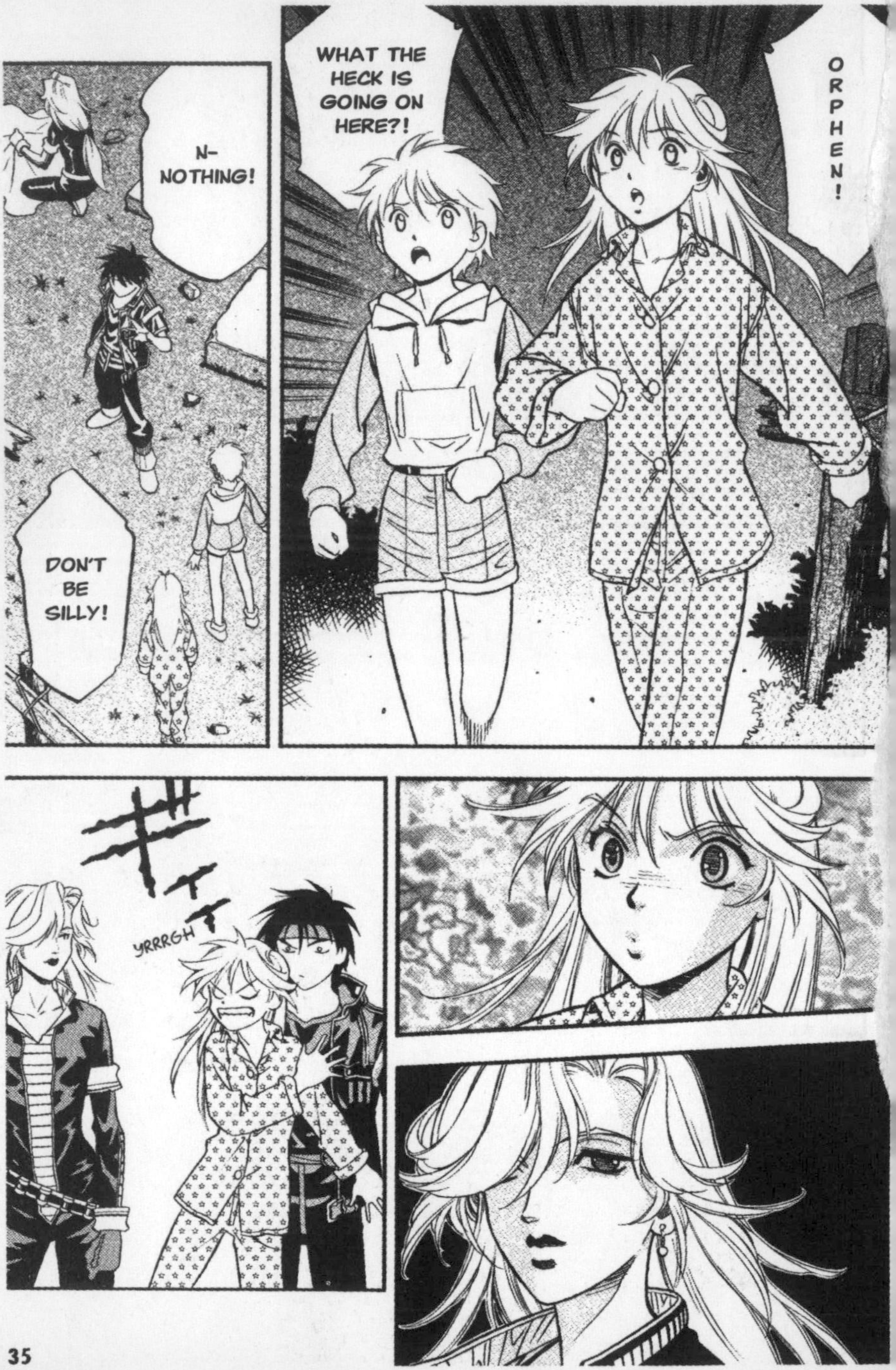
ORPHEN!
WHAT THE HECK IS GOING ON HERE?!
N-NOTHING!
DON'T BE SILLY!
YRRRGH

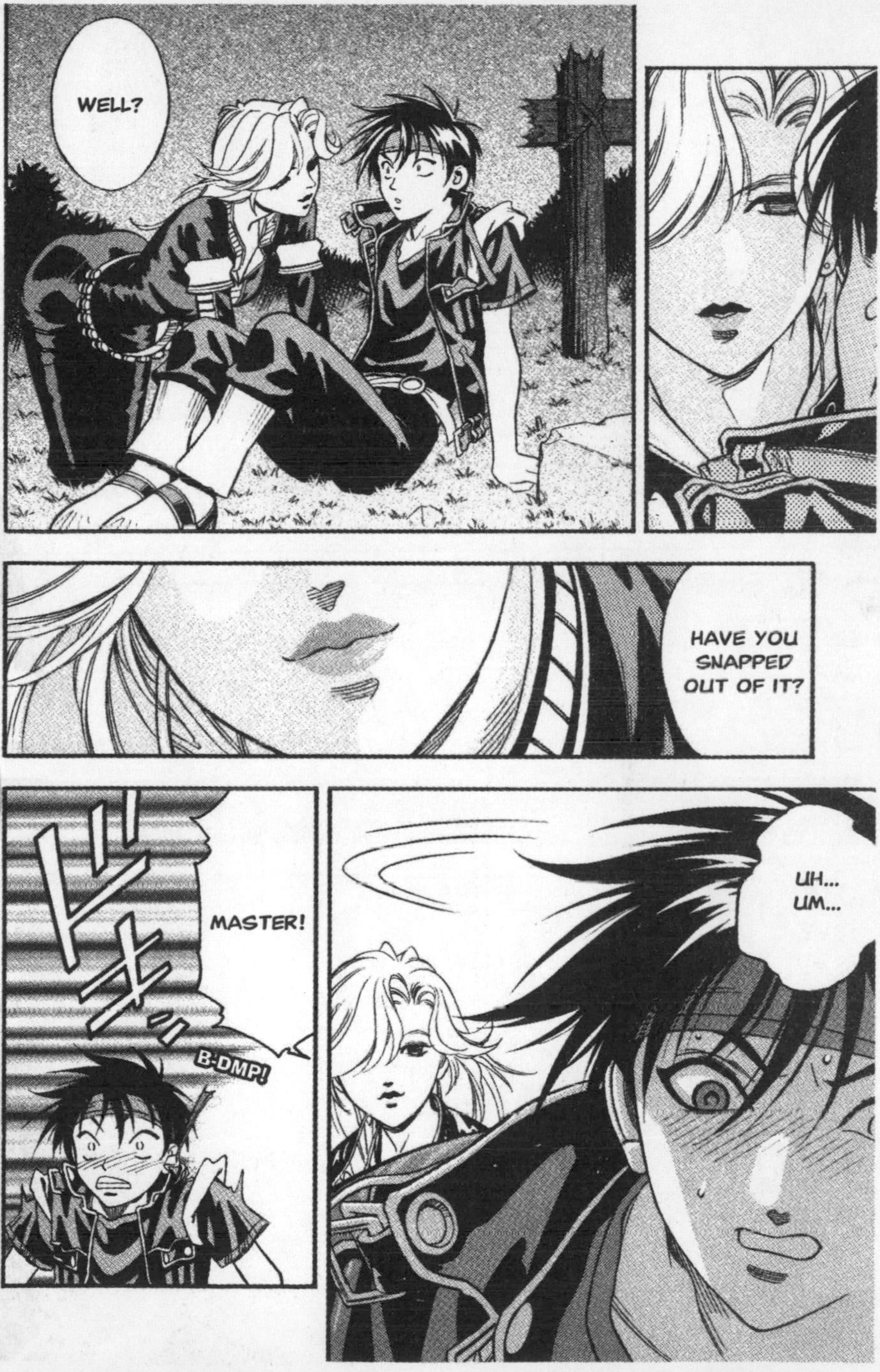
WELL?
HAVE YOU SNAPPED OUT OF IT?
UH... UM...
MASTER!
B-DMP!

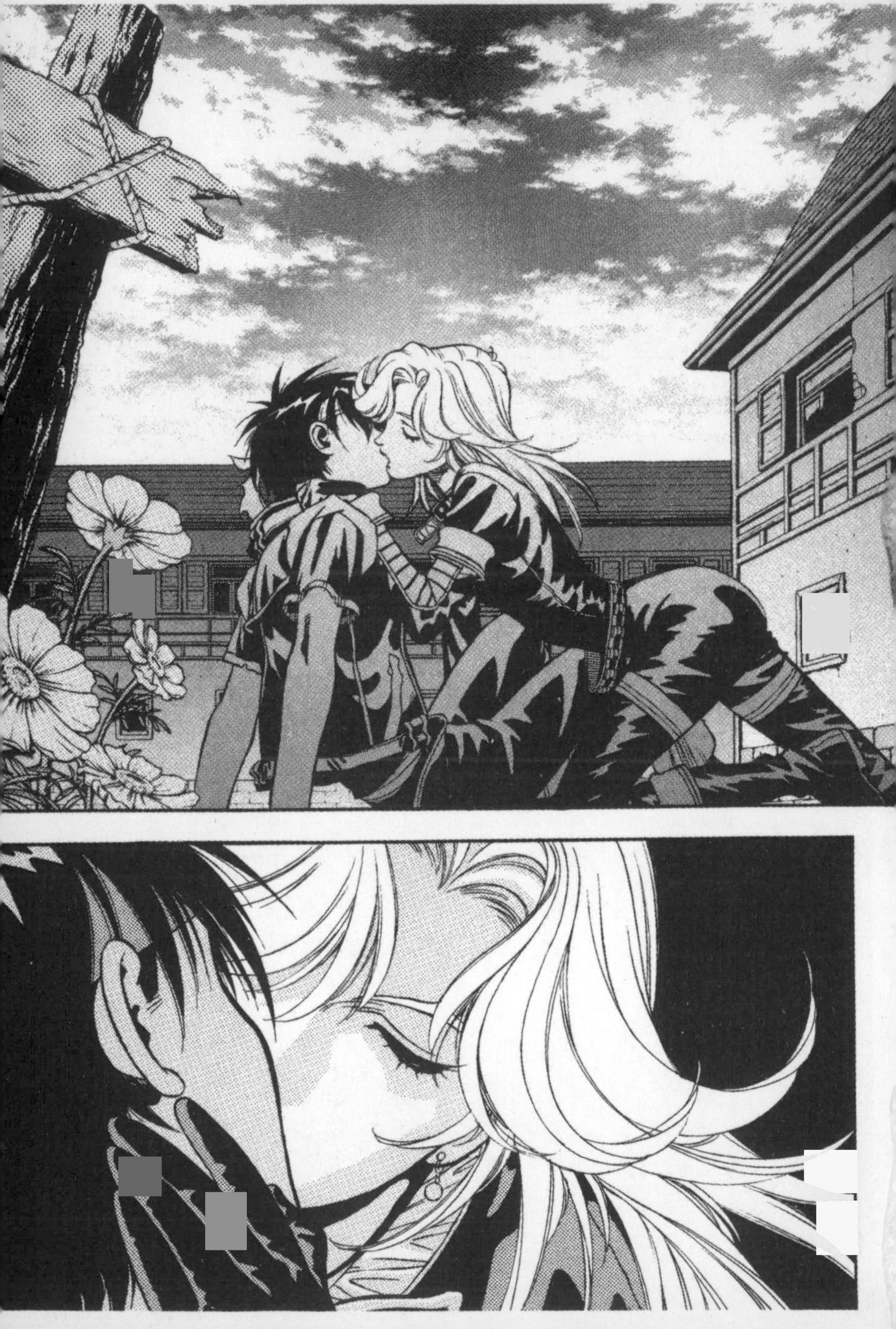

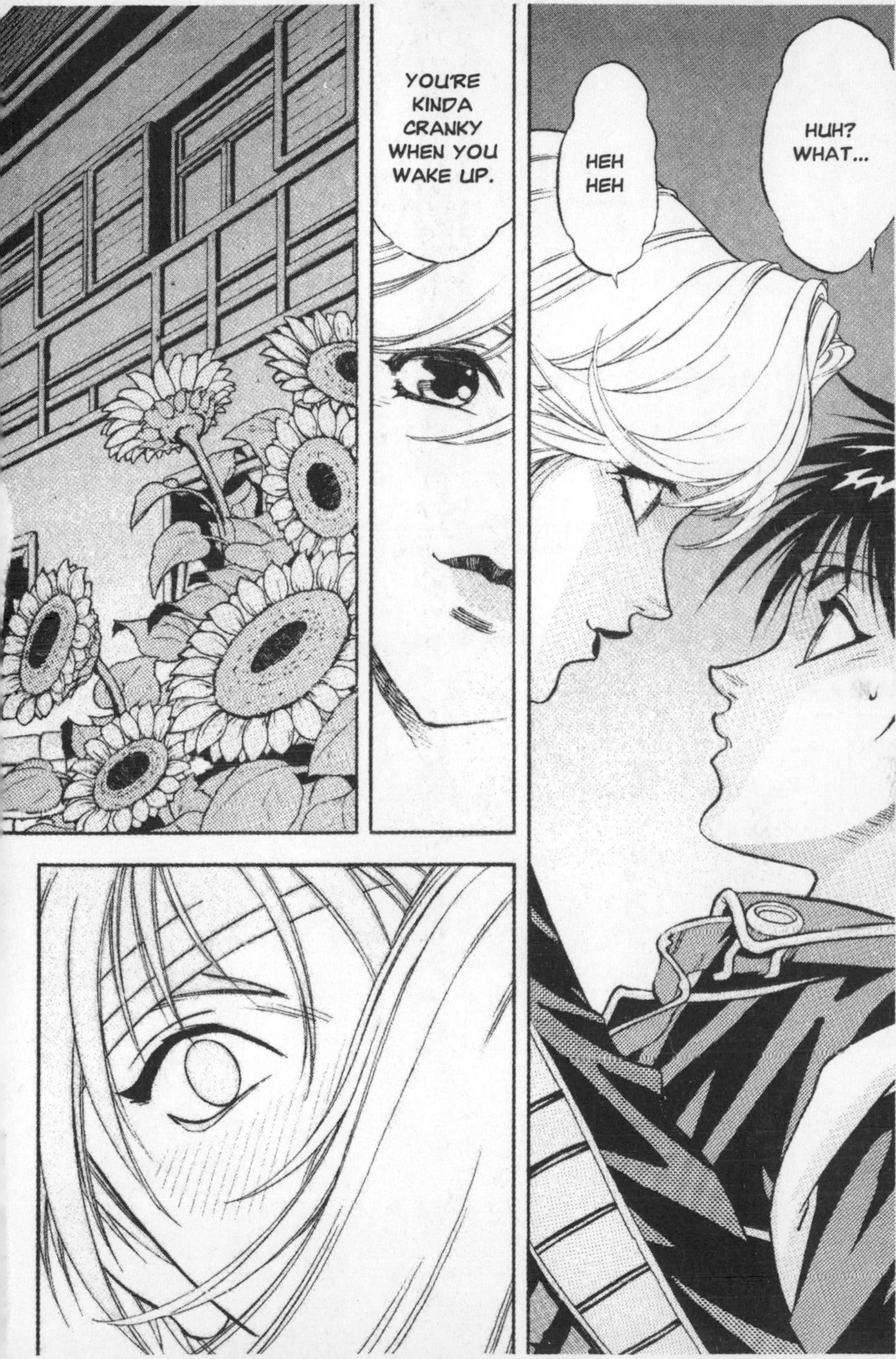
HUH? WHAT...
HEH HEH
YOU'RE KINDA CRANKY WHEN YOU WAKE UP.

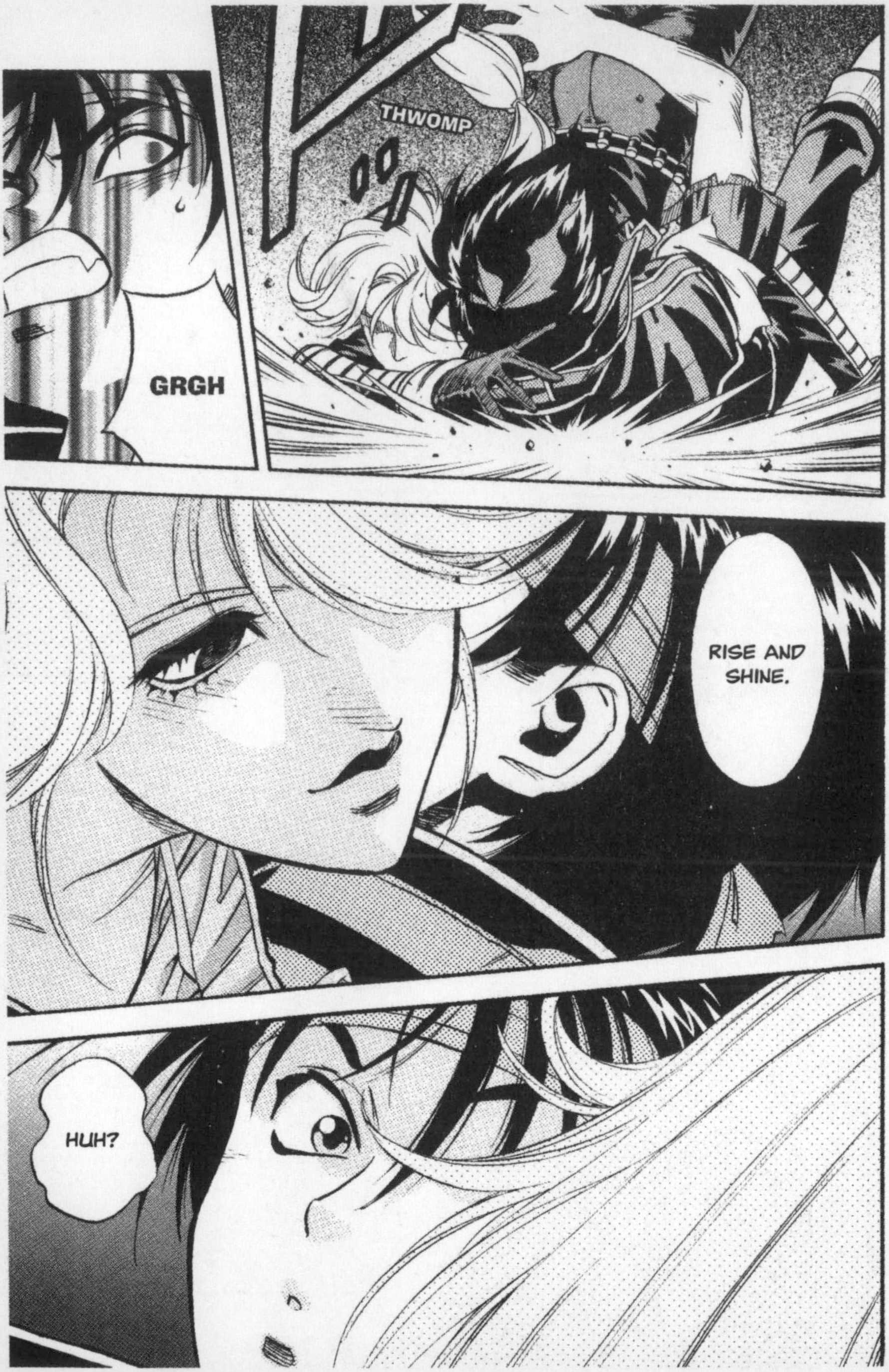
THWOMP
GRGH
RISE AND SHINE.
HUH?

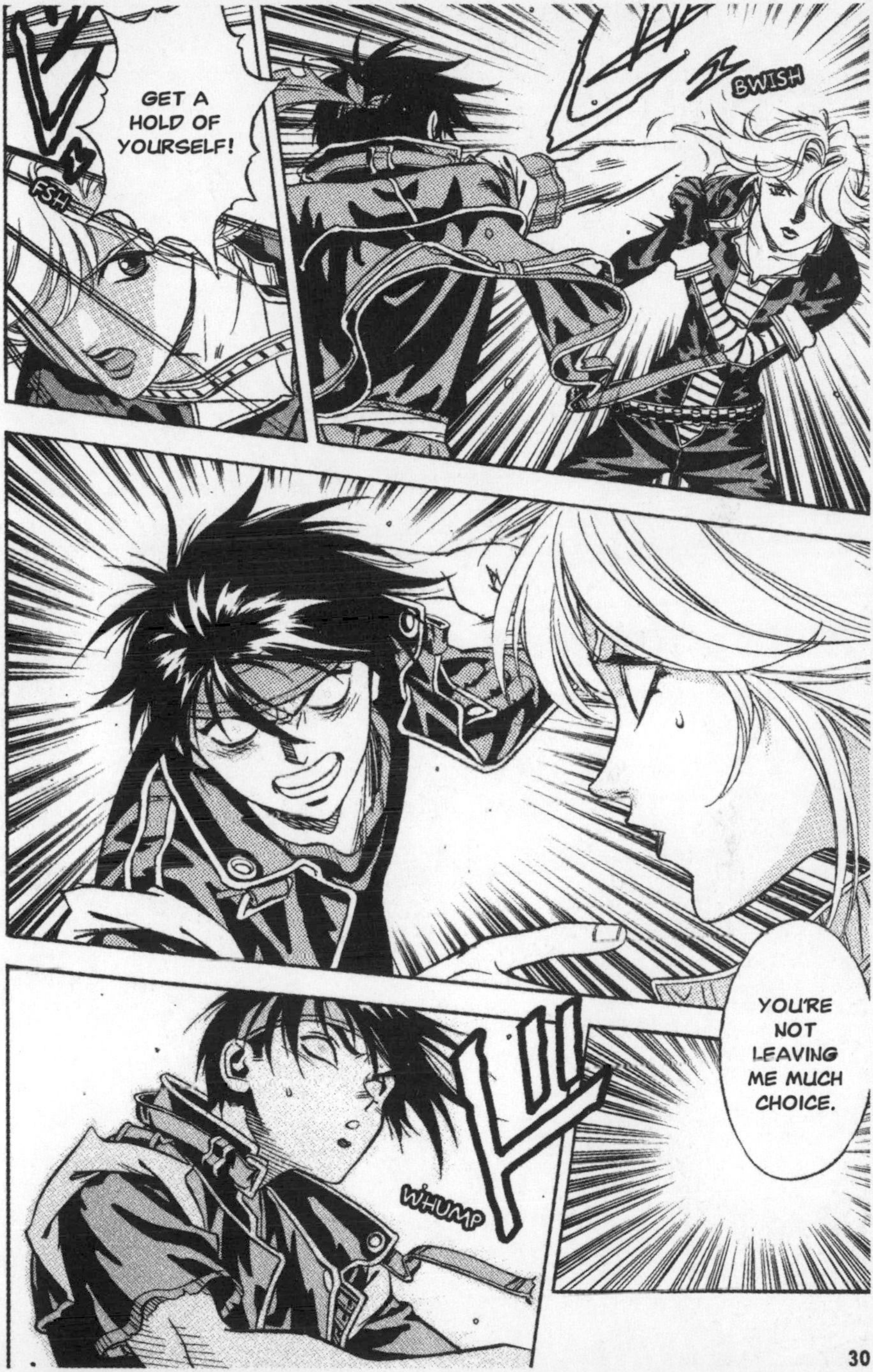
BWISH
GET A HOLD OF YOURSELF!
FSH
YOU'RE NOT LEAVING ME MUCH CHOICE.
WHUMP

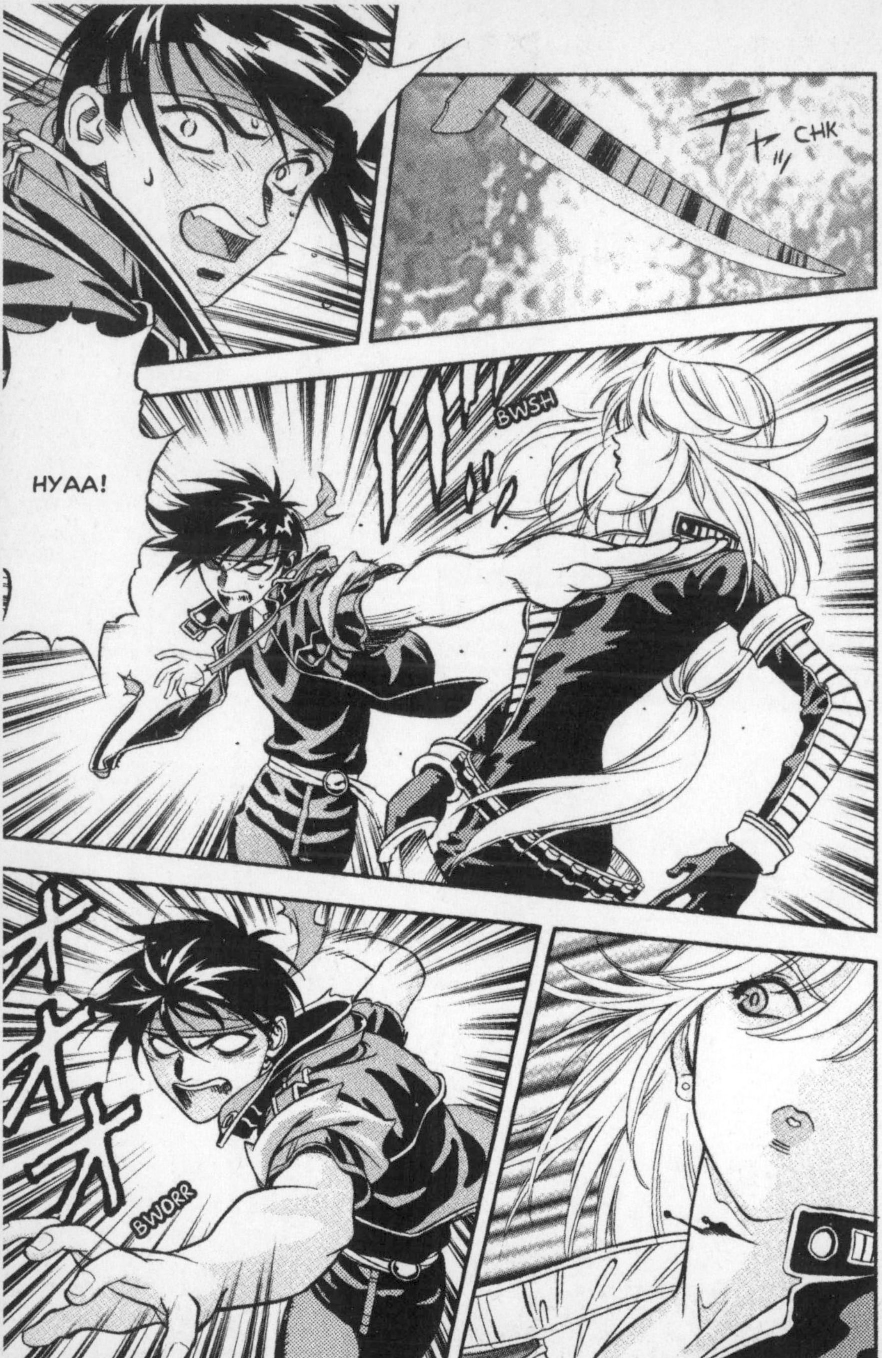

チャッ
CHK
BWSH
HYAA!
BWORR

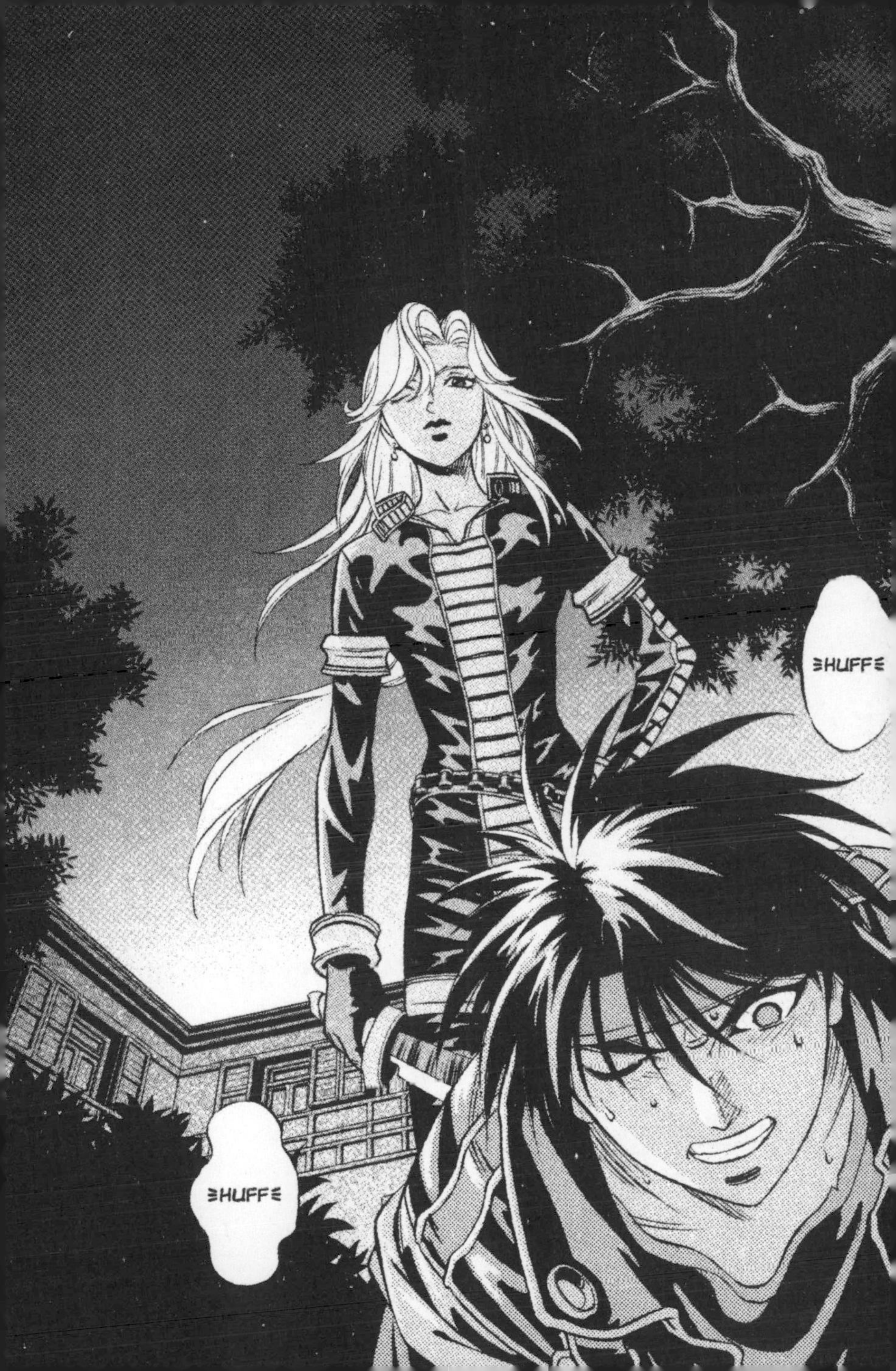
HUFF
HUFF

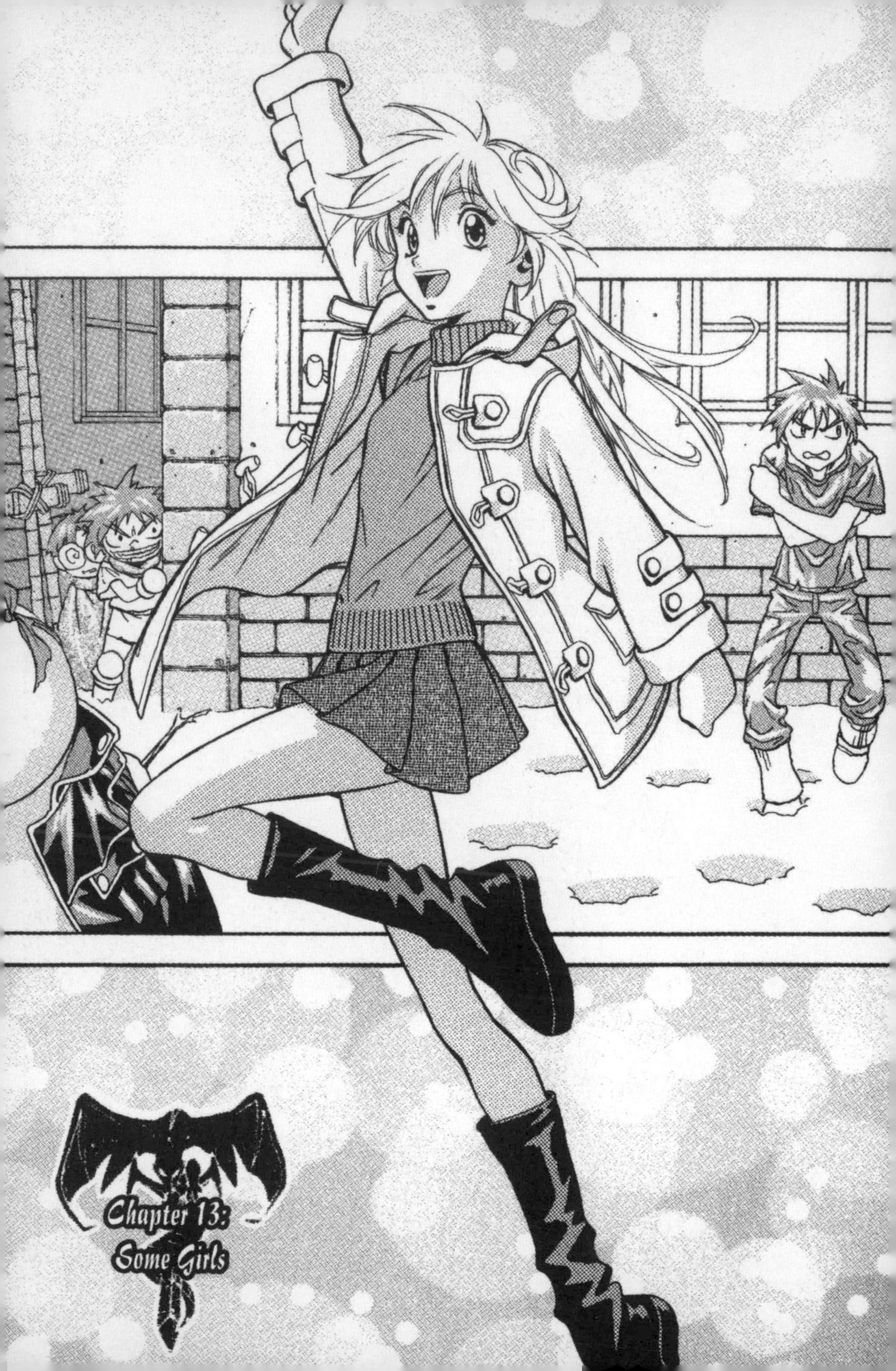
Chapter 13:
Some Girls

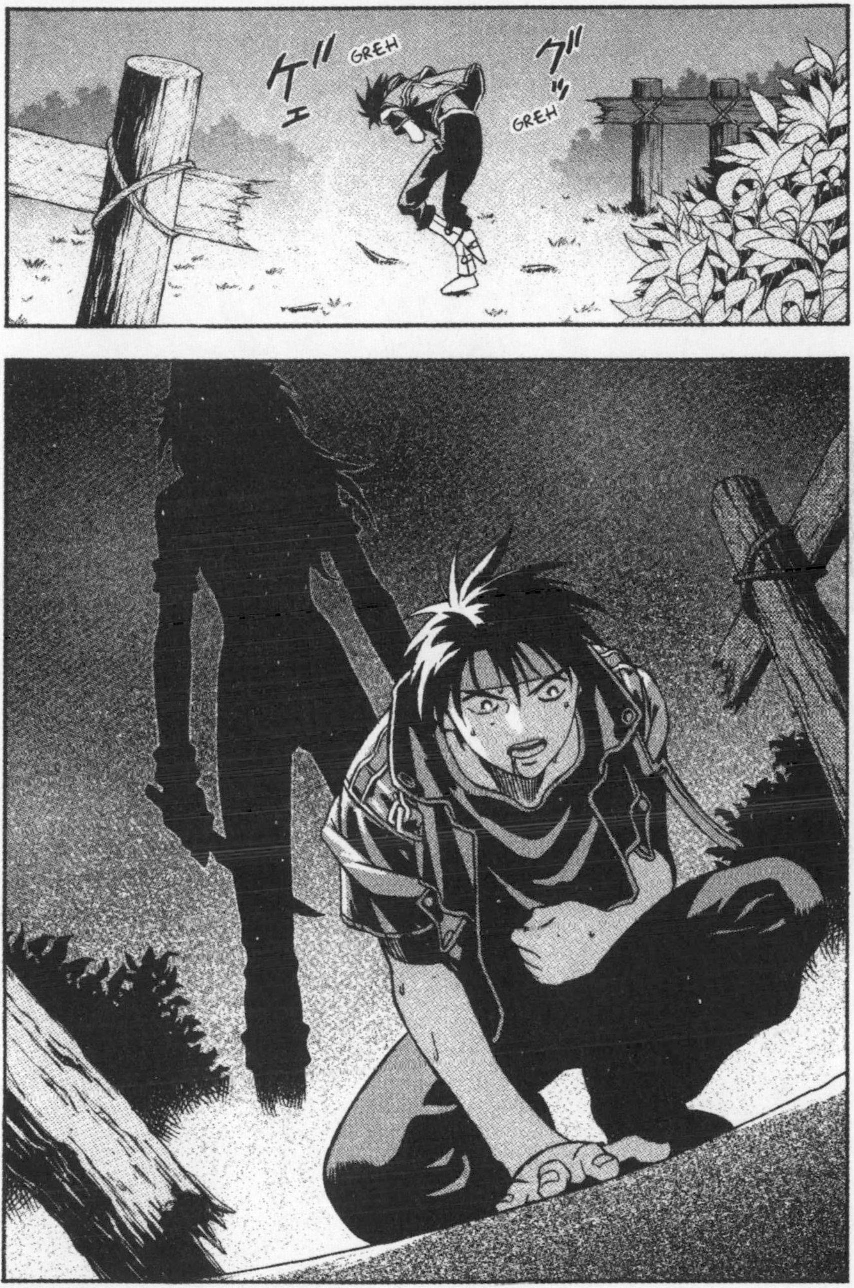
グッ
GREH
ゲエ
GREH

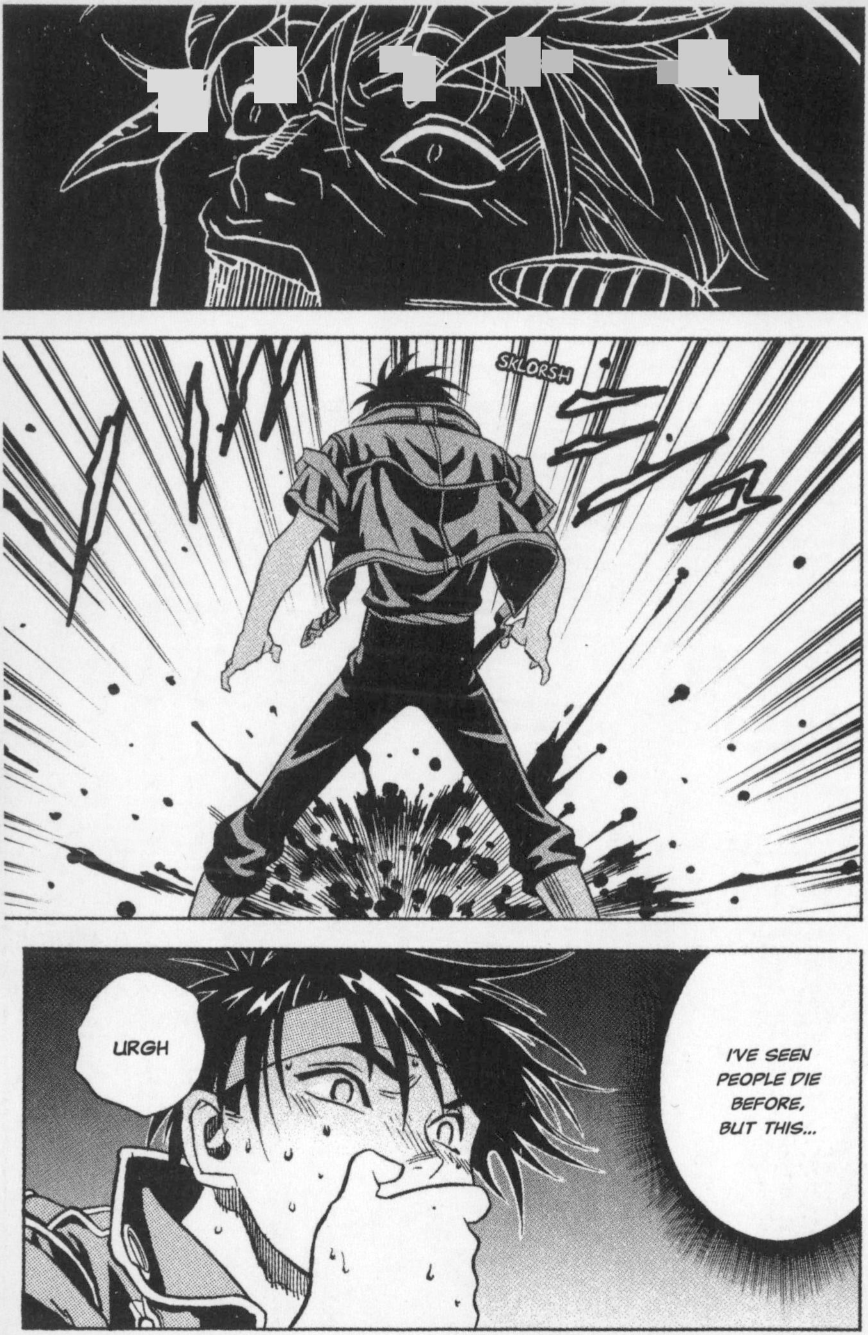
SKLORSH
URGH
I'VE SEEN PEOPLE DIE BEFORE, BUT THIS...

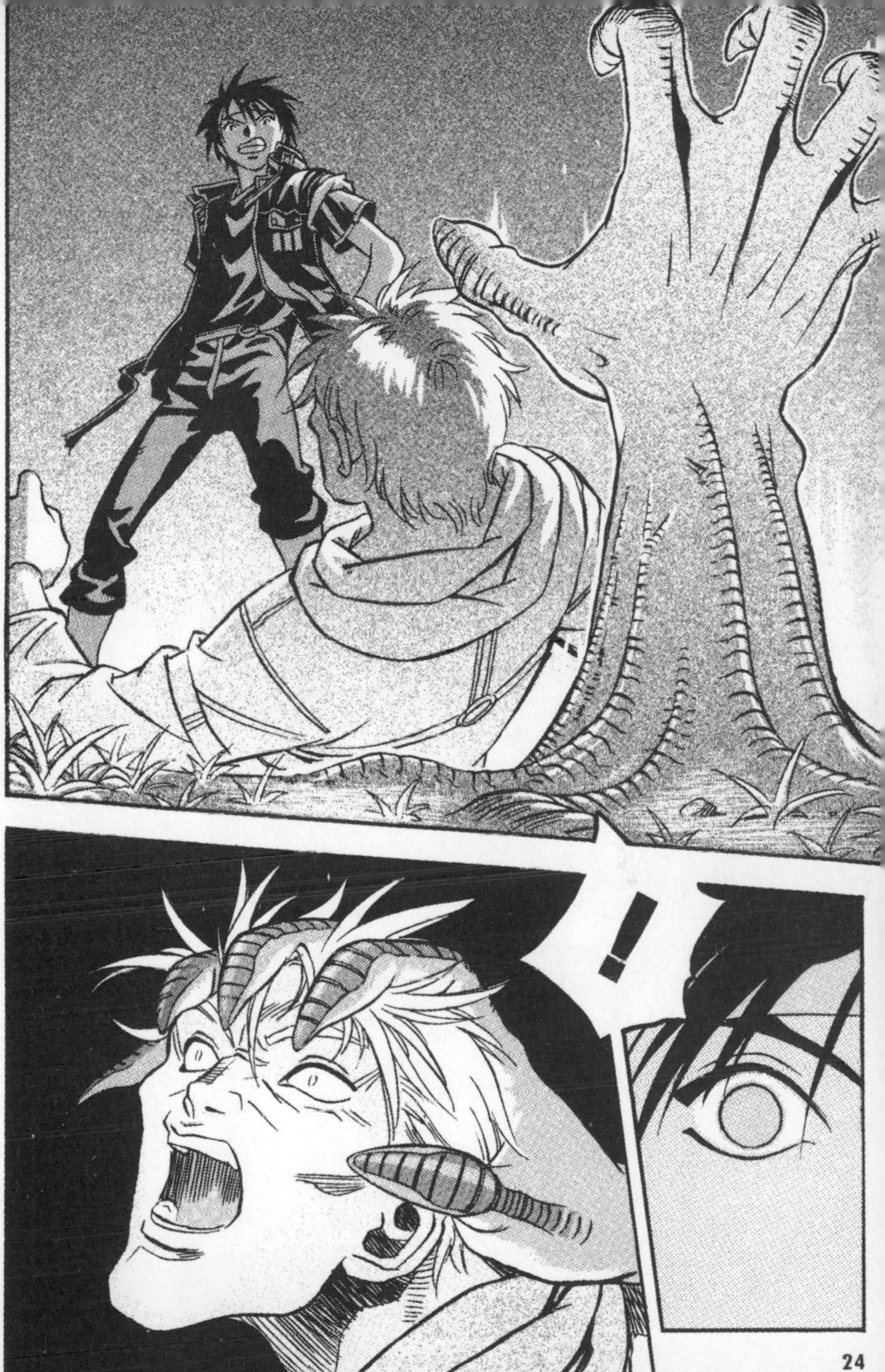
!

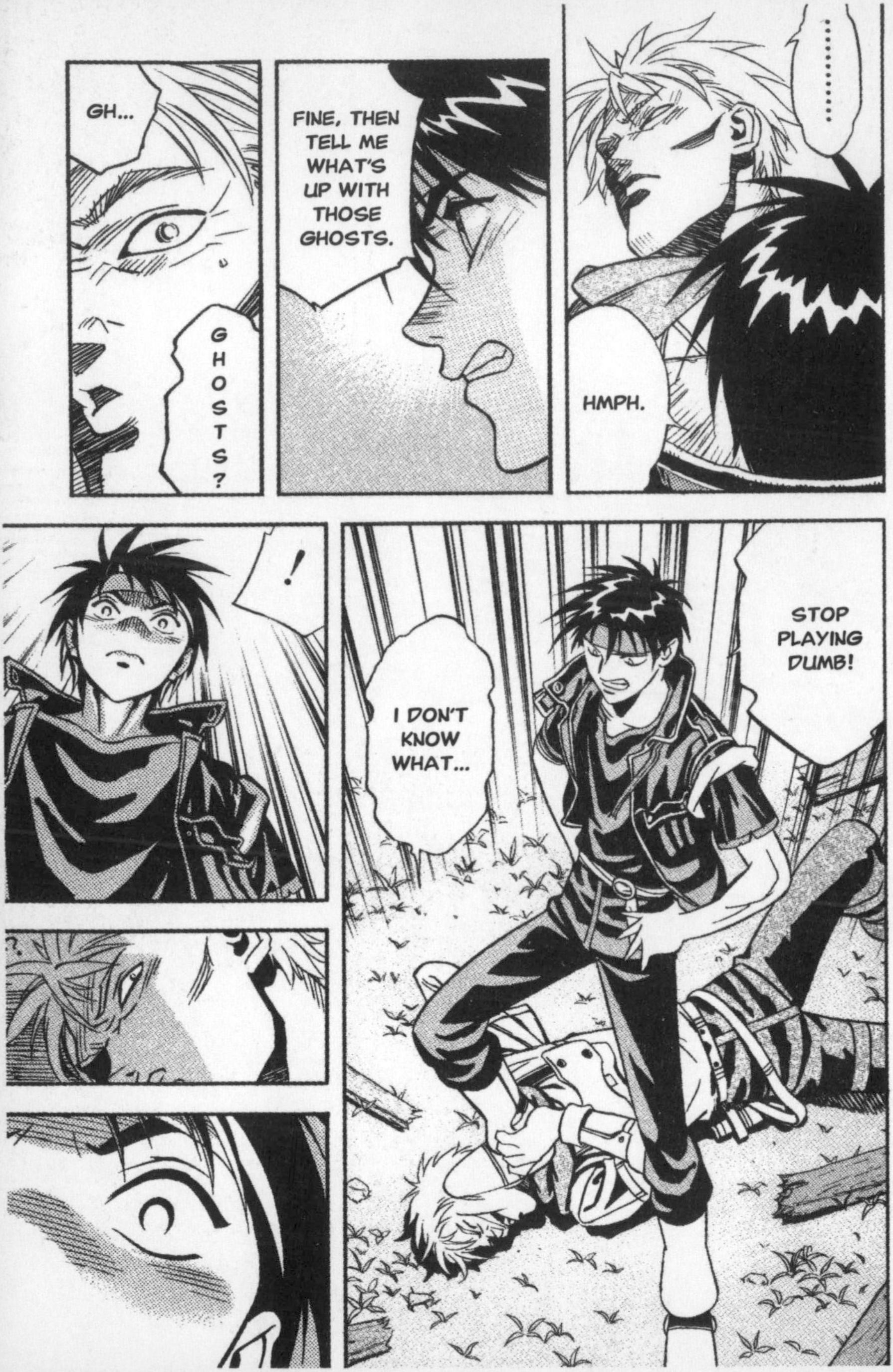
......
HMPH.
FINE, THEN TELL ME WHAT'S UP WITH THOSE GHOSTS.
GH...
GHOSTS?
STOP PLAYING DUMB!
!
I DON'T KNOW WHAT...
?

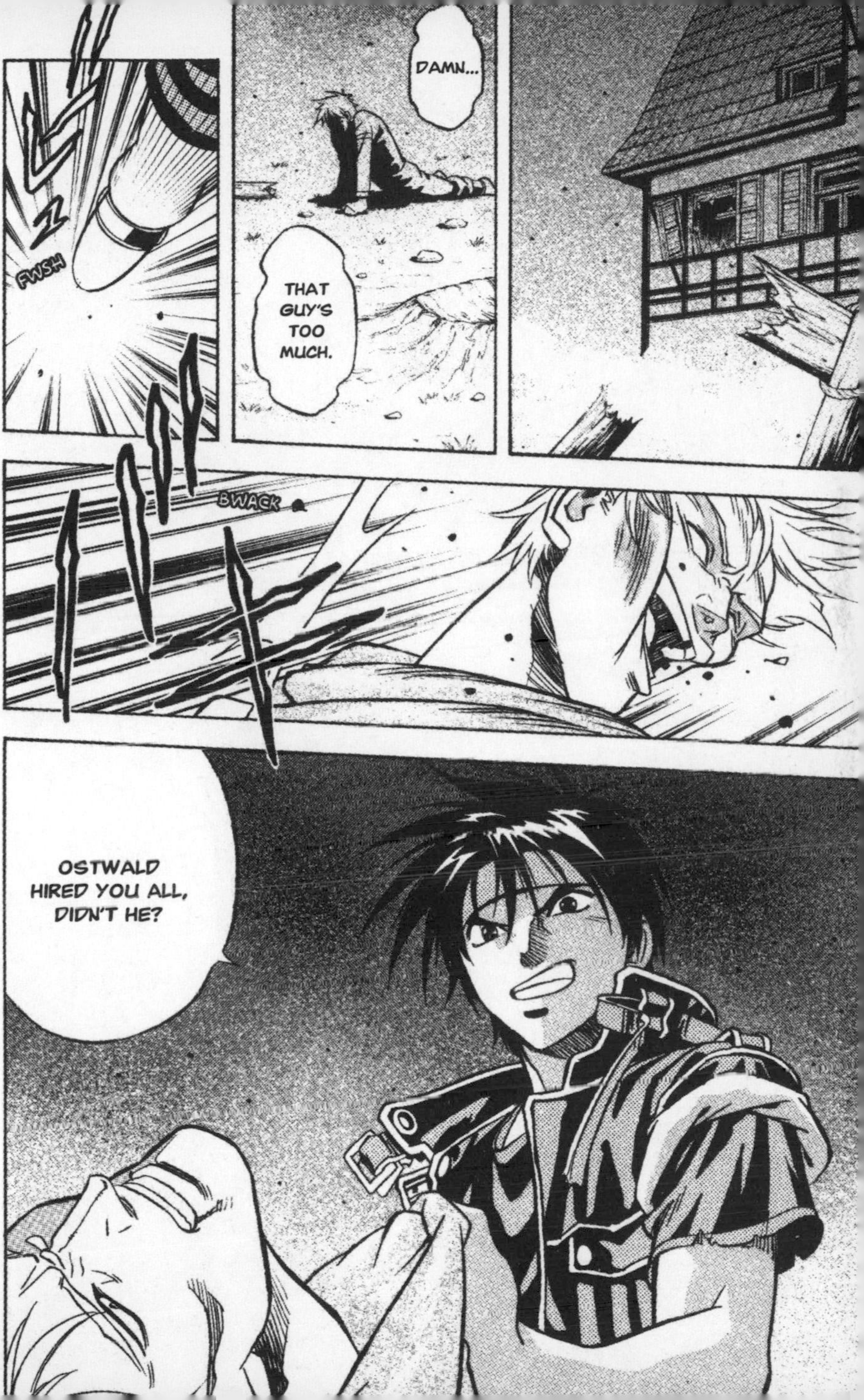

DAMN...
THAT GUY'S TOO MUCH.
FWSH
BWACK
OSTWALD HIRED YOU ALL, DIDN'T HE?

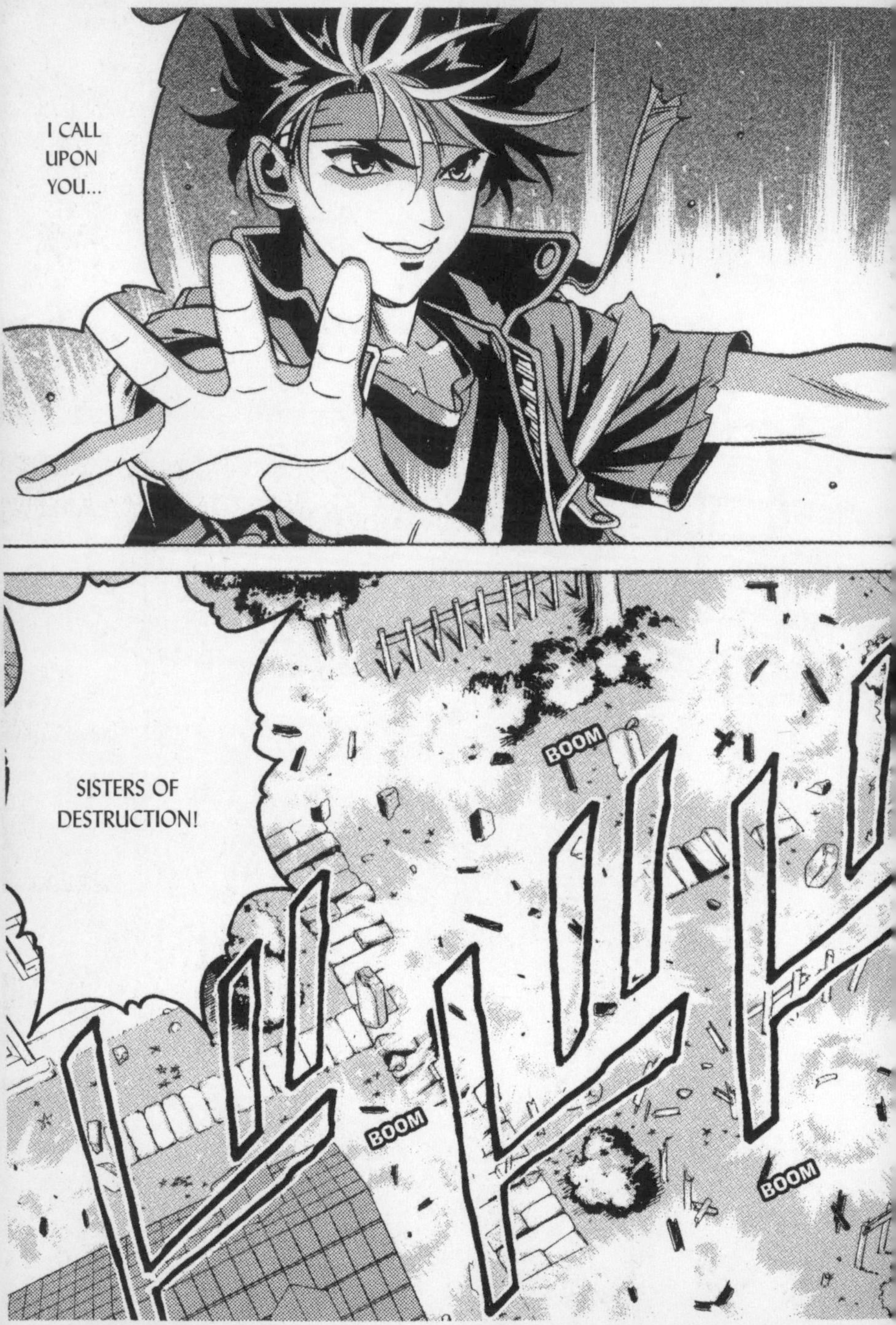
I CALL UPON YOU...
SISTERS OF DESTRUCTION!
BOOM
BOOM
BOOM

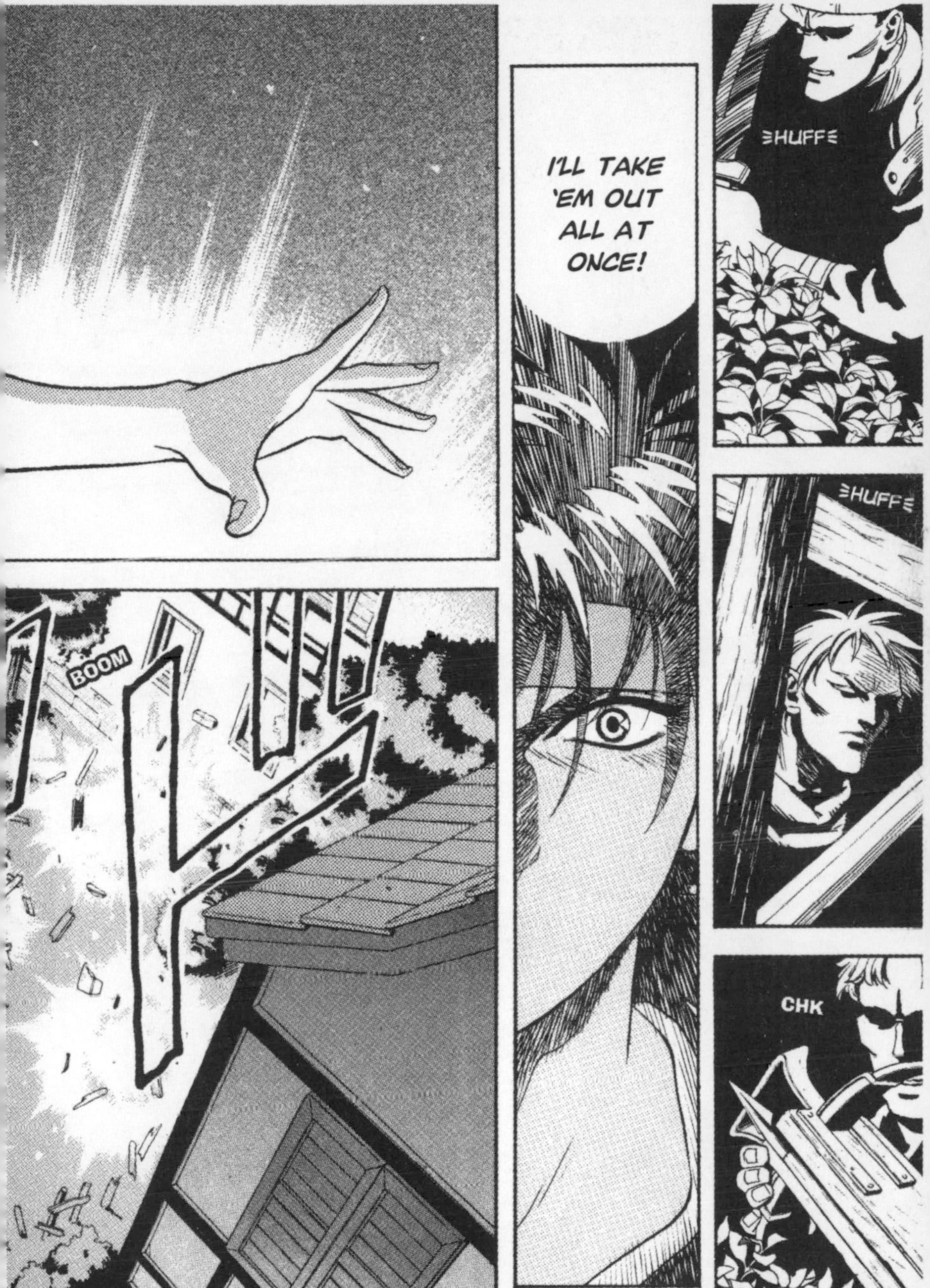
HUFF
HUFF
CHK
I'LL TAKE 'EM OUT ALL AT ONCE!
BOOM

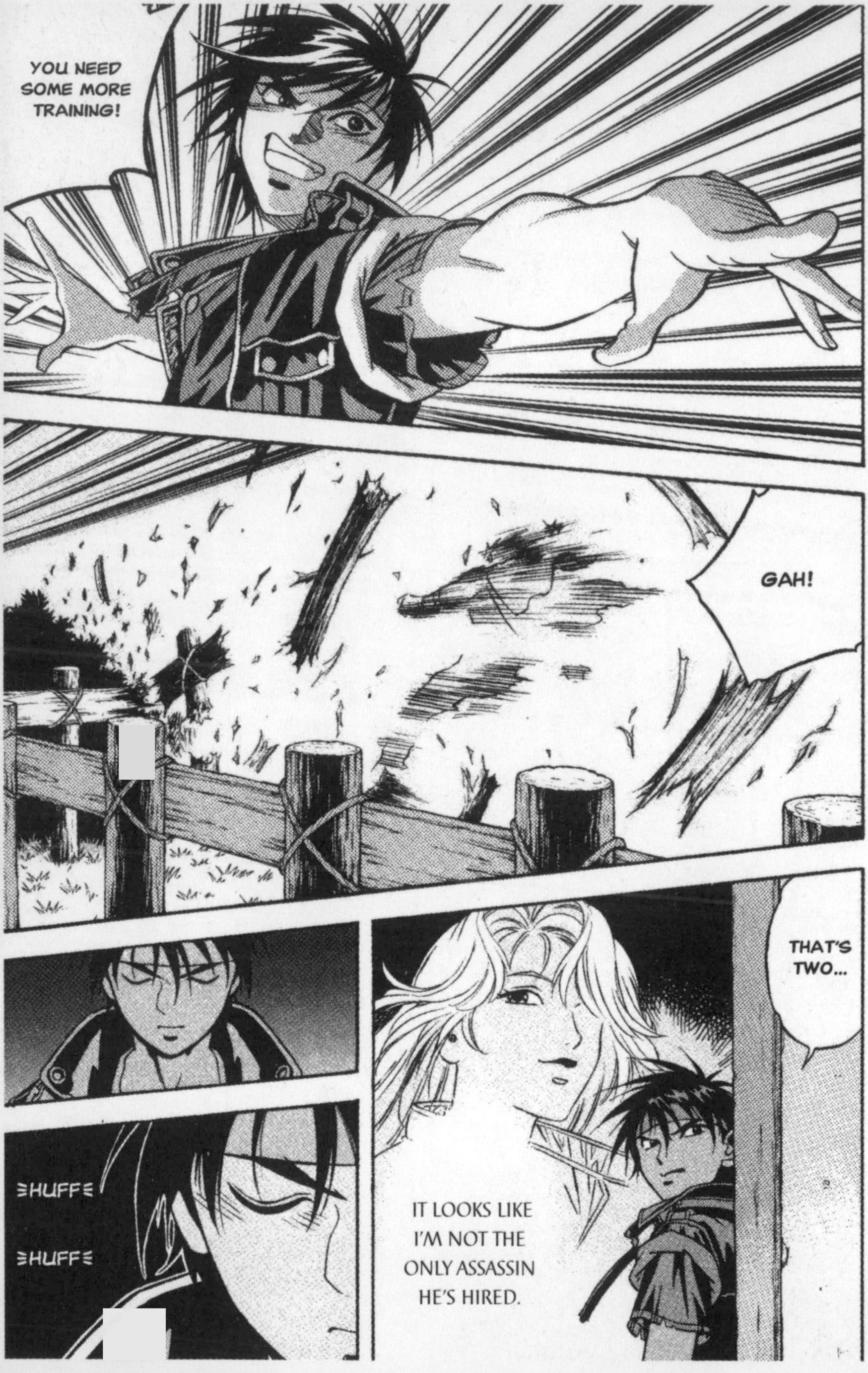
YOU NEED SOME MORE TRAINING!
GAH!
THAT'S TWO...
IT LOOKS LIKE I'M NOT THE ONLY ASSASSIN HE'S HIRED.
HUFF
HUFF

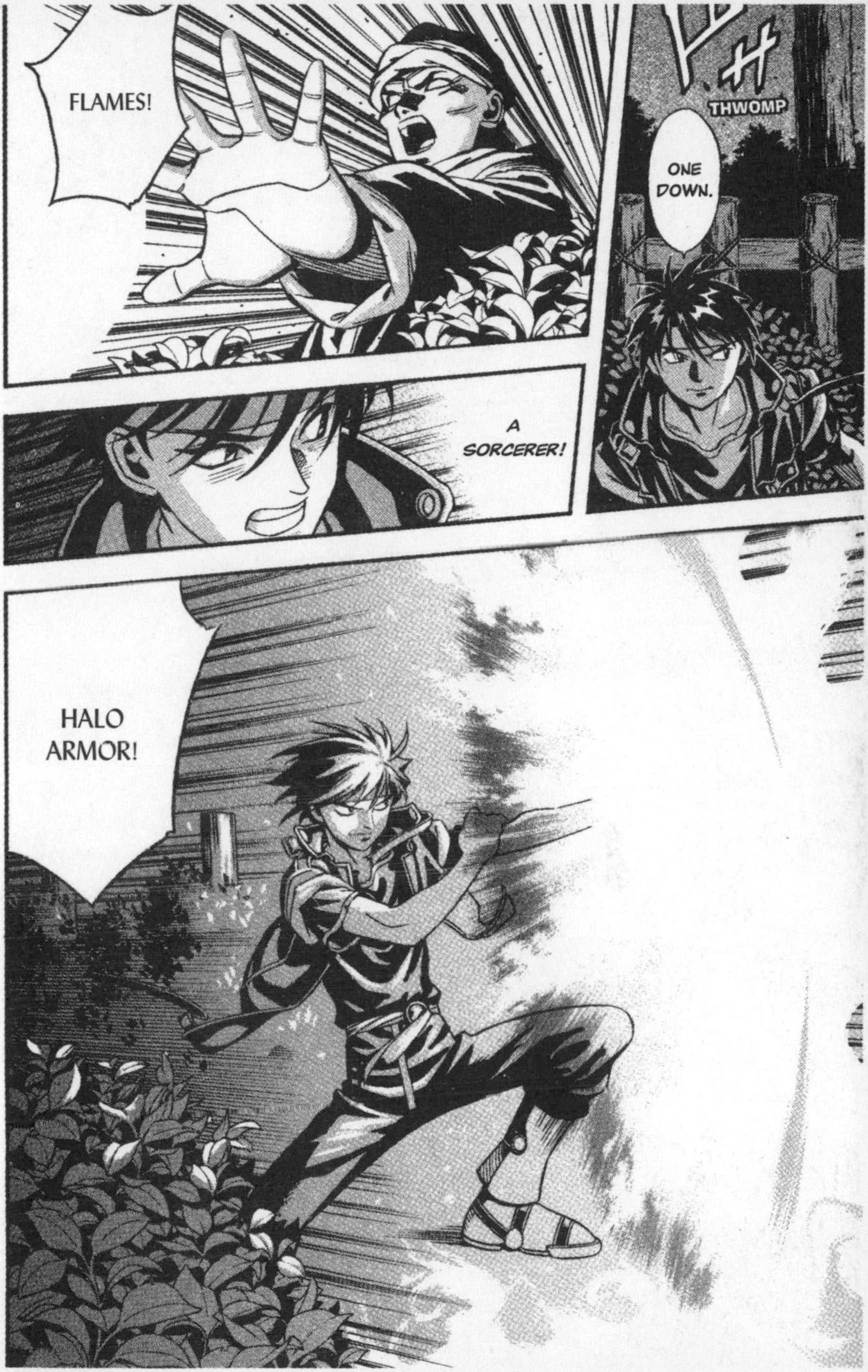
THWOMP
ONE DOWN.
FLAMES!
A SORCERER!
HALO ARMOR!

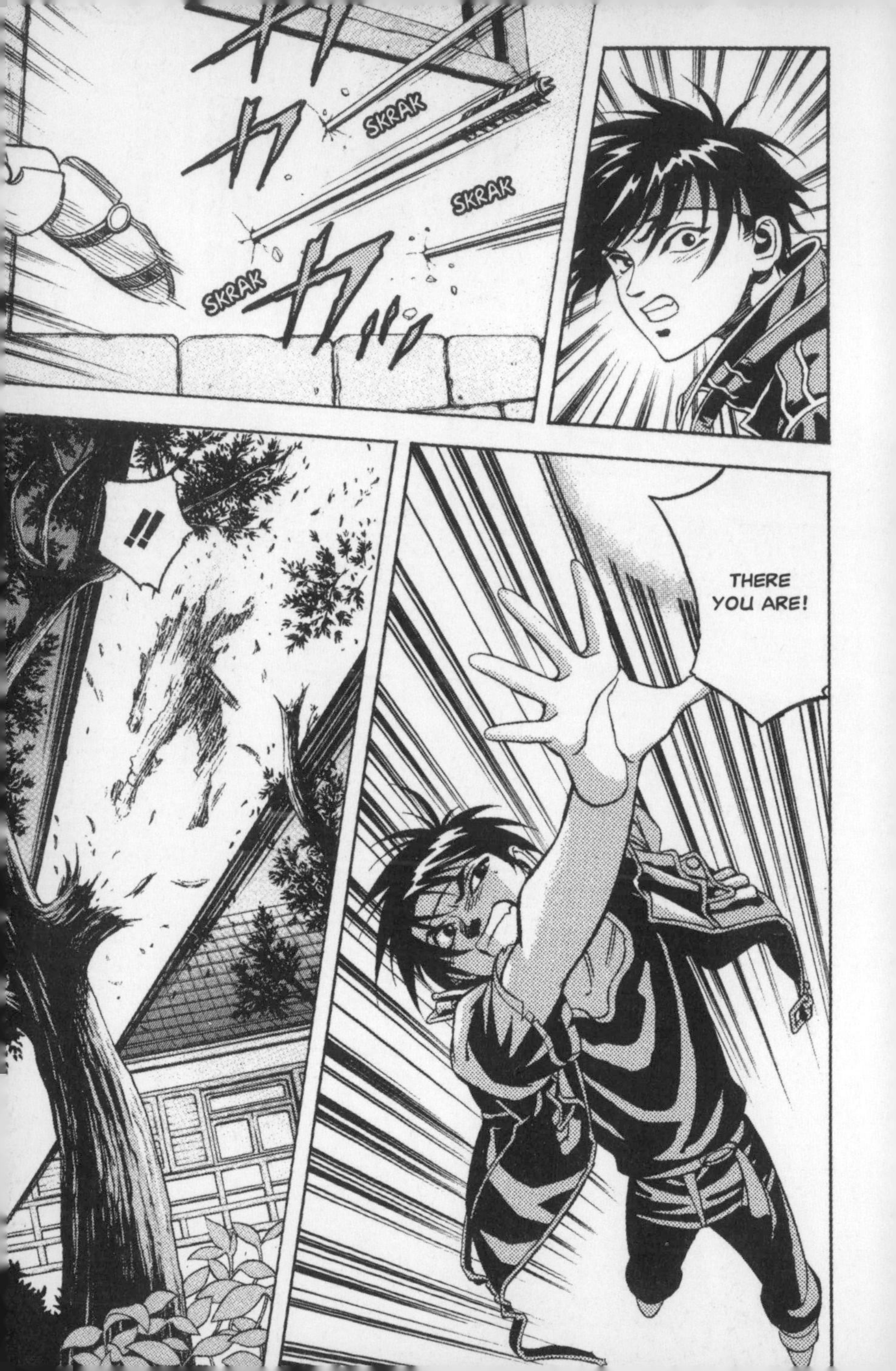
SKRAK
SKRAK
SKRAK
!!
THERE YOU ARE!

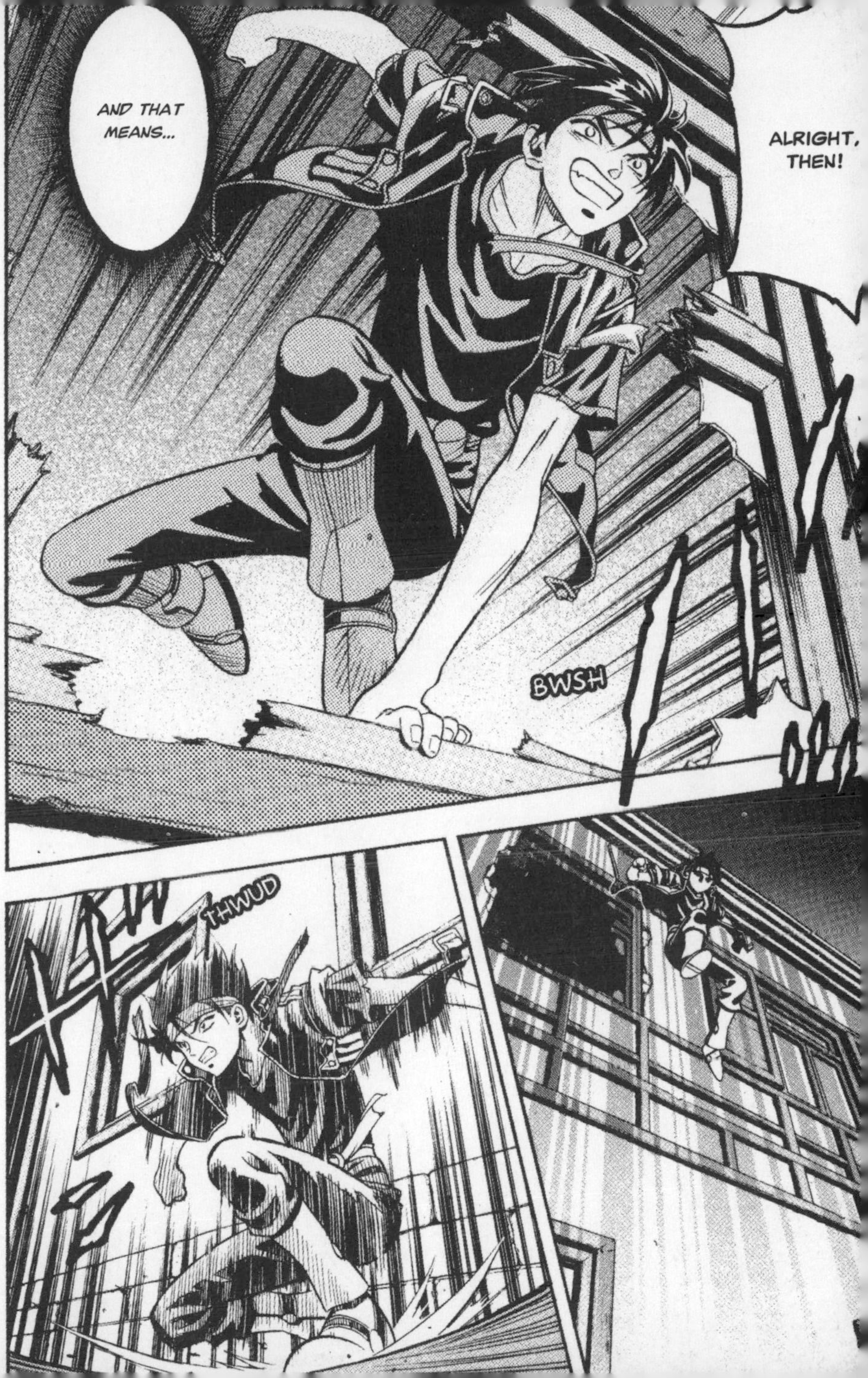
ALRIGHT, THEN!
AND THAT MEANS...
BWSH
THWUD

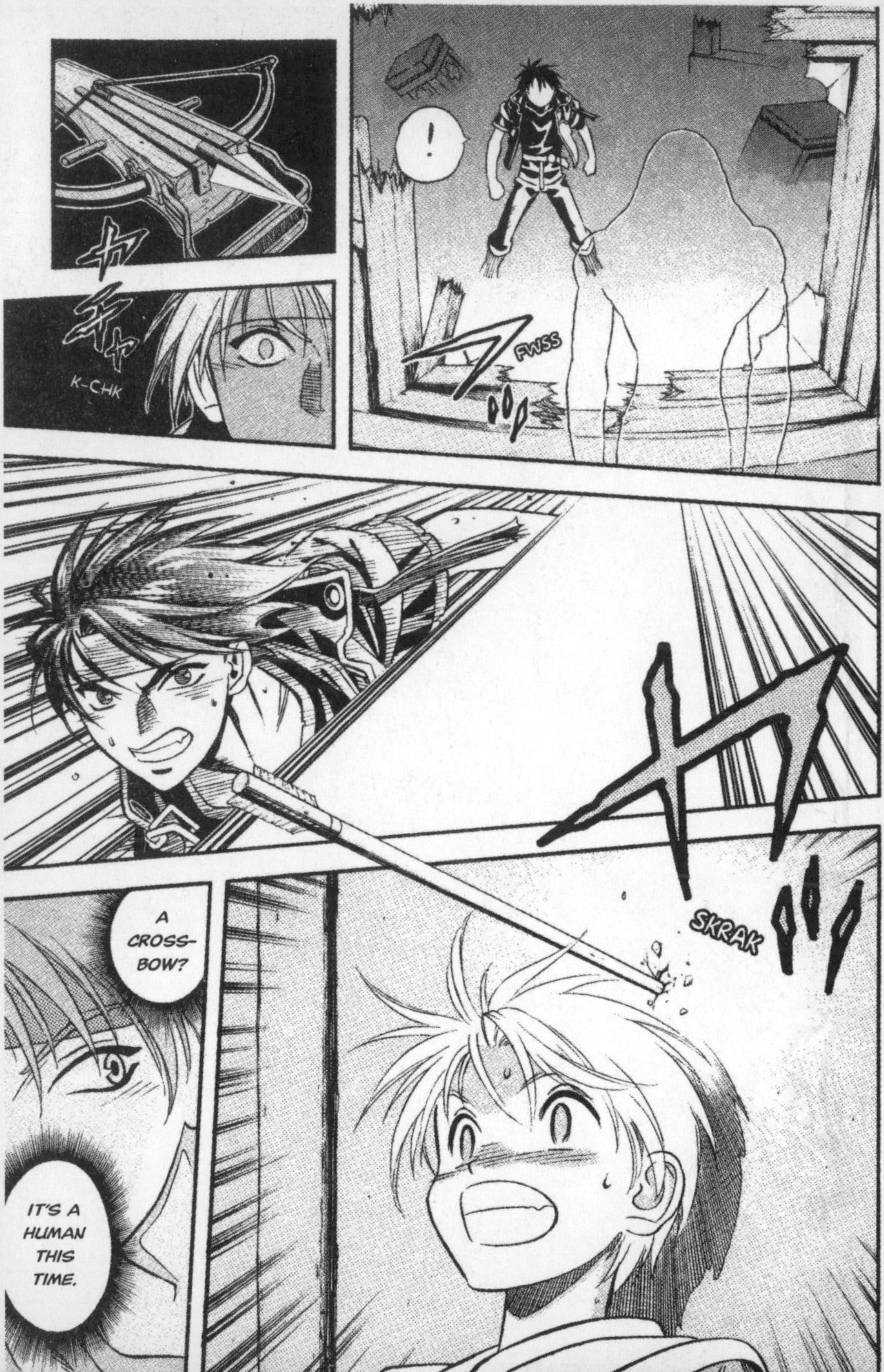
!
FWSS
K-CHK
SKRAK
A CROSS-BOW?
IT'S A HUMAN THIS TIME.

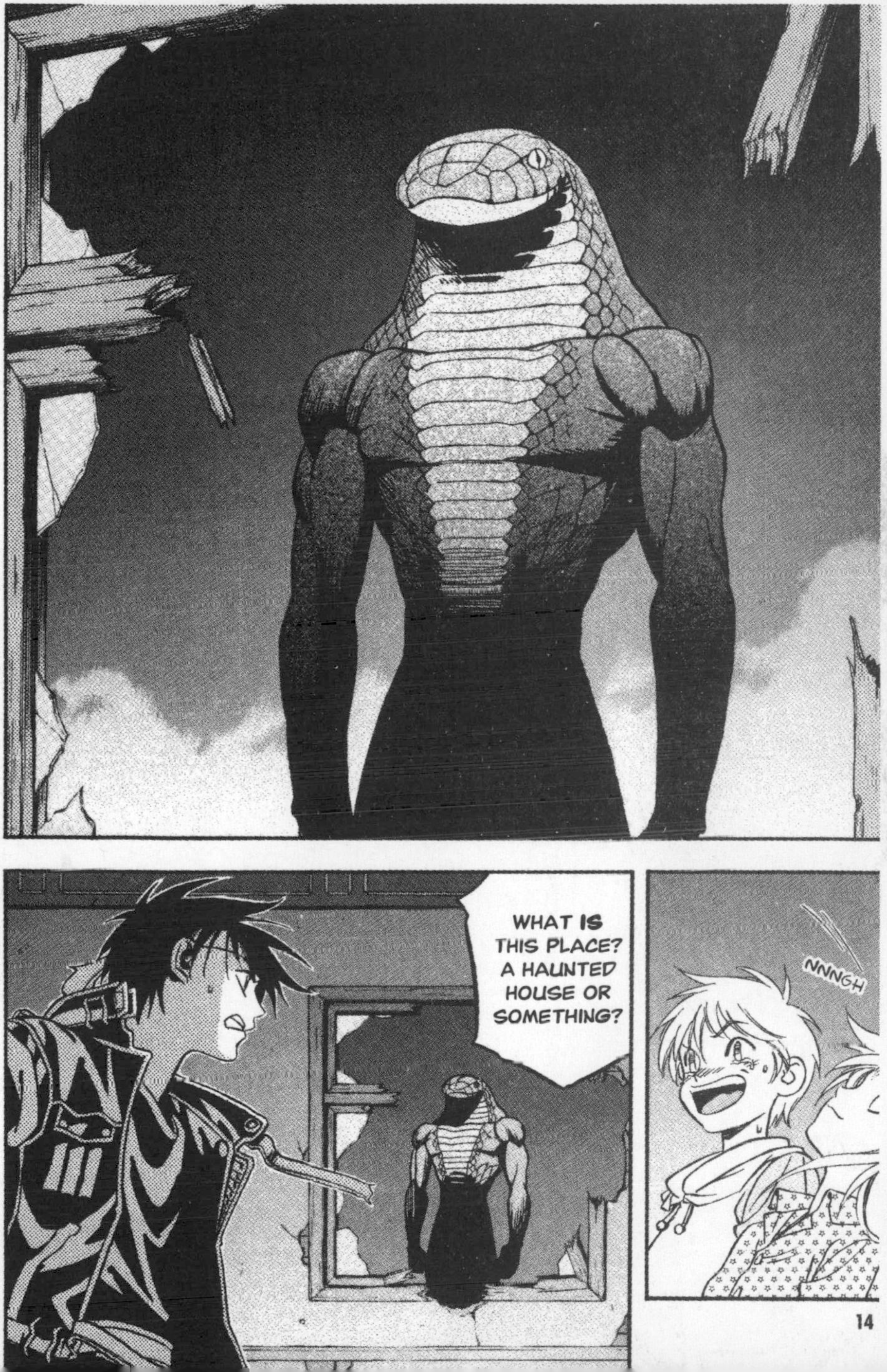
WHAT **IS** THIS PLACE? A HAUNTED HOUSE OR SOMETHING?
NNNGH

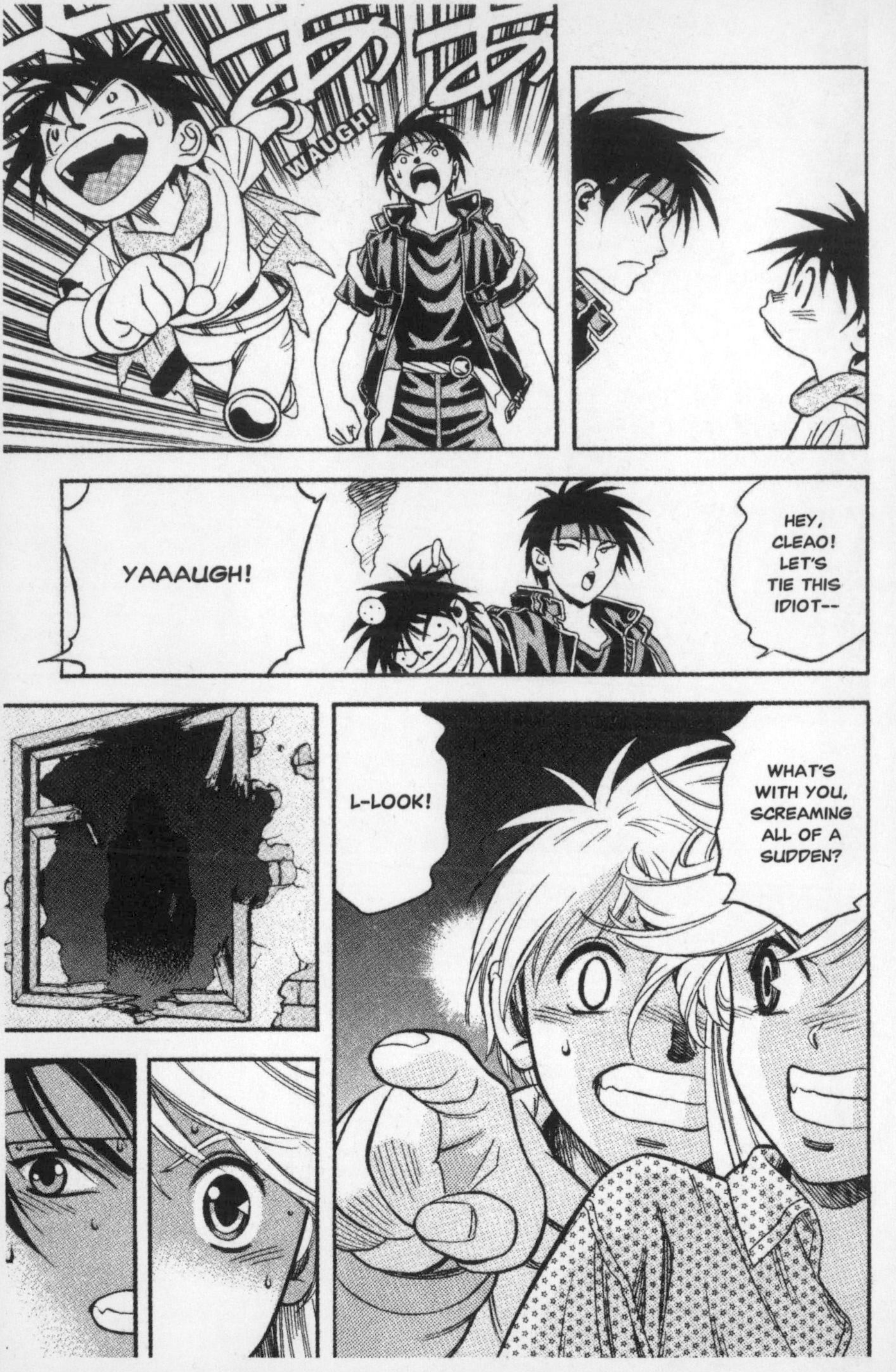
WAUGH!
HEY, CLEAO! LET'S TIE THIS IDIOT--
YAAAUGH!
WHAT'S WITH YOU, SCREAMING ALL OF A SUDDEN?
L-LOOK!

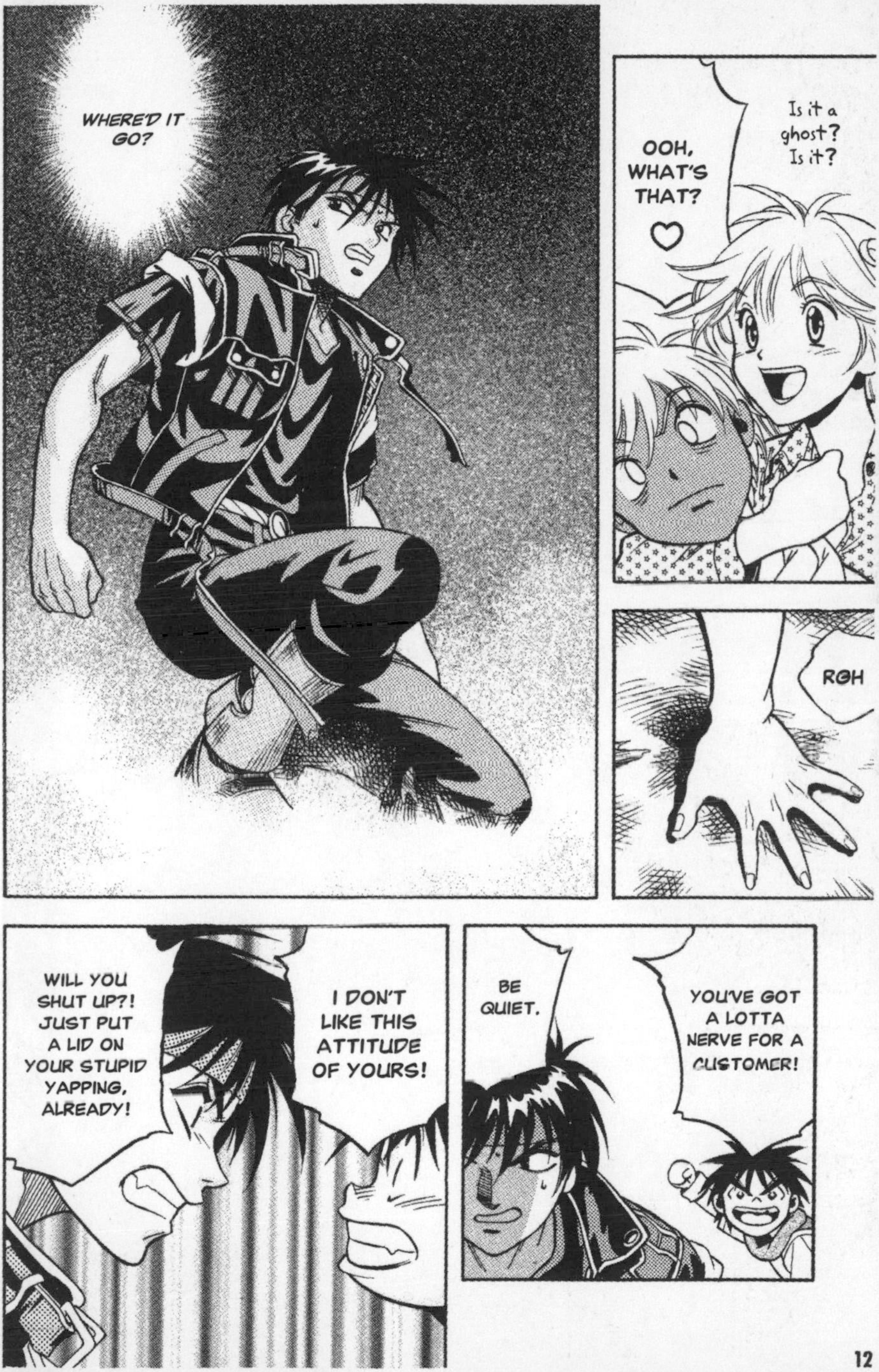
Is it a ghost? Is it?
OOH, WHAT'S THAT? ♡
RGH
WHERE'D IT GO?
YOU'VE GOT A LOTTA NERVE FOR A CUSTOMER!
BE QUIET.
I DON'T LIKE THIS ATTITUDE OF YOURS!
WILL YOU SHUT UP?! JUST PUT A LID ON YOUR STUPID YAPPING, ALREADY!

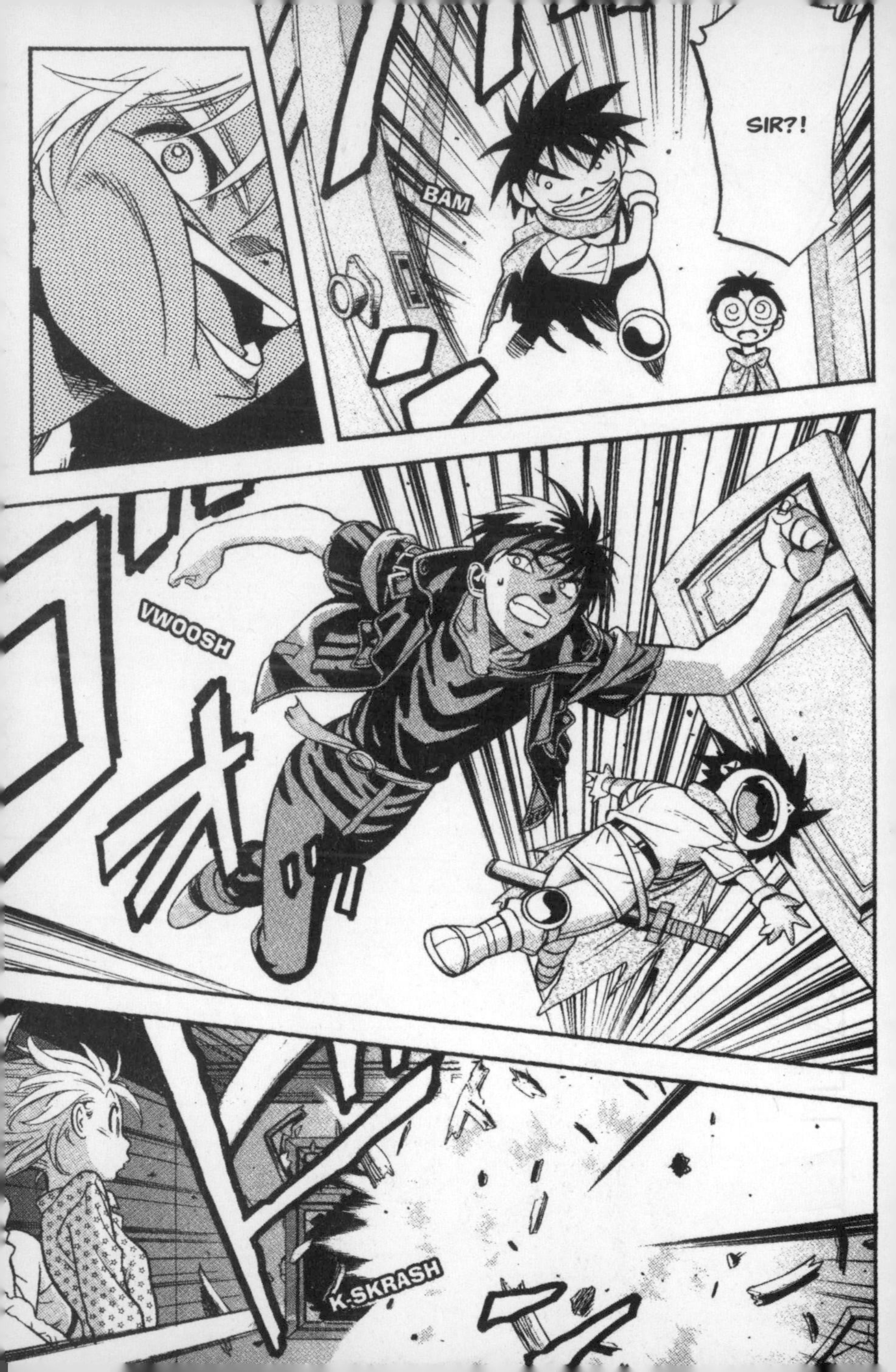
SIR?!
BAM
VWOOSH
K-SKRASH

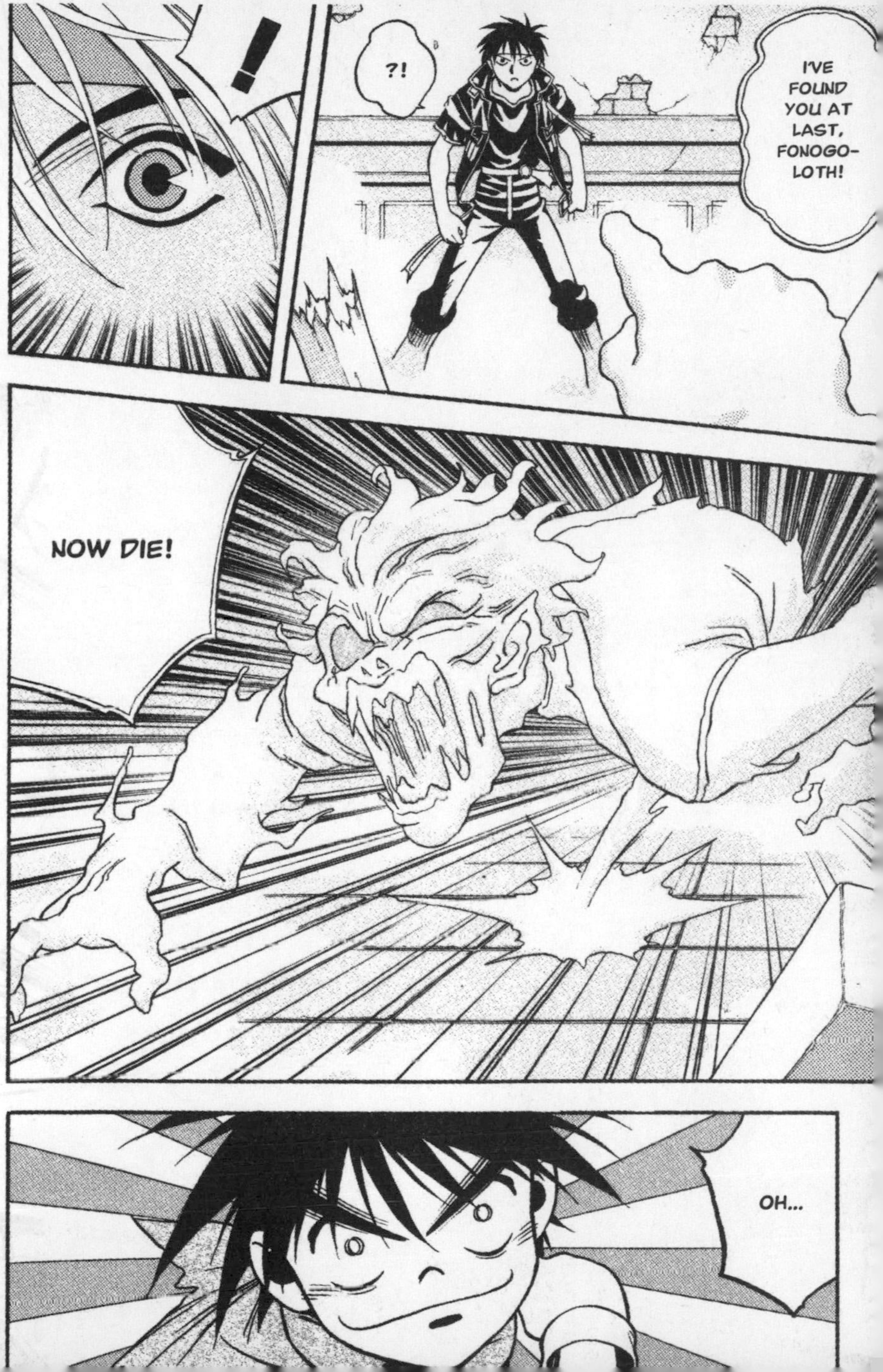
I'VE FOUND YOU AT LAST, FONOGO-LOTH!
?!
!
NOW DIE!
OH...

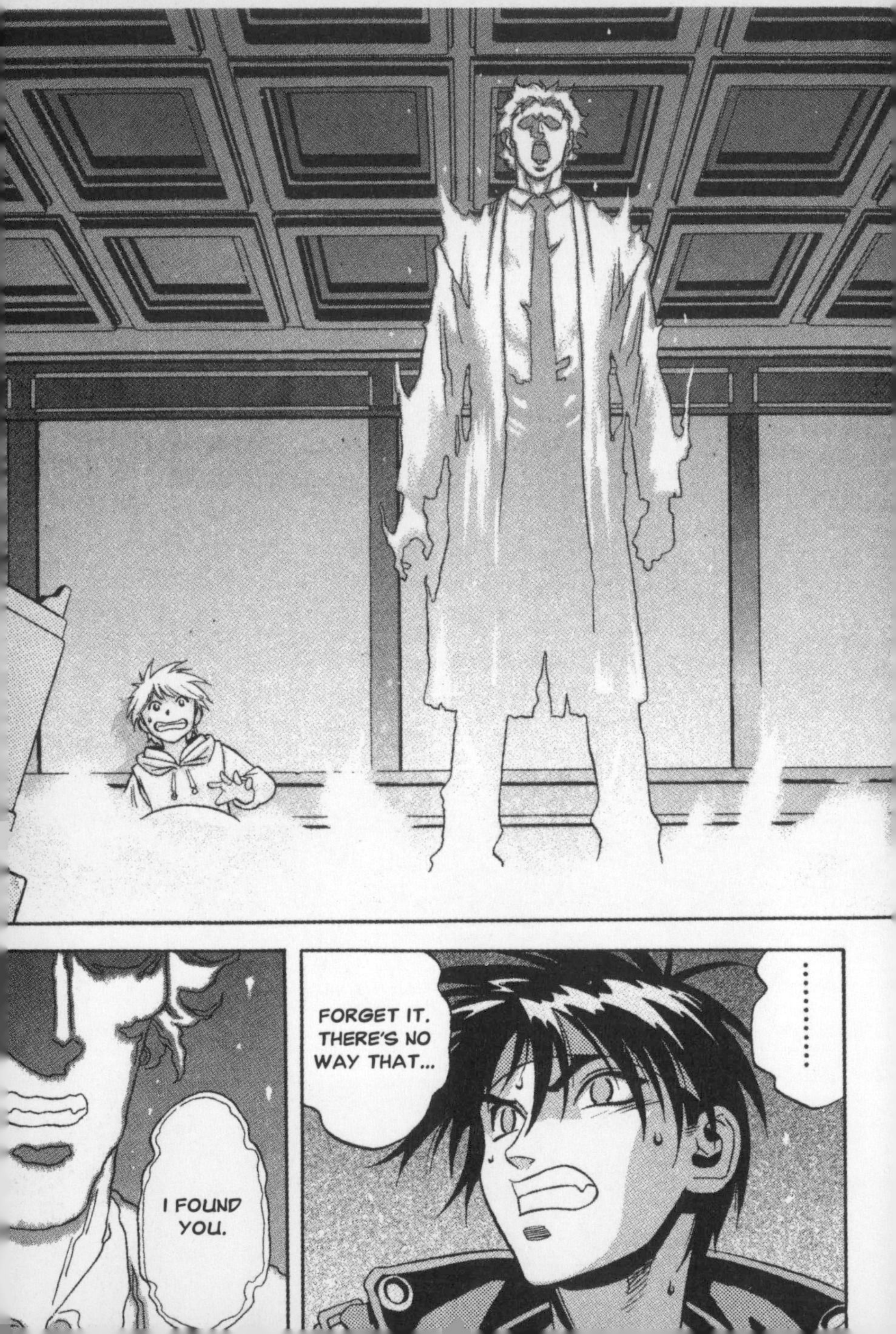
....
FORGET IT. THERE'S NO WAY THAT...
I FOUND YOU.

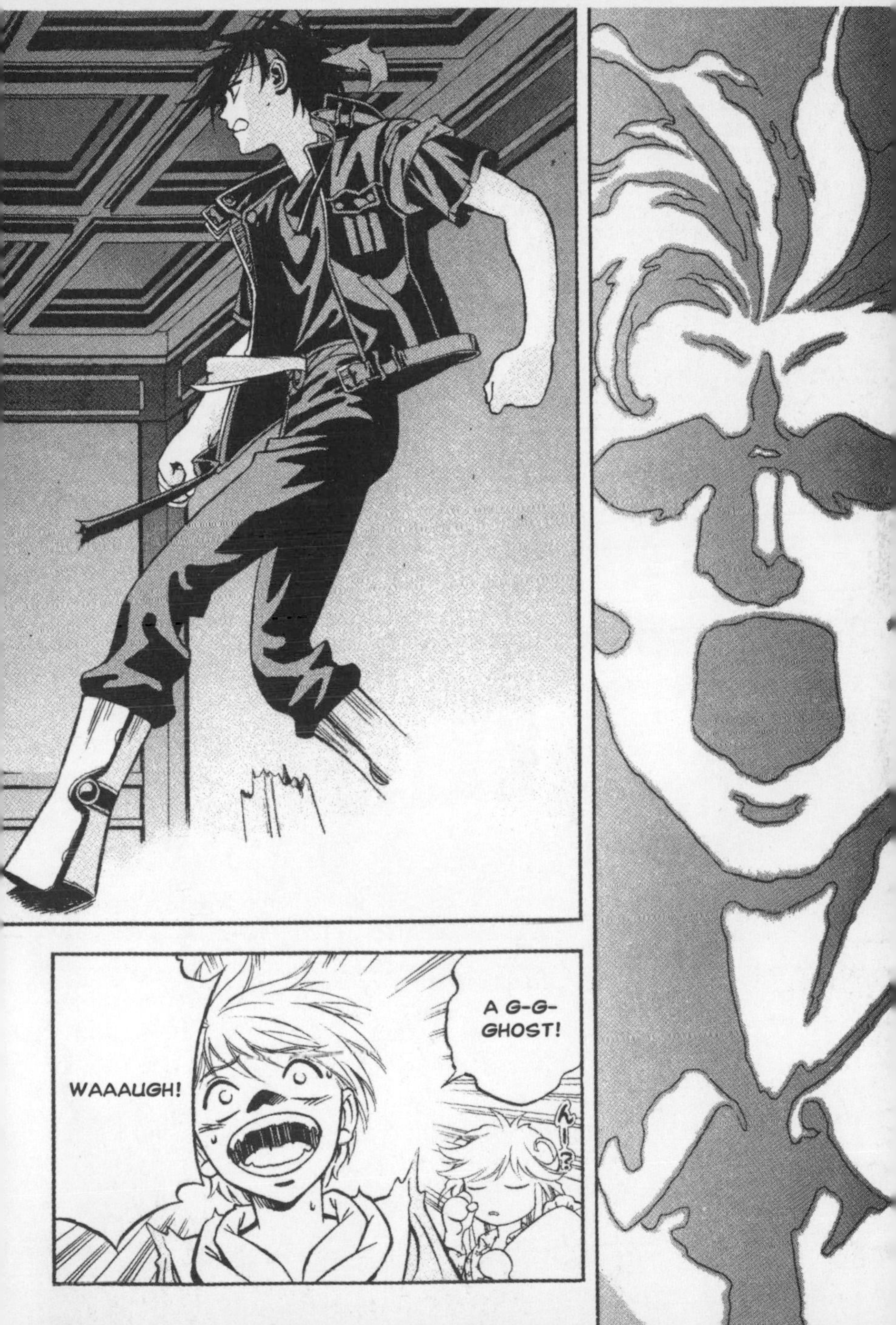
A G-G-
GHOST!
WAAAUGH!

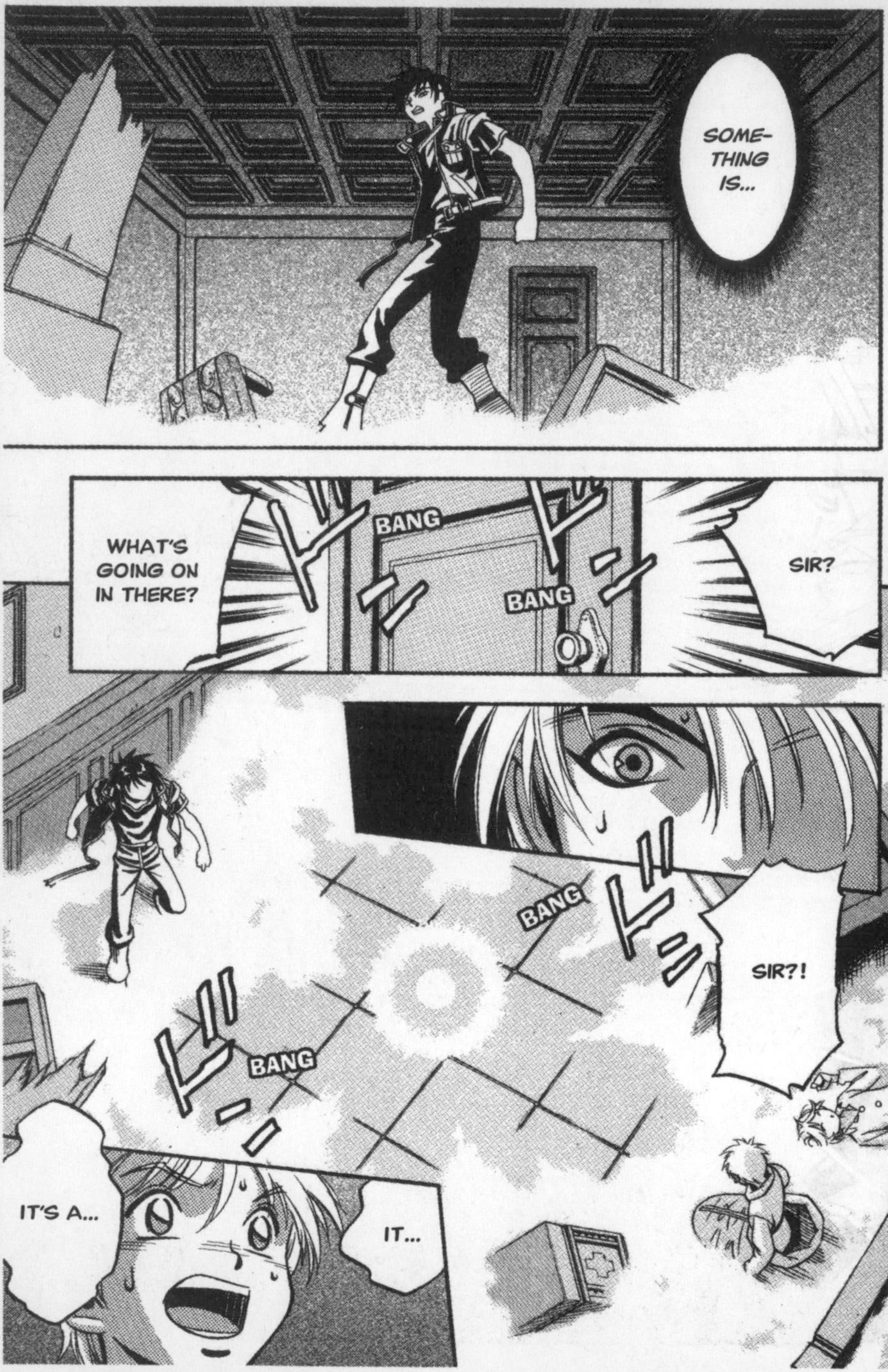
SOME-THING IS...
SIR?
BANG
BANG
WHAT'S GOING ON IN THERE?
SIR?!
BANG
BANG
IT...
IT'S A...

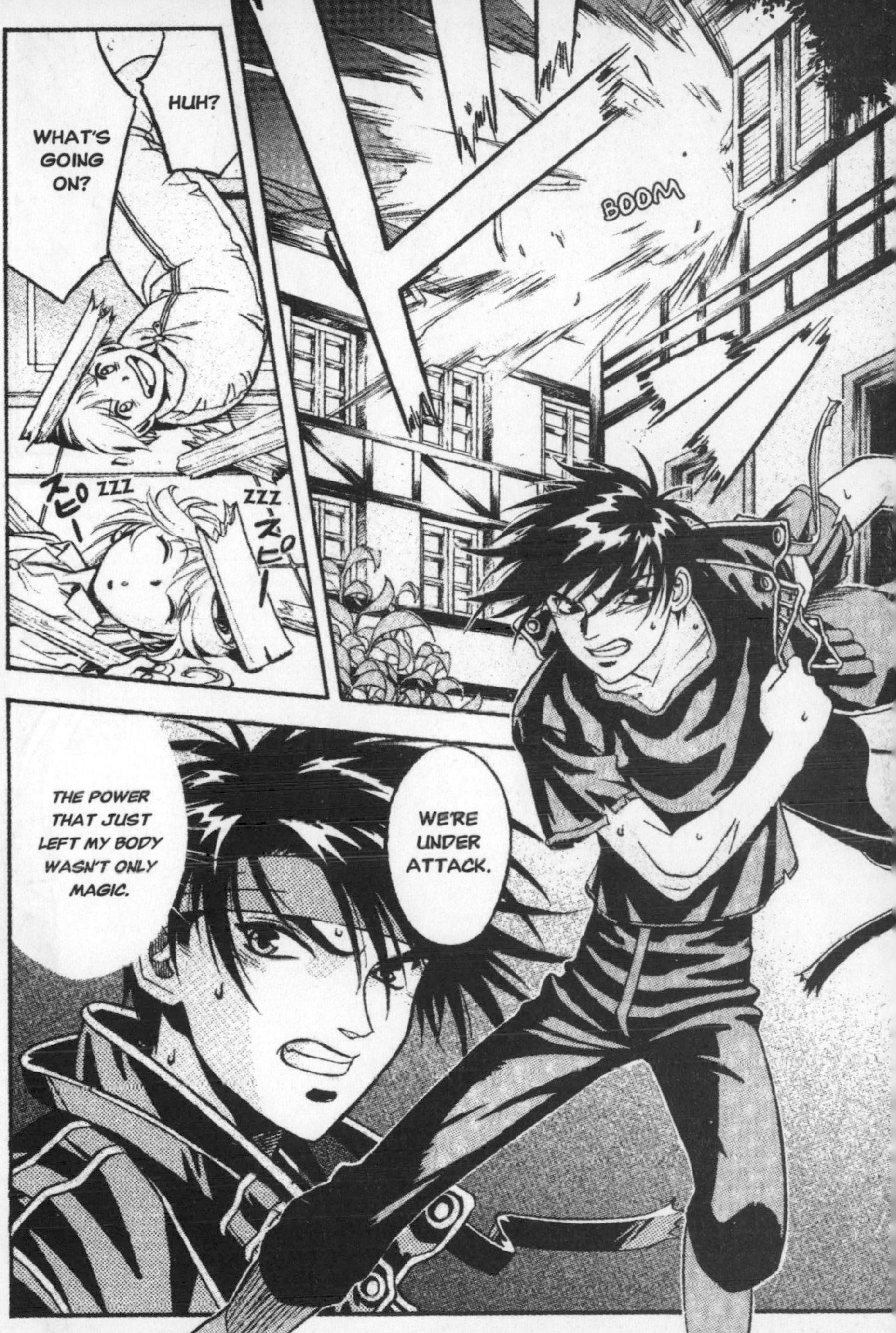
BOOM
HUH?
WHAT'S GOING ON?
ZZZ
スピー
ZZZ
スピー
WE'RE UNDER ATTACK.
THE POWER THAT JUST LEFT MY BODY WASN'T ONLY MAGIC.

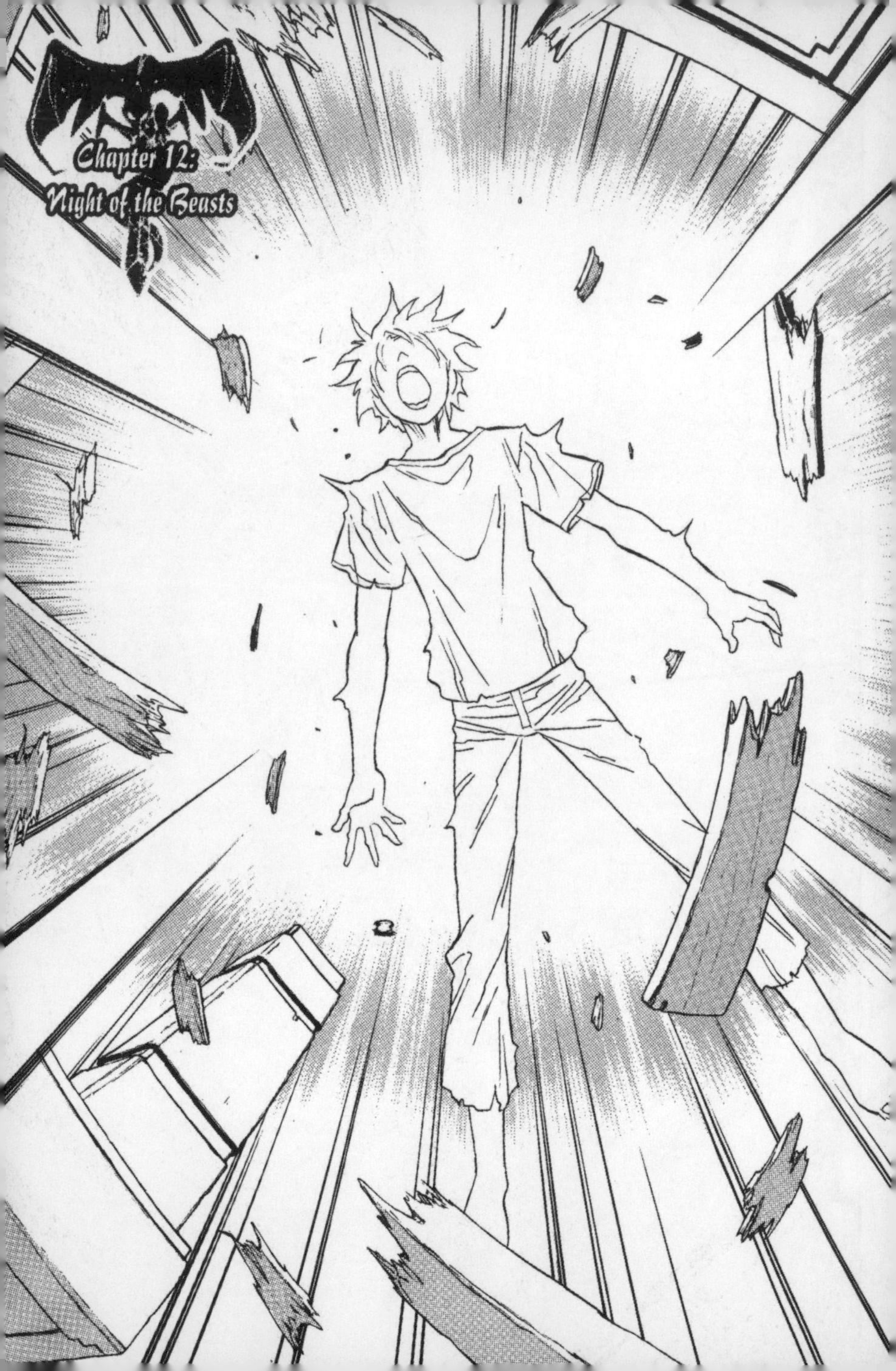
Chapter 12:
Night of the Beasts

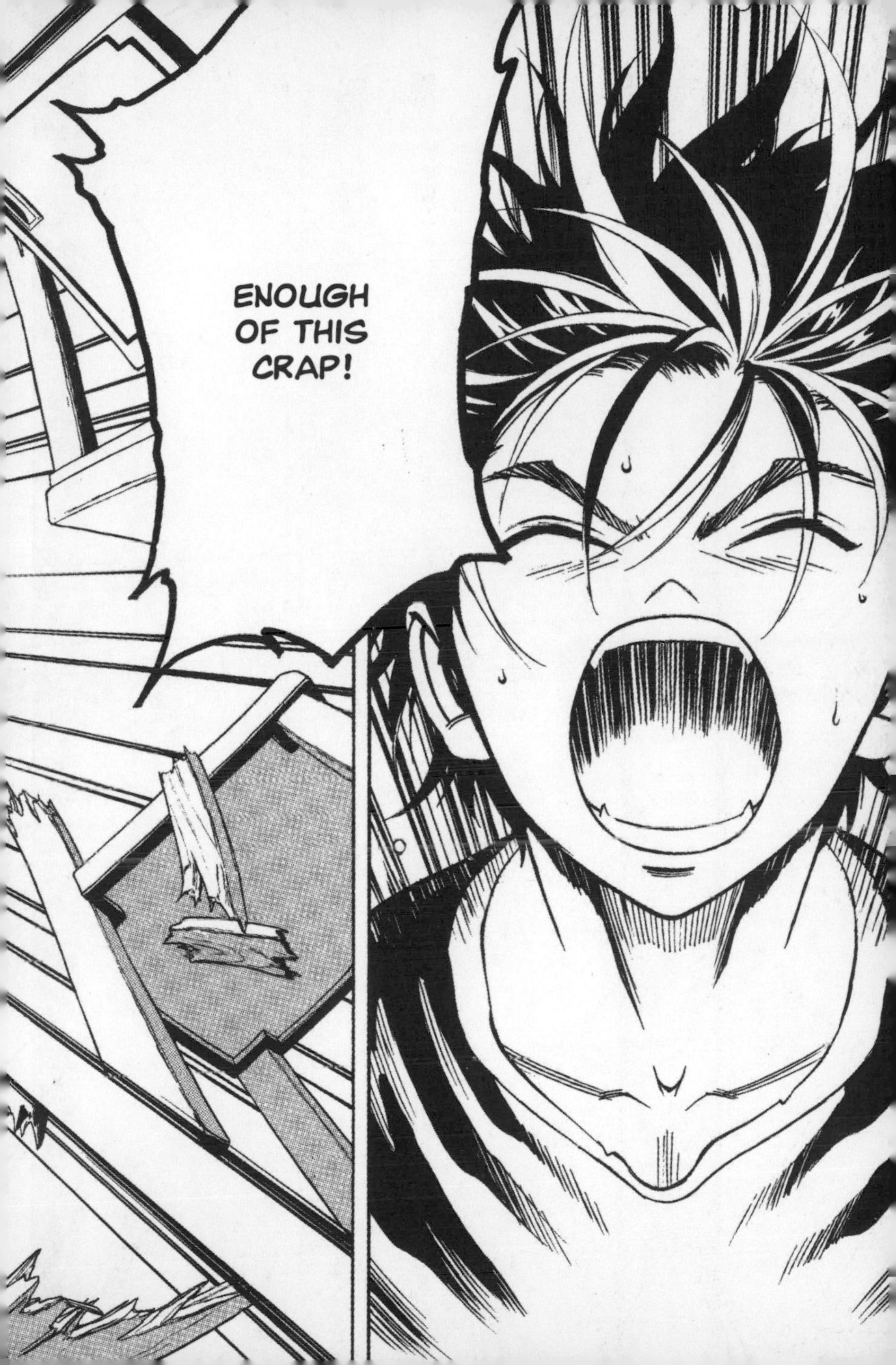
ENOUGH OF THIS CRAP!

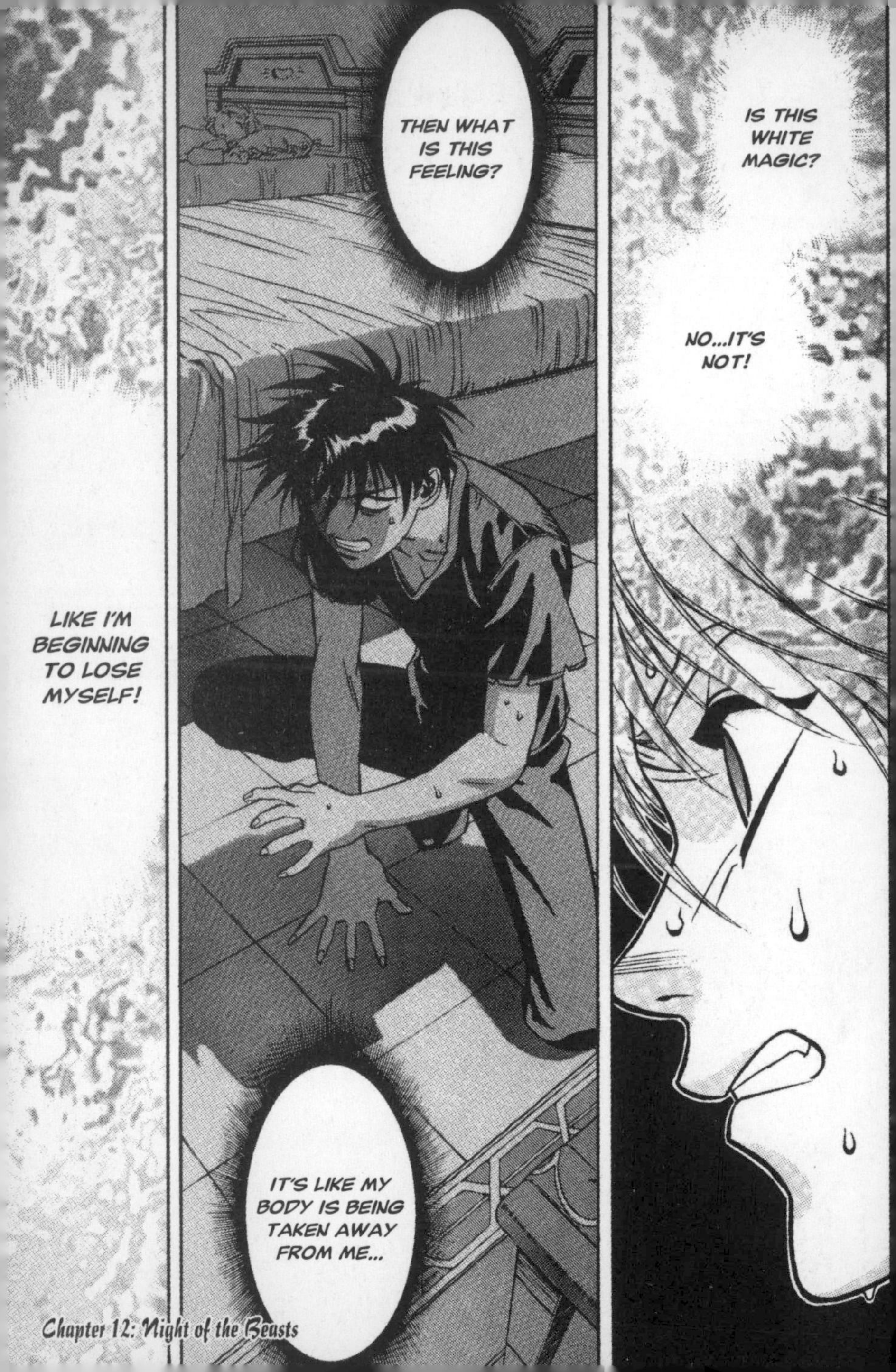
IS THIS WHITE MAGIC?
NO...IT'S NOT!
THEN WHAT IS THIS FEELING?
IT'S LIKE MY BODY IS BEING TAKEN AWAY FROM ME...
LIKE I'M BEGINNING TO LOSE MYSELF!

Chapter 12: Night of the Beasts

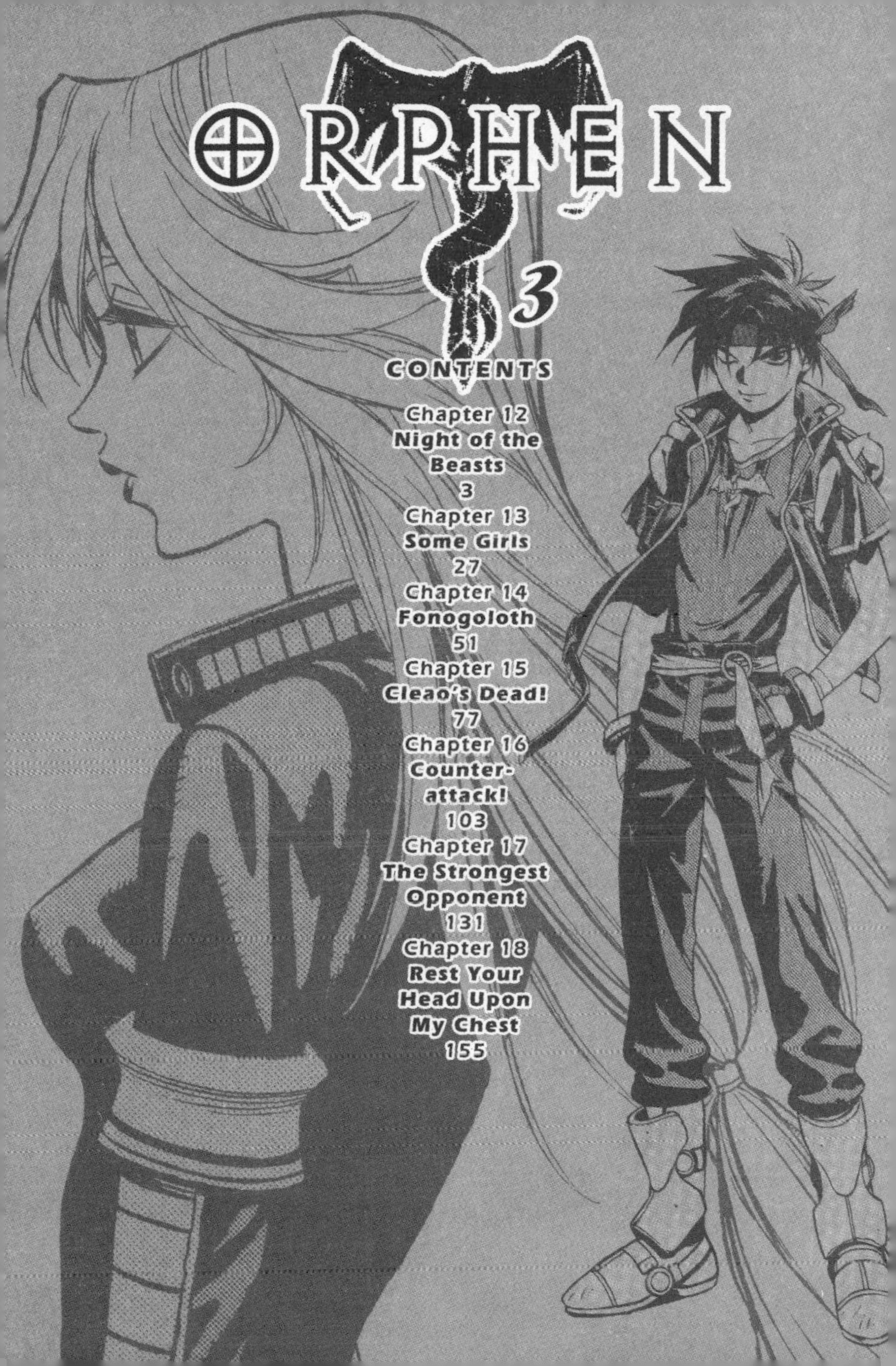

ORPHEN 3

CONTENTS

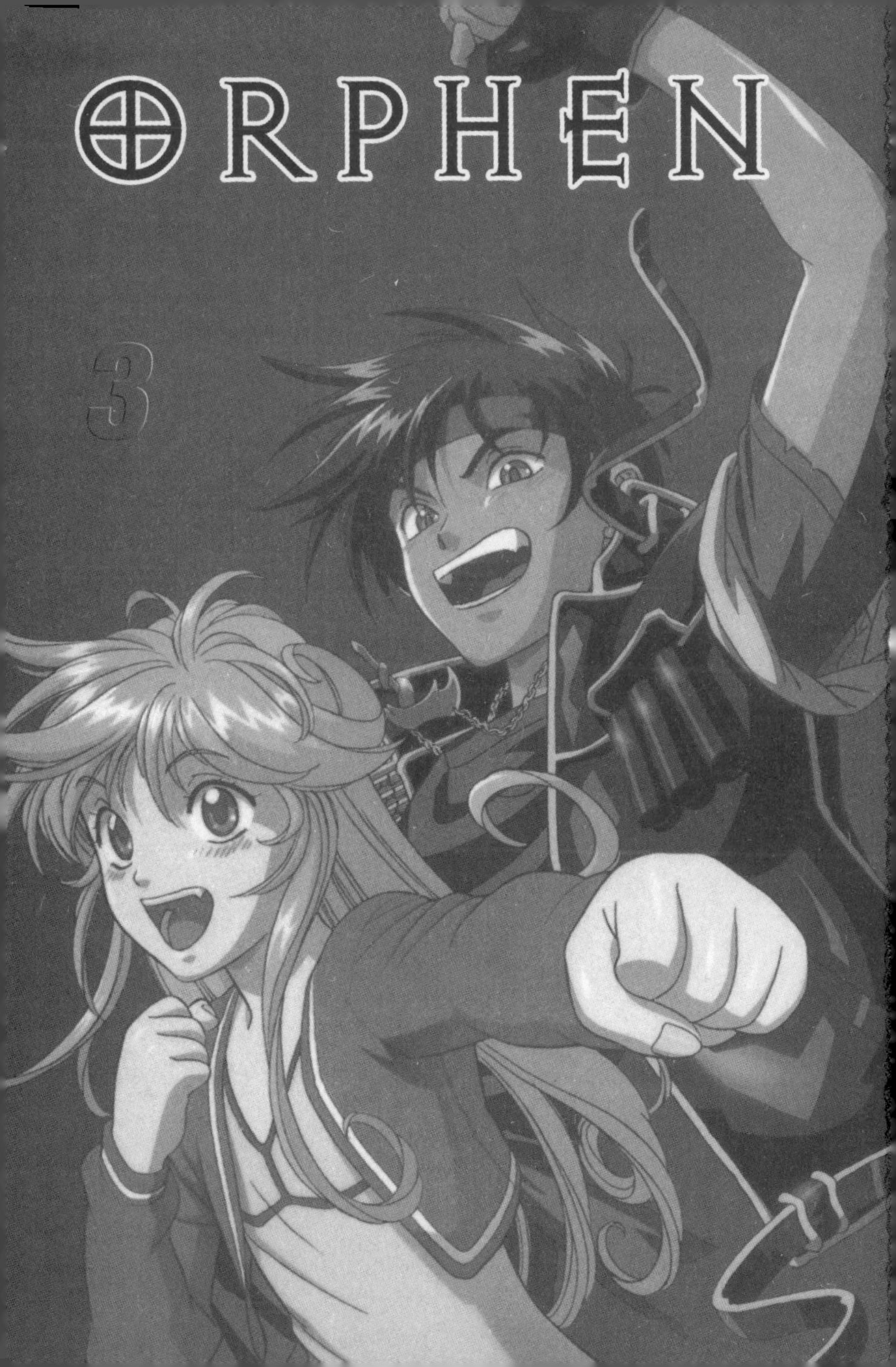
ORPHEN
3